The Early English Lyric

&

Franciscan Spirituality

Novel cantare   tutta l'humana gente
sempre de' fare   a Dio 'mnipotente
lui ringratiare   per te, flore aulente;
fosti fervente   di spirito sancto.

                   (MS. Cortona 91)

Vor þys day singeth a neowe song
and maketh blisfol mod:

Weole louerd beo wyth þe,
y-boren of may,
Wyth uader and þe holy gost
Wyþouten ende-day. Amen.

                   (MS. Phillips 8336)

The Early English Lyric

&

Franciscan Spirituality

David L. Jeffrey

University of Nebraska Press · Lincoln

Publishers on the Plains

UNP

Library of Congress Cataloging in Publication Data

Jeffrey, David L. 1941–
   The early English lyric & Franciscan spirituality.

   Bibliography: p.
   Includes index.
   1. English poetry—Middle English. 1100–1500—History and criticism.
   2. Franciscans—Spiritual life. I. Title.
PR351.J4   821'.04   74–78478
ISBN 0–8032–0845–6

The publication of this book was assisted by a grant from
The Andrew W. Mellon Foundation

Contents

Plates

Preface

THIS book attempts to understand a body of poetry by tracing it back to its particular roots and ethos, by seeing representative poems in their context of performance and then as much as possible letting them speak out of it, so secured, for themselves.

Partly because Middle English lyric texts depend more than most on context, I have used some terms of literary criticism in a generalized and contextual sense. For example, the word "style" is used not only in the sense of formal style but also to describe tone and aesthetic attitude, conveying in such cases a meaning akin to that suggested by the popular expression "life-style."

Similarly, the word "lyric," already one of the least precise of descriptive literary terms, is also used in a broad sense. Every student of medieval poetry will recognize that there are a great many forms and rhyme schemes for the lyric. As they have traditionally been classed, lyrics can actually be almost anything from very long poems— as, for example, some of the sermon-length poems in the Vernon Manuscript—to short two- or four-line tags inserted into a prose sermon or chronicle. But generally speaking they all have a recognizably "lyric" stanza form, often repeated, and most are only a few stanzas long. It is the larger more comprehensive sense of the term which I generally intend here. The word "lyric" itself, from the Greek word for lyre (whose principal use was for accompanying song and recitation), implies an association with music, and indeed, as I hope this study will in some measure illustrate, at least until after Campion this association is almost as appropriate for the general lyric as for the more explicitly musical carol. In a variety of forms, "medieval lyrics" were regularly sung.

I have not attempted in this study to distinguish "religious" lyrics from "secular" lyrics; traditional classification into camps of the worldly and the divine have seldom been useful and less often accurate. One of the achievements of this book, I hope, will be a demonstration that many lyrics heretofore thought secular are in fact distinctly religious in both emphasis and purpose.

Preface

When speaking of "Franciscan spirituality," I refer to a form of Christian spirituality which grew up in southern Europe in the late twelfth and early thirteenth centuries, and whose media and energies were channeled by the burgeoning Franciscan movement. This spirituality is reflected not in doctrinal statements which flirt with heresy, but rather in the structuring of orthodoxy according to particular devotional emphases within a generally Augustinian theological context. If I refer to a theological or devotional emphasis as "particularly Franciscan," I do not then necessarily mean that the particular idea was original with the Franciscans—for they were not often deliberately original—but usually that it was popularized and promulgated by them at a time when the general movement of Christian spirituality was in some other direction.

In most cases, my readings of the poems cited in this study represent independent consultation with the manuscripts. However, I have regularly cited published editions of the poems (or of versions of the poems) where that was possible. My general editorial practice has been to normalize the texts of all poems cited, to modernize punctuation, but to retain the original alphabet except for the wynn, which appears as *w*. All glosses and translations are my own unless otherwise indicated.

This study of Franciscan influences on the Middle English lyric was made possible through the generous assistance of several people and organizations whose contributions I should like to acknowledge. I am most indebted to Professor D. W. Robertson, Jr., whose judicious counsel has often afforded perspective to my cogitations, to Professor John V. Fleming, under whose tutelage the inspiration for my research was conceived, and to Professor Theodore Silverstein, whose careful reading of the manuscript for the University of Nebraska Press afforded much helpful criticism. Final preparation of the manuscript has been greatly facilitated through the cheerful dedication of my former student and research assistant, Miss Rose-Marie Silkens, as well as the patient editorial vigilance of Mrs. Ann Robinson of the University of Nebraska Press. Also, I am grateful for the hospitality of the Bodleian Library at Oxford, the British Library Manuscript Department, the Biblioteca Nationale in Florence, the Laurenzian Library, San Lorenzo, in Florence, and the Franciscan brothers of Ognisanti, also in Florence. I would like to thank the Biblioteca Communale in Cortona, the Master and Fellows of Corpus Christi College, Cambridge, the Trustees of the British Museum, and the Curators of the Bodleian Library for permission to use photographs of their manuscript material as illustrations.

Preface

To the Canada Council and to the Woodrow Wilson Foundation I owe my particular gratitude; without their assistance the European research which proved so invaluable—both in the present instance and for a forthcoming companion volume on medieval drama—could not have been achieved. My wife, Wilberta Johnson Jeffrey, typed her way through my first incursions into this study—part of a herculean, indispensable, and deeply appreciated contribution which words can only imperfectly acknowledge.

Victoria, B.C.

Abbreviations

Ageno	Franca Ageno, ed., *Laudi*, by Jacopone da Todi (Florence: Le Monnier, 1953).
Brook	G. L. Brook, ed., *The Harley Lyrics* (Manchester: University of Manchester Press, 1964).
BSFS	British Society of Franciscan Studies (ES = Extra Series).
Contini	Gianfranco Contini, ed., *Poeti del Duecento*, 2 vols. (Milan, Naples: Riccardo Ricciardi, 1960).
EEC	*The Early English Carols*, ed. Richard L. Greene (Oxford: Clarendon Press, 1935).
EETS	Early English Text Society (OS = Original Series; ES = Extra Series).
EL XIII	*English Lyrics of the XIIIth Century*, ed. Carleton Brown, corr. ed. (Oxford: Clarendon Press, 1962).
Fortini	Arnaldo Fortini, *La Lauda in Assisi e le origini del teatro italiano* (Assisi: Edizione Assisi, 1961).
HP XIV–XV	*Historical Poems of the XIVth and XVth Centuries*, ed. Rossell Hope Robbins (Oxford: Clarendon Press, 1959).
JEGP	*Journal of English and Germanic Philology*.
Little, *Documents*	A. G. Little, *Franciscan Papers, Lists, and Documents* (Manchester: University of Manchester Press, 1943).
Little, *Studies*	A. G. Little, *Studies in English Franciscan History* (Manchester: University of Manchester Press, 1917).
Liuzzi	Fernando Liuzzi, *La Lauda e i primordi della melodia italiana*, 2 vols. (Rome: La Libreria dello stato, 1934).

Abbreviations

Meditations	*Meditations on the Life of Christ: An Illustrated Manuscript of the Fourteenth Century*, ed. and trans. Isa Ragusa and Rosalie B. Green (Princeton: Princeton University Press, 1961).
MGH	G. H. Pertz, T. Mommsen, et al., *Monumenta Germaniae Historica*, Auspiciis Societatis Aperiendis Fontibus Rerum Germanicarum Medii Aevii, ser., LL (1826–1889); ser., Scriptores (1826–1934).
MLN	*Modern Language Notes.*
PL	*Patrilogia cursus completus, series Latina*, ed. J. P. Migne, 221 vols. (Rotterdam, 1878–1880).
PMLA	*Publications of the Modern Language Association of America.*
Raby	F. J. E. Raby, *A History of Christian-Latin Poetry from the Beginnings to the Close of the Middle Ages*, 2nd ed. (Oxford: Clarendon Press, 1953).
Reductione artium	St. Bonaventure, *De reductione artium ad theologiam*, ed. and trans. Emma Thérèse Healy, 2nd ed. (St. Bonaventure, New York: Franciscan Institute, 1955).
RL XIV	*Religious Lyrics of the XIVth Century*, ed. Carleton Brown, 2nd ed. revised by G. V. Smithers (Oxford: Clarendon Press, 1957).
Salimbene	Salimbene d'Adam, *Chronica*, ed. Oswald Holder-Egger in *Monumenta Germaniae Historica*, ser., Script., 32 (Hanover: 1905–13).
SATF	Société des anciens textes français.
SL XIV–XV	*Secular Lyrics of the XIVth and XVth Centuries*, ed. Rossell H. Robbins, 2nd ed. (Oxford: Clarendon Press, 1955).
Stevick	Robert D. Stevick, ed., *One Hundred Middle English Lyrics* (Indianapolis: Indiana University Press, 1964).
Zupitza	Julius Zupitza, "Die Gedichte des Franziskaners Jakob Ryman," *Archiv für das Studium der neueren Sprachen und Litteraturen* 89 (1892): 167–388.

The Early English Lyric
&
Franciscan Spirituality

Introduction

An Abbreviated History
of Approaches

THE DEVELOPMENT of theories concerning the origin of Western European vernacular lyrics has occupied the attention of three generations of scholars. The most efficient summation of these theories is that by Käte Axhausen.[1] She recounts the dozens of speculations that have been propounded, from naive notions that the whole genre emanates from Celtic religion and sarcophagi or from the effervescent personality of William the Ninth, Duke of Aquitaine, to more sophisticated if still unsatisfactory theories such as those which derive the genre from Ovid or from Arabic poetry.[2] Students of Middle English lyric poetry, accustomed to thinking of literary history as a general Western European evolutionary process, and noting that French and Provençal poetry preceded Middle English lyric poetry in time, have often turned to such theories for missing links in their own historical chain.

However, the characteristic features of the Middle English lyric are not those of its French or Provençal predecessors. Nor do early Middle English lyrics much resemble the short poems of Lydgate, Chaucer, Charles d'Orléans, or Machaut. To begin with, they were written for an entirely different audience. Composed in English during the reign of Anglo-Norman kings for listeners whose disposition, learning, and taste were considerably removed from that of the audience of the Anglo-Norman metrical romance, their language naturally reflects its own cultural style; they are popular, not courtly literature. Even more obviously, these lyrics are far more often than their courtly

1

counterparts overtly religious. Thematically concerned with traditional Christian subjects such as the nativity and Passion of Christ, they tend, like other poetry given to such subject matter, to develop what is sometimes called a spirit of "meditation."

Recent critics of the Middle English lyric have usually, in one way or another, seen this "meditative" quality as a chief distinguishing feature of the genre. But the adjective is potentially misleading: the poetry we usually think of as meditative—for example, that written in the early seventeenth century—is often highly intellectual, reflective, and personal. The medieval English religious lyric is seldom so intellectual, is more often physical than metaphysical, immediate than reflective, roughly simple than elaborately careful. It is usually characterized by emotion rather than thought, by force of style rather than by elaboration of argument, and by a dramatic movement toward radical identification of the "subject" with the object of the poem. And in this development it is quite likely to betray an ultimate connection with certain aspects of the Christian doctrine of repentance.

Penitential literature of the period is concerned with awareness of the vices and virtues, and with the three actions of penance—contrition, confession, and satisfaction. Yet while Middle English lyrics are often concerned with sin, guilt, and remission, and "penitential" is indeed more specifically characteristic of their tone than simply "meditative," few of the poems are narrowly penitential. It is possible to define in Middle English lyrics specifically not so much a paradigm of traditional doctrine as psychological *movement toward* penance. Through a consciousness of the dolor of Christ's atonement, the movement often tends first toward a dramatic identification with Christ. Then emotion concerning the person of Christ (and often the Virgin) is directed toward a necessary preparation for penance—that is, the experience of the poems becomes a kind of pre-penitential exercise. Especially where the poems seek to evoke a response to Christ's coming or present Passion, their spirit is what a medieval theologian would discuss under the heading "de contritione." Such a psychological movement can take place in a wide variety of lyric types, from those which seek to create a personal awareness of the problem of death, even to certain lullabies. While it is not then incorrect to regard Middle English lyric poems as "meditative" in a general sense, part of the argument of this book is that many of them can be more richly understood in terms of their emphasis on the immediate personal experience of contrition. In due course we shall consider the grounds of their concentration on this one aspect of penance.

A further notable feature of these poems its their incomplete character. Rosemary Woolf makes the excellent point that the Middle English lyric is often not complete as a self-sufficient story or poem, that "knowledge of an enclosing story is pre-supposed."[3] Hundreds of the lyrics come to us from the heart of exempla, homilies, and theological treatises, and are only fully comprehensible in the light of their "host" passages. One of the purposes of this study will be to explore the relationship of such poems to the materials from which they have been extracted.

Finally, many readers of Middle English religious lyrics have observed in them a view of nature which does not coincide with that in courtly poetry from similar periods. Rather than the extended intellectualizing of nature which reached its peak in poets from Alan de Lille to Jean de Meun, the medieval English lyric offers a simpler delight in nature, one which exists prior to intellectual considerations. The reasons for the difference are couched in an aesthetic which, when understood, can substantially improve our reading of the lyrics.

Scholarship devoted particularly to the English medieval lyric has in the past generation produced some noteworthy achievements. In his useful anthology *The Early English Carols* (Oxford: Clarendon Press, 1935), Richard L. Greene attempted, in introducing the carols there assembled, to relate them in some way to their function at the time of composition. Recognizing the obvious religious character of most of them, he set out to examine what seemed to be a likely source of primary influence for religious songs and poems—Latin hymn tradition. His analysis remains a valuable study of the Latin background of the English lyrics and carols. Greene demonstrates that there are a number of approaches to the medieval Latin hymn theory of Middle English lyric origins. First of all, the tenth century through the thirteenth was the period of greatest hymn-writing activity in Latin. The most obvious point of contact between the two forms is the scraps of Latin which actually occur in Middle English lyric verse. Some of these are fairly neatly worked into the fabric of their "host" poem; some are not. The assumption is that any clerk with a command of Latin would have at his disposal a number of hymn refrains or cliché phrases which might serve to spice a vernacular poem, or even to form its nucleus. Further, individual Latin hymns relate to the carol through a considerable number of lines which derive from some part of the liturgy.[4] But Greene notes significantly that the contribution from hymns of the Office is more evident in individual lines than in subject matter in general. Metrically, he feels, the two may have more in common; similarities of line and stanza seem to indicate an influence of the Latin hymn-poetry on English verse. The predominant Latin hymn-stanza of four four-measure lines appears to be imitated only to a limited extent, but may, Greene suggests, account for the specialized form of *a a a b* which relates to the dance. (Later we shall be able to see that the source of this form is definitely not the Latin hymn stanza.[5])

Another approach he examines is that which seeks inspiration for the Middle English lyric in the prose sequence of the Mass itself. The particular object of this hypothesis is that sequence from between the Gradual and the Gospel which when sung on feast days ended with an *alleluia* in which the final syllable was expressed in a prolonged series of notes called a *melisma*. The *melisma* was extended enough so that passages had to be provided for singers to take a breath. Then arose the practice of having each of these musical phrases sung twice by responsed choirs. Finally in the eighth century the single syllable stretched over such a long musical passage seems to have exhausted its appeal, and a series of Latin words were fixed to the notes instead. This became known as a "sequence," or "prose." The process did not stop there; once again the sequence developed with an increasing emphasis on accentual rhythm and rhyme, as in the famous *Victimae paschale laudes*. The final plateau observed by Greene is the regular or "Adamian" prose of Adam of St. Victor in which twin strophes are rhymed throughout. In it the rhythm is based on word accent and has a caesura. In this development Greene finds the evolutionary history of the prose sequence in the Mass.

With this history in mind, Greene draws attention to the "Laetabundus" sequence of St. Bernard, which he suggests might have influenced several English songs. He lists three examples. Two of the songs are by James Ryman, written very late in the fifteenth century, well over 250 years after the first Middle English lyrics, and are (as Greene admits) in any case not in true English carol form. Only one song (no. 14B in his anthology) appears to be part of a sequence fully transformed into a carol, with the "Alleluya" as burden. The point is that, in view of the evidence, there is little reason to suppose that prose sequences like the "Laetabundus" had much formative influence on the Middle English carol or lyric as a genre. Actually, Greene's examination of rhyme schemes concludes by demonstrating the effect of the already existing carol form, popular in origin, on the material of the prose, ecclesiastical in origin.

The final possible Latin source that Greene examines is non-liturgical Latin poetry, sacred and secular. Here he finds that there are many pieces resembling the carol in metrical form as well as in subject and spirit. Many of the *cantilenae* to which he refers are of the sort collected by G. M. Drèves in the monumental *Analecta hymnica*. Also, in the *Carmina Burana*, especially in songs in praise of spring and its joys, are found burdens typical of the carol form. But here again the evidence for Latin poetry as a direct progenitor of the English lyric fails to stand up. Many of the Latin pieces in this form have their tunes indicated by a few lines of English and French popular songs, demonstrating that the Latin poems derive from and are themselves in the verse form of a vernacular lyric.[6] Thus it is ultimately the popular nature of the carol genre which asserts itself here also. Greene's conclusion is that where the liturgy touches the carol it leaves only such effects as can be reconciled with the form already given by popular poetry. Behind the Latin *cantilenae*, which helped spread carol tradition, is still the vernacular carol form.

A more recent book, by Sarah Appleton Weber, *Theology and Poetry in the Middle English Lyric: A Study of Sacred History and Aesthetic Form* (Columbus: Ohio State University Press, 1969), carefully investigates the relationship of many Middle English lyrics to the liturgy. Noting the large number of lyrics which are composed after liturgical models or which have apparent liturgical value, Weber's book helps to place the performance contexts of many English lyrics in relationship to the theology of the Mass. In seeing these lyrics in their ecclesiastical setting, she does not, unfortunately, attempt to explain why so much material of liturgical value should so suddenly appear in vernacular verse form and not Latin (which clearly continued dominant in Church usage after this period), nor, regarding the concerns of her title, can she involve herself with the very large number of devotional lyrics which have no apparent liturgical connection. Nor does she face the question of why even the "liturgical" lyrics do not appear in regular missals and liturgy books, or in Books of Hours: the majority of extant lyrics written before 1350 appear either in special collections or in preachers' handbooks with clearly homiletical rather than liturgical organization, and most of the rest are found on flyleaves or as marginalia to a variety of Latin works. And it seems unlikely that liturgical themes account for the special style of the Middle English lyrics, with their spontaneous emotional apprehension of natural reality.

The most useful book to appear on Middle English religious verse is the one recently published by Rosemary Woolf, *The English Religious Lyric in the Middle Ages* (Oxford: Clarendon Press, 1968). A thematic study covering the thirteenth to fifteenth centuries, Woolf's is the first attempt to write a history of the religious lyric in medieval

England. She studies many of the important themes in this body of poetry, illustrates them, and recognizes that the poetry is fundamentally emotional and meditative in style and devotional in content; she concludes that "a history of the religious lyric that seeks to be comprehensive must become in part a history of medieval meditation and devotion."[7] Perhaps because it was outside the scope of her study, she does not develop any clear outline of such a history, or explore what it might mean for the poetry affected. This is unfortunate, as the perspective so afforded might have led her to qualify her thesis concerning the origin of the lyric: "The English religious lyric did not spring from the intention of putting secular conventions to the service of religion: it grew directly and unself-consciously from a Latin devotional movement, the authors using the vocabulary and verse forms conveniently at hand."[8]

I cannot, in view of the devotional history she suggests, concur with her view of the origin of the genre. Her attempt to support a Latinate theory and to discount a program of secular borrowings misses very much contrary evidence, which, when assembled, proves actually a complement to the main arguments of her book.

By comparison with Weber and in contrast to Greene, Woolf enlarges the argument somewhat, saying that the sources of Middle English religious lyrics "are invariably Latin works that are overtly and unmistakably meditations."[9] Generally speaking, however, she seems to have difficulty in showing the relationship between the specific Latin works she cites as sources and individual poems. I hope it will be possible to illuminate some of the reasons for the difficulty she encounters. For many of the cases (for example the *respice in faciem* she uses in her first chapter on Passion poetry), the likely reason that no close Latin source for the English poem has been discovered is that the poem is, with good reason, an independent response to the source Scripture (in that case Psalm 83:10), and this, I hope to show, is likely to be true for most Middle English lyrics—even those with liturgical themes such as *O vos omnes, Homo vide*, or the various *Improperia*. Woolf's study recognizes that the best English versions of the *Homo vide* are more like in feeling to other meditative vernacular verse than to their "source."[10] An awareness of the spirituality, the aesthetic, and the methodology of composition of these poems will help explain why this is so. In fact, even in those poems which are demonstrably close to a Latin original, it is the difference in the lyric style of the English version which is its really interesting feature.[11]

Where then may we turn to discover something more about the history and development of the popular Middle English lyric? As long ago as 1928, in his presidential address to the Modern Humanities Research Association, Carleton Brown suggested that one great influence on English culture remained virtually unstudied with respect to its particular influence upon literature:

> The historical facts concerning the coming of the Friars to England are well known, and the important influence which they exerted upon religious and social institutions has been pointed out so often that it does not need to be emphasized here. And yet no serious inquiry has been made, so far as I am aware, to estimate the service which they rendered in reviving vernacular literature. . . . The court . . . had its distinguished circle of poets, but the literature which they produced was written in an alien tongue and was recited before audiences composed entirely of the "high men" . . . . The monasteries had their profound scholars, but their learned treatises were in Latin. . . . Small provision was made for the instruction of laymen, and preaching was almost wholly discontinued in the parish churches. The friars immediately addressed themselves to these neglected laymen. . . . But no one has been able to tell us what they said.[12]

Eleven years later, R. H. Robbins began to investigate the provenance of early English carols. His discovery that what appeared to be the seven earliest religious carols were from Franciscan manuscripts of preaching materials seemed to him "unmistakable evidence that the Franciscans initiated the English religious popular carol." In a later article he examined the English carol manuscripts and discovered that possibly a majority of them were of Franciscan provenance. Robbins also quotes from correspondence with Brown in which Brown made the observation that the Middle English vernacular lyrics began to appear only after the first quarter of the thirteenth century, and then exploded into wide-ranging popularity within a very few years. The Franciscans, he reminded Brown, arrived in England in 1224.[13]

Following the lead of Robbins and Brown, most scholars treating the Middle English religious lyric have taken to referring vaguely to what is usually called "the Franciscan school"[14] when discussing carols and other lyrics of particularly obvious pietistic or devotional character. The most detailed explanation of what the term might mean has been offered by Walter J. Ong, in an article on medieval Latin religious poetry:

> Comparing [the "main tradition" of Latin religious] poetry . . . with what one finds in the *Dies Irae* and the *Stabat Mater Dolorosa*, one soon becomes aware that the textures of the two sorts of work are

quite different. . . . [They] both come into being within a distinctive current of mediaeval piety which may, for want of a more definitive characterization, be designated as the Franciscan school—both hymns are, as a matter of fact, attributed to Franciscans—although the school includes many non-Franciscan representatives, running back, as it does, to Bernard of Clairvaux and down into the renaissance *Following of Christ*. This school . . . characteristically finds the source of its rhetoric in the commonplaces of ordinary life—the love of son for mother, of mother for child, of brother for brother, St. Francis of Assissi's love of animals—encouraging the effort to transfer these or similar emotions to higher and nobler objects. This kind of piety seldom turns to theological elucidation . . . . In reference to Christ, such piety concentrates on His human nature, which provides it with a kind of bridge over which it can transfer to His Person responses, principally affective, with which it is familiar from elsewhere.

The existence of a Bonaventure shows that this school is not entirely averse to theological explanation; still, in fostering piety, far more readily than it takes to its theologians' findings, it takes to the conscription of popular notions and fashions which happen to be at hand.[15]

Franciscan spirituality is chiefly distinguished by its style. While Ong here speaks of Latin poetry, many of the stylistic attributes he enumerates are in fact characteristic of much medieval English poetry in the vernacular. Although it is clear that neither "Franciscan spirituality" nor the writing of lyrics was confined in this period solely to Franciscans, the specificial character of the Franciscan ministry significantly differs from that of other groups, for example, the Dominicans, in such a way as to suggest the English history of the Friars Minor as an appropriate contribution to this study.

Historians of the carol in particular have agreed in ascribing the initial impulse in its cultivation to the activity of the Franciscans.[16] The appearance of the earliest pieces of devotional polyphony set to English words was contemporaneous with the first period of their preaching in England; and compilations like the Franciscan *Book of Ossory* demonstrate an organized attempt to employ popular tunes for religious composition.[17] But the ascriptions remain vague because no one has yet shown why the Franciscans composed poetry or how they used it.

The discussion which follows attempts first to demonstrate substantial connections between the theology and methodology of the Order of Friars Minor and the form and content of extant Middle English lyrics, and subsequently to show ways in which an understanding of the nature of this connection can illuminate the style, content, and performance context of these poems. I do not presume in this book to propose a comprehensive *Ursprung* theory for the early English lyric. What this study indicates, however, is that any definitive history of this body of English poetry will need to fully engage the phenomenon of Franciscan spirituality, an influence which more than any other factor has decisively shaped early English lyric development. While the character of the Franciscan approach is distinctive in its own time, it agrees remarkably with the stylistic directions of English lyric poetry for many generations after the early Franciscan poets had ceased to write.[18]

Notes

1. *Die Theorien über der Ursprung der provenzalischen Lyrik* (Dusseldorf: Nolte, 1937). A more recent and also useful summary of *Ursprung* scholarship on the Provençal lyric and northern French lyric is Alfred Schossig, *Der Ursprung der altfranzösischen Lyrik* (Halle: M. Niemeyer, 1957).

2. See Robert Briffault, *The Troubadours*, ed. L. F. Koons, trans. by the author (Bloomington: Indiana University Press, 1965), chap. 2, which studies connections between Mozarab verse forms and those of the early troubadours; and his *Les Troubadours et le sentiment romanesque* (Paris: Les Éditions du Chêne, 1945). Another highly interesting work here is Leo Pollmann's *"Trobar Clus": Bibelexegese und hispano-arabische Literatur* (Münster im Westfalen: Aschendorff, 1965).

3. Rosemary Woolf, *The English Religious Lyric in the Middle Ages* (Oxford: Clarendon Press, 1968), p. 45.

4. Greene, *The Early English Carols*, pp. lxv–lxvii. See R. H. Robbins, "Friar Herebert and the Carol," *Anglia* 75 (1957): 194–98 for an example of limited hymn influence.

5. A century ago Édélestand Du Méril, *Poésies populaires latines du Moyen Âge* (Paris: F. Didot, 1847), suggested the debt of Latin hymnology to popular songs; this book will lend considerable evidence to that old theory.

6. Robbins discusses such a collection in *Secular Lyrics of the XIVth and XVth Centuries*, ed. Rossell H. Robbins, 2nd ed. (Oxford: Clarendon Press, 1955), p. xxxv.

7. Woolf, *English Religious Lyric*, p. 13.

8. Ibid., p. 2.

9. Ibid., p. 3.

10. Ibid., pp. 3, 30–31, 39.

11. See pp. 360 ff., 104. See also Douglas Gray's recent study, *Themes and Images in the Medieval English Religious Lyric* (London: Routledge & Kegan Paul, 1972). Of course, another option might seem to be the simple resignation of the Middle English lyric carols to that vaguest of historical shadows, "popular tradition." If we did not wish to delve anthropologically so fervently as Schossig, we might even let the quest go at that. Some carols, such as "Bring us in good ale," indicate a basis in folk-song, and folk-custom sufficient to titillate the anthropologists' irrefragable enthusiasm is suggested by the "Holly and Ivy" carols. (An amusing and effective warning against the pitfalls of over-zealous anthropologizing of medieval literature has been offered by C. S. Lewis, "The Anthropological Approach," in *English and Medieval Studies Presented to J. R. R. Tolkien* . . . [London: Allen & Unwin, 1962], pp. 219–30.) Here again, Greene's analysis checks undue generalization: the extant corpus of Middle English lyrics and carols evidences a written tradition largely, and the manuscript evidence, plus a study of form, combine to show that the carol as a genre was one step removed from the folk-song, if "lower" on the literary scale than the courtly lyric or scholarly Latin poem. The same could be argued for the popular lyric generally.

12. "Texts and the Man," *Bulletin of the Modern Humanities Research Association* 2 (1928):104. It should be noted that the thirteenth-century layman was probably not as neglected as has been sometimes thought; see D. W. Robertson, Jr., "The Frequency of Preaching in 13th Century England," *Speculum* 24 (1949):376–88. But the friars did draw large and enthusiastic audiences early in their ministry; see V. G. Green, *The Franciscans in Medieval English Life, 1224–1348, Franciscan Studies* 20 (Patterson, New Jersey: St. Anthony Guild Press, 1939), p. xi; also J. Huizinga, *The Waning of the Middle Ages* (New York: Garden City, 1954), pp. 12–13, etc. Their ability to draw such large crowds would seem likely to owe to their methods.

13. R. H. Robbins, "The Earliest Carols and the Franciscans," *MLN* 53 (1938):244–45; and "The Authors of the Middle English Religious Lyrics," *JEGP* 39 (1940):230–38.

14. E.g., Stephen Manning, *Wisdom and Number* (Lincoln, Nebr.: University of Nebraska Press, 1962), pp. 47, 49, 51, 78, 140–42, etc.

15. Walter J. Ong, "Wit and Mystery: A Revaluation in Medieval Latin Hymnody," *Speculum* 22 (1947):321.

16. *Early English Carols,* pp. cxxi–cxxviii. Greene notes that the Franciscans employed poetry in Italy, and also in France. See also E. K. Chambers, *English Literature at the Close of the Middle Ages* (Oxford: Clarendon Press, 1945), pp. 81–82.

17. Here the poems apparently set to popular tunes were composed in Latin. See Chambers, *English Literature,* pp. 108–9, 121; Robbins, *SL XIV–XV,* p. xxxv, but cf. Robbins, "Friar Herebert and the Carol," p. 194.

18. Patrick Grant explores the implications of the Franciscan tradition in "Augustinian Spirituality and the Holy Sonnets of John Donne," *English Literary History* 38 (1971):542–61.

Spiritual Revolution

&

Popular Poetry

ABOUT 1225, in what is usually thought to be the earliest recorded Middle English lyric, some long-forgotten troubadour, or his appreciative listener, inscribed on the leaf of a devotional handbook the following words:

> Mirie it is while sumer ilast
> wiþ fugheles song,
> oc nu necheþ windes blast
> and weder strong.
> Ej! ej! what þis nicht is long,
> and ich wid wel michel wrong
> soregh and murne and fast.[1]

The text is complete with music, and with its thoughts of summer, its artfully onomatopoeic "fugheles song" and even the "nighing" of winter's wind, offers a plangent and beautiful response to the cycles of nature. While a proverbial quality reaching back into Anglo-Saxon folk tradition reminds us of the English penchant for rustic maxim ("it's merry now while summer's here, but in winter then it's cold and drear"), the poem proves more skillful than proverb, more graceful

---

fugheles, birds'; *weder,* weather; *wid,* for, through, because; *soregh,* sorrow.

than cliché. At first glance a reader might, quite naturally, think of it as a secular poem.

Basic to the traditional classification of medieval poetry is a distinction between secular and religious realms of expression and experience.[2] The ground of this distinction was perhaps first forcefully suggested in the thirteenth century by St. Thomas Aquinas and others, who, in combining certain implementations of Aristotle's metaphysic with their continuing desire to pursue theology, found it necessary to a consistent dialectic to separate what they called the kingdoms of "nature" and "grace."[3] Subsequently, that separation has continued, with increasingly profound consequences for the history of art, culture, and criticism, to our own time, in many respects the most thoroughly "secular" age of our civilization. It is not surprising, therefore, forgetting how much of our understanding is acquired vocabulary and that the compass of our words may now be very different from what it used to be, that when we first look at "Mirie it is" we should refer it appreciatively to the realm of natural experience and turn to another poem. But in this poem the realm of natural experience is actually charged with implications for another and increasingly immanent kingdom.

Moving forward from the proverbial sense of the lines, we can appreciate on second examination how both in the dramatic shift of tone and emotion and in terms of natural imagery itself "sumer" readily figures the fullness of life, while the strong weather, howling winds, and long night suggest final winter, the barrenness of death. Here the tone of the poem disseminates a more ominous if not unusual foreboding; in the wind's warning is the anticipation of our mortality. The quickness with which the poet speeds our sense of the passage from life to death is one of his remarkable achievements: in five lines we slip away from the merry summer of birdsong to the "nighing" blast of winter's wind and reach an acute apprehension: "Yi! Yi! but this night is long . . ."—we may be dead a long while. The swift passage of time toward time's rough conclusion is beautifully apparent in the structure of the poem. But the series of emotions which begins with "mirie" does not conclude with "Yi! Yi!"; both proverbial and "metaphysical" senses of the poem are conditioned by the last two lines:

> and ich wid wel michel wrong
> soregh and murne and fast.

Here is where the difference begins. The poet's response to the inexorable course of the seasons, and of life itself, is not just recognition, or even alarm, but rather, personal remorse. His position is terminal. He looks backwards on the cycle of life—*his* own life—and in a consciousness of past wrongdoing says that he is sorry. He mourns, and he fasts. We have moved now from a poem about the cycle of the seasons to a shared consciousness of what a medieval theologian would unabashedly have called personal sin—and guilt. And so in this little seven-line poem we have natural, proverbial, "metaphysical," and now moral reference.

But there are fairly obvious theological implications in the poem as well. In the three terms of the last line are anticipated the three traditional steps involved in what Chaucer's Parson called "verray repentance"—true repentance:[4] *contrition* ("soregh"), *confession* (suggested by "murne"), and *satisfaction*, involving penitential action ("faste"). The poet's choice of words thus holds open two further possibilities: that the persona may be considered by us as languishing in the winter of death, gnashing his teeth in remorse, or, more hopefully, standing at the end of his own natural cycle, remorseful and repentant, engaging himself in penance while he has the opportunity. When one sings the song, of course, he "becomes" the persona, and the poem assumes a kind of evangelical self-prospect. The song's similarity to a popular biblical text is surely more than coincidental: Jeremiah 8:20 reads "Transiit messis, finita est aestas, et nos salvati non sumus" [The harvest is past, the summer is ended, and we are not saved]. And so it would seem possible to argue that "Mirie it is"—though not in a narrowly allegorical sense—is really a religious lyric.

Part of the obliquity in our critical perspective probably arises from the fact that the adjective "religious" can now have pejorative connotations when placed in apposition to the secular possibility. If we like "Mirie it is," we might prefer to exclude it from a classification with attendant dogmatic associations. It is clear that to do so would involve a distortion. And it is above all the apposition implied in the categories "secular" and "religious" which offers the most serious threat to the integrity of the poem. Certainly the vast majority of the Middle English lyrics left to us are "religious" in the sense that they are a form of religious expression; in fact about ninety per cent of the poems of known authorship were written by men in holy orders.[5] But to separate mechanically the two "kingdoms" in a medieval poem may obscure one of the most important premises of such a poem, which can be that there is no sharp discontinuity between secular and religious experience, or between the realm of God's created nature, including his highest creation, and God himself. Especially during the early thirteenth century this idea was viewed not just typologically, but "naturally."[6] The realm of nature was God's realm; it was also the realm of grace. Nature spoke to men about nature, about God, about sinfulness, and, when interpreted in the light of the Scriptures, about grace.[7] The ground of poetry, like the ground of experience, was spiritual, without a confusion between "religiosity" and "spirituality." There is nothing particularly new about this conclusion as a principle in medieval poetry; one can find it abundantly in earlier Latin verse.[8] What is notable here is that the connection of the two realms is not made in a labored allegorical sense: while patently informed by traditional theology, the associations are emotional and natural rather than intellectual and artificial. This subtlety may occasionally obscure for us the scope of the poem's comprehension. The method of "Mirie it is" is hardly so obvious as the method of poems by Prudentius, Alanus, or Jean de Meun.[9]

There is a second important observation to be drawn from a brief analysis of this little fly-leaf song. To make it, however, we need to have recourse to further historical comparison. The "Advent Lyrics" of the Exeter book (ca. 998) are the earliest English lyrics of note. The second lyric of the series begins:

> Eala þu reccend   ond þu riht cyning,
> se þe locan healdeð,   lif ontyneð
> eadgan upwegas,   oþrum forwyrneð
> wlitigan wilsiþes,   gif his weorc ne deag.

[You O Lord and true King who govern the locks, you open and reveal life. The exalted paths to another you deny, the glorious journey, if his acts are not worthy.][10]

Aside from the fact that it is a prayer to God the Father, designed after expressions of *comitatus* loyalty, its focus is outward, and the chanter of such an anthem does not feel so inescapably the implications of his words for his own life's condition. The tone of the poem does not play as subjectively upon the emotions. Unlike the longer Anglo-Saxon poems *Wanderer* and *Seafarer* (which even though not properly "lyric" poems in the later sense, do involve the reader in emotional response), the Advent Lyrics were designed to serve as a devotional exercise; they do not, however, lead to an urging of repentance in a way which is at once emotionally contrived and yet explicitly doctrinal. It is in fact the emphasis on repentance, and the poem's expression of remorse and contrition, which most sets a lyric like "Mirie it is" apart from earlier English lyric poetry.

If we move forward one hundred and fifty years we find, embedded

in a chronicle, the *Historia Eliensis* by Thomas of Ely, the following
poetic memory:

> Myrie songen the monkes binne Ely
> Whan Cnut Kyng rewe ther-by:
> Roweth, knightes, neer the lond
> And here we thise monkes song.[11]

Dated about 1150, it is the best known of a very few short poems in
English surviving from the first one hundred and fifty years of Norman
rule. It would be dangerous to make too much of it by way of representation. It is, however, much more a poem of objective, externalized
observation than "Mirie it is," like most of the poetry written in England between 1066 and 1200. We see King Cnut, supreme power of the
secular realm, pausing on his voyage to draw by the land and hearken
to the religious monks of Ely sing. It is a vignette of the ideal order
of things, one supposes, as the chronicler sees it. The reader is invited
to take some sense of satisfaction in this order, as in his pleasant
conjuration of the tranquil scene, but hardly to participate in any
critical personal way, and certainly not to the point of his own life's
evaluation and repentance. In the Cnut poem, the religious speaks
to the secular realm, but does not necessarily speak *in* it.

If we compare "Mirie it is" to poems written *after* 1225, however,
we find an abundance of similarity. From numerous tag-poems of the
memento mori type, through more artful and sophisticated versions
parallel to "Mirie it is" (such as "Death's wither-clench," "If man him
bithoghte inwardly and ofte," "Whan I see on rode i-don, Jhesus my
lemman," or "Wynter" [Harley MS.2253]), the extant corpus of Middle
English lyric verse is redolent with poems which urge immediate and
personal response to "michel wrong" and the long night of sorrow.[12]
Even a poem of devotion to the Virgin can end:

> A gult ig habbe, a weylawey!
> svnvvl ig am and wrege,
> by-sy to me, suete leuedy,
> þe no fend me ne dregche—
> to nyme bote ig am redy—
> and let me libbe and amendy,
> here deed me hvnne veȝge.
> for mine svnne ig am sory,
> þat lyues y ne regche,
> leuedy mercy! Amen.[13]

dregche, drag; *hvnne veȝge*, hence away.

The most striking feature of this poem is a sense of urgency, an emotionally intense, apparently contrition-bent mentality, thoroughly familiar to readers of the Middle English lyric. But the inspiration does not appear to be a literary inheritance. The spiritual tradition evident in the Advent Lyrics and in much medieval Latin poetry has not evolved into this new form; in fact, particularly in Latin verse, it continues side by side with the "new" religious lyrics in the vernacular.[14] Instead, there emerges in these poems a new sort of spirituality or religious expression which lends itself even more readily to articulation in vernacular poems and songs. If the generation of these qualities proves to be neither truly lineal nor truly native, it is natural that we should enquire after parallels.

On the continent, the most influential religious force on the popular arts had been the radical evangelical spirituality of St. Francis of Assisi. Earlier in the thirteenth century, it had provided the dynamic scintilla which ignited an explosion of Italian vernacular poetry, primarily in the religious lyric.[15] In that country, accomplished ecclesiastical and secular poets had turned to devotional composition in *vulgari eloquentia*, and the resulting poems in simple vernacular were often beautiful compositions. There is an interesting point of contact here, for while we might expect that the earliest Middle English lyrics would be in rough, untutored, or simple verse forms (like Ely's lines on King Cnut), in fact we find just the opposite.[16] These poems, their vocabulary so deliberately attuned to a popular and un-Latinate audience, are often highly skilled exercises in courtly verse forms. "Mirie it is while sumer ilast," for example, is composed in an early variety of *rhyme royale*.

If the tradition of the Middle English lyric is not initially a native one, it invites tracing all the more insistently when so many of its chief qualities can be discovered in a near contemporary tradition of spirituality and poetry which extends from the wayside exhortations of the first Friar Minor through the fire-and-brimstone preaching of St. Anthony, Bernardino of Siena, and John Pecham, on to Franciscan poets from the Italian Jacopone da Todi to the Englishman James Ryman. In this body of writing, akin in so many ways to the tone and feeling of Middle English lyrics, a distinctive spirituality, with primary emphasis on contrition and personal repentance, is everywhere apparent.[17] Preachers and poets from this tradition—some more skillfully than others—continually admonished their listeners to "wid wel michel wrong, soregh, and murne, and faste," or to:

Amende we us while we haue space
For why nowe is the tyme of grace.[18]

These same friars, as we shall see, felt some reason to believe that the "tyme of grace" was drawing to a close. "Mirie it is while sumer ilast," probably only the first stanza of a longer song, is itself only the beginning of a longer—and most intriguing—story.

English Franciscans were not, of course, the first in their order to use poetry as a channel for evangelical purposes. The first of their celebrated *ioculatores Dei* was in fact St. Francis himself.[19] But in tracing the Franciscan poetic tradition, we must first attempt to appreciate the general conditions which produced not only the revolutionary Franciscan response to traditional Christian gospel, but also the response of other movements of reform spirituality which employed poetry at the close of the twelfth century.

At the beginning of the eleventh century, the organized Church was showing advanced symptoms of encroaching dry rot. Nowhere was this more true than in the profound ecclesiastical turmoil of Languedoc and northern Italy. For years it had been common for priests to practice concubinage and simony, and despite the intense antipathy of ordinary parishioners, there was little they could do except refuse to attend Mass and other sacraments, which in any case were offered with remarkable infrequency.

Facing this confusion, Pope Gregory VII, already disturbed by the lack of papal control over France, considered an encyclical against simoniac and adulterous bishops, one which would sever the responsibility of obedience incumbent upon those under their sinful example.[20] For a time his action was delayed by the efforts of a few clerics, notably Sigebert of Gembloux, who urged that there should be some other way of negotiating reform of the churches than by such a decree. In his *Chronics* (1074) he expressed the fear that it might push the people to "Donatism"—a willful rejection of the established Church on the basis of the quality of its local representatives.[21] Sigebert apparently knew the condition of the European churches better than did the Pope.

In the same year, Gregory issued his proposed encyclical. It required all Christians to renounce their obedience to those bishops who showed indulgence to the clergy in the matter of celibacy. In the following year, 1075, he commanded the laity to accept no official ministrations from married priests, to refuse the sacraments from them and in fact to "rise against" them; he also deprived reprobate clerics of their revenues.[22] In 1109 he declared consecration by a simoniac to be null and void. Needless to say, these changes met with vigorous protest on the part of the affected clergy, especially since the number and extent

of infected parishes had grown so great that the decrees now served as
a license for whole populations to disown the official representatives
of the Church. With papal authority on their side, long repressed
feelings of animosity toward the clergy burst open. Some communities
indeed refused the sacraments, some stoned and even killed accused
priests, and laymen whose sincerity was respected by their peers began
to fill the function of the displaced priests—in open defiance of
injunctions against their doing so—even to the administration of the
sacraments. Priests were burned in their own money, and communion
elements "blessed" by married priests were overturned. Sigebert of
Gembloux cried out in a pamphlet: "Where is the Catholic who would
not be grieved . . . at the beauty of the Church being turned into
folly . . . clerics are objects of public derision and persecution, they
are castrated, mutilated . . ." and he adds, "as evident testimony to
the considerable wisdom of their chastisers." Yet, "some priests do not
repent if they are so fortunate as to escape public violence, and therefore . . . dealing fiercely with their pastors is now regarded as 'good
works' by the people."[23]

Despite institutional attempts to control excesses, the situation
continued largely unremedied to the end of the twelfth century. St.
Bernard's description of some of the churches of his own time is
hardly more commendatory:

> The churches are without preachers: the priests do not have the
> respect which is their due; Christians deny Christ, and their temples
> pass for synagogues. They disavow the sanctity of the sanctuary of
> God, and the sacraments are no longer regarded as sacred. Holy days
> pass without solemnity; men die in their sins, and their souls are
> borne before the redoubtable tribunal without having been recon-
> ciled to the Savior by penitence, and without the aid of the final
> sacrament. The grace of Baptism is denied, the children of Christians
> no longer learn to know Christ, they are no longer permitted to walk
> in the way of Salvation.[24]

In a society which was warp and woof the garment of the Church,
such abuses were bound to produce unrest. Since the first quarter of
the tenth century heretics had been increasingly a problem, and execu-
tions by burning were becoming increasingly frequent.[25]

Many of the conditions which favored the development of art and
literature also nourished a tendency to political and ecclesiastical rebel-
lion. No area offered a more favorable environment for the growth of
heresy than the south of France. Wealth, practical independence from
the central power of the French kings, a broadly based merchant trade,
the natural spirit of the inhabitants—all of these had fostered a degree

of what with caution we might call "individualism" and consequently a tendency toward fragmentation unmatched in northern feudal Europe. And many aspects of the social analysis of southern France cross over the Piedmont to equal pertinence in the provinces of northern Italy.

At first the heresies were largely "non-doctrinal," and according to the usually accepted view were principally manifestations of two phenomena: anticlericalism and religious "zealotism."[26] Men like Tancheln, Piere de Bruis, Henri de Lauzan, Clement and Edwardus, Éudes, or Éon d'Étoile, the Publicani, the Patarines, the Poor Men of Lyons, and their brothers the Poor Men of Lombardy, were basically people who would have much preferred to continue within a revitalized Church.[27] Many of them, in fact, continued to seek out "pure" clergy from whom to obtain the sacraments.[28] Although inevitably doctrinal differences of varying importance crept in, the Inquisition's condemnation focused on their insistence on "holy poverty" and "failure to submit to ecclesiastical authority."[29]

That there were many of these groups with doctrinal tendencies often quite distinct from one another is a fact that has been confused (and was even by the Inquisition) through lumping all heretics under the title "Albigensians."[30] Collectively, to be sure, the heretics did provide an extreme problem for the Church. For a brief period they eclipsed the Church as the major religious power in an area extending from Padova to the Loire, and opposing them was often difficult because of the remarkably exemplary lives many of them led. It is in this latter respect that some groups of heretics had much in common with the later movement of St. Francis. High ideals, a professed love of absolute honesty and poverty, and a vigorous proclamation of Christian love as the basis for human conduct combined in many cases to produce a distinctive pursuit of the *vita apostolica*.[31]

Among these groups of heretics the Waldensians, or Vaudois, are particularly interesting. In 1173, in Lyons of Gaul, a burgher named Peter Valdes, or Waldo, who had accumulated great wealth through the practice of lending money at interest, was living peacefully in the enjoyment of his success. As he walked along the road one day he stopped to listen to a *jongleur* telling the story of St. Alexis. It had a profound effect upon him. Waldo invited the *jongleur* to his house and, troubled by their conversation, later went to the local school of theology to seek advice for his soul's struggle toward God. The advice was "go and sell all that you have, and give to the poor." Unlike his biblical predecessor (Matt. 19:16–24), Waldo did just that. The poor rejoiced, his wife left him in disgust, and to this point he was regarded by the Church as favorably as any "religious"—except that they were concerned about the somewhat indiscriminate distribution of his money.[32] By 1177, the Chronique du Canon de Lyons reports of Waldo that he had taken vows of "eternal poverty," and had gathered around himself several enthusiastic followers who had vowed the same. Soon the group became large enough to be known as a sect, called at first not Waldensians or Vaudois, but "Poor Men of Lyons," and later also the "Poor Men of Lombardy." Little by little they began to expand their influence. Despite a protective Lateran decree,[33] the Bishop of Lyons soon conceived an acute distaste for their disturbing insistence on holy poverty, and instead of offering the cooperation of the Church, subjected the Poor Men of Lyons to intense and unhappy scrutiny. Yet such hostility apparently only served to cause a more rapid expansion of their movement.

In doctrine, Waldensians were considerably less unorthodox than most other "heretical" groups. Their principal deviation derived from their heavy emphasis on poverty, on chastity, and particularly on the Holy Scriptures: God's word was regarded as more authoritative than man's. Consequently, there was a doubled tendency toward disobedience of ecclesiastical authority when it was thought to contradict Scripture. At first the Poor Men of Lyons had preferred to have all sacraments administered by the Church; they wanted only to live and to preach primitive Christianity—the apostolic life.[34] Later on, specific doctrinal deviations that developed included a rejection of belief in prayer to the saints, in prayer for the dead, and in infant baptism.

In order to effect their program of spreading belief to others, the early followers of Waldo had turned to a vehicle which seemed to lend itself best to the problems of transmitting scriptural and doctrinal instruction to an un-Latinate people—vernacular poetry. Their idea was hardly original: Waldo himself had first been moved to repentance by the vernacular song of the *jongleur*. The process of vernacularization had had an early start in Provence; as early as 840 there are records of monks inserting vernacular pieces into antiphons and the liturgy, some of these described by the more traditional clergy as of "indecent character." In the tenth and eleventh centuries the practice had become common, and critics were complaining of the "prodigious ignorance" and "astonishing liberty of imagination" of the priests who rendered scriptural tales into poetical narrative. Monastic poets had written amatory and Song of Solomon-styled poems as well as hymns of the nativity,[35] and there was, of course, already a healthy tradition of Christian Latin poetry by this time.[36]

But the most relevant key to the storehouse of vernacular poetry of the turn of the thirteenth century is probably Waldo's *jongleur*. Thriving trade routes, increasingly popular fairs, expanding travel, the success of traveling groups—all of these offer a plausible incentive for folk entertainment, and records from the period show an ever increasing number of troubadours and minstrels. While in the past it has been argued that monastic poetry in the vernacular gave rise to the new *poésie populaire*,[37] by the late twelfth and thirteenth centuries the tide was really flowing the other way. All over Provence and northern Italy the Church found itself resorting to the vernacular, both in sermons and in poetic inserts, to compete with a vernacular tradition already well geared to meet popular demand.[38] How far back this Church borrowing reaches we can only guess, but presumably at least to the last quarter of the eleventh century.[39]

That the subject matter of the very earliest troubadour poetry was dominantly religious[40] also follows more naturally from its (popular) cultural environment than from a tradition of monastic poetry. For a pious people frustrated by the decadence of their local churches, the rhythms of worship and yearning for religious knowledge would seem to have been conditioned and sustained by lyric adaptations of Scripture into their native language:[41] it might well be that Waldo's *jongleur* was not at all unusual in his repertoire. Certainly Waldo himself worked to obtain translations of Scripture almost immediately,[42] and sent out his Poor Men of Lyons to preach from translated passages, chanting religious verse based on scriptural paraphrase but in the style of the mendicant *jongleurs*. The verse form served, or so we are told by a contemporary chronicler, as a memory device for both the preachers and their audiences.[43]

Publicity by popular poetry, unfortunately for the Waldensians, proved not much to their long-term advantage. As we have seen, they concluded their theological dispute with the Church at one critical point: their belief in each man's efficacy as his own priest in approaching God directly opposed the Church's insistence on the primacy of the hierarchic priesthood. Since this deviation and others less significant were said to be derived by Waldo from recourse to the Bible in his own language, the efforts of his followers to get vernacular Scripture or a reasonable facsimile thereof into the hands of their followers and would-be converts as quickly as possible was soon to be seen by the Church as a partisan objective.

Aside from Scripture, parts of the liturgy,[44] and perhaps a commentary on the Canticles, little religious poetry of the Provence Waldensians has survived. Chief among the remnants are *The Noble*

Lesson, The Scorn of the World, The Bark, The New Comfort, The New Sermon, The Lord's Prayer, The Parable of the Sower, and *The Father Eternal.* An account of these may be had elsewhere;[45] I should like to indicate here only two or three of the most interesting aspects of the poems.

First of all, this is religious poetry in the tradition of what Bayle called "vraie poésie populaire"—poetry of penitence, praise, narrative instruction, and adulation. There is evidence that a large body of poems no longer extant, like those mentioned above, concerned itself with paraphrasing "les plus touchantes histoires de la Bible."[46] Secondly, the poetry is not properly lyric: the pieces range from two to over four hundred lines, and since most are fragments, there were presumably some which were much longer. *La Nobla Leyczon* in particular resembles the sort of thing we have in the English *Cursor mundi,* but is even more like certain rhymed sermons and poetic homilies of the type of the "Seven Petitions of the Pater Noster" (MS. Bodl. Add. E.6).[47] Others of the poems are reminiscent of the Anglo-Norman poetic "homilettes" and didactic verse of Franciscan Friar Nicholas Bozon[48] more than they are of most Middle English Franciscan lyrics, although there is frequent use of lyric stanza forms.

Since these poems were primarily constructed as rhetorical teaching devices, there is every reason to believe that they were delivered in the manner of a sermon.[49] *La Nobla Leyczon,* written between 1190 and 1240,[50] also the period of the most revolutionary Franciscan activity, has a clearly didactic rather than simply narrative thrust, emphasizing that the true follower of Christ will practice the three virtues of spiritual poverty, chastity, and humility. This emphasis on a life consistent with that of Christ and the apostles runs throughout the poetry. The *New Comfort* begins with an injunction to abandon self and serve God with fear, "per l'amor del Segnor." Then follows a description of the wretchedness of this fleeting life, and after that a series of quatrains on faith and works. These verses lay heavy stress on the doctrine which

> San Jaco [St. James] mostra e aferma clarament,
> Qu l'ôme non se salva per la fé solament
> Se el non es cum las obras mescala fidelment.[51]

The *Parable of the Sower,* in the same stanza form, is a clear attempt to tell a biblical story in the vernacular poetic idiom, with highly interesting efforts to enhance immediate and local application through allusions to contemporary places and events. The likelihood that such biblical poetry owes partly to a vernacular oral tradition seems the more probable in that while Waldo's followers sang such songs and told such tales, we also know that they themselves were for the most part illiterate, and there remains no convincing record of actual "trouvering" among them.[52] The application of existing poetic traditions to their own proselytizing purposes may well have been chiefly the work of a learned minority, especially since the first converts were mostly among the laity.

The balance of early Waldensian poetry which is recorded but not extant was also typically religious: hymns to the Trinity, "souvenirs de la vie miraculeuse du Christ," legends adapted from prose Latin sources, acts of ancient heroes, saints' miracles, and pieces where "sous prétext d'invocation à Dieu le poète rapelle les principeaux évenements de l'ancien et du nouveau Testament."[53] Waldo and his followers seem to have regarded the instrument of vernacular poetry as a means to the end of learning more Scripture; when they could not obtain copies of translations they often passed on the passages orally, committing them to memory.[54] Reinerius Saccho tells us that out of six causes to which he ascribed heresy, four were directly involved with the *learning* of the heretics. "They teach and learn, without books . . . night and day. . . . To those who would excuse themselves, as not being able to learn, they say, 'Learn only one word every day, and in a year's time you will know three hundred, and you will get on'." The result was that Saccho had "seen and heard a certain lay countryman, who repeated the book of Job word for word, and many who perfectly knew the whole New Testament."[55] Saccho reports that their "learning" (he clearly means practical scriptural knowledge) was in fact often superior to that of the clergy. The poetic instrument apparently served its masters well.

The influence of Peter Waldo and his followers is not to be equated with that of the more immediately relevant movement of St. Francis.[56] What the Poor Men of Lyons have most to teach us is that, with respect to the conditions of their times, the essential spirituality and orientation of the early Franciscans were not unique. Waldo preceded Francis by scarcely a generation. Their areas of geographical and cultural influences correspond or overlap. They both lived in the area where the Church was suffering most from spiritual stagnation. Both men became interested in the spiritual regeneration of men. In their methodologies they both employed poetry for teaching; in fact, it may well be that some Franciscans took direct inspiration from their predecessors in this matter. One noteworthy difference between them however is that the early Franciscans, not under the same pressure from official ecclesiastical authority as the harried Waldensians, put primary emphasis on the development of another poetic form—the shorter popular song—more suited to their characteristically different needs and approach, while the suppressed Waldensian poetry, calculated to carry a greater body of specific scriptural knowledge, itself more quickly went the way of all things. Waldensian methodology, however, was to survive in the adaptations of more orthodox groups, including especially the Franciscans. And the shorter Franciscan poetic form, produced by an essentially coeval revolutionary climate of reform spirituality, became by virtue of a trick of history the major shaping influence in English lyric poetry of the Middle Ages.

St. Francis was born and raised in Assisi, a town which in 1203 had chosen an "Albigensian" for *podestà*, a fact suspicious enough to disturb some of the Pope's advisers.[57] And while the Franciscan movement is not to be confused with that of the Waldensians, it is undeniable that many of their basic objectives were identical.[58] Like the Poor Men of Lyons, St. Francis demanded absolute poverty; like them, his group were wandering preachers and singers—the *ioculatores Dei* who sang men into the Kingdom of Heaven.[59] Franciscans likewise considered themselves an apostolic and penitential order, and the scriptural passage that had convinced St. Francis of the necessity of poverty was the same as that espoused by Peter Waldo.[60] Theologians have said that St. Francis himself may have reflected an "heretical" influence in some of his teachings; and that he may have had some sympathy for heretics—though I suggest for reasons of Christian charity and not of heretical prejudice—may be suggested by the "Portiuncula Indulgence."[61] It is clear however, that the facts of both their similarity and their one crucial difference—the Franciscans were obedient to Rome—were not lost on Innocent III.[62]

St. Francis began with an intense mystic adoration fixed on the person and Passion of Christ, an adoration revealed both in the early biographies and in the songs of his followers. But in other Minorite themes and perhaps especially in their poetic forms, sources antedating St. Francis probably play a part. We know that in the years of the most severe persecution of heretical and unorthodox groups many of the returning "fraternities" as well as individual heretics, mystics, and vagrant clerks did attach themselves to the Franciscans.[63] Many of these, especially the clerks, may have been *jongleurs* in their own right. As for St. Francis himself, we learn from his early biographers that he first learned to write poetry in Provençal, and that for many years whenever he composed songs it was in the tongue of Languedoc and not his own native Umbrian.[64] In view of these considerations, it seems not entirely unjustified to make allowance in the Franciscans—especially of the time just after St. Francis' death—for religious and even literary influences of diverse origins.

The first years of the thirteenth century saw a steadily mounting papal pressure succeed in launching an offensive against numerous heretical groups, principally the Cathari and Vaudois who populated southern France and northern Italy. Significantly, recriminatory actions were taken at the same time against the "Spiritual" Franciscans, who, despite the opposition not only of the Holy See but of the majority in their own Order ("Conventuals"), persisted in their insistence on holy poverty, mendicant evangelism, and Joachimite apocalyptic speculation. (Notable among the *zelanti*, who unless they repented were forced to flee into hiding as heretics, was the English Franciscan theologian William of Ockham.) During and immediately after the Inquisition and the "crusades" the Popes were successful in obtaining the reintegration of many of the heretical groups back into the Church. The reconciliation was accomplished in a variety of ways. In 1208 and 1209 some Franco-Spanish Vaudois under the urgings of Innocent III were led back into the fold by their poet-preacher Durandus de Huesca. Many of the Lombard Waldensians, despite their intense emphasis on the personal relationship between man and God and the "priesthood of believers," were nevertheless won back to local parishes in Lombardy. The Humiliati, a heretic group with much the same emphasis on poverty and spirituality as the Franciscans or the Waldensians, were reclaimed under Innocent III as an entire order, and remain so today.[65] Confraternities like that of the Rosary or the Puy evidently received a variety of spiritual refugees.[66] But the crusade did not prove entirely effective; many of the ordinary laity among the heretics, especially in the more isolated areas, simply went underground, only to reassert themselves later on.[67]

Altogether, the number of "heretic" poets who ended their lives in reconciliation with the Church, or died in cloisters, is considerable.[68] But perhaps most relevant to our immediate concern is the tremendous amount of borrowing from materials of the errant poets by either sympathetic or competitively minded clergy as well as by Franciscans. The sudden prevalence of the use of rhyme in thirteenth-century French sermons and the new emphasis on religious poetry did not develop out of thin air. Lecoy de la Marche describes a trend: "La chaire n'échappe pas à la contagion: tantôt le prédicateur s'empare d'un texte de chanson vulgaire pour en faire un commentaire de fantaisie, tantôt il revêt son discours même d'une forme rythmique."[69]

A case in point is Étienne de Bourbon, Dominican priest and Inquisitor. Faced with the success of his opponents, he began to adapt and compose verses, making them "objects que de rappeler à l'orateur les principaux points de son sermon." What he used for this purpose was four or five rhymes which he called *versus colorati*; others of his compatriots began to use longer poetic insertions or even metrical sermons.[70] It is in these forms, of course, that the real influence of the suppressed poetic tradition of the Waldensians and other heretic groups survives. Soon both poetic sermons of the type first used by groups like the Poor Men of Lyons one hundred and fifty years earlier and the sermon-tag lyrics of the Franciscans had spread over France and appeared also in England.[71]

As late as the Irish *Red Book of Ossory* (begun by the Franciscan Richard de Ledrede in 1316, and continued by his successors till the sixteenth century) the reorientation of secular vernacular songs was a short route to providing religious music on short notice—in this last case for the use of the clerics themselves. Among the Latin songs and scraps of vernacular verse in the book is a Latin rubric which explains the presence of the early fourteenth-century songs. As Robbins has observed, in the course of their contact with the local people the clerics had picked up various *cantilene teatrales turpes*, and their superior, not wishing to forbid what was enjoyed, "substituted pious words for the secular, and thereby reproduced in Latin the original form of the vernacular pieces. So that his clergy would recognize the tune for the new Latin verses, Ledrede headed some of his sacred parodies with lines of the corresponding vernacular song."[72] This practice had its hazards: Gerald of Wales in his *Gemma ecclesiastica* tells how one day an absent-minded priest got up before his congregation and began to chant—but the words that first came to the music were "swete lemman, dhin are." That kind of "are" not being the sort of thing his bishop thought the Church should be dispensing, a ban on the song ever being sung again within the parish was promptly proclaimed.[73] For all that, even from the limited examples adduced here we can see that while the borrowing of poetic forms for original religious composition by friars and others may have been more common in the thirteenth century than the bishop would have approved, it is certain that when occasion suited the regular Church itself was decreasingly averse to borrowing tavern songs to meet a growing competition. Most of the evidence, however, points to the Franciscans as first and chief among clerical borrowers of the popular vernacular song.

It could be observed, of course, that flexibility for the adaptation of whatever most effective materials are at hand has always been

characteristic of effusions of Christianity at their moments of greatest
spiritual strength. The history of liturgical music is replete with instructive examples. It may be recalled that the organized introduction
of music into Christian worship has been claimed for Arius, who
curiously enough is now also known as a heretic. Arius collected songs
of sailors, millers, and travelers and set them to liturgical texts. Gibbon
made the story popular in the eighteenth century, telling how Arian
singers paraded the streets of Constantinople, beguiling the ignorant
with indoctrination by popular song, until Chrysostom effectively
countered them with his own group of singers.[74] In a similar vein,
many dance tunes of the Renaissance have been preserved to us
through their incorporation into a Mass. For example, the tune
"L'homme armé" ("The armed man") was a popular French folk
song of the fifteenth century, and was made into a polyphonic song by
Antoine Busnois. Over the ensuing generations thirty writers adopted
it for newly polyphonic liturgical music; Palestrina's *Missa quarta* of
1582 is based on it. During the Reformation, likewise, many popular
tunes found their way into hymns. Siegmund Levarie, in his book
on the fourteenth-century French composer Guillaume de Machaut,
describes such a process:

> Students used to sing a ditty when leaving their university town at
> the end of a term; substitution of one word changed "Innsbruck, I
> now must leave thee" to "O world, I now must leave thee," and reli-
> gion gained new adherents by the adoption of a melody. A popular
> tune, "Mein mut ist mir betrübet gar" ("My heart is very sad") opens
> a song collection written down by a Nurnberg citizen around 1450.
> The composer Hans Leo Hasler, of the same town, used the melody in
> a small piece for chorus, which was widely sung around 1600 as a
> lament to the words "Mein G'mut ist mir verwirret" ("My heart is all
> confused"). For this secular "hit," the Protestant poet Paul Gerhardt
> found a new text by freely translating St. Bernard's mystical "Salve
> caput cruentatum" into "O Haupt, voll Blut and Wunden" ("O head,
> full of blood and wounds"). And in this version one hears it today,
> as the often recurring and deeply moving chorale in Bach's *Passion
> According to St. Matthew.*[75]

Many more highlights could be cited, including the one to which
Protestants are still heir, the eighteenth-century revival hymns adapted
under the influence of the Wesleys. One wonders with Levarie how
many modern congregations think of "Rock of Ages" as a pastorale,
Handel's "And the Glory of the Lord" as a minuet, and "Oh That
Will Be Glory For Me" as a waltz. Despite some failing in the nine-

teenth century, vigorous adaptations of secular music for religious purposes have continued to mark revivals of Christian spirituality. The Negro spiritual is an excellent case in point, and in fact in its turn has reinfluenced contemporary secular music.

In the thirteenth century this kind of adaptation was a vigorously thriving enterprise, and while Franciscans and groups like the Waldensians were chiefly catalytic to the process, the secular clergy was also beginning to respond to the challenge. Indeed, they soon saw that here too, just as in the more exalted genres of narrative poetry, there was ample justification for such a methodology in the early Fathers. St. Augustine, in particular, commenting on the Exodus, had noted that "just as the Egyptians had not only idols and grave burdens which the people of Israel detested and avoided, so also they had vases and ornaments of gold and silver" which the Israelites took with them, as God's commandment, to put to a better use (*De doctrina Christiana* 2.40.60). This passage, along with passages in Origen and St. Jerome (*Epistle* 70 in particular), received a popular audience through preaching guides like John Bromyard's *Summa praedicantium*, and became for the centuries which followed a guarded injunction to borrow from the world whatever could be rendered serviceable to furthering the message of God's love found in Scripture.[76] We will see that no group developed this aesthetic and theological methodology more fervently or thoroughly than the Franciscans. It is interesting that at the very time when certain elements of the Church, particularly in northern France, were rediscovering this principle, it was already being implemented far more pervasively at the grass-roots level in the south of France and in northern Italy, and by groups of which many would prove to be an actual threat to the established Church. The threat, however construed, seems to have been very much a motivating force behind extensive competitive borrowing of the poetic medium, and also the various reclamation movements besides the friars (e.g., confraternities like those of the Rosary and Puy, and the ordo Humiliati) which were instituted to redeem and to prevent if possible errants like Waldo and his followers.

It is as the most significant of the Catholic "reclamation" groups that we now regard the Franciscans. That they were able to fulfill this role owes in great part to their natural affinity to the heretical sects with their emphasis on *vita apostolica* and evangelical spirituality. When St. Francis was recognized by Innocent III in 1210, the recognition was made in an attempt to bring his group under the wing of the Church before it, too, went the way of the Poor Men of Lyons.[77] Based like that of the Cathari and Waldensians on poverty and renunciation, while emphasizing a thoroughly personal and evangelical content, the doctrine of Francis avoided the charge of heresy largely because of his own simple obedience to the constituted powers of the Church.[78] There is however substantial evidence to suggest that, if not St. Francis himself, then certainly those who continued to insist on following his "pure rule"—the *zelanti*—were profoundly influenced not only by many of the same conditions as the Waldensians, but also by more radical theological aberrations, such as certain of their apocalyptic expectations which will be considered in the next chapter.

Yet for practical purposes, St. Francis was not himself in any real doctrinal dispute with the Church. In fact, one could almost say that he and most of the early Umbrians who followed his example were "sublimely ignorant" of strictly theological questions. For him the issues at hand were the urgency of repentance and conversion in face of what seemed to be the imminent end of the "tyme of grace" and the coming of Judgment, and the necessity of fulfilling Christ-like service in the pursuit of evangelical objectives. Therefore, doctrinal content in the songs, whether traced in Umbrian, Provençal, or English, is as simple, traditional and direct as popular songs—a "mass media" approach directed towards moving ordinary people to spiritual reform. This was the key motivation for Franciscan preaching, and for Franciscan song. Uniquely sanctioned by Rome, and generally unhindered by official persecution, the friars could wander from town to town in the manner of minstrels, from market place or street corner sing the old songs which had become new, and in so doing draw townsfolk for a characteristically simple penitential sermon.[79] They offered their poetry as a waysong, the appetizer as it were, but seldom as the main course. Once we have understood the Franciscan method it is not then difficult to understand why the poetic tool the Franciscans developed was lyric, and not narrative like that of the Waldensians.

St. Francis was schooled in the language and forms of the Provençal poets, and himself wrote the earliest surviving Umbrian lyric in the vernacular ("The Canticle of the Sun").[80] One of his original followers, Brother Pacifico, in the world a composer of wanton songs, had been crowned by the emperor as *Rex versum* before joining the Order.[81] In Umbria and elsewhere in Italy lay brotherhoods of *laudesi* soon sprang up, giving employment to *jongleurs* and poets who would "with more devotion than art . . . frame rude songs or dramatic pieces on the ever popular events of the Gospel story, especially on the Passion, the miracles of the Virgin, and the joys of Paradise."[82] Out of these groups also came Latin hymns of lasting fame: the magnificent *Dies irae* of Thomas of Celano, the plangent *Stabat mater* of Jacopone da Todi, and the graceful *Philomena* of John of Pecham, the brother minor who became Archbishop of Canterbury in 1279. But as we shall see, the vast body of Franciscan poetic production remained popular and in the vernacular dialect. In it the emotional atmosphere of early Franciscan Christianity is continually present. In the vernacular poems as much as in the Latin, the two principal themes of Franciscan spirituality continued to be repentance and contrite identification with the passion of Christ.

Jacopone da Todi was one, for example, who like Franciscan poets after him was keenly aware of the impetus given to repentance by an awareness of the decay of the flesh. In his vernacular poems, like the dialogue between the Soul and the Body, or the ghoulish *Quando t'aliegri* (an address to a decaying corpse), we see a rationale behind the call for spiritual reorientation which is less dramatically if perhaps more succinctly stated in the first stanza of his Latin *De contemptu mundi*:

> cur mundus militat sub vana gloria,
> cuius prosperitas est transitoria:
> tam cito labitur eius potentia,
> quam vasa figuli, quae sunt fragilia.[83]

[Why does the world go on struggling for vainglory, whose prosperity is so short-lived: its power is as quickly broken as the fragile vessels of the potter.]

Yet penance is not the ultimate goal, but rather the crucial turning point after which, by grace, man may identify himself with Christ and so reach for salvation; man is called not only to the actions of penance but to "ammendement."[84] Identification with Christ in his death on the cross is the means, as St. Paul said, of putting to death the old man in ourselves, and being reborn into the new life which is Christ in us (Galatians 2:20). This kind of identification is ultimate, and in his *De passione Domine* Jacopone's final cry capsulizes the point of his whole poem:

> in hac tua passione
> me agnosce, pastor bone.[85]

[In this your suffering recognize me, good shepherd.]

These lines, recalling the words of the repentant thief in Luke 23:42, remind us that the kind of cognition implied in "me agnosce" is that which St. Bernard, for example, had suggested in his treatment of

John 10: 27–28[86] ("My sheep hear my voice and I the Lord acknowledge them, and they follow me; and I give to them eternal life") and which in the Vulgate reads, "Oves meae vocem meam audiunt et ego Dominus *agnosco* eas, et sequuntur me; et ego vitam aeternam do eis . . . ," that is, it is an "identification" involving new birth and eternal life as the consequence of a shared dying.

The Franciscan poets were to see the most powerful appeal of the atonement as emotional, and envision the basis of that appeal as concretely manifested in the physical details of the crucifixion itself.[87] In this bias they were departing substantially from previous tradition, taking the sometimes remote biblical doctrine and infusing it with vivid, even gruesome descriptions of the pain and suffering of Christ. Almost always, Christ's bodily agony becomes overtly symbolic of the infinitely greater magnitude of his spiritual suffering on behalf of sinful mankind, but to drive the spiritual message home the physical point was graphically portrayed as perhaps never before in Christian art.[88] Christ crucified became the supreme image and focus for the universal tension between Love and Death. The appeal of the new, spiritual approach was explosive, ultimately helping to instigate a stylistic revolution which changed the course of European art.[89] In the new expression, in the psychology of motif as well as in theme, we begin to see that the spirituality manifested in Franciscan art is double-edged: vividly portrayed, man's fear of death moves him toward penance, and vivid manifestations of the greatest love and pity move him toward love. The latter response, evoked in visions of the Passion of Christ, could often be most sensitively realized from the vantage of Mary, who in the literary iconography of Franciscan poetry is not alone the abstract Virgin, or the bride of the Song of Songs, but an effective presence, a vital referent for personal, human identification. F. J. E. Raby has aptly said that "the Franciscan singers, from Bonaventura to Jacopone, sang always with their faces set to the scene of this double passion, where

> Under the world redeeming rood
> The most afflicted mother stood
> Mingling her tears with her Son's blood."[90]

He might easily have made the boundaries larger—from St. Francis to the authors of the early English lyric.

Notes

1. Carleton Brown, ed., *English Lyrics of the XIIIIth Century*, corr. ed. (Oxford: Oxford Univ. Press, 1962), no. 7 (hereafter cited as *EL XIII*). A musical setting of 'Mirie it is' is recorded: *Medieval English Lyrics*, Argo #2RG5443.

2. The title of the general English lyric collections reflect this distinction. Those which will be most often referred to here, in addition to the work cited above, are: *Religious Lyrics of the XIVth Century*, ed. Carleton Brown, 2nd ed. rev. by G. V. Smithers (Oxford: Clarendon Press, 1957), hereafter cited as *RL XIV; Secular Lyrics of the XIVth and XVth Centuries*, ed. Rossell H. Robbins, 2nd ed. (Oxford: Clarendon Press, 1955), hereafter cited as *SL XIV–XV; Historical Poems of the XIVth and XVth Centuries*, ed. Rossell H. Robbins (Oxford: Clarendon Press, 1959), hereafter cited as *HP XIV–XV; The Early English Carols*, ed. Richard L. Greene (Oxford: Clarendon Press, 1935), hereafter cited as *EEC; One Hundred Middle English Lyrics*, ed. Robert D. Stevick (Indianapolis: Indiana Univ. Press, 1964), hereafter cited as Stevick; *The Harley Lyrics*, ed. G. L. Brook (Manchester: Univ. of Manchester Press, 1964), hereafter cited as Brook.

3. For the handling of these terms by St. Thomas, see the convenient collection edited and translated by A. M. Fairweather, *Nature and Grace, Selections from the Summa Theologica of St. Thomas Aquinas* (London, 1954); see also D. L. Jeffrey, "From Plato's Academy to 'The School of Athens,'" in *By Things Seen: The Ordering of Experience in Medieval Culture*, ed. D. L. Jeffrey, R. W. Kaeuper, and R. A. Peck (forthcoming).

4. *Parson's Sermon*, line 85, in *The Works of Geoffrey Chaucer*, ed. F. N. Robinson, 2nd ed. (Cambridge, Mass.: Houghton Mifflin, 1961), p. 229. The Parson's full treatment of penitential doctrine is a good example of a medieval treatise on penance.

5. Rossell H. Robbins, "The Authors," p. 230.

6. Cf. M. D. Chenu, "Nature and Man: The Renaissance of the Twelfth Century," in his *Nature, Man, and Society in the Twelfth Century* (Chicago: Univ. of Chicago Press, 1968), pp. 1–48.

7. See chap. 3 below, the discussion of Bonaventure's *De reductione artium ad theologiam*.

8. See the study by F. J. E. Raby, *A History of Christian-Latin Poetry from the Beginnings to the Close of the Middle Ages*, 2nd ed. (Oxford: Clarendon Press, 1953), hereafter cited as Raby.

9. I do not mean to suggest, of course, that because the allegorical method of a poet like Jean De Meun makes his intentional indirection more apparent, his meaning is always obvious. See the excellent study by John V. Fleming, *The Roman de la Rose: A Study in Allegory and Iconography* (Princeton: Princeton Univ. Press, 1969).

10. *The Advent Lyrics of the Exeter Book*, ed. J. J. Campbell (Princeton: Princeton Univ. Press, 1959), pp. 48–49.

11. Stevick, no. 1.

12. E.g., *EL XIII*, nos. 10, 13, 20, 30, 35A, 35B, 38; *RL XIV*, no. 133; Brook, no. 17.

13. *EL XIII*, no. 32.

14. Raby, pp. 376–414; W. Ong, "Wit and Mystery: A Revaluation in Medieval Latin Hymnody," *Speculum* 22 (1947):310–41.

15. See A. F. Ozanam, *Les Poètes franciscains en Italie au trezième siècle* (Lyon, 1913).

16. See Sabino Casieri, *Canti e liriche medioevale inglese del MS. Harley 2253* (Milan: La Goliardica, 1962), esp. pp. 8–27.

17. Raby, pp. 419 ff.; François Vandenbrouke, in J. Leclercq, F. Vandenbroucke, and L. Bouyer, *The Spirituality of the Middle Ages*, pp. 283 ff. (vol. 2 of *A History of Christian Spirituality*, 3 vols., newly trans. and ed. [London: Burns and Oates, 1963–69]), the most important study of medieval Christian spirituality; see also Pierre Pourrat, *Christian Spirituality*, 4 vols. (London: Burns, Oates and Washbourne, 1922–55), vol. 2.

18. Franciscan friar James Ryman, who died at Canterbury in 1492, is a late practitioner of the Middle English lyric who manifests a number of the traditional traits of Franciscan spirituality and poetic style. This is the burden of one song, quoted entire in chapter six below, from the complete poems edited by J. Zupitza, from MS. Cambridge University Library, HS. Ee. I, 12, in "Die Gedichte des Franziskaners Jakob Ryman," *Archiv für das Studium der neueren Sprachen und Litteraturen* 89 (1892):167–338, no. 49 (hereafter cited as Zupitza).

19. *Speculum perfectionis*, ed. Paul Sabatier (Paris, 1898), p. 197.

20. P. Jaffé, *Regesta pontificum*, 2 vols., 2nd ed. (Paris, 1865), 1:594–649.

21. J. P. Migne, ed., *Patrilogia cursus completus, series Latina* (hereafter cited as *PL*). 221 vols. (Rotterdam, 1878–80), 160: 217.

22. See n. 20 above.

23. A further colorful detail from the same source: some confirmations were performed with a substitute oil of confirmation made from ear wax (G. H. Pertz, T. Mommsen, et al., *Monumenta Germaniae Historica*, Auspiciis Societatis Aperiendis Fontibus Rerum Germanicarum Medii Aevii [1826–89]—hereafter cited as *MGH*—ser., LL., 2:436). St. Bonaventure echoes the same complaints vigorously. Jacopone, in one of his satires (*Lauda LII*, "Jesu Cristo se lamenta"), says that Christ weeps because of the ungrateful Roman Church, that her unworthy priesthood "murders Him afresh, and wastes the fruits of His labors for men."

24. "Basilicae sine plebibus, plebes sine sacerdotibus, saderdoes sine debita reverentia sunt, et sine Christo denique Christiana. Ecclesiae synagogae reputantur; sanctuarium Dei sanctum esse negatur: Sacramenta non sacra censentur: dies festivis frustrantur solemniis. Moriunter homines in peccatis suis: reapiuntur animae passim ad tribunal terrificum, heu! nec poenitentia reconciliati, nec santa [al. sacra] communione muniti. Parvulis Christianorum Christi intercluditur vita, dum Baptismi negatur gratia [etc.]" (*Epistle 241*, in *PL* 182: 434).

25. Steven Runciman, *The Mediaeval Manichee: A Study of the Christian Dualist Heresy* (Cambridge: Cambridge Univ. Press, 1947), p. 117.

26. J. Guiraud, *Histoire de l'Inquisition au Moyen Âge* (Paris: A. Picard, 1935).

27. For accounts of these groups, see Peter the Venerable, *PL* 189: 719, 850; St. Bernard of Clairvaux, *PL* 182: 434 ff.; Georges Bourgin, ed., *Guibert de Nogent, histoire de sa vie* (Paris: A Picard, 1907), bk. 3; see *MGH*, ser., Scrip. 19: 131 ff.; also "William of Newburg," *Rerum Britanica Medii Aevi Scriptores* (London, 1858–98), 82: pt. 1, 60; and for the Poor Men of Lyons, see Jean Jalla, *Histoire des Vaudois des Alpes et de leurs colonies* (Paris: Pignerol, 1904), chap. 1.

28. See Runciman, *Manichee*, passim; also Étienne de Bourbon, *Anecdotes historiques, légendes, et apologues*, ed. A. Lecoy de la Marche, Société de l'histoire de France (Paris: Renouard, 1877), pp. 327 ff., nos. 274–314. Étienne was a Dominican of the early thirteenth century; his is probably the closest thing to an objective account of the heretics in an Inquisition-minded age. Although he was a Dominican, he took considerable interest in the heretics, even to the point of later being among the first to imitate them in the use of verse from the pulpit.

29. C. Sc! midt, *Histoire et doctrine de la secte des Cathares ou Albigeois* (Paris: J. Cherbuliez, 1849), 1:7–24.

30. A. S. Turberville, *Mediaeval Heresy and the Inquisition* (London: C. Lockwood, 1921), p. 22. (This tendency has behind it St. Augustine's treatment of Manicheanism, thus Runciman's title *The Mediaeval Manichee*.) Pierre Belperron (*La Croisade contre les Albigeois et l'union de Languedoc à la France* [Paris: Plon, 1945], pp. 61–63) observes the various distinctions relevant to the period. He divides the Albigeois into their constituents, principally Cathars and Vaudois, plus the many unassociated groups.

31. See Turberville, *Mediaeval Heresy*, pp. 20–21. For a list of charges sometimes made against the Waldensians, see the transcription of English MS. Cott. Jul. D, xi, fol. 84r (14th century) published by T. Wright in *Reliquae antiquae*, 1 (London: J. R. Smith, 1845): 246.

32. Étienne de Bourbon, *Anecdotes*, pp. 290 ff. (The St. Alexis referred to is the anchorite who died in 412.) See also Jalla, *Histoire des Vaudois*, pp. 121 ff. Cf. the ME life of St. Alexis in four versions from six MSS, late fourteenth century, ed. Frederick J. Furnivall (EETS OS 69 [London: Trübner, 1878]), pp. 17–79. It also appears in the Franciscan-authored *Gesta Romanorum*, where Alexis is referred to as the "mendicant stranger"; see Charles Swan's translation of one of the Latin MSS, ed. T. Wright (New York, 1871), 1:72. There is a *lauda* to St. Alexis in Italian MS. Cortona 91 (Franciscan confraternity) where Alexis is similarly referred to as "Come pellegrino andave" (Fernando Liuzzi, *La Lauda e i primordi della melodia italiana*, 2 vols. [Rome: La Libreria dello stato, 1934], 2:319—hereafter cited as Liuzzi). See also chap. 4.

33. Jalla, *Histoire des Vaudois*, pp. 13 ff. The Third Council of the

Lateran in 1179 (Pope Alexander III) condemned many heresies (Cathar, Publicani, Patarenes, Albigensians of Toulouse, etc.) but not the Vaudois. The Pope approved Waldo and the vows of poverty, but forbade his followers to preach except by invitation of a priest. This prohibition was obeyed for a short time only.

34. See documents in S. R. Maitland, *Facts and Documents Illustrative of the History, Doctrine, and Rites, of the Ancient Albigenses and Waldenses* (London, 1832), pp. 342 ff. Lucie Varga, in "Peire Cardinal était-il hérétique?" *Revue d'histoire des religions* 117 (1938):213, says that they were trying to return "vers un catholisme primitif."

35. See C. C. Fauriel, *History of Provençal Poetry* (New York, 1860), pp. 155, 158–63.

36. This has been well documented by Raby.

37. "La poésie monastique devait produire la poésie populaire. Les jongleurs après avoir répété les hymnes et les récits qu'ils avaient appris dans les cloîtres, composaient euxmêmes des chants naïfs qui bientôt passaient de bouche en bouche, voyageaient d'une province à l'autre, étaient répétés dans toutes les campagnes par les pâtres gardant leur troupeau, par les laboureurs poussant leur charrue, par les femmes rassemblées autour du lavoir ou occupées à la cueilleté des olives. On ne savait pas quel était l'auteur de ces couplets si promptement gravés dans toutes les memoires. Inspirés par le peuple, ils retournaient au peuple, après avoir reçu d'un ménestrel ambulant une forme rythmique et un air facile à retenir" (M. A. Bayle, *La Poésie provençale* [Aix, 1876], p. 194).

38. Fauriel, *Provençal Poetry*, pp. 162–63.

39. This is where Fauriel (pp. 351 ff.) places the real upsurge of vernacular poetry in Provence. It is fair to suspect that among the traveling *jongleurs* and minstrels vernacular songs and poems were a venerable tradition. However, since it was orally carried more often than written we do not have extant MSS (see Ernst Hirsch, *Beiträge zur Sprachgeschichte der württembergischen Waldenser* [Stuttgart: W. Kohlhammer], 1962).

40. Bayle, *Poésie provençale*, pp. 241 ff.

41. Étienne de Bourbon records another instance, where a *jongleur* meets a woman known for her beauty and concupiscent love of many suitors, and converts her to the love of God, a love greater than all others: "Audivi quod, cum quidam domina pulcritudine speciosa, a multis impetita, multos amore pernicioso adamasset, et multi eam, quidam joculator per hanc viam eam ad amorem Dei convertit. Sollicitabat eam quod amorem suum poneret in quemdam magnum maxime pulcritudinis, probitatis, largitatis, curialitatis, etc. Cum autem illa diceret quod ipsa habuisset tot impetitores et habuisset amatores tam magnos et divites et probos, cum ille intulisset quod ille pro quo rogabat omnes gracias aliorum excedebat, illa tandem consenciente quod, si talem eum probaret, amorem suum ei daret, intulit: 'Nullus nobilior, divicior, curialior Virginis filio, in quo sunt omnes gracie sine defecto.' Cum ergo ostendisset ei eorum quos ipsa dilexerat defectum et christi comple-

mentum graciarum omnium, movit eam ad contemptum vanitatis et amorem veritatis" (*Anecdotes*, p. 186, no. 214).

42. Jalla, *Histoire des Vaudois*, chap. 2.

43. It is an Inquisitor and a Franciscan who indicates the object of these rhymes, and he adds that they are not the only attempts of this kind. "They shrewdly intermingle their own rites and heresies so that they might better allure for the purpose of teaching these things, and so that they might memorably and more thoroughly inculcate them. Just as we with good reason propound to laymen the Creed, the Lord's Prayer, and other things, so they devise beautiful songs for the same purpose" (from David of Augsburg, chap. 17, as quoted in Emilio Comba, *History of the Waldenses of Italy*, trans. T. E. Comba [London: Truslove and Shirley, 1889], p. 338, n. 801). David was a Franciscan mystic whose notable pupil and friend was Berthold von Regensburg, the Franciscan preacher who so eloquently urged the Franciscans to expedite the spreading of their message by borrowing the heretics' poetic technique (see chap. 4, nn. 52–55, below).

44. One early Waldensian MS contains "the Gospels appointed for the last fortnight in Lent, with some Epistles for the same season, and the gloss attributed to Haimon" (Comba, *History of the Waldenses*, p. 171). The language is definitely Provençal (Comba, pp. 163–66, and nn. 327, 328; and François J. M. Raynouard, *Choix des poésies des troubadours* [Paris: F. Didot, 1816–21], 2:140).

45. Comba, *History of the Waldenses*, pp. 215–31. There is a reproduction of most of these in Antoine Monastier, *Histoire de l'Église Vaudoise* (Lausanne: G. Bridel, 1847), pp. 245–379. See also his catalogue of "known" Vaudois items, most of which are not now extant (pp. 232 ff.).

46. *Poésie provençale*, p. 193.

47. Ed. H. G. Pfander, *The Popular Sermon of the Medieval Friar in England* (New York: New York University Press, 1937), pp. 41 ff.

48. See *Les Contes moralisés de Nicole Bozon, Frère Mineur*, ed. Lucy Toulmin Smith and Paul Meyer for the Société des anciens textes français (Paris: Firmin Didot, 1889); also Bozon's poems, edited by Amelia Klenke in *Three Saints' Lives* (New York: Franciscan Institute, 1947).

49. Pfander, *Popular Sermon*, p. 40.

50. Comba, *History of the Waldenses*, p. 233.

51. Ibid., pp. 219–21.

52. Ibid., pp. 223–5.

53. Joseph Anglade, *Les Troubadours* (Paris: A. Colin, 1908), p. 203; see also Bayle, *Poésie provençale*, pp. 193 ff.

54. Étienne de Bourbon, *Anecdotes*, pp. 307–8.

55. Maitland, *Facts and Documents*, pp. 400 ff. The early prose translations attempted to be "word for word": they were given that kind of literal interpretation as well (Comba, *History of the Waldenses*, p. 187).

56. See E. S. Davison, *Forerunners of St. Francis and Other Studies* (Cambridge, Mass.: Houghton Mifflin, 1927), pp. 283–4.

57. Johannes Jorgenson, *St. Francis of Assisi* (New York: Longman's, Green, 1912; rpt. 1955), p. 81.

58. One notable exception is the emphasis on translation of Scripture into the vernacular, although even in the thirteenth century Franciscans were interested enough to make translations directly from the Hebrew text; see Beryl Smalley, *The Study of the Bible in the Middle Ages* (South Bend, Ind.: Univ. of Notre Dame Press, 1954), p. 341.

59. *Speculum perfectionis*, ed. Sabatier, p. 197.

60. See also Matt. 10:7–13 (Jorgenson, *St. Francis*, pp. 57 ff.). St. Francis heard it read and expounded by a priest. See the forthcoming book by Ciriaco Arroyo on the historical tradition of the Gospel of Matthew in medieval conversions to poverty.

61. See Runciman, *Manichee*, p. 129. Portiuncula was the town where St. Francis had heard the famous reading of Matt. 10:7–13. In 1216, in the height of the antiheretical activity, St. Francis came to the Pope (Honorarius II) and begged for the Portiuncula church the same indulgence granted to the Crusaders in the Holy Land: "That everyone who, with penitence for his sins, comes into this church and confesses his sins and is absolved by the priest, shall be free from all guilt and *punishment* [italics mine] for the sins of his life from the day of his baptism to the day when he entered the said church" (as quoted in Jorgenson, *St. Francis*, p. 145). Not surprisingly, Honorarius depicted the injury it might do to the Indulgence of the Crusade, but grudgingly let it pass in a modified form. This sort of an indulgence would naturally be of great benefit to former heretics wishing to escape reprisal. See Raphael M. Huber, *The Portiuncula Indulgence, Franciscan Studies* 19 (New York: Wagner, 1938).

62. The *Chronicon Uspergense*, explicitly connecting the two movements, sees Innocent III's acceptance of the Friars Minor as a counter-move to the Waldensians. It occurs in *MGH*, ser., Script., 23:376: "Eo tempore mundo iam senescente exortae sunt duae religiones in ecclesia, cuius ut aquilae renovatur iuventus, quae etiam a sede apostolica sunt confirmatae, videlicet Minorum fratrum et Praedicatorum. Quae forte hac occasione sunt approbatae, quia olim duae sectae in Italia exortae, adhuc perdurant, quorum alii Pauperes de Luduno se nominabant, quos Lucius papa quondam inter haereticos scribebat eo quod supersticiosa dogmata et observationes in eis reperirentur; in occultis quoque predicationibus, quae faciebant plerumque in latibulis, ecclesiae Dei et sacerdotio derogabatur. Vidimus tunc temporis aliquos de numero eorum, qui dicebantur Pauperes de Luduno, apud sedem apostolicam cum magistro suo quodam, ut puto Bernhardo, et his petebant, sectam suam a sede apostolica confirmari et privilegiari. Sane ipsi dicentes, se gerere vitam apostolorum nichil volentes possidere aut locum certum habere, circuibant per vicos et castella. Ast domnus papa quaedam supersticiosa in conversatione ipsorum eisdem obiecit, videlicet quod calceos desuper pedem precedebant et quasi nudis pedibus ambulabant; preterea cum portarent quasdam cappas quasi religionis, capillos capitis non attendebant nisi

sicut laici; hoc quoque probrosum videbatur in eis, quod viri et mulieres simul ambulabant in via et plerumque simul manebant in domo una, et de eis diceretur, quod quandoque simul in lectulis accubabant, quae tamen omnia ipsi asserebant ab apostolis descendisse. Ceterum domnus papa in loco illorum exurgentes quosdam alios, qui se appellabant Pauperes minores, confirmavit, qui predicta supersticiosa et reprobrosa respuebant, sed precise nudis pedibus tam aestate quam hieme ambulabant et neque pecuniam nec quicquam aliud preter victum accipiebant et si quando vestem necessariam quisquam ipsis sponte conferebat; non enim quicquam petebant ab aliquo. Hi tamen postea attendentes, quod nonnunquam nimiae humilitatis nomen gloriationem importet et de nomine paupertatis, cum multi eam frustra sustineant, apud Deum vanius inde gloriantur, maluerunt appellari Minores fratres quam minores Pauperes, apostolicae sedi in omnibus obedientes." Ronald A. Knox, *Enthusiasm* (New York: Oxford Univ. Press, 1950), p. 104, writes: "It is permissible to suggest that if St. Francis had lived a century earlier there would have been no Waldensians," to which Bernard Marthaler replied in "Forerunners of the Franciscans: The Waldenses," *Franciscan Studies* 18 (1958):133–42, that "if it weren't for Peter Waldo there would have been no Franciscans." I agree with Felix M. Bak, whose article takes its title from Marthaler's conclusion, "If it weren't for Peter Waldo, there would have been no Franciscans," (*Franciscan Studies* 25 [1965]:4–16) that both statements are logically indefensible; however, the striking similarity of the two groups bespeaks a response to common cultural stimuli which leads to their methodological similarity. The fact of their historical relationship is sufficiently established in the sources cited.

63. See R. W. Emery, "The Friars of the Blessed Mary and the Pied Friars," *Speculum* 24 (1949):218–28; and G. Meersseman, "F. F. Prêcheurs et le mouvement devôt en Flandre au xiiie siècle," *Archivum fratrum praedicatorum* 18 (1948):73 ff.

64. *Legenda trium sociorum* (trans. in Otto Karrer, *St. Francis of Assisi* [New York: Sheed and Ward, 1948], pp. 14, 18); also see *The Writings of Brother Leo*, p. xxxiv.

65. C. Guerrieri Crocetti, in *La Lirica predantesca* (Florence: Vallecchi, 1925), pp. 61 ff., discusses the impact of this reclamation on Franciscan and other religious poetry in Italy during the thirteenth century. See also n. 77 below.

66. It is my conviction that further work in the role of the thirteenth- and fourteenth-century confraternities in France and England will prove to be of critical importance to our understanding of Middle English poetic development. For the Puy in particular, one might look initially to É. P. Du Méril, ed., "La Confrèrie des clercs Parisiens du Puy de l'Assumption de Douai" *Mémoires de la Société Nationale d'Agriculture, Sciences, et Arts*, ser. 3, bk. 2 (Douai, 1914), pp. 1–93; and H. J. Chaytor, *The Troubadours and England* (Cambridge: Cambridge Univ. Press, 1923), p. 29.

67. Jalla, *Histoire des Vaudois*, chaps. 12, 13; Belperron, *La Croisade,*

chap. 4. It is even suggested by Jeanroy (*Savaric de Mauleon: Baron and Troubadour* [Cambridge: Cambridge Univ. Press, 1939], p. 49) that by 1224 the Albigensian heretics had for all practical purposes regained almost all ground lost in the crusade.

68. Anglade, *Les Troubadours*, devotes a whole chapter to this (chap. 3). There were a few heretics who had been reclaimed long enough before their death to do some damage; Folquet de Marseilles, the one-time bishop troubadour, became the most zealous of anti-heretical persecutors.

69. De la Marche, *La Chaire française au Moyen Âge* (Paris: Renouard, 1886), p. 479.

70. Lecoy de la Marche (pp. 479–80) feels that Étienne's use of the term *versus colorati* was "sans doute par opposition aux vers *blancs*, et qui ne sont qu'une suite de récits ou citations à l'appui." Étienne had been a member of the Inquisition for twenty years, yet the tone of his anecdotes and the type of material he covers indicates that he was, if not a sympathizer with the heretics, at least interested in them on a slightly more "academic" level than most of his colleagues. Consequently he makes a very useful source for this sort of study. See also n. 28 above.

71. Pfander, *Popular Sermon*, pp. 20 ff.

72. *SL XIV–XV*, p. xxxv. A graphic modern example of how this adaptation from the secular to the religious probably worked out in practice is afforded by a modern novel, John Steinbeck's *Grapes of Wrath*. In it, Steinbeck introduces the preacher Jim Casey sitting under a tree "whistling solemnly the tune of 'Yes, Sir, That's My Baby.' His extended foot swung slowly up and down in the tempo. It was not dance tempo. He stopped whistling and sang in an easy thin tenor: 'Yes, sir, that's my Saviour,/ Je-sus is my Saviour/ Je-sus is my Saviour now./ On the level/ 'S not the devil,/ Jesus is my Saviour now!' " (New York: Viking, 1939). See also Bruce Wardropper, *Historia de la poesia lirica a lo divino en la cristianidad occidental* (Madrid: Revista de Occidente, 1958). Medieval poets were not shy of dance tempo.

73. Geraldus Cambrensis, *Opera* (Rolls Series 21), 2:120.

74. *Decline and Fall of the Roman Empire* (New York: A. L. Burt, 1845), 2:537.

75. *Guillaume de Machaut* (New York: Plenum, 1954), p. 57.

76. For a concise study of the "Egyptian gold" concept, see D. W. Robertson, Jr., *A Preface to Chaucer* (Princeton: Princeton Univ. Press, 1962), pp. 337–43.

77. Herbert Grundmann, *Religiöse Bewegungen im Mittelalter* (Berlin: Verlag der Emil Ebering, 1935), shows that until the end of the twelfth century the official church had consistently frowned upon those religious movements which entailed preaching of the Gospel by laymen (pp. 59 ff.). Under Innocent III's change of policy efforts were made not only to win over heretically inclined Humiliati and Waldensians, but consistent with this trend approval was given to the new fraternities of Francis and Dominic (pp. 70–100). Aware that excommunication, the stake, and crusade were

not the answer to "Albigensian" and kindred heretic groups, Innocent sought, especially after 1198, to direct the mendicant movement into orthodox channels (pp. 70, 100, 156, etc.). The most important tool at hand for the job of reclamation was the Franciscan Third Order, the Tertiaries, into whose ranks came many of the Waldensians and Humiliati. This was not regarded without reservation by some, like Ugolino, for "Plusiers, parmi eux, avaient versé dans l'hérésie"—quoted by P. Godefroy in "Le Tiers-Ordre de Saint-François," *Études Franciscaines* 29 (1927):479. Jacques de Vitry, writing while Francis was still alive, could still call them the revivers of religion, which he said had almost died out of a world whose end was near, and which was threatened by the coming of Antichrist (*Historia occidentalis,* esp. p. xxxiii). Still to be seen in the Basilica of St. John Lateran is the following description of the "Dream of Innocent III":

> Tertius Ecclesiae Pater Innocentius, hora
> Qua sese dederat somno, nutare ruinae
> Hanc videt Ecclesiam, mox vir pannosus et asper
> Despectusque humerum supponens sustinet illam,
> At pater vigilans Franciscum prospicit, atque
> Vere est (inquit) quem vidimus, iste ruentem
> Ecclesiam; fidemque; feret, sic ille petitis
> Cunctis concessis liber, lactusque; recessit.

See V. Forcella, *Iscrizioni delle chiese e d'altri edifici di Roma* (Rome, 1869–84), 8:15, no. 16.

78. See Paul Sabatier, *Life of St. Francis of Assisi,* trans. Louise Seymour Houghton (New York: Scribner's, 1894), pp. 97–102, 97, n. 3.

79. See Chapter 4 below.

80. J. R. H. Moorman, *The Sources for the Life of St. Francis* (Manchester: Univ. of Manchester Press, 1940), p. 17.

81. Sabatier, *Life of St. Francis,* p. 210. See below, chap. 4.

82. Raby, p. 430.

83. This poem was translated into ME, and appears in at least ten MSS from the thirteenth and fourteenth centuries (*RL XIV,* p. 287) with slight variants in the translation. The following is from Trinity Coll. Camb. MS. 181, (printed in *RL XIV,* no. 134):

> Whi is þe world biloued, þat fals is & vein?
> Siþen þat hise welþis ben vncertein.

> Al so soone slidiþ his power away
> as doiþ a brokil pot, þat freish is and gay.

The intriguing phrase in the Latin is "quam vasa figuli." While *figulus* means "potter" or "seal maker," *vas figuli* is a poetic expression used by the Vulgate (Psalms 2:9) to allude to the fate of the builders of the brick walls of Babylon: "Thou shalt break them with a rod of iron, thou shalt dash them in pieces like a potter's vessel." Juvenal in his Tenth Satire, made doubly famous by Dr. Johnson's imitation in "The Vanity of Human Wishes," employs the same usage (line 171). Another ME translation follows the

Latin original, which was edited by Henry A. Person, *Cambridge Middle English Lyrics* (Seattle: Univ. of Washington Press, 1953), p. 18.

84. The theological significance of the particular Franciscan emphasis on "identification" with Christ is relevant to our examination of the Middle English lyric and will be discussed in the next chapter.

85. Raby, p. 441.

86. *Epistle* 221, *PL* 182: 413.

87. See A. G. Little, *Franciscan History and Legend in English Medieval Art*, BSFS 19 (Manchester: Univ. of Manchester Press, 1937).

88. For a concise treatment of this revolution in style see Émile Mâle, *L'Art religieux du xiiie siècle en France* (Paris: A. Colin, 1935). One of the most significant Franciscan documents for study of the "new style" is the *Meditations on the Life of Christ*, ed. and trans. Isa Ragusa and Rosalie B. Green (Princeton: Princeton Univ. Press, 1961), hereafter cited as *Meditations*.

89. Raimond van Marle, *The Development of the Italian Schools of Painting* (The Hague: Nijhoff, 1923–38), 1:258–363.

90. Raby, p. 421.

Franciscan Spirituality

B Y THE TIME Franciscan friar John Pecham had been raised to the Archbishopric of Canterbury in 1279, the real spade work of Christian theology was being done not in the cloistered gardens of contemplatives but amid the noisy controversies of university towns. Further, in contrast to the relative calmness and harmony with which the old order had proceeded, a spirit of intense competition was developing between two main factions of university theologians, the enthusiastic proponents of neo-Aristotelianism—chiefly Dominicans— on the one hand and, on the other, an alarmed coalition vigorously defending a patristic tradition whose major emphases they saw threatened by the new philosophy.[1] The latter group, not always without misgivings, followed the academic lead of the Franciscans who, because of their natural rivalry with the Dominicans and established presence at Oxford, Cambridge, and Paris, were forced into leadership among those defending the old order.[2] Pecham found the opinions of the Dominicans and Franciscans now sharply opposed on all but the most basic matters of faith, and he charged that the former, by rejecting the traditions of the saints and relying instead exclusively on philosophical dogmas, had filled the Church of God with idols. His chief modern biographer reports that "taking a leaf from the book of William of St. Amour, he warned the pope that this was the danger of the last days, foretold by the apostle; for, if the doctrines of Augustine and the other fathers were scorned, the whole fabric of Christian philosophy would crumble, and truth submit to falsehood."[3]

Pecham was not deliberately advertising himself as an enemy of philosophy as handmaid to theology, but rather opposed what he saw as academic excesses and "profane novelties," which in the last twenty

43

years had gained undue heights of grandeur, threatening the essential role of theology as he understood it. For him, truth and right perspective resided with a tradition of saints whom he had little difficulty identifying: "What could be more solid and more sound doctrine than that of the sons of blessed Francis, Brother Alexander of sacred holy memory, and of Brother Bonaventure and his sort, in whose treatises is applied all holy and philosophical art, teaching with Augustine the eternal rule and unchanging light, in complete contrast to that new stuff?"[4] The Franciscans, he believed, were chief among those who strove to safeguard the Augustinian tradition, the basic occupation of which was simply the teaching of scriptural exegesis, scriptural commentary, and the sacraments. In other words, what Archbishop Pecham defended was a concept of theology which saw as its chief object the elucidation and transmission of revelation—the delivered Word of God. Among theologians of his school Scripture was granted priority; even where other guides to spiritual understanding were recognized, Franciscan theology was usually characterized by more attention to the processes of divine revelation than, for example, Dominican theology. But a further refinement of this distinction is possible.

In any assessment of Franciscan theological interests, St. Bonaventure must rank as the principal authority. Born at Bagnorea near Viterbo in 1221, he entered the Franciscan Order in 1243, studied about the same time under Alexander of Hales, the founder of the Franciscan school at Paris, lectured there as *Magister regens* until 1255, and by 1257, at the age of thirty-six, was elected Minister General of the Friars Minor. In 1265 he was offered the Archbishopric of York, but refused it in order to continue as Minister General and to write. As a systematic philosopher-theologian he is not generally considered a match for St. Thomas, with whom he is often compared; the difference in the method and objective of the two men, however, is instructive. Paschal Robinson approximated a summation when he said, "Thomas extended the Kingdom of God by the love of theology, Bonaventure by the theology of love."[5] The distinction is well taken, if the latter half receives some qualification. The theology of Bonaventure is not merely a sequence of mystical rhapsodies, but a relatively complete philosophical system, propounded chiefly in four books: the *Commentarium sententiarum, Breviloquium, Itinerarium mentis,* and the *De reductione artium ad theologiam.* In these works the basic Franciscan position on scriptural revelation is defined.

When St. Bonaventure undertook to describe an epistemology, he distinguished four "lights" to human knowledge:

Notwithstanding the fact that every illumination of knowledge is within, still, we can properly distinguish what we may call the *external* light, or the light of mechanical skill; the *lower* light, or the light of sense perception; the *inner* light, or the light of philosophical knowledge; and the *higher* light, or *the light of grace and of sacred Scripture.* The first light illumines in the consideration of the *arts and crafts*; the second in regard to *natural form*; the third in regard to *intellectual truth*; the fourth and last, in regard to *saving truth.*[6]

Within this schema St. Bonaventure frames an ordered perspective for the pursuit of matters both of faith and of aesthetics. It is important to note the hierarchy of "lights" that he establishes. The fourth and highest light is not, as some have mistakenly reported, "the knowledge of theology"[7]—at least with respect to the understanding of theology as pursued by Aquinas; rather, in Bonaventure's own words, the highest light is "lumen gratiae et sacrae Scripturae." A significant difference for the understanding of Franciscan theology and aesthetics is involved.

For the "Seraphic Doctor," much more than for St. Thomas for example, the starting and finishing point for investigation in theological matters is not the natural light of reason and the evidence it discovers, but the content of scriptural revelation, accepted as true by a voluntary act of faith.[8] There existed a firm precedent for this viewpoint in the earliest history of the Order, though the emphasis on the facts is often misplaced: St. Francis's warnings against the possession of books and such apparently anti-intellectual pronouncements as Jacopone da Todi's poem about the threat of Paris to Assisi are often cited as evidence of a fundamental anti-theological bias in the Franciscan Order, and as support for accusations of ignorance and illiteracy among the friars.[9] Though such allegations are not entirely without foundation and are particularly supported by the behavior of Franciscans like those satirized in fourteenth-century England, they nevertheless tend to obscure what is really a much more balanced disposition. The records of even the fervent *spirituali* are quick to add to St. Francis's injunction against the possession of books his directive that the brothers study the Scriptures carefully, particularly the New Testament.[10] St. Francis himself was well versed in the Scriptures, quoting from them profusely in his preaching and pronouncements,[11] and Celano, his early biographer, reports that learned men were continually astonished at the biblical knowledge of the Franciscans (*II Celano* 103). In short, among the early Franciscans the choice was made to give scriptural knowledge priority over the discipline of theology per se.

G. H. Tavard has noted that St. Bonaventure's conception of theology "rests on a fourfold basis." First, it assumes objective continuity between theology and Scripture: the knowledge of Scripture attained by an individual through progressive exegesis of its senses becomes the starting point for further and yet concurrent search after the "reality hidden behind the Creed." Secondly, his notion of theology implies that the temporal and supernatural worlds are viewed as telescoping "congeries of symbols" which focus on the Trinity a patterned universal harmony whose key becomes accessible through faith. "Third, it entails a discontinuity between theological and philosophical reason; by nature philosophy is blind to the symbols upon which theology thrives." Fourth, it requires that the development of theology itself be seen as dependent upon insight into those symbols, upon the acuteness of spiritual vision, or, from a practical viewpoint, upon the progression of an individual's spiritual life.[12]

Tavard further points out that a comparison with St. Thomas ought to lay stress on these particular points, for it is from this divergent pattern of perceptions that the Franciscan school cut its theological garment:

> Happen what may to the Augustinian tradition after St. Thomas, a staunch party of Franciscan theologians carried on their work upon the lines adopted by St. Bonaventure. Men like John Peckham, Walter of Brugghe, William of Mare and also, to a smaller extent, Matthew of Aquasparta and Richard of Middleton, vigorous theologians as they were, stood firmly by the Bonaventuran conception. To give an instance, Richard of Middleton, having admitted that theology was a science, esteemed all the same that it was more "practical" than "speculative."[13]

For St. Bonaventure and his successors scriptural knowledge has an almost prerequisite importance to faith, since, as he says in the *Breviloquium*, it "describes the whole universe insofar as it is useful to know it for salvation." But faith is the essential guide to Scripture: "It is impossible to enter Scripture with a view to studying it if one has not, beforehand, the infused faith of Christ, as this is the light, the door, and even the basis of all Scripture." Faith sifts the contents of Scripture, "for faith itself, while we are pilgrims far from the Lord, is the foundation, guiding light, and entrance door to all supernatural illuminations. By its standard all God-given wisdom ought to be gauged, lest it extend beyond what is seemly; it must be gauged soberly, according as God has dealt to everyman the measure of faith."[14] Personal faith as guide to the revealed Word of God, and

Scripture expounded as guide to community faith: the progression characterizes the orientation of Franciscan theology toward practical evangelism.

This traditional emphasis was more vigorous among English Franciscans than their continental counterparts. Friar Roger Bacon indicates that Robert Grosseteste, an early protector of the English Franciscan province, along with two of his successors in the office of lecturer to the friars—Thomas of Wales and Adam Marsh—form a special tradition of learning which was founded by Grosseteste and "prevailed for several generations in the Franciscan school."[15] The overwhelming emphasis of this school was on Scripture. The "Auctoritas irrefragabilis" (Grosseteste) is definite on this point in a letter to Agnellus in 1233, and we have Bacon's express statement that "Grosseteste and Adam Marsh [Marisco] invariably used the text of Scripture for the subject of their lectures in preference to the Sentences of Peter Lombard," later the favorite textbook in the schools of theology.[16]

In view of their marked emphasis on Scripture one might ask why the Franciscans did not devote more energy to preparing translations, perhaps in the manner of the Waldensians. In the past it has in fact sometimes been popular among scholars of a certain sympathy to criticize the friars for failing to transmit an early and textually accurate Bible into the hands of thirteenth-century English laymen. A notable voicing of this opinion was that of G. G. Coulton:

> The Friars did study the Bible, in the earlier generations at least . . . .
> But they did little to spread the knowledge of the actual text among
> the people, who were fed on glosses and pious embroideries rather
> than on the plain facts of Bible history. One of the most popular books
> of this kind, St. Bonaventura's *Hundred Meditations on the Life of
> Christ*, contains a good twenty per cent of glosses from the Fathers,
> or else of sheer romance, based upon the saint's own surmises of what
> might have happened, or on revelations vouchsafed to "a holy Brother
> of our Order." In spite of a general warning at the beginning of the
> book, and several others elsewhere, there is nothing in most cases to
> mark the transition from Bible fact to pious fancy. The Virgin Mary
> is constantly brought in as acting and speaking without the least Bib-
> lical authority. And the example thus set by one of the first men of
> the century was naturally followed by others: e.g. by the friar who
> wrote the very pretty but utterly unbiblical romance of the Magdalene
> . . . . Chaucer's keen eye noted this tendency on the Friar's part. St.
> Bonaventura's book apparently was designed for the immediate use of
> the clergy, through whom it would filter to the people: but in this
> indirect process it would be just the extraneous features of these Bib-
> lical romances which would catch the hearers' fancy, and stick most

surely. At the best, therefore, the great bulk of the people knew the Bible story only with a strong admixture of modern Franciscan notions. Here again Chaucer helps us: his clerk Nicholas, reminding the carpenter of Noah's flood, has no doubt that he will remember the least Biblical feature in that event as conceived in the later Middle Ages— the refusal of Noah's wife to embark until she had drunk one more pot of ale with her jolly gossips ashore.[17]

Here Professor Coulton has provided us with a table of the very strengths of Franciscan "translation" of the Scriptures. Yet the attitude he expresses needs to be challenged, for it fails to understand the key facet in Franciscan programs for making Scripture available in the vernacular, which is in fact the use of extra materials to corroborate and strengthen the exegetical sense while at the same time providing a personalizing referent, thus sharpening the doctrinal point and purpose of the scriptural narrative. This concept is absolutely essential to the understanding of all vernacular literary tools employed by the Friars Minor.

First, let us consider the method employed by the foremost book of "pious fancy" cited by Coulton, the pseudo-Bonaventuran *Meditations on the Life of Christ*. This work, one of the formative influences in the late medieval stylistic shift in the graphic arts, contributed greatly to and helped to inspire the devotion to the Passion, the central element in Franciscan spirituality.[18] Ascribed to Joannes a Caulibus, a Tuscan, it was translated into Middle English at least seven times in the first hundred years after Bonaventure's death in 1274, besides once into Anglo-French; in some of these translations it survives in several manuscripts.[19] Perhaps the most familiar and accessible modern translation is from an Italian manuscript, *Meditations on the Life of Christ: An Illustrated Manuscript of the Fourteenth Century*, edited and translated by Isa Ragusa and Rosalie B. Green.[20]

In the *Meditations* are many examples of interpolations or fabrications extraneous to the text of the Gospels; Coulton is certainly right about that much. But the supra-biblical materials are not included entirely fortuitously, or irresponsibly, as he implies. In fact we can isolate several categories of interpolation which may be classified according to their theological or psychological function in elucidating or sharpening the practical spiritual application of biblical narrative. For example, in one fictional passage, at the circumcision of John the Baptist, a deliberate attempt is made to underscore the theological significance of his role as forerunner to Christ, linking it at the same time with liturgical hymns which express the prophetic tradition looking toward the Incarnation:

On the eighth day, when the child was circumcised and named John, Zacharias spoke and prophesied, saying, "Benedictus Dominus Deus Israel" etc. (Luke 1:68), "Blessed be the Lord, the God of Israel, for He has visited His people and wrought their redemption." Thus two beautiful canticles were created in this house, the Magnificat and the Benedictus. Our Lady, who was standing behind a curtain that she might be invisible to the men attending the circumcision of John, listened intently to the hymn in which her Son was mentioned and secured everything in her heart, most wisely (*Meditations*, p. 25).

Another category of interpolation carries reminders of the continuity between Old Testament prophecy and New Testament revelation, and corresponds to what one would find appropriated to the relevant Gospel passages by the *Glossa ordinaria* or the gloss of Franciscan friar Nicholas of Lyra. Thus in the *Meditations'* detailed "return from Egypt," which incorporates traditional pilgrimage motifs and is intended to be reminiscent of a larger pilgrimage, the Holy Family is pictured as having to cross the Jordan:

> It is said that the site on the Jordan where John baptised is the same place where the children of Israel crossed when they came from Egypt through the desert and that near this spot in that desert John did penance. Thus it is likely that the boy Jesus, passing it on His return, found him there. Meditate on how he received them joyfully . . . (*Meditations*, pp. 82–83).

The reader will recognize that the passage is replete with liturgical and sacramental significance: the spiritual baptism which the fathers saw prefigured in the crossing of the Red Sea (which is here by a subtle felony transmitted over a few hundred miles of desert) is explicitly linked to another prefigurement of spiritual baptism, that of the forerunner John; and though specific reference is omitted to John's baptizing of Christ in the Jordan, the mind of the reader might dart ahead to complete the chain of baptisms in remembering that penultimate and vicarious spiritual baptism which prepared the way for his own. Many other examples of interpolation explicitly relate New Testament happenings to Old Testament prefigurement for the obvious theological and liturgical connections. As in the entire ninetieth chapter, "Of the Lord's return to the Holy Fathers after the Resurrection," the interpolations serve to strengthen the idea of continuity between the Testaments, and, in the absence of those parts not translated, call their spiritual significance to mind.

Another kind of additional material found in the *Meditations,* though less frequently, is that sort which, when read exegetically, illuminates the spiritual meaning of its host passage. In Franciscan works the practical, surface meaning of the interpolation is usually forthrightly spiritually instructive as well. Following the prologue to the *Meditations,* Friar John gives a version of the dispute between the four daughters of God from St. Bernard's sermon on the Annunciation. (It should be noted that though the *Meditations* roughly translates the Gospels, the authority most frequently cited for gloss is St. Bernard, whose name appears on nearly every page; no figure is of greater influence on Franciscan spirituality.) The dispute over the fate of Man, between Truth and Justice on the one hand, and Mercy and Peace on the other, offers an ideal crucible for resolution of the Divine Nature: Justice tempered by Mercy is presented in one perfect "median" who is the spirit of Truth and Peace. The role of the Savior in relation to the death-deserving sinfulness of man and the unalterable righteousness of God is made explicit. "Thus," says Friar John, "we can imagine what may have happened in heaven!"[21]

If these examples illustrate the theological and catechal construction of the *Meditations,* some other passages have added details which are not textual, but function primarily to inculcate an affective piety. That is, often their purpose is simply to enjoin a sympathetic response to the Cross for the spiritual virtues inherent in the response.[22] Since this emphasis on the "affectual" is perhaps the most significant aspect of Franciscan spirituality in response to the details of the Gospel story, it is worthwhile to note the care with which Friar John states the importance of affectual as well as intellectual contemplation, particularly as it is directed to the *humanity* of Christ:

> You have also seen how there are three kinds of contemplation, that is, of the humanity of Christ, of the celestial court, and of the divine Majesty. You must know that in each of them there are two heights of the mind, that is, the *intellectual* and the *affectual* . . . . You will not be introduced to these three kinds if you do not know how to enter, unless you first meditate on the humanity of Christ which is given you in this little book.

Friar John goes on to quote St. Bernard's sermon on the ascension:

> There are two things that we must purge with us, that is, the intellect and the affection: the intellect so that one may understand; the affection so that one may will . . . . But Christ illuminates the intellect; Christ purges the affection (*Meditations,* pp. 262–63).

Since Christ's humanity is the aspect of his person which the Franciscans wished to emphasize in order to clarify the surrogative nature of his suffering, the love and compassion of a human mother for her suffering child would naturally have a compelling emotional effect in actuating this realization. The *stabat mater* motif in Franciscan spirituality is representative of the effective "affectual" use of non-biblical additions to the Passion scene, as, for example, in the usually conservative Middle English translation of the *Meditations* ascribed to Robert Manning:

> A! with what sorow hys modyr was fedde,
> Whan she say hym so naked and alle bled!
> Fyrþer more, þan gan she to seche,
> And say þat þey had left hym no breche.
> She ran þan þurgh hem, and hastyly hyde,
> And with here kercheues hys hepys she wryde.
> She wulde do more, but she ne myȝt,
> For fersly here swete sone ys from her plyȝt.[23]

The original account gives alternate descriptions of the crucifixion. In the first, Christ climbs on a ladder up the cross, then is affixed. In the second version, the cross is first laid on the ground, Christ affixed, and then raised up, "if this suits you better," says Friar John, launching into an equally detailed and imaginative account of the proceedings in such a method. In other words, it is not literal fact that counts, but the derivation of spiritual benefits concomitant with the overall story. The object is not simple reenactment of the crucifixion for recreation: that would be morbid. It is spiritual actualization in the heart of the observer that is desired:

> Thenk now, man, how hyt ys down
> Yn þe oure of syxte of none.
> Beholde þe peynes of þy sauyour,
> And crucyfye þyn herte with grete dolour.[24]

This would be as true of the "revelation" Friar John includes of the physical details of Christ's birth (*Meditations*, pp. 33–35) as of the "additions" to the Passion.

In all of these examples, that Christ was also a man is the ground of man's identification. A variant expression of the humanizing tendency may be seen in the simple desire for physical contact with the life of the Lord. In one place Friar John refers to a stone column to which Christ was fastened before His trial, averring that it was preserved to his day, as he knew "from a brother of ours, who saw it" (*Meditations*, p. 326). Again he describes the table of the Last Supper, which he says he saw and measured at the Lateran Church in Rome (*Meditations*, p. 277). The Middle English translator considerately omits this personal reference, but faithfully transcribes the description of the table and seating arrangements in the manner of an explanatory commentary:

> So þat here by þou mayst lere
> þat of o dysshe þey etyn yn fere,
> þarfore þe myȝt nat vndyrstonde
> Whan cryst seyd, "he þat hys honde
> Yn my dysshe putteþ furþ ryȝt,
> He shal betraye me þys nyȝt."[25]

Basically, the above examples illustrate the kinds of interpolations one finds in Franciscan treatments of Scripture, not only in the *Meditations* but elsewhere, and are representative of the kinds of uses to which the additional materials are put. Instead of a Latin Bible with a Latin marginal gloss, a vernacular highlight of the Gospel harmonized[26] was created, with gloss interlaced. In the running commentary and manner of presenting the Gospel story we may regularly observe basic elements of Franciscan spirituality and theological bias.[27] Yet the added materials were in no way meant to supplant, rival, or even to claim proximate authority with the actual scriptural accounts; Friar John, in concluding his work, makes that point clear:

> Therefore you ought to know that it is enough to meditate only on what the Lord did or on what happened concerning Him or on what is told according to the Gospel stories, feeling yourself present in those places as if the things were done in your presence, as it comes directly to your soul in thinking of them. The moralities and authorities that I placed in this work for your instruction need not be used in the meditations, unless the virtue to be embraced or the vice to be avoided occurs of itself to your thoughts. Therefore, in this meditating, choose some quiet hour. Afterwards, later in the day, you can take the moralities and authorities and studiously commit them to memory. It is fitting to do so, for they are most beautiful and can instruct you on the whole spiritual life (*Meditations*, p. 387).

A place for each and each in its place: the commentary, like a devotional work, is ancillary to the revelation itself.

We see in the *Meditations* a thoroughly representative Franciscan work entirely consistent with the tradition championed by Grosse-teste, Bonaventure, and Pecham: Friar John's work is simple, dramatic exposition of Scripture, plus exegesis (complete or implied) and com-mentary. The thematic center toward which all other elements point is the atonement, the Passion of Christ.

The Franciscan theologians believed with St. Anselm that the reason for the incarnation was the Fall of Adam. "Cur Deus homo," they asked, "si Adam non peccasset?"[28] If man had not sinned, there would have been no need for the Virgin birth. But since human nature had sinned, human nature had to atone for the sin, and it was in his human nature that Christ was able to become a truly surrogative sacrifice; his divine nature chiefly served to grant his suffer-ing acceptability as a substitute before God.[29] Thus the idea of the necessary centrality of Christ's human nature, so dramatically intrinsic to the life of St. Francis, receives consistent development in the hands of Franciscans, whether theologians such as Alexander of Hales, Robert Grosseteste, Saint Bonaventure, Richard of Middleton, and Scotus, or evangelists in the vernacular like Saint Bernardino of Siena, Berthold von Regensburg, William Melton, and Nicholas Philipp. It is particularly relevant to Franciscan doctrine on the sacraments.

The effect of saying that if Adam had not sinned there would have been no need for the incarnation is, of course, to say ultimately that the redressing of sin by redemptive grace in the Passion is the chief object of the incarnation.[30] This idea was extended somewhat further by the Franciscans than by anyone else. Alexander of Hales, for example, develops two principles with respect to the sacramental grace appropriate to each sacrament. The first is that the sacramental grace as such of each sacrament has as the font of its efficacy a par-ticular virtue of the Passion of Christ; the second states that by sacra-mental grace we become conformed to the "Suffered-Christ."[31] These two principles suggest a useful tactic and framework for detailing Franciscan doctrine in that they briefly encompass the flow of Fran-ciscan theological thought, which for practical purposes, with respect to the sacraments as well as Scripture, flows in concentric circles around the Cross.

Alexander's first principle relates specifically to the removal of eternal punishment. That is, the grace of each sacrament relates to a virtue of the Passion in such a way as to create a purgatorial effect like that of the sacrament of penance:

Above all the virtue of the Passion of Christ blotted out the penalty for original sin, and baptism by virtue of grace blots out guilt, and

in such manner the full remission for our guilt and fault grows out
of the resurrection of Christ.[32]

Here we have an idea of Alexander's breakdown of the elements
responsible for complete efficacy of the sacrament. The remission of
actual guilt depends on the infusion of grace by God, while the remission of punishment, or removal of the "carentia temporalis visionis
Dei" finds its causality in the Passion of Christ: "virtus Passionis
Christi delevit poenam originalis peccati." K. F. Lynch has shown that
this idea is corroborated in the Codex of Alexander's *Glossa* and elsewhere in his works.[33]

The idea that the Passion is in itself the font of effectual grace
in the sacraments strengthens its position even more in Franciscan
thought. St. Francis, as Friar John notes at the beginning of his
Meditations, had insisted on continuing devotion to the Passion as
essential in achieving conformity to the Person of Christ, a focus
maximized in His suffering, and had illustrated the intensity of his
devotion with the stigmatization on La Verna. This idea closes a circle
with Alexander's second principle, that by the sacramental grace
inherent in the virtues of the Passion we become conformed to the
suffered Christ. Lynch notes:

> The Redemption for Alexander was not something once accomplished,
> but something which through the sacramental system remains perpe-
> tuated such as to continue to flow in a very precise way into the
> spiritual life of each recipient of a sacrament.[34]

In this way the recipient of sacramental grace is able to "glory in
the Passion" (Alexander, *Quaestio de Sacramentis*), just as he may by
virtue of contemplation of the Passion in the participation invited by
Friar John's *Meditations*:

> We must now treat of the Passion of our Lord Jesus. He who
> wishes to glory in the Cross and the Passion must dwell with con-
> tinued meditation on the mysteries and events that occurred. If they
> were considered with complete regard of mind, they would, I think,
> lead the meditator to a (new) state. To him who searches for it
> from the bottom of the heart and with the marrow of his being,
> many unhoped-for steps would take place by which he would receive
> new compassion, new love, new solace, and then a new condition of
> sweetness that would seem to him a promise of glory (pp. 317–18).

The goal of the sacraments, then, is the same as the goal of meditation; both focusing (like Franciscan treatments of Scripture) on

the Passion, they move toward conformation of the individual to Alexander's "Suffered-Christ." But as the passage above suggests, it is not necessarily the intellectable theological virtues deriving from the Passion which come first in time; rather, Friar John's affectual, or emotional "height of mind" can take temporal precedence over the intellectual. This expression of relationship between the two spheres is fundamental to Franciscan thought. The intellectual-theological content of Franciscan literature is seldom absent. It is however almost invariably subservient to the appeal of affectual piety and its consequent morality. The emotional aspect is manifest, the intellectual invites a more diligent reading.

A summary point of significance concerning the Passion transcends its sacramental and devotional importance, yet in such a way as to highlight the critical value of devotional attention. Conformity to the Suffered-Christ, or *Leidensnachfolge*, as Bonifatius Strack puts it,[35] becomes in Franciscan theology an imperative for salvation. Through Christ's suffering alone God's will is turned favorably toward man; moreover, the way which He shows to eternal life leads through His suffering.[36] As Strack has pointed out, what Bonaventure interprets this to mean, effectively, is that God the Father, "der König, hat geradezu als Dekret aufgestellt das niemand ihn sehen werde, der nicht mit ihm mitgekreuzigt ist."[37] This of course is spiritual crucifixion, as the passage from Bonaventure quoted immediately below makes clear, but the immediate connection made between vicarious *Leidensnachfolge* and salvation adds substantive purpose to the pursuit of both *imitatio Christi* and devotion to the Passion. Bonaventure dramatizes this:

> Notice the fact that Christ, the King of Kings, makes a decree that none may see him, unless he is crucified with him. And this decree is applicable to all without exception; moreover it is binding on all, and none may ignore it. And whosoever holds back from accepting the mortification of the cross in his body so that the life of the Lord Jesus in his own body is not manifest in imitation, is not worthy in other respects, without that banner of victory, to follow him to the crown.[38]

The concentric circles revolve closer and closer to the Cross.

Penance, as we shall come to see, was the sacramental form with which the Friars Minor were most concerned. Alexander of Hales provides a convenient example of the Franciscan theological emphasis on penance. For him the removal of the guilt of mortal sin must find its place in contrition. Though he recognizes that contrition along with confession and satisfaction are all involved in the "sacramentum-Ecclesiae," he singles out contrition as principally retaining the essence of the sacrament;[39] that is, he finds in contrition the realization of penance which alone can provide for its personal completion, or "satisfaction." In fact, he attributes to the grace infused in contrition the effect of remitting guilt:

> Penance is virtue, or grace. In the same way that virtue is one part of the essence of penance, so in the same fashion grace is the other. There are in fact two operations of penance; one is the remission of guilt, and the other the remission of the penalty. For in contrition is remitted the guilt, and penalty through confession and satisfaction, yet at some times both are remitted through contrition alone. In so much as grace pertains to the remission of guilt the proper operation of grace is the blotting out of guilt altogether. On the other hand, by the same token virtue pertains to the remission of penalty; whereupon a man living in charity in so doing renders up to God what is owed to Him, and in that much certainly satisfies, and is justified. Contrition is therefore that action proceeding out of charity and justice.[40]

From this point it is but a small step to style contrition itself as a sacrament: "nam ut sacramentum ita potest compleri in contritione" (*Glossa*, 4. 16. 253). The sacramental sign is in annihilation: as a man spiritually annihilates himself in contrition, God then annihilates his guilt in the remission of sin.[41]

A concluding illustration of the direction Franciscan sacramental theology takes toward the Passion and the humanity of Christ is available in ordinary descriptions of the Eucharist. With reference to the contribution of the Passion of Christ conveyed by the Eucharist, Alexander of Hales states:

> In the Eucharist is granted a similar virtue, for as much as is experienced from the love of the Passion, so much the greater becomes the union through love of the members of the mystical body to the Head.[42]

The charity of the Passion expresses itself in the Eucharist, and constitutes the form of the Church. St. Bernardino of Siena, in a 1425 sermon on the Eucharist, used Psalm 110:4 as his text: "Memoriam fecit mirabilium suorum, misericors et miserator Dominus: escam dedit timentibus se" (He has made his wonderful works to be remembered, the Lord gracious and full of compassion: he has given meat unto them

that fear Him). Why did God grant this gift? asks Bernardino rhetori-
cally, then answers that it was for the same reason that the Passion
itself occurred. "I answer that being enamored of human nature, not
being able to show greater generosity than this which is the greatest,
He gave Himself to be eaten and drunk, and He transformed us into
Himself." The memorial is of his love, of the transformation which
he effects on our behalf, and particularly of the Passion, which expresses the love and makes the transformation possible.[43] Pecham's
hymns on the Eucharist, proposed in honor of the feast of Corpus
Christi, point in the same direction,[44] and the connection is obvious
in the title Manning gives to his translation of the *Meditations:
Medytacyuns of þe soper of oure lorde Ihesu. And also of hys passyun.*

But the particular genius of Franciscan spirituality is seen in the
theology of contrition as personal discipline. Christ is seen as a champion knight "struggling for us bravely on the cross against His enemies," and through involvement in the sacraments of contrition and
penance we become conformed to him in his struggle, and by the
infused grace of the sacrament become strengthened as athletes in
the combat of the Lord, soldiers against the adversary, and thus distinguished from those who have merely put on Christ in baptism.[45]
Contritional response is not therefore appropriated to one occasion of
conversion alone, but is a part of the continuing Christian life. This
is the vital force of Alexander's second principle of sacramental grace.

In this theological light it is possible to consider certain basic
elements of Franciscan spirituality in a more enlightened way. When
St. Bernard contemplated the wounds of Christ, he would do so from
the perspective of a potential martyr who saw in the contemplation
fortification against possible trials and adversity. That is, in observing the spiritual fortitude of Christ he recognized its source, and
learning thus that his hope lay in the same source and not in his own
strength, he would be able to bear the adversity. But as we have
seen, Franciscan contemplation goes beyond this to involve participation in the more purely theological values described above, all the
more particularly when these values are derived from a process of
affectual piety. When Friar John in prefacing his *Meditations* quotes
from St. Bernard on this point, he acknowledges the virtue which
Bernard cites but goes further to say that not only the martyrs but
"also the confessors bore their tribulations and infirmities with great
patience, and have to this day" (*Meditations*, p. 2), what he means is
that the virtues of contemplating the Passion extend beyond fortification for martyrdom, as the "confessors," the Franciscans, had discovered, to the psychology of daily Christian experience.

One obvious goal of an evangelical Christian movement is to effect a penitential response on the part of those to whom it ministers. The Friars Minor were fully traditional in this respect, in fact often justifying their existence in terms of the need to urge people to penance.[46] Feeling as they did that contrition was the genuinely essential aspect of penance it is natural that their methodology as much as their spirituality should have been directed toward evoking a spirit of contrition on the part of their listeners. The techniques for fulfilling this objective were varied, but had a common psychological basis: Thomas Eccleston reports that one English friar, when hearing confessions, "was so full of kindness and compassion that if he saw that penitents were not showing sufficient signs of repentance, he used to move them to contrition by his own sighs and tears."[47] But for those with less control over their tear ducts a simpler and theologically more relevant model was available: they could direct the penitent or should-be-penitent to the scene of the Passion.

In eliciting a proper contritional response to the Passion, few holds were barred. Friar John, when describing the progress of the crucifixion in some detail for the affective benefits that might be derived thereby, remembered suddenly that he was addressing himself to a young female religious. In a small aside he clears his throat— "We must not be repelled at the thought of those things that our Lord Jesus did not hesitate to bear to redeem us and rescue us from the hands of our old enemy" (*Meditations*, p. 320)—and then begins to recount every possible aspect of the suffering with much vigor. We must not suppose that medieval readers shared the squeamishness about death and physical suffering which belongs to the generation satirized by Evelyn Waugh; such explicit treatment was calculated to inculcate empathetic response to Christ's pain, and though some Franciscans like Ubertino da Casale and Bartholomew of Pisa (see Appendix A) would intricately spiritualize every scratch and wound, for the most part the gruesome details were intended simply as an emotional shock to produce contrition. The reader of Franciscan literature is deliberately invited to imagine himself present at Calvary, and to recreate mentally each detail so as to achieve the most realistic visual and emotional effect (*Meditations*, pp. lxxv, 320).

For contrition-producing detail with regard to suffering, it seems natural to appeal to the perspective of those who viewed the crucifixion. Another example from Manning's translation of the *Meditations* will serve to show that the English spirit at this point was not fainter than the Italian. Manning manages to color a little of both the scriptural account and his source text:

Whan þey to þe hondes come were,
Pryuyly with here pynsours sore þey plyȝt,
Lest marye shulde gryse sore of þat syȝte,
þey haled harde ar hyt wulde be
þe nayles stokyn so fast yn þe tre;
Ful faste þey wrastyn, no þyng þey wounden,
Nedes þey mote brese foule hys honden;
But ryȝtwus god accepteþ alle þyng
Of eche man, mekely aftyr hys menyng.[48]

In its expansion the Middle English version illustrates both the ever-present bent to contrition-producing detail, and the tendency which we noted earlier to use supra-biblical materials so as to give a moral or allegorical gloss to the host narrative, as here in the last two lines.

The theology of contrition was essential to the message of mendicant Franciscan preachers in England. It is not necessary to suppose that they would have to have read Alexander of Hales, Grosseteste, or St. Bonaventure to have acquired it either (though very many probably did read their theologians in any case: see pp. 84–85 below). English Franciscan preaching guides such as the *Liber exemplorum, Speculum laicorum,* and *Fasciculus morum* all have a central chapter, entitled like that in the *Speculum laicorum* "De Contricione [et ejus bonis]" (chap. 19), which begins:

Contrition is sorrow for sin assumed by free will, with the intention of confessing and making satisfaction. Therefore, contrition is "saying it from the heart," and I polish the point, so to speak, with a universal illustration. Take, for example, Mary Magdalene . . . .[49]

After citing the Magdalen as example, the author suggests various qualities appropriate to contrition. The contrition of a penitent ought to be great, because his spirit properly deserves death; it ought to be most bitter because the suffering of Christ was most bitter. It is in the practical shaping of the theology of contrition that the tone of Franciscan homiletics really develops. After each suggestion the author characteristically leaves space to indicate that the preacher should at that point wax eloquent in hell-fire and graphic examples of his own. "Effectus ergo viro contricionis est anime sanatius," he points out, and continues with suggestions for examples to make this clear, as well as more blank spaces for inclusions of the preacher's own choice—often, from the evidence of surviving manuscripts, vernacular poetry.

In view of the Franciscan bent to contrition we can begin to appreciate how the humanity of Christ became the important aspect of his person relevant to the Passion. To reinforce this idea comes also the belief that Christ could not have suffered in his divine nature because divinity is impervious to temporal adversity:

> A lytyl from aungels he ys made lesse:
> Whyl he ys yn þys valey of dyrknes;
> þys wo he suffred yn hys manhede,
> But god suffred naght yn hys god hede.[50]

"Made a little lower than the angels," the poet says, reminding his audience of the biblical description of created man, the first Adam; so the significance of the second Adam's identification with first Adam's heirs in submitting to the same frail flesh is understood. It is the sharing of human flesh which renders the sacrifice meaningful, the human nature of Christ a bridge over which individual piety transfers to his person responses, principally affective, with which it is familiar from personal experience.[51]

It was not, then, only Christ himself in whom the Franciscan artists and poets saw wide scope for their imaginative representations of the *agapé* love of Christ. For no matter how much the humanity of Christ was emphasized, it was still difficult for the contrite spirit to relate its own human responses of love or suffering to the figure on the cross while remembering Christ's "god-hede." As St. Bonaventure noted, some referent for computing the nature of God's love for man is required. The divine love is not only in Christ, but in the Father, and the Father's love for the Son. Other points of comparison promptly present themselves: great is the love which a mother has for her son; greater is the love which Christ has for us; greater than mother-love is the love of a husband for his spouse; Christ's love surpasses this too. The greatest love which man can imagine, says Bonaventure, is the love of the body for the soul, but this also is less than the love of Christ for everyman.[52] But at least the lesser loves are a point of reference, and because of the incarnation they can be regarded as differing more in intensity than in quality from the love of Christ for men. Therefore, the Franciscans, preachers and poets, were able to employ instructively the lesser loves. But what better technique than to employ all of these in one natural image? So it was that the Blessed Virgin Mary, swooning at the foot of the cross, became a popular aid to the affectual piety promulgated by Franciscan spirituality.

St. Anthony of Padua suggests in his exegetical interpretation of the Blessed Virgin several of the spiritual and symbolic characteristics which help to constitute in her a proper channel for devotion to the Passion.[53] In the first place, she is a symbol for the Church, the *Sponsa* of Christ, the "Flower of the Field" (Cant. 2:1) which flourishes openly without losing its beauty, the "garden enclosed" (Cant. 4:12) by the walls of humility and poverty, and the Temple.[54] She is also the "Refuge of Sinners" foreshadowed by the cities of refuge which God commanded to be built (Numbers 35:13).[55] In this role she relates to the Christian in the world as he is part of the Church. Secondly, she is the Queen of Heaven, who receives, as in St. Bernard, the crown from her triumphant Lord, and she contributes by her loyalty and devotion to the victory, in a manner prefigured by Queen Esther and King Assuere.[56] But finally, and most persuasively, she is the agent whereby Christ took on human nature. "Out of the sackcloth of our nature Jesus Christ made a tunic for Himself which He made with the needle of the subtle work of the Holy Spirit and the thread of the Blessed Virgin's faith."[57] In her obedience, humility, solicitude for Christ, compassion, and ultimate trust in Christ's power she provides above all a moral influence, exemplary to human conduct, and a powerful point of personal identification.[58]

> Nou goth sonne vnder wod,—
> me reweth, marie, þi faire Rode.
> Nou goþ sonne vnder tre,—
> me reweþ, marie, þi sone and þe.

> (*EL XIII*, no. 1)

And after the storm, under the cross, in the stillness of the sun's setting, Mary becomes the dramatic representative of the contrite sinner, the secondary tragic figure with whom the contrite is invited into close response, and her psychological function in effecting contrition is charged with the doctrine explained most clearly by Bonaventure, that she feels in her own body the pain of Christ's suffering[59] (see Plate 1). Also, significantly, she experiences the highest spiritual joy at man's redemption, and becomes a focus for this emotion as well.[60] The Italian Friar John reports the prayer of the Virgin under the cross, concluding, "The Lady prayed in these and similar words with all her feelings and mind and with great bitterness in her heart. Have compassion now for her whom you see thus afflicted."[61] Mary's compassion is such that she would herself die with Christ on the

---

wod, forest, wood; also (entire line). "Now clouds the sun in stark distress"; *reweth*, pity; *Rode*, face, Cross.

Plate 1. "Plange Maria cum dolore" (MS. Cortona 91)

cross—not exchange places with him—so keenly does she desire to identify with her Son in his suffering.

> She swouned, she pyned, she wax half dede,
> She fylle to þe grounde, and bette here hede.
> .   .   .   .
> "A, my sone! my socour! now wo ys me:
> Ho shal graunte me to deye wyþ þe?
> þou wrecched deþ, to me þou come,
> And do þe modyr dye with þe sone;
> Aboue alle þyng y desyre þe:
> Com deþ, and to my sone þou brynge me.
> My fadyr, my former, my mayster, my make,
> Why, swete sone, hast þou me forsake?"[62]

This scene, more vivid than in the Latin original, has as its ultimate source St. Bonaventure, whose treatment is slightly less violent, though as dramatic:

> "Jesu, fili mi, Jesu, quis mihi det, ut ego tecum et pro te moriar, fili mi, dulcissime Jesu!" Quoties ipsam ad illa immitia vulnera verecundos, putas, occulos levasse; . . . Quomodo ipsam prae immensitate doloris cordis, credis, non potuisse deficere, a quo ipsam summe miror etiam mortuam non fuisse? Commoritur vivens, vivendo ferens dolorem morte crudeliorem.[63]

> ["Jesus, my son, Jesus permit me to die with you and for you, my son sweetest Jesus." How often does she do reverence, raising her eyes to the cruel wounds: . . . Can you believe that in the face of her immense sorrow of heart, she did not faint, or still greater wonder, did not die? Living to die together, she endured life as cruel sorrowful death.]

It would be unfair to leave the impression that portrayals of the Virgin beneath the cross are always this emotional. The great *Stabat mater* of Jacopone da Todi is much more restrained than the example just cited; but then, it is a hymn. Interestingly enough, it is in the vernacular poems and songs and not in the Latin versions that the emotion is most evident. Some of the Latin pieces, like the long poem of Ubertino da Casale printed in Appendix A, show a clear attempt to expand the monologue of the Virgin into a controlled dialogue between Mary and her Son in which the theological significance of the Passion is spelled out. When translated into the vernacular, and hence directed to a popular and not clerical or fraternal audience, the tone is qualified. For example, in the notes of a sermon delivered by an English Franciscan, William Melton, the *stabat mater* scene is appealed to:

> Audiens hec dolorissima mulier sche pleyned hir of mankynd': I make my mone to all "world" sene I had neuer child but Christe þat he xall þus deye from me, I gete no mo, pytusly I plene me of mankynde. *Bernard* ubi supra: O mulier dulcissima, mollis ad flendum, mollis ad dolendum, tu scis quod ad hoc veni, ad hoc carnem de virgine assumpsi, ut per crucis patibulum saluarem genus humanum; quod placet deo patri, quomodo displicet tibi, dulcissima mater? Respondet mater: O appellacio, vere dei nate, tu michi pater, tu michi sponsus, tu michi filius, nunc orbor patre, nunc vicuor sponso, desolabor prole, omnia perdo. But ʒif I apeel from þe lawe of scripte to þe lawe of grace I fynde no mercy in none place.[64]

> [Hear now the most sorrowful woman . . . . or to follow Bernard: O sweetest woman, mild in weeping, mild in sorrow, you know that I came to this, for this assumed flesh of the virgin, so that through cruci-fixion on the cross I might save mankind; since it pleases God the father, why should it displease you, sweetest mother? The mother replies: O I appeal, true God born, you my father, you my spouse, you my son; now bereft of father, now deprived of spouse, I am for-saken by my offspring, I have lost everything . . . .]

We may observe three things here: first, the dramatic quality suggests a vigorous homiletic presentation; second, the vulgar nature of Mary's dialogue in the English version contrasts with the polished style of St. Bernard's Latin; third, the last English phrase suggests that it came as a couplet from some vernacular poetic rendition of the sub-ject. Melton's sermon would have been delivered in English, despite the Latin notes. In it, whether through Bernard or through poetry, the object remains constant: through an intense response to the Pas-sion, the hearer moves toward conformation to the Suffered-Christ.

Occasionally the ideal of conformity was carried to remarkable extremes. Salimbene describes the behavior of Gerardino Segarello, who when refused by the Friars Minor tried to found his own Order of the Apostles, despite the prohibitive Fourth Lateran decree (1215). His appeal was based upon even more literal imitation of the life of Christ than that of the most fervent Franciscan *spirituali*, and his excesses were often ghoulish.[65] Among the friars themselves a few of the more simple-minded religious occasionally were guilty of literal-minded absurdities. Salimbene records in his chronicle an incident recounted to him by an English friar, one Richard, in which the Devil tempted a brother into believing that he still lacked one thing

Plate 2. St. Francis and the Seraph of the Stigmata (MS. C.C.C. Cambridge, 16)

for his salvation, that he should literally crucify himself. Shortly after the brethren found him, half-dead, with one hand and both feet nailed to a cross.[66] In another instance, Walter of Madely, a companion of Agnellus, envisioned the corpse being taken from the cross above the altar and laid in the choir; on drawing nearer he discovered that it did indeed have five wounds, but was the body of Agnellus.[67] The suggested parallel to the stigmatization of St. Francis (see Plate 2) is obvious, and raises a point. While the Franciscans generally were not carried to so blatant and literal an imitation of the life of Christ and the Apostles as some radicals, they were nevertheless predisposed to imitation as a mode of life. This is revealed not only in the Franciscan habit and Rule, but also in the hagiographical tradition rapidly built up by the early biographers of St. Francis and adapted into iconographic detail by contemporary artists. One is surprised to see among the *legenda* which border the cross of St. Francis in the Bardi Chapel of Santa Croce, Florence, a depiction of St. Francis standing in a fishing boat a little off shore, preaching to a crowd there assembled. Such a story does not appear to have survived in extant Franciscan legend, but even if it could be found, the express likeness of both story and representation to the story of Christ preaching from the boat in Galilee (Mark 4:1) and its graphic representations has transparent purpose. The connection is simply one more item in an articulated program of hagiography and iconography intended to dramatize the conformity of St. Francis to the life of Christ.

Nowhere is this program more evident than in the thaumaturgy developed in early biographies of the Saint, as well as for St. Anthony of Padua. With respect to St. Francis, the "conformity" seems occasionally to extend beyond the life of Christ. An illustration might be his Pauline vision on the road to Spoleto (*Legenda trium sociorum*, chap. 1). But there is another, more consistent pattern of hagiographical events which have striking historiographical overtones. Before concluding that the attempts at conformity to Christ recorded by Francis' biographers[68] are merely an expression of the drive for Christian perfection (they of course are that), we might pick up some further clue from the opening lines of the *Fioretti*:

> It is first to be considered that the glorious St. Francis in all the acts of his life was conformable to Christ the Blessed. And that even as Christ, at the beginning of his mission, chose twelve Apostles who were to despise all worldly things and follow Him in poverty and in the other virtues, so St. Francis in the beginning chose for the foundation of his Order twelve companions who were possessed of naught save direst poverty. And even as one of the twelve Apostles of Christ, being reproved by God, went and hanged himself by the neck, so one of the twelve companions of St. Francis, whose name was Friar John della Cappella, became a runagate and at last hanged himself by the neck. . . . And even as those holy Apostles were, above all, wondrous in their holiness and humility and filled with the Holy Ghost, so those most holy companions of St. Francis were men of such saintliness that, since the days of the Apostles, the world hath never beheld men so wondrously holy. For one among them was rapt, like St. Paul, up to the third heaven, and he was Friar Giles; another, to wit, Friar Philip, was touched on the lips by an angel with a coal of fire, even as the prophet Isaiah was . . . .[69]

There is no mistaking the conviction of the brothers that this was not casual coincidence. Notice further among the other early biographies as well, that Francis in the preface to the *Legend of the Three Companions* is compared to the morning star; in addition to choosing twelve companions he also went in the company of sinners (*I Celano* 1. 29); like Christ he maintained a forty-day fast (*Fioretti* 1.7); he healed a woman possessed of a devil (*Fioretti* 2.4); he was no scholar, but understood excellently the Scriptures (*II Celano* 2. 5, 16); he healed a leper (*Fioretti* 1. 25); he was said to be recognized by sheep who revered him as a shepherd;[70] on thinking his death at hand, and that it was Thursday, he held a last supper in which he broke bread to his followers in the manner of Christ;[71] he received the stigmata—the marks of Christ's crucifixion after apprehension of the fire of the Holy Spirit and an apocalyptic (Isaiah 6:2) seraphim (*Fioretti* 2.2); afterwards he was confronted with one Jerome "that was incredulous, and doubted much, even as St. Thomas the apostle doubted the wounds of Christ," and resolved his doubts in the same fashion (Fioretti, 2.5).

Other situations for comparison could be adduced as well as instances where the early biographers make a strained comparison:

So it happened that He who inspired the Kings to bring gifts to honour his son in the days after His nativity, also inspired that noble and saintly lady [Jacoma] to bring gifts to honour his beloved servant in the days before his death, which was his true nativity.[72]

As late as the fifteenth century, the legend was rounding out to include the suggestion that Francis was born in a stable and laid in a manger.[73]

There are other notable scriptural analogies in the Franciscan accounts as well: the names of Paul and Isaiah have already been mentioned here. Additional resemblances to scriptural personalities include allusions to Old Testament figures such as Jeremiah the "weeping prophet." One day Francis is said to have been walking alone and weeping and moaning aloud. When asked what was the matter, he replied:

Plango passionem Domini mei Iesu Christi, pro quo non deberem verecundari alta voce ire plorando per totum mundum [I weep for the passion of my Lord Jesus Christ, for whose sake I would not be ashamed to go lamenting loudly through the whole world] (*Legenda trium sociorum* 5. 14).

But more particularly among these Old Testament allusions, attention is drawn to the rather remarkable pattern of correlation between miracles performed by St. Francis and his follower, the famous preacher and thaumaturgist Anthony of Padua, and miracles performed by Elijah and Elisha. Elijah, like Francis, is among the prophets noted for his intense piety (1 Kings 19:10, 14; Luke 1:17, where he is compared with Christ; Rom. 11:2; James 5:17); Elijah foretells a plague sent as judgment on the people (2 Chronicles 21:12–15), and Francis does the same;[74] Elijah fasts forty days in the wilderness (1 Kings 19:8), as did Christ, as did Francis (*Fioretti* 7) and no one else of note on record; Elijah had a special kinship with the birds, was fed by ravens (1 Kings 17:1–7) and Francis' relationship with the birds is legendary (*Fioretti* 16.22; *Speculum perfectionis* 12.113); Elijah was given to extremes of spirit, exuberance, and despondency (1 Kings 19:10–18) and such is the character of Francis throughout the biographies; Elijah is sustained in the household of the widow of Zerephath, whose meal and oil are miraculously increased despite the extra burden (1 Kings 17:8–16), while Francis and his followers are so great a burden on their host, the parish priest of Rieti, that they strip the vineyard, but on Francis' prayer the vineyard is restored to bring forth more wine than before (*Fioretti* 19). One final point about Elijah is worth noting: like Christ, Elijah was translated, did not experience a natural death, but was borne off in a flaming chariot (2 Kings 2:11); St. Francis appeared to the brethren at Rivo Torto in a flaming chariot. Elijah then reappeared with Christ at his transfiguration, after which Christ explained to the disciples that Elias (Elijah) who "must first come and restore all things" has already come in the person of John the Baptist (Matt. 17:3–13; 11:13–14), the forerunner.

The other pairing is equally interesting. Elisha was called into service under Elijah (1 Kings 19:19); Anthony was called into service under St. Francis, and likewise followed in his footsteps; Elisha was the great preacher among the prophets, Anthony was the great preacher of the Franciscan order; Elisha neutralized the poison in a potage for his brethren (2 Kings 4:38–41), Anthony did the same;[75] Elisha healed a leper (2 Kings 5:1–19), and Anthony also;[76] Elisha increased a woman's oil (2 Kings 4:1–7), so also does Anthony;[77] Elisha's bones restore a dead man to life (2 Kings 13:21), and the same is said for Anthony.[78]

What the early "Spiritual" biographers intended by this extensive and evidently conscious extension is probably similar to the intention which informs the *Meditations*. Nothing happens for the first time. There is nothing of spiritual significance in the Old Testament which does not recur in the New Testament, and again in the personal present. This is the *concordia Scripturarum*, the mysterious correspondence between the Scriptures to be seen by those who have eyes to see. Its effect is to make Old and New contemporaneous; to transform time into eternity; history *sub specie aeternitatis*. Or history as poetry: it is, as we shall see in a companion volume, the time sense of medieval drama. And, for hagiography, as for poetry, drama, and Scripture itself, these become exegetical principles whereby the recurring details are spiritually understood.[79] The resulting juxtapositions relate also to an historical and apocalyptic consciousness dramatically shaped by eschatological traditions in Franciscan thought.

The apocalyptic teachings of Joachim of Fiore, a Cistercian abbot who died in Calabria in 1202, had brought into the world of St. Francis's time a startling new conception of history. Derived from an historiographical exegesis of the Apocalypse, its main tenet was the now famous theory of the three ages of the world, a "trinity of ages" corresponding to the divine Trinity. Salimbene described the extensive influence of the abbot's teachings on Franciscans in his own day, his own thoughts after an inconclusive A.D. 1260,[80] and then summarized the central doctrine:

> . . . he divides the world into a three fold state; for in the first state the Father worked in mystery through the patriarchs and sons of the prophets, although the works of the Trinity are indivisible. In the second state the Son worked through the Apostles and other apostolic men; of which state He saith in John "My Father worketh until now, and I work." In the third state the Holy Ghost shall work through the Religious.[81]

Each subsequent age follows the pattern of the first age. The Old Testament is the pattern and key to the meaning of history. Joachim estimated that each age lasted, as he thought that the Old Testament age did, for forty-two generations, and had a precursor or germinator as well as an initiator or fructifier. Hence, around 1260 would begin the final age which would presumably last for about forty-two generations—a sort of millenial kingdom of the Spirit characterized by love and peace—until the *terminus ad quem* of the "tyme of grace," the final judgment.[82] The birth throes of each age were to be violent, especially the third age, giving rise to antichrists in the immediately preceding period.[83] However, "each age . . . is an advance over the preceding one, explains it, and gives a rationale to its pattern. Human history is divine fulfillment. The human race progressively receives a fuller revelation of the meaning of time and historical existence and progressively becomes more perfect."[84]

King Uzziah (Ozias: Isaiah 6:1, 2—the same passage from which comes the seraphim of St. Francis) was the precursor of the second age, which was initiated by Zacharias, the father of John the Baptist. St. Benedict of Nursia was the precursor of the coming age, which would be a spiritual (monastic) age.[85] The first age was dominated by the Law—and is characterized by married men; the second by Grace—and clergy; the third by the Holy Spirit—and *viri spirtuales* living a monastic form of life. The Church would continue to exist, but the sacraments would be spiritualized. In Joachim's historiography, the age of Grace was about to end, and that of the Holy Spirit now to be ushered in with the new Elijah, who was assigned to the order of monks. As St. John the Baptist had prepared for the coming of the Son, so St. Benedict prepared for the new age of the Spirit.[86] The monks of the second age had been imperfect—even the Cistercians spent too much time in the care of multiplying flocks and herds; hence it was necessary that "the true likeness of apostolic life should succeed them."[87] Joachim predicted the coming of twelve holy men, prefigured by the twelve patriarchs and the twelve Apostles. The opening of the *Fioretti* may suggest that the Franciscan Spirituals thought they knew the identity of that final dozen.

The influence of Joachimism among the Franciscans was methodologically significant and very widespread. Notable Spiritual Franciscans espoused the Joachimite cause: the renowned Hugh de Digne, a "great Joachite," was a friend of Grosseteste, Adam Marsh (Marisco) of Oxford, and John of Parma, and a formative influence upon the Franciscan Tertiaries of Provence;[88] John of Parma, Minister General of the Order before St. Bonaventure, and friend of the English province, was called by Salimbene "a very mighty Joachite," a singer and composer of songs.[89] John was also a close friend of Gerard de Borgo San Dennino, whose *Introductorius ad evangeliam aeternum* was so roundly condemned by Jean de Meun in his *Roman de la rose*;[90] and it was even charged by some that John of Parma wrote the work himself.[91] While this seems doubtful, there was apparently enough reason to believe he influenced the book that he was forced to resign as Minister General in 1257.[92] Joachimite influence crept into Franciscan commentaries: in 1240, an English friar, one Brother Aymon, employed Joachim's method in a commentary on Isaiah, and the same flavor is detectable in Friar Alexander's historical interpretation of the Apocalypse, written in 1242.[93] Remarkably, despite all the storm of dispute and eventual charge of heresy laid against Gerard's *Introductorius*, Joachim's own prophecies were never condemned. Too many had long held him for a prophet, and the immense popularity and authority of his prophecies continued well into the seventeenth century.

Even if we reduce the size of the apocalyptic spectre to avoid extravagant interpretation, we must still allow for its influence on the early Franciscans. And, with or without Joachim, there is ample evidence that the Order from St. Francis himself down through the Middle Ages was apocalyptically or Judgment oriented.[94] The Rule itself (*1 Reg.* 23. 16) and the great *Dies irae* attest to this expectation.[95] "Now is the time of mercy, later the time of justice," was a familiar cry.[96] It is not simply that the Franciscans may have felt some impetus toward hastening their work in the face of an impending curtain call whose date (whether 1233, 1260, 1300, 1333, 1366 or whatever)[97] was constantly before them, though the sense of urgency thus derived was an important influence on their method. Rather, it seems probable that what lies behind the legend-building and Joachimite prophecy is a particularly acute consciousness of the progress of history, literal history infused with a spiritual syntax, which was not commonly so dramatically articulated in the time, and which relates to their theological thought in other areas. The Franciscans did not, like the Dominicans, set much value on their sermons, and so, unhappily, preserved very few. Instead, and unlike the Dominicans, they preserved chronicles. There are many of these, from those of Brother Jordan of Saxony and Thomas Eccleston, which simply record the early history of their provinces,[98] through general historical compilations like the Melrose and Lanercost chronicles,[99] to deliberate spiritual interpretations of history. One instance of the latter kind is afforded by the historical interpretation of the Apocalypse by Friar Alexander, mentioned above.[100] Another is the *Historia septum tribulationis ordinis minorum* of Fra Angelo Clareno, which, in conformity with the chronological methods of the Joachimites, summed up in six epochs of tribulation the struggles and wars of the Spirituals from the middle of the thirteenth century.[101] All of these compilations have at least one thing in common: an acute sense of history, and the belief that the Franciscan Order stood at a particularly critical point near the end of the calendar of God's time—the penultimate day. Moreover, this idea extends beyond the chronicles to other Franciscan works, including Franciscan "translations" of Scripture, in prose, pantomime, and poetry.[102] More than a generation ago it was observed that the influence of Joachimism is apparent in Friar John's *Meditations*.[103] Since that work in turn will be seen to have had a profound influence on Middle English poetry, it is in order that something of the shape communicated to that poetry by a "Joachimite" sense of the end of all things be fairly appreciated in its style.

If we summarize the elements of Franciscan theology and spirituality touched upon in this chapter, the features achieving prominence are: Scripture, the humanity of Christ, affectual response, and the sacramental grace in contrition and identification (or conformity). The Franciscans gave to the Scriptures first authority in their theological and spiritual world, and with respect to doctrine and handling of the Scriptures organized biblical materials so that they focused on

the Passion of Jesus Christ. They gave second priority to the sacraments, and when elaborating their sacramental doctrines traced all
investment of effective grace to the Passion of Christ. The most notable aspect of their evangelical spirituality was contrition-evoking,
affective contemplation of the Cross, sometimes through the inter-
mediary Virgin, prescribed in such a way as to promote spiritual conformity to the Passion of the Suffered-Christ. Finally, the historiographical consciousness of the early Friars Minor seems to have
prompted them not merely to urgency in proclaiming their message,
but to seeing themselves juxtaposed to their immediate social and
political world, and that world in the perspective of a dawning New
Age of which they were harbingers.[104] Theirs was a theology of history
which included both prophetic tradition and coming Apocalypse, and
which pointed to one single event as the center of it all—not the birth,
but the death of Christ. All else in history led up to and prepared for
that moment, all afterwards followed it and fulfilled its prophecy.
For contemplation, edification, sanctification, and salvation they turned
to the Cross.

> In hac tua passione
> me agnosce, pastor bone!

cried Jacopone da Todi, and his plea for recognition was to be echoed
and re-echoed on down to the fifteenth century.

Notes

1. See Beryl Smalley, *English Friars and Antiquity in the Early Fourteenth Century* (New York: Barnes and Noble, 1960).
2. Decima L. Douie, *Archbishop Pecham* (Oxford: Clarendon Press, 1952), p. 281; see also M. D. Chenu, "La Première Diffusion du Thomisme à Oxford," *Archives d'histoire doctrinale et littéraire du Moyen Âge* 3 (1928):185–200.
3. Douie, *Pecham*, pp. 292–93.
4. "Praeterea noverit ipse quod philosophorum studie minime reprobamus, quatenus misteriis theologicis famulantur; sed profanas vocum novitates, quae contra philosophicam veritatem sunt in sanctorum injuriam citra viginti annos in altitudines theologicas introductae, abjectis et vilipensis sanctorum assertionibus evidenter. Quae sit ergo solidior et sanior doctrina, vel filiorum beati Francisci, sanctae scilicet memoriae fratris Alexandri, ac fratris Bonaventurae et consimilium, qui in suis tractatibus ab omni calumnia alienis sanctis et philosophis innituntur; vel illa novella quasi tota contraria, quae quicquid docet Augustinus de regulis aeternis et luce incommutabili, de potentiis animae, de rationibus seminalibus inditis materiae et consimilibus innumeris, destruat pro viribus et enervat pugnas verborum inferens toti mundo?" (*Reg.* 3. 901). All translations are my own unless otherwise indicated.
5. In *The Catholic Encyclopedia* (New York: Robert Appleton, 1907–12), 2:653a.
6. "Licet autem omnis illuminatio cognitionis interna sit, possumus tamen rationabiliter distinguere, ut dicamus, quod est lumen *exterius*, scilicet lumen artis mechanicae; lumen *inferius*, scilicet lumen cognitionis sensitivae; lumen *interius*, scilicet lumen cognitionis philosophicae; lumen *superius*, scilicet lumen gratiae et sacrae Scripturae. Primum lumen illuminat respectu *figurae artificialis*, secundum respectu *formae naturalis*, tertium respectu *veritatis intellectualis*, quartum et ultimum respectu *veritatis salutaris*" (St. Bonaventure, *De reductione artium ad theologiam*, ed. and trans. Emma Thérèse Healy, 2nd ed. [St. Bonaventure, N.Y.: Franciscan Institute, 1955], p. 38—hereafter cited as *Reductione artium*).
7. *Reductione artium*, p. 47.
8. ". . . sicut scientiae philosophicae super prima principia sua fundantur, ita scientia Scripturae fundatur super articulos fidei" (*De donis S. S.* 4. 13, in St. Bonaventure, *Opera omnia*, ed. F. Fanna and I. Jelier [Quaracchi, 1883–1902], 5: 476).
9. *Legenda trium sociorum*, chaps. 67, 69; *Jacopone da Todi, Laudi*, ed. F. Ageno (Florence: Le Monnier, 1953), *Lauda* XXXI; cf. Hilarin Felder, *Geschichte der wissenschaftlichen Studien im Franziskanerorden* (Freiburg im Bresgau: Herder, 1904), p. 64. Actually, the passages which contain injunctions against owning books add: "He [St. Francis] did not despise sacred science, for indeed he had a great veneration for those learned men of the

Order and for all scholars" . . . (p. 69). Jacopone, of course, was well read in theology: see E. Underhill, *Jacopone da Todi, Poet and Mystic* . . . *1228– 1306* (London: Dent, 1919), pp. 230–40.

10. J. R. H. Moorman, *A New Fioretti* (London: SPCK, 1946), pp. 60 ff.

11. P. Eugène d'Oisy, in "François et la Bible," *Études franciscaines* 39 (1927):498–529, 646–56; 40 (1928):69–80, shows that, significantly, St. Francis alludes to or quotes from the Psalms twelve times more frequently than from any other book in the Old Testament, and that in the New Testament he refers to Matthew eleven times for every three references to the next most popular gospel, Luke. Despite this concentration, he shows familiarity with both Testaments. (Interestingly, the Old Testament book quoted most frequently by Christ was also the Psalms—as much as all others together.)

12. G. H. Tavard, *Transiency and Permanence: The Nature of Theology According to St. Bonaventure* (St. Bonaventure, N.Y.: Franciscan Institute, 1954), pp. 252, 253–58.

13. Ibid., p. 252.

14. The translations are from the *Breviloquium* (pr. 3; pr. 2—a paraphrase of Romans 12:3), the prologue to which work Tavard says is "something like a charter of the status of Scripture in Christian culture" (p. 40).

15. A. G. Little, "The First Hundred Years of the Franciscan School at Oxford," in *St. Francis of Assisi: 1226–1926: Essays in Commemoration*, ed. Walter Warren Seton (London: Univ. of London Press, 1926), p. 172. The most recent treatment of Franciscan writings on Scripture is to be found in J. R. H. Moorman's definitive *History of the Franciscan Order* (Oxford: Clarendon Press, 1968), pp. 256–77, 390–405.

16. *Fr. Roger Bacon Opera* (Rolls Series), ed. J. S. Brewer, pp. 328–29; translated in Little, "The First Hundred Years," p. 173.

17. George G. Coulton, *From St. Francis to Dante* (London: D. Nutt, 1906), p. 303.

18. P. Ubald d'Alençon, "La Spiritualité franciscaine," *Études franciscaines* 39 (1927):287; he says that Friar John was "professeur de théologie à Milan." See also Pierre Pourrat, *La Spiritualité chrétienne* (Paris: J. Gabalda et fils, 1928), 2: 229. See chap. 3 below.

19. See M. Deanesly, "The Gospel Harmony of John de Caulibus or St. Bonaventura," *Collectanea Franciscana*, vol. 2, ed. C. L. Kingsford et al., (BSFS 10: Manchester: Univ. of Manchester Press, 1922), pp. 10–19.

20. The manuscript they translate is from the Bibliothèque Nationale, Paris, but many MSS existed in England in Latin, besides several translations into English and French among illustrated MSS alone (p. xxiii). This was a work of immense popularity, receiving many adaptations and part translations in addition to the one ascribed to Manning and cited below (n. 23). Notable is the translation/paraphrase of Nicolas Love, done in 1400, entitled *The Mirrour of the Blessed Lyf of Jesu Christ*, ed. Lawrence F. Powell (London, 1908).

21. *Meditations*, pp. 6–9.

22. See here *Magistri Alexandri de Hales, Glossa in quatuor libros sententiarum Petri Lombardi*, Bibliotheca Franciscana Scholastica Medii Aevi 15, vol. 4 (Quaracchi, 1957), dist. 3170; 4. 83–86.

23. *Medytacyuns of þe soper of oure lorde Ihesu. And also of hys passyun. And eke of þe þeynes of hys swete modyr, Mayden marye. þe whyche made yn latyn Bonaventure Cardynall*, ed. J. M. Cowper, EETS OS 84 (London: Trübner, 1875), lines 619–26. Cowper ascribes the translation to Robert Manning of Brunne and gives it a date between 1315 and 1330. It occurs along with *Handlyng Synne* in Harley MS. 1701; see also Luigi Cellucci, "Il Poemeto inglese tratto dalle 'Meditationes,'" *Archivum Romanicum* 22 (1938):67–73.

24. Manning, *Medytacyuns*, lines 605–8.

25. Ibid., lines 65–72.

26. Friar John often collates accounts from three or four evangelists for his rendition, as for example in his account of the annointment of Christ by Mary Magdalene, which is a representative gathering of Matthew 26, Mark 4 and 14, and John 12. Robert Manning in his translation naturally follows Friar John, but what he adds illustrates another harmonizing tendency of Franciscan literature, homogenized quotation of and allusion to numerous scriptural verses in a homiletic medley of verse:

> þenk, also, þe greete dede of hys powere:
> He myȝt ha sent an angel to saue vs here,
> But þan of oure saluacyun we shulde nat þanke hym,
> But calle þe aungel sauer of alle man kyn.
> þarfor hys fadyr so hertly loued vs,
> He ȝaue vs hys owene gete sone Ihesus;
> þan we onely hym þanke and do hym onoure,
> As fadyr, as former, socoure and sauyoure.
> þank we now oure sayoure, þat salue vs haþ broȝt,
> Oure syke soules to saue, whan synne haþ hem soȝt,
> Of hys grete godenes gyn we hym grete,
> Seyyng þe wurde of sakarye þe holy prophete:
> "Lorde god of Israel, blessed mote þou be,
> þy peple þou hast vysyted and boȝt hem to þe.
> Whych setyn yn derkenes of deþ and dysese,
> þou lyȝtest hem and ledest yn to þe wey of pese."
> To þat pes pereles we prey þou vs bryng.
> þat leuyst and reynest with oute endyng.

(*Medytacyuns*, lines 1125–42)

Cf. *Meditations*, p. 82.

27. Yet there is usually restraint when it comes to particular "party" issues. The spiritual Franciscan ideal of poverty is the only such example in the *Meditations*, where it is noted that the Holy Family was in "dire poverty," and that "the Lord found this the highest virtue; this is the heavenly pearl for which it appears one must exchange everything. It is the main founda-

tion of the whole spiritual edifice" (pp. 35–36). This quotation suggests that Franciscan exegesis when prolix could become a little strained.

28. St. Anselm, *Cur Deus homo*; a modern translation is in *Trinity, Incarnation and Redemption: Theological Treatises*, ed. J. Hopkins and H. Richardson (New York: Harper Torch Books, 1970).

29. See for example D. J. Unger, "Robert Grosseteste . . . on the Reasons for the Incarnation," *Franciscan Studies* 16 (1956): 1–37. Also St. Bonaventure, in *Tractatus de preparatione ad missam* 1, 10 (Quaracchi, 8:1026);*Feria sexta et Parasc.*, Sermo I (9:259b); and *Dom. II pro Pascha*, Sermo I (9:295a), etc. Also see Jean Bonnefoy, "La Question hypothétique: Utrum si Adam non peccasset . . . au xiiie siècle," *Revista española de teologia* 14 (1954):327–68, esp. 334–35.

30. K. F. Lynch, "The Doctrine of Alexander of Hales on the Nature of Sacramental Grace," *Franciscan Studies* 19 (1959): 355.

31. Ibid., pp. 354, 364.

32. "Praetera, virtus Passionis Christi delevit poenam originalis peccati, et baptismus ex virtute gratiae delet culpam, et ita plena remissio quoad culpam et poenam fit praetur resurrectionem Christi" (Alexander of Hales *IV Glossa* 4. 86).

33. Lynch, "Doctrine," pp. 340 ff.

34. Ibid., p. 364.

35. Bonifatius Strack, "Das Leiden Christi im Denken des hl. Bonaventura," *Franziskanische Studien* 41 (1959):129–62.

36. *Com. in Jo.* 12. 36 (Quaracchi, 6:417b): ". . . quia passio non habet effectum nisi in imitatoribus Christi . . ."—*Com. in Jo.*, c. 20. 73. 3 (6:621a): "In passione ascendit Christus ante nos, ut iter nobis expediret." *Apol. Paup.*, c. 1. 2 (8:235b): ". . . cum ipse magister omnium Christus non ad solatia carnis, sed ad supplicia crucis discipulos suos semper invitat."

37. Strack, "Leiden Christi," p. 148.

38. "Ecce, quod Christus, Rex regum statuit decretum, quod nullus possit eum videre, nisi sit secum crucifixus. Et hoc decretum est tantae generalitatis, ut nullus excipiatur; tantae autem necessitatis, ut cum nullo dispensetur; sed quilibet tenetur accipere crucem mortificationis in suo corpore, ut et vita Domini Jesu in corpore suo per imitationem manifestetur, alioquin non est dignus sequi eum ad coronam sine vexillo victoriae" (St. Bonaventure, *Dom. IV in Quadrag.*, Sermo I [Quaracchi, 9:323b]).

39. Cf. *Glossa* 4. 16. 253: "Si vero quaeratur cuiusmodi partes, dicendum est quod sunt partes quoad esse, et sunt partes quoad bene esse. Quoad esse est pars contritio; quoad bene esse est pars confessio cum satisfactione, prout satisfactio est praeter contritionem. Nec est hoc contrarium, quod poenitentia secundum sui rationem potest praedicari de contritione, quia in ipsa contritione consistit esse poenitentiae secundum quod est causa delectionis peccati."

40. "Respondemus: poenitentia est virtus vel gratia. Secundum unum esse est virtus, secundum alterum est gratia. Sunt enim duo effectus; unus est remissio culpae, et alter remissio poenae. Nam in contritione remittitur

culpa; per confessionem et satisfactionem poena, quae etiam remittitur quandoque per solam contritionem. Quantum ergo ad remissionem culpae est gratia; effectus enim delendi culpam est gratiae proprius. Quantum autem ad remissionem poenae est virtus; tunc enim homo existens in caritate satisfacit, et ita reddit Deo quod ei debetur, quod scilicet est iustitiae. Est ergo opus illud ex caritate et iustitia procedens" (*Glossa* 4. 14. 210).

41. *Glossa* 4. 22. 382: "Propter hoc videtur potius esse dicendum quod in contritione est principaliter esse poenitentiae secundum quod est sacramentum. Et est ibi quiddam quod est sacramentum tantum, scilicet contritio exterior; quiddam sacramentum et res, scilicet interior contritio; res vero tantum, remissio peccati. Et consistit similitudo in annihilatione. In contritione enim annihilat se homo; in remissione peccati Deus annihilat culpam." See K. F. Lynch, "Doctrine," and "The Sacramental Grace of Confirmation in Thirteenth-Century Theology," *Franciscan Studies* 22 (1962):32–149, 172–300. John Lathbury, in the "de Constantia" section of his *Commentary on Lamentations*, describes penance in terms of the Flagellation: "Iuvat enim servatque dupliciter: sive Flagelli loco, cum peccavimus; sive Fraeni, ne peccamus. Flagelli quidem quia paterna manus est quae lapsos crebro verberat: carnificis, quae tarde sed semel punit" (chap. 9, "de castigatione").

42. "In eucharista similiter datur virtus, quia quantum est de caritate passionis, major fit unio per caritatem membrorum corpis mystici ad Caput" (*Glossa* 4. 8. 132).

43. Cuthbert Gumbinger, "St. Bernadine's Unedited *Prediche Volgari* (Florence, 1424 and 1425; Siena, 1425; Padua, 1443)," *Franciscan Studies* 25 (1944):26–27.

44. Note *Rythmus de corpore Christi*, and *Ave vivens hostia*, ed. E. Blume, *Analecta hymnica*, 31:111–12. For Pecham's other hymns in praise of the Holy Sacrament see pp. 597–98.

45. Alexander of Hales, *Introitus*, pp. 7: 131, lines 58 ff.; also *Quaestiones disputatae antequam esset frater* (Quaracchi, 20:851): "Per confirmationem reformatur ad similitudinem Christi pugnatis contra inimicos."

46.   "Thise curatz been ful necligent and slowe
      To grope tendrely a conscience
      In shrift; in prechyng is my diligence,
      And studie in Petres wordes and in Poules.
      I walke, and fisshe Cristen mennes soules,
      To yelden Jhesu Crist his propre rente;
      To sprede his word is set al myn entente."
                  (*Summoner's Tale*, lines 1816–22)
Chaucer's Summoner's friar might as easily have been a Dominican, for on this point both orders advanced much the same argument.

47. The passage, in context, reads: "Floruit quoque apud Lenniam famosissimae sanctitatis vir, frater Galfridus de Saresburia, qui in austeritate vitae se alterum, si dici potest, Franciscum exhibuit, in conformitate virtutis et suavitatis ac simplicitatis gratia secundum Antonium. Tantae vero pietatis

fuit et compassionis in confessionibus audiendis, ut, ubi non videret confitentes congrua signa compunctionis ostendere, ipse eos potius ad fletum suis fletibus et singultibus (C. fol. 79ᵇ) commoveret; sicut de viro nobili domino Alexandro de Bissinburne contigit; quia cum sibi confiteretur quasi narrando quandam narrationem, flens amarissime frater ipsum flere coegit et ad propositum intrandi minorum ordinem suis meritis et salutaribus consiliis provexit . . ." (*De adventu fratrum minorum in Angliam*, ed. A. G. Little [Manchester: Univ. of Manchester Press, 1951], p. 63).

48. Manning, *Medytacyuns*, lines 906–14. Comparison with the original (*Meditations*, p. 341) will reveal the additions.

49. "Contricio est dolor voluntarie assumptus pro peccato cum proposito confitendi et satisfaciendi. Contricio ergo dicitur a cor et tero quasi universalis tractio. Exemplum de Magdelena . . ." (ed. J. Théodore Welter [Paris: A. Picard, 1914], pp. 26–27).

50. Manning, *Medytacyuns*, lines 409–12.

51. Pourrat, *La Spiritualité*, 2:229, 253, 275.

52. *Com. in Jo.* 15. 20 (Quaracchi, 6:405b).

53. See "The Blessed Virgin in Antonian Exegesis," chap. 4 in Louis F. Rohr, *The Use of Sacred Scripture in the Sermons of St. Anthony of Padua* (Washington: Catholic University of America Press, 1948), pp. 67–81. Rohr gives a good catalogue of Antonian iconography for the Virgin.

54. St. Anthony of Padua, *In Dominica XV post Penticosten*, in *S. Pat. Thaumaturgi Ineliti Sermones Dominicales et in Solemnitatibus*, ed. Locatelli (Patavii: Societas Universalis Sancti Antonnii Patavini Edit., 1895), 2:453a–b; *Sermo in Purificatione Sanctae Mariae*, p. 722a.

55. *Dominica II in Quadragesima*, 1:91a.

56. "*Esther* Beata Virgo Maria est . . . *Egeus custos virginum* est Iesus Christus . . . Hic *Egeus* nostram Esther idest Beatam Mariam, eo copiosius ornavit quo ipsa *cultum muliebrem non quaesivit*; nec enim se vel alium habere voluit ornatorem, sed totam se commisit *custodis* arbitrio, a quo tam decenter est *ornata*, ut hodierna die super Angelos sit exaltata"; and, "Ista nostra gloriosa *Esther* hodie per manus Angelorum *ducta est ad cubiculum regis Assueri*, idest aethereum thalamum, in quo rex regum beatitudo Angelorum, stellato solio residet Iesus Christus, qui eamdem gloriosam Virginem super *omnes mulieres amavit* . . . Vere omni gratia praestantior fuit Beatiae Mariae gratia, quae Filium cum Deo Patre habuit, et ideo hodierna die in caelis coronari meruit. Unde subditur: *Et posuit diadema regni in capite eius*" (*In Assumptione S. Mariae Virginis*, 3:732b, 732a). Cf. pp. 236–37 below.

57. "Jesus Christus ex sacco nostrae naturae fecit sibi tunicam quam acu, idest subtili opere Spiritus Sancti, et filo, idest fide Beatae Virginis, consuit et seipsum induit; et super ipsam cinerem vilitatis et paupertatis aspersit" (*In Dominica XIII post Pentecostem*, 2:409a—this figure is an allusion to Job 16:16).

58. *In Dominica II post Epiphanem*, 2:667b–668a.

59. St. Bonaventure, *I Sent.* 48. 4 (Quaracchi, 1:861b), "Dicendum, quod dolore de aliquo est dupliciter: aut ita quod dolens voluntate rationis absoluta velit contrarium eius, de quo dolet; et sic nulli licet dolere de passione Christi . . . . Alio modo dolere de aliquo est ferri ad contrarium voluntate pietatis, tamen nihilominus hoc velle voluntate absoluta; sic bonum est condolere Christo et pie affici circa eum, et sic afficiuntur viri sancti, qui magnas gratias agunt Deo de passione Christi; sed tamen moventur pie in consideratione dolorum. Sic etiam piessima anima beatae Virginis dilectissimo Filio suo patienti, quantum sustinere poterat, compatiebatur. Nullo tamen modo est dubitandum, quia virilis eius animus et ratio constantissima vellet etiam Unigenitum tradere pro salute generis humani, ut Mater per omnia conformis esset Patri. Et in hoc miro modo debet laudari et amari, quod placuit ei, ut Unigenitus suus pro salute generis humani offeretur. Et tantum etiam compassa est, ut, si fieri posset, omnia tormenta quae Filius pertulit, ipsa multo libentius sustineret."

60. "Ipsa [Maria] enim ad similitudinem Filii sui sub cruce et iuxta crucem habuit summum gaudium et summum dolorem, sicut Filius in cruce et per crucem summum habuit dolorem naturalem de morte et summum gaudium rationale de humani generis redemptione . . . . Maria benedicta summum habuit dolorem naturalem ex dilectione Filii pro morte, quam praesens aspexit: summam dilectionem rationalem super eo, quod ille qui de ea natus fuit, tanta caritatis ostensione humanum genus redemit" (*De Assumptione Beatae Virginae Mariae* 6 [Quaracchi, 9:705a]).

61. *Meditations*, p. 327; also p. 335. Similarly St. Bonaventure: "Audiamus Virginis Matris Mariae lamentabilem vocem et attendamus eius vehementem dolorem, et videbimus, quia non est dolor sicut dolor eius, excepto dolore Filii, ad cuius exemplar dolor suus assimilatur. Mira enim et incredibili compassione tenebatur atque verbis nostris inexplicabili sermone. Dolores namque, plaga et opprobria Filii in se retorquens, in suam propriam personam recipiebat, sentiens quod et in Christo Jesu. In animo enim illi martyri commartyr astabat, vulnerato convulnerata crucifixo concrucifixa, gladiato congladiata. Nam suam ipsius animam pertransivit gladius passionis Christi" (*Domenica infra Octavan Epiphanem* I [Quaracchi, 9:172a–173b]).

62. Manning, *Medytacyuns*, lines 786; 789–96.

63. *Vitis myst.* 9. 1 (Quaracchi, 8:174b–175a).

64. A. G. Little, ed., *Studies in English Franciscan History* (Manchester: Univ. of Manchester Press, 1917), pp. 250 ff. (hereafter cited as Little, *Studies*).

65. Salimbene d'Adam, *Chronica*, ed. Holder-Egger, in *MGH*, ser., Script., 32 (Hanover: 1905–13): 255 ff. (hereafter cited as Salimbene).

66. Salimbene, p. 570.

67. F. Gilbert, *B. Agnellus and the English Grey Friars* (London: BSFS, 1937), p. 88.

68. In addition to the translation of the *Fioretti* cited below, see the *Legenda trium sociorum* (chap. 1, n. 64, above), and the translations of Brother Leo in Karrer, *St. Francis*, pp. 72 ff.

69. Trans. Damian J. Blaher, in *The Little Flowers of St. Francis* (New York: Dutton, 1951).

70. St. Bonaventure, in Karrer, *St. Francis*, pp. 161–62.

71. Brother Leo, in Karrer, pp. 142–44.

72. Ibid., p. 145.

73. Paschal Robinson, in *The Catholic Encyclopedia*, 6:221d.

74. Brother Leo, in Karrer, *St. Francis*, p. 93.

75. *Catholic Encyclopedia*, 1:556–57.

76. *Leggende Antoniane*, ed. Roberto Cessi (Milan: Società editrice "vitea pensiero," 1936), p. 74.

77. *Catholic Encyclopedia*, 1:557c.

78. *Leggende Antoniane*, p. 63.

79. Cf. Ernst Benz, *Ecclesia Spiritualis: Kirchenidee und Geschichtstheologie der Franziskanischen Reformation* (Stuttgart: W. Kohlhammer, 1934), p. 6; see also N. O. Brown, *Love's Body* (New York: Random House, 1966), p. 201. On the reading of hagiography see Jean Leclercq, *The Love of Learning and the Desire for God: A Study of Monastic Culture*, trans. Catherine Misrahi (New York: Fordham Univ. Press, 1961), pp. 162–84, 199–201; and "L'Écriture sainte dans l'hagiographie monastique du haut Moyen Âge," in *La Bibbia nell' alto medioevo, settimone di studio del centro italiano di studi sull' alto medioevo* 10 (Spolento, 1963): 103–28. The methods Leclercq elaborates are more suited to the following example from Franciscan legend (*Fioretti*, 24) concerning Francis' missionary trip to Egypt (Old Cairo). With twelve of his holiest companions Francis apparently went straight to the palace of the Soldan of Babylon, and preached vigorously many times before an impressed but unrepentant Soldan, who nevertheless allowed him license to preach to the Saracens. Francis then spent the night in a nearby inn, wherein was a woman "most fair in body but foul in soul, who, accursed one, did tempt him to sin. And St. Francis, saying he consented thereto, she led him into a chamber. Said St. Francis, 'Come with me.' And he led her to a fierce fire that was kindled in that chamber, and in fervour of spirit stripped himself naked and cast himself beside that fire on the burning hearth; and he invited her to go and strip and lie with him on that bed, downy and fair. And when St. Francis had lain thus for a great space, with a joyous face, being neither burned nor even singed, that woman, affrighted and pierced to the heart, not only repented of her sin and of her evil intent, but likewise was wholly converted to the faith of Christ; and she waxed so in holiness that many souls were saved through her in those lands." The conscious a-literal use of Babylon and the introduction of the fair whore would not be without power of association for a medieval Christian audience. Similarly, the legend in which St. Anthony, rebuffed by the heretics, turns to preach to the fishes (*Leggende Antoniane*, pp. 36–38) has its own simple allegorical interpretation. But the Elijah-Elisha parallels are another story.

80. Salimbene, pp. 323–34, 236, 466; 302.

81. Trans. in Coulton, *From St. Francis to Dante*, p. 151.

82. See Joachim de Fiore, *L'Évangile éternel*, trans. Emmanuel Aegerter, 2 vols., Des Textes du Christianisme 3–4 (Paris: Rieder, 1928), 1:90–115; cf. Apocalypse 11:3. During this period the Saracens and Jews would be converted and the world returned to the pre-lapserian harmony.

83. See the summary by F. Kampers, in *The Catholic Encyclopedia*, 6:256d. Many thought that Fredrick II was the Antichrist, others that it would be Alphonso of Spain. Fredrick's death in 1250 did not destroy apocalyptic expectation by any means; predictions as to the actual dates were merely advanced to 1333, 1366, and so on, so that the Apocalypse was always just around the corner. See Morton W. Bloomfield, *Piers Plowman as a Fourteenth-Century Apocalypse* (New York: A. A. Knopf, 1963); and Émile Gebhart, *Mystics and Heretics in Italy at the End of the Middle Ages*, trans. Edward M. Hulme (New York: A. A. Knopf, 1923), pp. 86–94. While he lived Fredrick was widely believed to be the Antichrist, from Italy (Salimbene, p. 236) to England (Matthew Paris, *Chronica majora*, ed. H. R. Luard, trans. J. A. Giles, 3 vols., 2nd ed. [London: H. M. Stationery Office, 1872–83; Kraus Rep., 1964], 3:215). Fredrick hated the Franciscans for the part they took against him in Italy (Paris, *Chronica majora*, 3:636); later he and his son Conrad placed guards around the country to intercept friars traveling to and from the papal court in disguise. When captured they were tortured and hanged (3:256, 278, 551). With this kind of opposition one can imagine the force of Brother Elias' defection recorded by Eccleston: "When Brother Elias (first Minister-General after Francis) learned that the Pope required him to obey the new Minister-General in the same way as any other friar, he would not humble himself, for he had never learned to obey. So he left for Arezzo and joined the Emperor Fredric, and for this action justly incurred the Pope's public excommunication" (trans. in Little, *Documents*, p. 54).

84. Bloomfield, *Piers Plowman*, pp. 66–67.

85. See Joachim de Fiore, *L'Évangile éternel*, vol. 1, Introduction: see here also Paul E. L. Fournier, *Études sur Joachim de Fiore et ses doctrines* (Paris: A. Picard, 1909).

86. Beryl Smalley, *The Study of the Bible*, p. 288.

87. *Concordantia, Novi et Veteris Testamenti* (Venice, 1519), fol. 59v, as quoted by Smalley, *The Study of the Bible*, p. 288.

88. Salimbene, pp. 232–34. The best account of the influence of Joachim among the Franciscans is that given by Marjorie Reeves, *The Influence of Prophecy in the Later Middle Ages: A Study of Joachimism* (Oxford: Oxford Univ. Press, 1969), pp. 175–241.

89. Salimbene, pp. 294–96.

90. Guillaume de Lorris and Jean de Meun, *Le Roman de la rose*, ed. Ernest Langlois, 5 vols., SATF (Paris: Firmin-Didot, 1914–24).

91. Gebhart, *Mystics and Heretics*, pp. 183–85.

92. Patrick Cowley, *Franciscan Rise and Fall* (London: J. M. Dent and Sons, 1933), p. 181; see also Coulton, *From St. Francis to Dante*, p. 152.

93. Gebhart, *Mystics and Heretics*, p. 176; see J. P. Gilson, "Friar Alex-

ander and his Historical Interpretation of the Apocalypse," in *Collectanea Franciscana*, vol. 2, ed. C. L. Kingsford et al. (BSFS 10; Manchester: Univ. of Manchester Press, 1922), pp. 20–36.

94. Ray C. Petry, "Medieval Eschatology and St. Francis of Assisi," *Church History* 9 (1940):54–69; and "Medieval Eschatology and Social Responsibility in Bernard of Morval's *De Contemptu Mundi*," *Speculum* 24 (1949):207–17.

95. See the introduction of P. C. Clair to his edition, *Le Dies Irae, histoire, traduction, commentaire* (Paris, 1881).

96. St. Bonaventure, quoted in Karrer, *St. Francis*, p. 168.

97. See n. 83 above.

98. Trans. Emma Gurney-Salter, *The Coming of the Friars Minor to England and Germany* (London: Dent, 1926).

99. See the discussion by A. G. Little, "Chronicles of the Mendicant Friars," *BSFS ES* 3 (1932):85–103.

100. Ibid., p. 94.

101. Gebhart, *Mystics and Heretics*, p. 167.

102. Little, "Chronicles," p. 94.

103. P. Guido Bondatti, *Gioachinismo e Francescanesimo nel dugento* (S. Maria degli Angeli: Porziuncula, 1924), p. 147.

104. Franciscan historiography bears a considerable relationship to their political interest—and is thus important to any analysis of the "political poems" of known Franciscan provenance or authorship.

Aesthetics & Spirituality

I HAVE already suggested that it would be too early to conclude from their constitutional wariness of purely academic endeavor that the Friars Minor were content to live and work in strawberry fields, singing the doctrine that ignorance is bliss.[1] On the contrary, the remedy of certain kinds of ignorance was their particular occupation. Franciscan commentaries on Scripture like that of Nicholas of Lyra, and symbolic dictionaries directed to exegetical purposes, like that of Bartholomew the Englishman, testify to an articulated interest in illuminating knowledge of the Scriptures; Roger Bacon's extensive work in philosophy and pre-science has long been recognized; and the reputation of Alexander of Hales, Grosseteste, Duns Scotus and Bonaventure as master theologians is secure.[2] Religious education became the foremost activity of mendicants in England during the late thirteenth and fourteenth centuries. As late as the fifteenth century the Friars Minor were attacking ignorance with vigor; for St. Bernardino of Siena it remained the cause of all evils:

> Dear Brethren, during this Lent we wish to stress that which is more contrary to the salvation of souls than all other things in the world, that which is the cause of all evils in the world, the cause of all wars, of all pests, of all sickness, of all sins that men commit and of all the evils and harm that come upon souls and bodies.
>
> And what is this thing? It is ignorance. *Quia omnis peccator ignorat.* All sinners are ignorant. Who was to blame that Adam sinned? Ignorance. Who caused the death of Christ? Ignorance. All the sins and evils that ever happened in the world all have come from ignorance.
>
> And therefore we shall use our strength to conquer this beast of ignorance; and every day we will give him a beating. Because we

83

cannot give place to light, if we do not chase away ignorance. Then there will be light.[3]

Bernardino goes on to say that the beast of ignorance is that of the Apocalypse 11:7, which comes out of the abyss of darkness, and the darkness he means is the same to which the "four lights" of St. Bonaventure had been directed.

The Franciscans were concerned primarily with Scripture and those things immediately relevant to religious knowledge. But their world was wide, and despite St. Francis' arguments against owning books, Franciscan libraries soon grew to include a magnificent spectrum of classical and medieval writings. The extent of the holdings of even a small friary, that at Rimini, is remarkable. In addition to five complete or partly complete Bibles, certain appropriate books of which were glossed (Job, Canticles, Psalms, Proverbs, Wisdom, Ecclesiasties, the Apocalypse, and Daniel), there were three "Concordantiae Bibliae," many "legenda sanctorum" and a host of particular commentaries. These latter include thirteen works by St. Jerome, two commentaries by Ambrose, eleven works by St. Augustine including two copies of Augustine on the Psalms, *De civitate Dei, De Trinitate, Super Genesi ad litteram, Confessiones, Enchiridion, Sermones,* and *Retractiones.* Also included in the list of commentaries and patristic writing are two works by Eusebius, Rabanus on Jerome, several of the most important works of Pope Gregory the Great, Lombard's *Sententiae,* seven works of St. Bonaventure, works by Anselm, Lactantius Firmianus, Richard of St. Victor, Duns Scotus, Ockham, Damascene, Petrus Cardinalis, John of Wales, Nicholas of Lyra, Boniface, Strabo, St. Bernard, the Decretales of Innocent, and the summas of Godofredi and the Spiritual (or heretical) Rainerus Fasani. In short, the library of one small Franciscan friary possessed a worthy representation of the great exegetical works and commentaries in the Augustinian tradition.[4] But the list does not stop there.

In the classics of Greek and Latin literature and philosophy the library was scarcely less adequate. Many of the works of Aristotle, including his *Ethics, Metaphysics, Physics, Poetics, Logic,* and *Politics* are listed, some with commentaries, along with works of Hippocrates, Alexander of Alexandria, Sallust, Pliny, Seneca (letters and tragedies), Tully, Cato, Marcus Aurelius, Valerius Maximus, Lucan, Terence, Martian, Plutarch, Priscian, Herodotus, Cicero, Livy, Martianus Capella (*De nuptiis Phylologiae et Mercuri*), Macrobius (*Saturnalia* and *De somnio Scipionis*), Apuleius, Cassiodorus, Boethius, Lucretius, Statius (*Thebiad*), and Alan de Lille (*Anticlaudianus; De planctu Naturae).* Also notable are the *Gesta Alexandri magni,* Boccaccio's *De montibus et fontibus* and *Genealogia Deorum,* a "Comentarum Virgilii super 6 pulchrum," Petrarch's *De re familiari, De rebus senilibus, De remediis utriusque fortunae, De rebus memorandis, Aphricum carmen,* and *De viris illustribus,* the commentary on Dante by Benvenuti, a "Liber vulgare in gallico," and numerous "mirrors", including one "Ionnis Angeli speculum speculorum." In addition to all of this there are about fifteen sermon cycles, symbol dictionaries like the *De proprietatibus rerum* of English Franciscan Bartholomaeus Anglicus, and many interesting items not now readily identifiable, such as the "Proverbia vulgaria eleganter latinizata."[5] In the composition of this list as a whole is revealed ample evidence of the Franciscans' interests, not only with respect to scriptural commentary, but with respect to the *moralia* to be delved for in the pagan classics.[6]

The British brothers of the Order were apparently not less given to learning than their Italian counterparts; the great Franciscan schools at Oxford and Cambridge are sufficient evidence. Hilarin Felder noted that England had given to the Order "a greater number of eminent scholars than all the rest of the nations put together . . . . Indeed, if we consider the real leaders of the schools of the Friars Minor, they belonged to England, with the exception of Bonaventura."[7] Though the dissolution destroyed nearly all Franciscan records and holdings, the number of medieval volumes we now trace to the Greyfriars' Library at Oxford attests to the remarkable extent of its early catalogue. There were also large holdings at Cambridge and Hereford, and it is reasonable to conclude that other friaries would have had good, if smaller, libraries.[8] A Franciscan register compiled by Bolton, an early fifteenth-century librarian of Bury St. Edmunds,[9] shows substantial record of the Latin classics, and the Franciscan Library at Killiney is of particular interest. It owned a considerable collection of Italian Franciscan materials, among them sermons of St. Bernardino of Siena and poetry and hymns of Italian friars, including one lyric by Jacopone da Todi.[10] Further indication of once-rich Franciscan libraries may be seen in the many Franciscan manuscripts which turn up later in Austin friaries.[11] The records make clear that the contents of these libraries are consistent with Franciscan interests in commentary and exegesis, and it is appropriate that from them should come illustrations of the basic exegetical principles which Franciscan friars could be expected to recognize.

Among the early Franciscans, and indeed in St. Francis himself, a penchant for apparently literalistic interpretation of the Bible is often noted, and we have already cited some extremes of this tendency among his followers. Yet while Francis often took the Bible literally, he was quick to emphasize the apostle's warning "litteram occidit, spiritus autem vivificat":[12] "the letter kills, the spirit gives life." The apparent contradiction in approaches may be partially resolved with an example. When he read Psalm 21:7, "But I am a worm and no man; the reproach of men, and the outcast of the people," Francis identified the sufferer with Jesus. This identification was a function of his finding the Old Testament a prophetic prologue to the New, and accords with Augustinian tradition in exegesis. But Francis went further, and in "anguished memory of the Christ thus humbled," refused to tread upon worms.[13] Here he has made a symbolic or allegorical association in his exegesis, but proceeded from that to what we might unwarily call a "literalistic" personal response. Actually, we need to distinguish in this particular kind of situation between *littera* as "letter," and "literal." A truly literal response of the sort the Apostle Paul and Augustinian exegetes warned against erred in seeing only the literal, once-in-time historical significance of the biblical words and law, thus failing to be attuned to the spirit of the law and ultimately to the spiritual meaning of the words in Scripture. Francis himself was not guilty there; his "literalism" in fact arises from what might seem to be a too-vigorous extrapolation of the spiritual principle, the same tendency which caused him to find spiritual merit and evangelical value not only in conforming to Christ inwardly, but in conforming to him outwardly as well, the external action serving as reinforcement to the internal attitude.[14] This kind of response is then really a part of exegesis on the spiritual plane, which Franciscan friar Thomas Docking would call *moraliter*,[15] and which becomes the most immediate of Franciscan exegetical objectives. As in all exegesis which develops Augustinian principles along similar lines, the other spiritual levels are often employed, but it is usually the moral concern which predominates. Where traditional medieval exegesis involved the concordance of the two Testaments—a concordance of symbols, of spiritual truths[16]—Franciscan exegetes extended the concordance to current events and ultimately to personal history. The point of interpretation, and its appropriate conclusion, was participation. This principle had already been developed in the work of Joachim of Fiore.[17] Where Hugh of St. Victor in his *De arca Noe morali* and *De arca Noe mystica* carefully separated letter and spirit, emphasizing literal details and then systematically allegorizing them,[18] the eschatologically-minded Franciscan commentator Nicholas of Lyra would subsume the entire history of the Church under the same symbols, drawing them forward to embrace the personal present at the point of an historical *Dei et animae unionem*.[19] It is this progression, and its attendant degree of tropological emphasis, that often helps to distinguish the exegetical—and aesthetic—intention of the "Franciscan school" from that of most of its contemporaries.[20]

In chapter two we saw that in his discussion of the "four lights" of true understanding, St. Bonaventure distinguishes as fourth and highest the "lumen gratiae et scripturae." In Bonaventure's system it is the light of knowledge which grants dignity to the soul. Innate illumination gives the soul still more dignity, since God himself patterns it to his own image. "The soul is capable of God in its memory, intelligence, and will. This is the same as to be made to the likeness of the Trinity, with unity in essence and trinity in faculties."[21] But such illumination is cast by the combined forces of grace and Scripture properly received. Here Bonaventure invokes, like all medieval thinkers and Fathers of the Church, a fourfold reading system which distinguishes in addition to the literal sense three kinds of spiritual senses: allegorical, moral (or tropological), and anagogical:

> Although in its literal sense, it is *one*, still, in its spiritual and mystical sense it is *threefold*, for in all the books of Sacred Scripture, in addition to the *literal* meaning which the words clearly express, there is implied a threefold *spiritual* meaning: namely, the *allegorical* by which we are taught what to believe concerning the Divinity and humanity; the *moral* by which we are taught how to live; and the *anagogical* by which we are taught how to keep close to God.[22]

Here the priorities of procedure in Franciscan exegesis are made explicit. In its literal sense, Scripture is one, both in the limited and all-encompassing senses. Paradoxically, it is the limited sense of the literal which offers the only place of beginning. No one comes to the spiritual fully without first really grasping the literal: "The Holy Ghost does not provide the spiritual sense before man has filled his urn to capacity with the water of the literal sense. Then God changes the water of the literal sense into the wine of the spiritual sense" (*In Hexaëmeron* 19.8).[23] Yet if Franciscan exegesis always begins emphatically with the literal sense, it is not as a kind of absolute subject upon which the other senses are predicated. There is no real discontinuity between the senses; each is a fully present significance of the *signum*. The resolution of the one and the many of senses is in the plenary experience of the pregnant urn, the water of the literal sense. In it rest all the others, poised, incarnate to him who drinks. "Hence," says St. Bonaventure, all of Sacred Scripture teaches these three truths: namely, the eternal generation and Incarnation of Christ, the pattern of human life, and the union of the soul with God. The first regards *faith*; the second *morals*; the third, the *purpose of both*. To the study of the first the doctors should devote themselves; on that of the second, the preachers should concentrate; and to the attainment of the third, the contemplatives should aspire.[24]

We can expect therefore that Franciscan preachers would naturally tend to concern themselves most with *mores* and *finem utriusque*, and this is in fact the case. Augustine, Bonaventure continues, is chief exponent of the first class, Gregory and Bernard of the second, Dionysius and Richard of St. Victor of the third class; Hugh of St. Victor excels in all three.[25] The prominence of St. Bernard in Franciscan thought here relates to the practical moral concerns of Franciscan preaching.

Beyond the four categories, "the subject matter to which all is reduced as a *totum integrum* is Christ." This is the one reality which fulfills all conditions. Echoing St. Paul's *Letter to the Colossians*, Bonaventure is emphatic, repeating himself: "The subject matter to which all is reduced as to a principle is God himself."[26] God alone, as the principle of all things, is absolutely irreducible, and God in Christ is the ultimate focus for all of Scripture's spiritual illumination. This conclusion might seem to relate to the allegorical spiritual sense most of all, but that is actually not the case. As we have seen, it was in the person of Christ that Franciscan spirituality found the "pattern of human life," and *imitatio Christi* is in principle a moral occupation. Thus, a friar like Thomas Docking is typical in that while he often alludes to the complete exegetical system, he usually begins any spiritual interpretation with "moraliter," and like a typical Franciscan preacher is interested in practical morality more than anything else, for it is in the pattern of life that the literal word becomes flesh.[27]

Allegorical interpretations occupy a position of some importance, even if second to tropology. The anagogical sense usually receives the least attention in Franciscan exegesis. This may be observed particularly in Franciscan sermons from St. Anthony[28] onwards, perhaps because the immediate purpose of such sermons was the correction of errors in doctrine and morals (and such an objective would not necessarily entail elaborate delineation of the heavenly life to come). This order of emphasis outlines the general approach to texts described by Franciscan exegetical activity—a concrete appreciation of the literal level, followed by a movement to spiritual understanding of the physical or historical reality.

Another feature of Franciscan exegesis is that attitude toward the Old Testament which seeks to explain it not only in terms of implicit faith, but in terms of "preparation"—an emphasis previously noted in the discussion of the *Meditations* and of the Old Testament parallels in the life of St. Francis.[29] With respect to Christ and the Virgin particular foreshadowings are continually, sometimes laboriously noted.[30] Louis F. Rohr, in his study of the sermons of St. Anthony of Padua, finds Anthony's heavy preference for the Old Testament a significant departure from typical twelfth-century practice, and provides a likely reason for the emphasis; he notes that many in Anthony's audience "had either accepted or were in danger of accepting the Albigensian heresy which was overrunning France and Italy in the early years of the thirteenth century." He continues:

> One of the primary tenets of this heresy was the denial of all worth to the Old Testament. To its adherents the God of the Old Law was essentially evil, and the great historical figures of the Old Testament— the prophets and the patriarchs—were His minions in carrying out His evil designs; the Old Law could not produce justice, and all those who had lived according to it were buried in hell; the New Law alone was the true law. Moreover, the Albigenses maintained that ecclesiastical authority was to be condemned. The very character of these doctrines demanded that they be attacked on scriptural grounds, because the authority of the Word of God was the only authority that the heretics recognized, if they recognized any at all. St. Anthony therefore began his assault with a defense of the value of the very Scriptures (the Old Testament) which the heretics had denied. To this end he endeavored to find his answers to their challenge in the words of the Old Law itself, and he upheld its divine origin by citing it with the same reverence that he accorded the words of the New Testament. He pointed out that there is no difference between the wisdom of the Old Testament and that of the New: the same God is the God of both. In effect, therefore, the heretics were placed in a dilemma: they must either recognize the wisdom which is found in the Old as well as in the New Testament, or they must deny the New Testament along with the Old—a denial which would have undermined their teachings completely.[31]

St. Anthony cites the Old Testament twice as often as the New Testament in his sermons, quoting most frequently from Isaiah and the Psalms, and strongly preferring the former to the more traditional favorite, the Canticles.[32] The prophecies of Isaiah were of particular value to Anthony because the many references to Christ countered the heretical claim that only the New Testament spoke of Christ and

the Father. The effectiveness of this approach to the arguments of
the heretics led St. Anthony to favor allegorism as a technique in
asserting the exegetical continuity of the Scriptures, and subsequent
Franciscan exegetes usually followed his practice.

The view of nature held by St. Francis was not, as sometimes
romantically imagined, a proto-Romantic worship of the universe.[33]
G. K. Chesterton contends rightly that Francis was not a lover of
nature in the sense of accepting the "material universe as a vague
environment, a sort of sentimental pantheism."[34] He saw in all creatures an expression of God, but did not view that creation as something vague and undifferentiated. Franciscans following him were
characterized in their aesthetic by rejoicing not merely in the lofty,
noble, or grand, but equally in a particular flower, leaf, or pebble.
Faith made it possible for the simplest of men to read the Book of
Nature; only the literate could attempt the Book of God's Word.
The most insignificant of God's works was still a divine signpost, and
one element of the typical Franciscan message in the thirteenth century was precisely a call to the simplest people to know God in his
works. St. Bonaventure merely set out, in his usual fashion, to give
intellectual development (perhaps he thought also respectability) to
St. Francis' theology of nature. The distinctive idea thus codified was
that the uneducated Christian is better able to listen to the voice of
creation than the philosopher, that simple faith in such a case could
work through proven principles to express the objective reality of
this world and its intrinsic relationship to the Creator. This was an
idea remarkable in its time, and spectacular in its effect upon the
development of the arts.

All four senses of exegesis were applied to the study of nature.
St. Bonaventure asserts of all creation that "as faith, hope and
charity bring to God, likewise all creatures suggest what is to be
believed, expected, and done. Accordingly there is a threefold spiritual
sense: *allegory* concerns what is to be believed; *anagogy* what is to be
expected; *tropology* what is to be done, for charity overflows into
action" (*In Hexaëmeron* 13.11) This illuminates the Bonaventuran
view of Scripture discussed in chapter two above: Scripture partakes
of the meaning of creation. The Bonaventuran doctrine is explained
again in another definition of the subject matter of theology, which
affords a deliberate complement to his view of the object of biblical
exegesis: "The subject matter to which all is reduced as a *totum universale* . . . is a thing or sign."[35] This old idea, coming from St. Augustine[36] and adopted by Peter Lombard[37] (on whose work Bonaventure

is commenting), affirms that theology deals with "things and signs." In the view of the universe favored by Bonaventure and Grosseteste *all* things are referred to a transcendent archetype which in ultimate analysis is God himself.

A study of creation as a complex of indicators pointing to God gives rise to Franciscan emphasis on the signs of God that are to be found in nature. Most important, however, is not, as in the developing neo-Aristotelian school, identification of the formal principles which constitute the images, but their interpretation. The lower part of the reason can exclude the symbolism of creation from its view of things; this happens not only when there occurs a wrong intentionality ("entente") toward the sensual world, but also when short-sighted literalism fails to take account of the symbolic value of creation. As soon as the likeness of God is embodied in a being, there is a possibility of misunderstanding. "Vel dicendum, quod aliae creaturae possunt considereri ut res, vel ut signa."[38] It is as signs that they are ultimately worth knowing; things are made merely for the glory of God, not to acquire or amplify it, but to communicate it.[39] While men write with signs, God writes, so to speak, with things and signs—men and events. Since God is to be met within it, the content of the Book of God's Works requires as diligent a study as the content of the Book of his Words.[40] This is the fundamental animus in the Oxford empiricist movement of the thirteenth century, nearly all of whose leaders were Franciscans. John Pecham, Richard of Middleton, Robert Grosseteste, Thomas of York, Roger Bacon, and even Duns Scotus and William Ockham believed with Bonaventure that a way of reading should be discovered that leads naturally from the created to the Creator, revealing nature as a transient passage to the higher reality which is Christ. Natural knowledge of the universe is a necessary and useful guide, a figure of the divine person which may ultimately be exchanged for the reality it portrays.

> Indeed, in every creature there is a refulgence of the divine exemplar, but mixed with darkness: hence it resembles some kind of opacity combined with light. Also, it is a way leading to the exemplar. As you notice that a ray of light coming in through the window is colored according to the shades of the different panes, so the divine ray shines differently in each creature and in the various properties. Again, it is a trace of God's wisdom. Wherefore the creature exists only as a kind of imitation of God's wisdom, as a certain plastic representation of it. And for all of these reasons it is a kind of book *written without*. When therefore the soul sees these things, it seems to it that it should go through them from the shadow to the light, from the

way to the end, from the trace to the truth, from the book to veritable
knowledge [which is in God].[41]

The figure itself is, however, a vital pathway or window, an indispensable signature of the higher reality, the pilot *lumen, speculum,*
and *imago* to the enquiring soul (*In Hexaëmeron,* 12. 16). Now we see
through a glass darkly, but we see.

In exploring the images of nature the exegetical system is applied
to one of three basic interests: Nature as *speculum,* Nature as moral
law, and Nature as nature. Robert Grosseteste's *Dictum* 60, *Omnis
creatura speculum est,*[42] is consistent with his statements about value
in nature elsewhere, and representative for Franciscan thinkers in general. "The artifice of the world is a manifestation of the art by which
it is made . . . as the spoken word is but the sign of the inner word,
so the sensible works of creation are signs of the invisible and eternal
Word," he says, and again, "Omnis enim creaturae species exemplar
est honesti alicuius in nostris moribus et veri alicuius in divinis et
aeterni rationibus."[43] Admittedly, these statements were common doctrine to the tradition which traced its inheritance from Plato to
Augustine, but which was now being defended against the corrosion
of neo-Aristotelianism, according to Archbishop Pecham, by the Franciscans. A century before, Alain de Lille had expressed one shade of
it when he wrote:

> Omnis mundi creatura
> quasi liber et pictura
> nobis est in speculum:
> nostrae vitae, nostrae mortis,
> nostri status, nostrae sortis
> fidele signaculum.[44]

[All the world's creatures, as a book and a picture, are to us a mirror:
in it our life, our death, our present condition and our passing on are
faithfully signified.]

But the doctrine expressed, generally known as exemplarism, was in
the thirteenth century particularly developed by Franciscans such as
Bonaventure and Grosseteste.[45] It does not end with reducing creatures
to the eternal ideas, but reveals itself in the enlightened search of the
Christian thinker who finds embedded in every detail of the created
world the image of the Trinity: "Omnis creatura speculum est, de
quo resultat similitude Creatoris, unitatis scilicet et trinitatis."[46] For
Grosseteste, all creation in some way expresses the trinitarian nature

of the Creator. The creature is less than the Creator, and thus falls greatly short in its representation, but its function must be viewed as a limited imitation, a "shadow," as Bonaventure has it (*In Hexaëmeron* 3. 8), of the Creator.[47] Grosseteste then gives a list of trinitarian examples which progresses from the smallest fleck of dust whirling in the sunlight to the Augustinian triad of memory, intelligence, and love (or will), which is the closest figure of the Trinity itself (*Hexaëmeron* 7. 4. 5). He is careful to say that the examples are not only figures or poetic fictions (though they certainly are that) but real arguments from which the Trinity can be proved: "non solum sunt exempla, sed evidenter summae Trinitatis collata sunt argumenta, ipsa Trinitem efficaciter probantia":[48] that is, the Trinity impinges upon a real world with real correspondence. Yet he goes on: "non tamen, propter vitandem prolixitatem, afferimus illa nunc sicut argumenta, sed sicut exempla imaginationem iuvantia."[49] Leaving the examples to the vigorous imagination of individual Franciscan preachers is a common device of their handbooks, and as we shall see in the chapters following, the imaginative *exemplum* turned to by the preachers was frequently expressed as a poem. The technique of poetry is to speak in metaphor, implying more and stating less than the more elaborated *exemplum*. But compression is appropriate to the Franciscan method. Each facet of creation is in effect a *figura* of the Truth, so that metaphor everywhere is a consistent device for reflecting the nature of truth.[50] Herein lies a key to Franciscan lyrical methods, which instead of systematically intellectualizing and at once dematerializing nature, chooses instead to develop its symbolical value as a figure for the objective intelligible reality to which the tangible naturally points.

The eye which sees the holly as a figure for Christ looks down essentially the same plane as that which approves Queen Esther as a type of the Virgin: one applies itself to Scripture and the other to nature. But inherent in nature as well as Scripture is the tropological plane, and it should not surprise us to find that at the end of his dictum *Omnis creatura speculum* Grosseteste adds some moral reflections based upon the construction of a medieval looking glass. We are warned that the soul itself is a mirror, whose spiritual condition dictates the rectitude with which it records the figures of nature, and that only the soul/mirror which is able to subject itself to the will of Christ will be free of distortion. If distortions and lack of correspondence in the *speculum* of nature occur, it is not that there are distortions in creation, but rather in the attitude of the observer.[51] Nature, as well as Scripture, reveals and is controlled by the moral law, and is to that extent consistent. The easy movement from nature

Plate 3. St. Francis Preaching to the Birds (MS. C.C.C. Cambridge, 16)

as *speculum* to nature as moral law is similarly illustrated by Thomas Docking, who, commenting on Galatians 6:2, describes how man is invited by all creatures into communion effectively and affectively ("corde et opere") with nature. All the elements, he says, earth, air, fire, and water, communicate even through their various properties. "Quapropter luce liquet clarius quod omni creatura peior probatur homo nisi ad omnis creature invitationem, quantam exposcit utilitas, se studeat communicare":[52] the light shines clearly for those who have eyes to see.

The transition from nature as *speculum* to nature moralized is perhaps most simply suggested by St. Bernardino of Siena, in a sermon from his Florence course for 1424. Speaking of the sun, he says that its rays signify the virtuous state, and that it itself has three properties: "the first that it shines, which signifies faith; the second that it is strong, which signifies hope; and the third that it is warm, which signifies charity."[53] Initially, St. Francis had responded to the same kind of exegesis, following from his seeing in the sun a symbol for Christ, and produced the *Cantico al sole*.[54] Subsequently, Friar John in his *Meditations on the Life of Christ* is able to speak in the same vein of the nativity, saying that "today the Sun of justice, which has been hidden behind the clouds, shines brightly,"[55] and to elaborate on the consequences of that light for the life of man.

Grosseteste ends his *Dictum* 60 with a few brief anagogic conclusions,[56] but these are only a small fraction of the treatise, which is dedicated to demonstrating that nature is a complex of *figurae*, a *speculum* of the eternal being. And metaphysical dependence upon eternal being[57] is a logical precursor to metaphors that characterize creatures as "words announcing the hidden mysteries of God," or "copied books" from which the character of Deity can be understood.[58]

But all of these are not the only reasons for the focus on nature in Franciscan literature. Just as we noted with respect to Scripture that there was a characteristic Franciscan appreciation for the dramatic qualities of the literal story itself, so also here there is an equally distinctive love of nature simply as nature. God created the world for man's pleasure, and to the spirit in tune with Christ nothing is more natural than to delight in God's bounty. Jacopone da Todi sings:

> Terra, erbe con lor coluri,
> arbori e frutti con sapuri,
> bestie, miei serviduri,
> tutte en mia bevolcarìa.

Acque, fiumi, lachi e mare,
pescetegli en lor notare,
aera, venti, ucel volare,
tutti me fo iollarìa . . . .

Trees, plants, fruits, beasts of the field, rivers, lakes and sea, little
birds and fishes are a source of his particular joy. Jacopone is caught
up in the immediacy of his response to literal nature, and in this
poem takes only a moment for moral reflection, and to hint his
agreement with St. Bonaventure that nature also leads, through sub-
mission of the will, to the "third truth," the union of the soul with
God:

Puoi che Deo ha lo mio velle,
possessor d'onne chevelle,
le mie ale ò tante penne,
de terra en ciel non m'è via.[59]

[Since God has my will, I am possessor of all-will (i.e., I am truly free);
my wings have so many feathers that my flight from earth to heaven
is nothing.]

Franciscan poetry frequently suggests that it is appropriate to delight,
inarticulate, in the details of creation; it is a legitimate occupation
in itself, and the relationship of creature to Creator need not always
be systematically spoken when it is so axiomatically implied.

In its fullest understanding, *"omnis creatura speculum est"* is an
idea profoundly central to an especially Franciscan concern with the
details of created life. The peculiarities of this concern prove to be
directly relevant to the kind of influence Franciscans were to have
on developing English art forms, already inclined to relate to nature,
but in different ways. As noted earlier, Old English poetry had responded to nature, but in reaction; courtly Middle English poetry
largely intellectualized or stylized nature. But popular Middle English poetry springing up in the thirteenth century paid more attention
to nature, almost "for its own sake," than any other contemporary
English art form, or any other literature which came into contact
with English life.[60] Exegetically, Franciscan spirituality provided
itself with allegory and symbolism for extensive lists of English flora
and fauna in the *De proprietatibus rerum* of Bartholomew; psychologically it responded to spring with a

Svmer is icumen in,
Lhude sing cuccu!

lhude, loudly; *wde,* wood.

> Groweþ sed and bloweþ med
> and springþ þe wde nu.
> Sing cuccu!

or saw in the *speculum* of autumn a not so hazy portent:

> Nou shrinkep rose ant lylie-flour
> þat whilen ber þat suete sauour
> in somer, þat suete tyde;
> ne is no quene so stark ne stour
> ne no leuedy so bryht in bour
> þat ded ne shal by glyde . . . .[61]

Whether in one tiny flower of the field or in the season of spring itself, a poet in the Franciscan tradition could find an exemplar. Each encounter offered its own delight, and in a world of such infinitely varied revelations, it became not only possible but desirable to figure each streak of the tulip.

In his *De reductione artium ad theologiam* St. Bonaventure explicitly undertook to develop a "Franciscan aesthetic" consistent with a Franciscan view of revelation. Characteristically, he began with a statement about Scripture. It should be recalled again:

> Unde tota sacra Scriptura haec tria docet, scilicet Christi aeternam generationem et incarnationem, vivendi ordinem et Dei et animae unionem.[62] [Hence all of sacred scripture teaches these three truths: namely, the eternal generation and Incarnation, the pattern of human life, and the union of God and the soul.]

We have already observed that this applies equally well to the "Book of God's Works," nature. But here Bonaventure says:

> By the same process of reasoning is Divine Wisdom to be found in the illumination of the mechanical arts, the sole purpose of which is the *production of works of art*. In this illumination we can see the *eternal generation, and Incarnation of the Word*, the *pattern of human life*, and the *union of the soul with God*. And this is true if we consider the *production*, the *effect*, and the *advantage* of the work, or if we consider the *skill of the artist*, the *quality of the effect produced*, and the *utility of the advantage to be derived therefrom*.[63]

stour, strong; *by glyde*, overtake

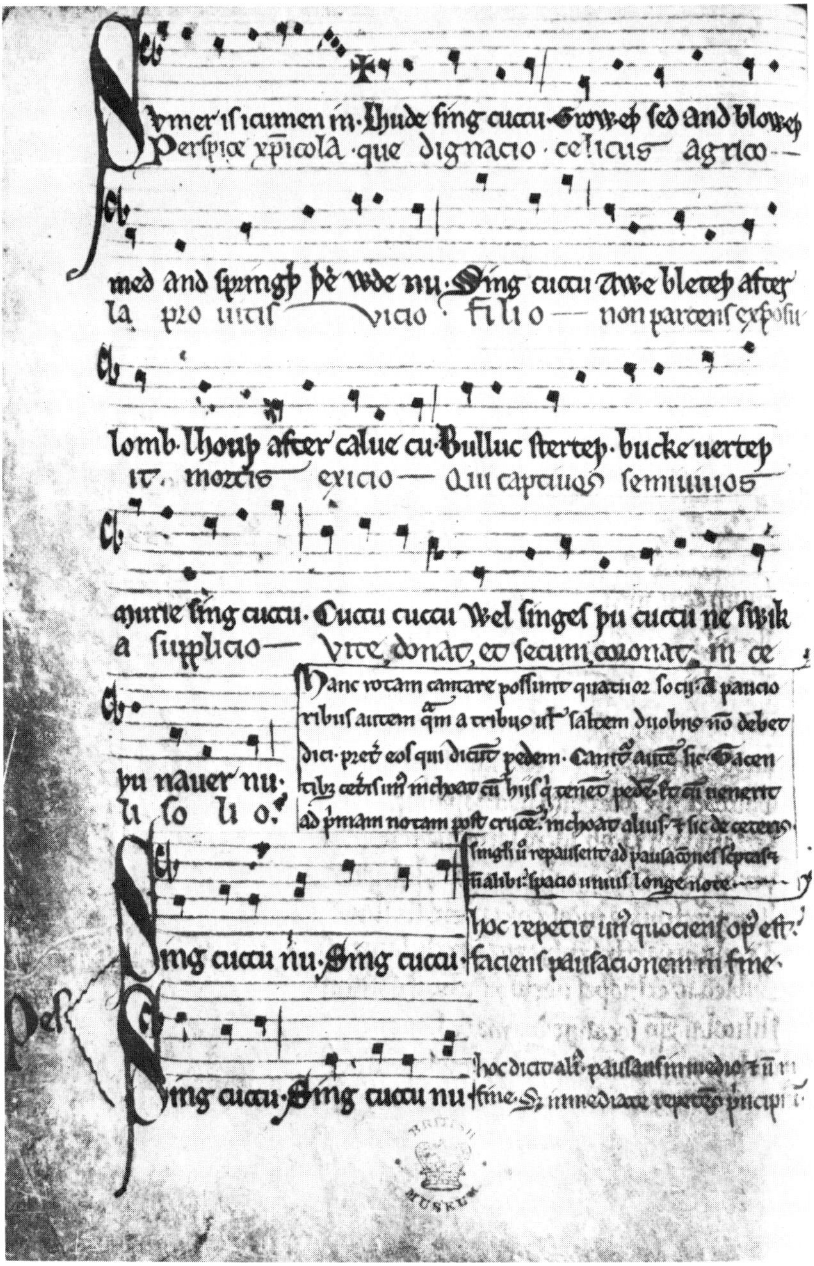

Plate 4. "Sumer is icumen in" (MS. Harley 978)

What he is saying, in short, is that in art as well as Scripture and nature, the image of the Creator may be discerned. This is to go much further afield with exemplarism,[64] or concepts of the *imago Dei*, than most of his predecessors and contemporaries. St. Augustine had not ventured so much. But Bonaventure develops his extension with scholastic thoroughness. He begins with the parallel of the human artist to the Creator:

> If we consider the *production*, we shall see that the work of art proceeds from the artificer according to a model existing in his mind; the pattern or model the artificer studies carefully before he produces and then he produces as he has predetermined. The artificer, moreover, produces a work bearing the closest possible resemblance to the interior model . . . .[65]

Thus the basic concept of creation is formulated by analogy and in the fusing of will with material substance Bonaventure implies the incarnation of the word as well as of the Word. This of course is a logical application of Augustinian doctrine on the Logos, and has been seized upon, through Bonaventure, by modern "Christian existentialists" such as Gabriel Marcel and Nicolai Berdiaev.[66] Yet Bonaventure does not stop with the production of works of art, but also considers their effect:

> If we consider the *effect*, we shall see therein the *pattern of human life*, for every artificer, indeed, aims to produce a work that is beautiful, useful, and enduring, and only when it possesses these three qualities is the work highly valued and acceptable. Corresponding to the above-mentioned qualities, in the pattern of life there must be found three elements: knowledge, will, and unaltering and persevering toil" [Aristotle, II *Ethic*, c.4]. *Knowledge* renders the work beautiful; the *will* renders it useful; *perseverance* renders it lasting. The first resides in the rational, the second in the concupiscible, and the third in the irascible appetite.[67]

Herein lies the pedagogical potential of art, and Bonaventure does not hesitate even to seize upon the opportunity his statement provides.

Finally, he sees the "fruit" or advantage of art to be the same as the final purpose of Scripture and nature:

> If we consider the *advantage*, we shall find the union of the soul with God, for every artificer who fashions a work does so that he may derive *praise, benefit,* or *delight* therefrom—a threefold purpose which corresponds to the three formal objects of the appetites: namely, a *noble*

good, a *useful* good, and an *agreeable* good. It was for this same three-fold reason that God made the soul rational, namely, that of its own accord, it might *praise* Him, *serve* Him, *find delight* in Him, and be at rest; and this takes place through charity.[68]

The ultimate objective of all three dimensions of revelation is clearly evangelical; in all of their triune properties the final message of Scripture, nature, and art should be exactly the same.

Bonaventure suggests the possible third, or "evangelical" function of art in another way. It begins with the problem of finding a place for dramatic art in a classification of what he has referred to as the mechanical arts:

> Furthermore, as an aid in the *acquisition of each of these necessities,* the mechanical arts contribute to the welfare of man in two ways: either by *supplying a want,* and in this case it is *navigation,* which includes all commerce of articles of covering or of food; or by *removing impediments* and ills of the body, under which aspect it is *medicine,* whether it is concerned with the preparation of drugs, potions, or ointments, with the healing of wounds or with the amputation of members, in which latter case it is called surgery.—Dramatic art, however, is unique.[69]

Here the "seraphic doctor" has followed the enumeration of Hugh of St. Victor,[70] except that he bases his classification not upon the nature of the arts but rather upon their purpose—either utility or pleasure. It has been suggested that "dramatic art is the only one in the second division, all the others supply man with the necessities of life."[71] But that is not quite Bonaventure's point, I think, in placing dramatic art in a class by itself—*theatrica autem est unica.* The nature of the relationship of the enumerated arts to the needs of mankind is made more explicit in the lines which follow:

> That these [the above-mentioned arts] *suffice* is to be accepted [in this way]: every mechanical art is intended for man's *consolation* or his *comfort*; its purpose, therefore, is to banish either sorrow or want; it either *benefits* or *delights,* according to the words of Horace:
> "Either to profit or to delight is the wish of poets."
> And again:
> "He has gained universal applause who has combined the profitable with the pleasing."
> If its aim is to afford consolation and amusement, it is *dramatic art,* or the art of putting on plays, which embraces every form of entertainment, whether song, music, fiction, or pantomime.[72]

The quotation of Horace is not fortuitous. We should notice Bonaventure's careful phrasing: that every (*omnis*) mechanical art is
intended for human consolation or comfort; its purpose is to banish
either sorrow or want, that is, consolation; and it either benefits or
delights "secundum illud Horatii." Dramatic art, he says, has the
aim of both consolation and amusement (*solatium et delectationem*).
The words of Horace are: "he who has combined the profitable with
the pleasing gains universal applause." Dramatic art is peculiar in its
ability to combine the two properties, and this is the true source of
its unique value, "to teach and to delight." Now this is interesting,
for two reasons: first, because by *theatrica* he says he means the art of
exhibiting plays, and that this art embraces every form of entertainment (*omnem modum ludendi continens*), song, music, fiction, and
pantomimes; second, because he elsewhere explicitly states that the
delight to be achieved in *sense perception* (of art or nature) leads to
the union of the soul with God.[73] We may then reasonably draw two
conclusions from Bonaventure's statements about art, and particularly
what he calls *theatrica*. The first is that the arts identified may act
as a *speculum* of the divine revelation in the same manner as Scripture
or nature, and in such a case are subject to the same exegetical proce-
dures. Second, drama, music and lyric (*cantilena*) are legitimately set
to function according to the threefold purpose of scriptural and
natural revelation: to demonstrate the "eternal Incarnation of the
Son of God," to illustrate the "pattern of human life," and to orient
towards the common evangelical objective of "union of the soul
with God."

Nor does Bonaventure rest merely with establishing exegetical
principles for any art which happens to be at hand, but he goes on
to suggest that the *production* of a work of art can also lead one to
an understanding of the union of the soul with God. The illumination
of mechanical knowledge thus acquired "via est ad illuminationem
sacrae Scripturae."[74] The implication of official favor for Franciscan
"production" of art is strong, and, as we shall have occasion to see,
amply acknowledged in practice.

One or two further characteristics of the Franciscan aesthetic are
worth noting. In detailing how the other illuminations of knowledge
which he mentions are to be reduced to the light of sacred Scripture,
Bonaventure significantly first considers that one which is most basic
and literal, the illumination of sense perception. This process, he says,
concerns itself exclusively with the cognition of sensible objects, and
occurs in three phases: "cognoscendi *medium*, cognoscendi *exercitium*, cognoscendi *oblectamentum*."[75] Here the consistent triune pat-

tern unfolds again. If we consider the *medium* of perception, he says, we shall see therein the word begotten from all eternity and articulated, made flesh, in time—because of generic, specific, or symbolical likeness to the Creator. Words inhere in the Word: in language and in vision the processes of creativity are analogous to the form of the creator. When the contact between organ or faculty and object is established, there results a new percept, an expressed image by means of which the mind reverts to the object.[76] The *exercise* of sense perception reveals, accordingly, the pattern of human life. But in the *delight*, as we have already observed, is opened the union of the soul with God.

> Indeed, every sense seeks its proper sensible with longing, finds it with delight, and seeks it again without ceasing, because "the eye is not filled with seeing, neither is the ear filled with hearing" [Eccl. 1:8]. In the same way, our spiritual senses must seek longingly, find joyfully, and seek again without ceasing the beautiful, the harmonious, the fragrant, the sweet, or the delightful to the touch. Behold how the Divine Wisdom lies hidden in sense perception and how wonderful is the contemplation of the five spiritual senses in the light of their conformity to the senses of the body.[77]

The potential of sense perception expressed here is remarkable. It says that the spiritual senses not only may, but must "seek longingly, find joyfully" the divine wisdom hidden in it. Sense perception begins in delight and ends in transcendent delight, as language and desire converge in the metaphor of the body.

Finally, Bonaventure calls upon works of art—music and poetry—to illustrate the necessary harmony of the universe, in which the part is subordinate to the whole. In the case of music played upon the harp, he says that the chords should be so proportioned that if any one should be altered so as to give it prominence no harmony at all would remain. With poetry, the words can be so ordered that from the same words it would be impossible to make poetry that would be better.[78]

This highly articulated Franciscan interest in the harmonious beauty of specific physical details of creation—especially as an avenue to union with God—was not universally shared in the thirteenth and fourteenth centuries. The Dominican school, with its great doctors Albert and Aquinas, showed little interest in created beauty, even in its transcendental character, except in accidental instances.[79] Albert, for example, with very pragmatic interests in the natural world and serious reservations about the value of mystical contemplation, when it came to theology was less interested in sense experience than in logic: "God is he who is proved to be, more than he who is experienced."[80] This implicit division was made explicit in the work of his pupil, Aquinas, who thought that the will of man was fallen, but that his intellect was not[81]—an idea which, once developed, had the effect of suggesting that man's intellect was in some sense autonomous. There are various results of this in his thought, one of which is the development of natural theology—a theology that could be pursued independently of the Scriptures. While Aquinas hoped for unity, and argued for a correlation between natural theology and the Scriptures, what really happened was that an autonomous sphere was set up, in which theology became a study of the operations of the intellect.

Bonaventure, on the other hand, in this respect a classic Augustinian, saw unregenerate man as imperfect in all of his faculties of memory, intellect, and will. There was no development of an autonomous sphere. His exemplarism found itself equally involved in the realms of nature, Scripture, and art. In his perspective theology became the study of remedial grace flowing through all of these realms simultaneously. Following this, one may readily distinguish between the aesthetic of the Dominicans, reflected in St. Thomas for example, and that of the Franciscans, represented in Bonaventure. The experience of the beautiful for St. Bonaventure embraces not only the senses of sight and hearing, as for St. Thomas, but also the other three senses of touch, smell, and taste, all of which can stimulate enjoyment in the individual without any immediate consideration of the intellectual role of their object.[82] Enjoyment derived from the senses is the primary Franciscan aesthetic experience.[83] In the system of St. Thomas the aesthetic impression rests on an intellectual act,[84] and consequently the object of the aesthetic becomes "the form of the thing as the end."[85]

Further distinctions between Dominican and Franciscan responses to nature may be made on the basis of their relative spontaneity, and the varying faces of nature they choose to countenance. E. J. M. Spargo has characterized some of these respective differences, and her summary is worthy of quotation in full:

The delight experienced in the presence of the beautiful is spontaneous and without reflection. Only afterwards does there follow an act of the intellect inquiring why these objects produce their pleasant effects and what constitutes the pleasure that results from their perception. That is, it does not inquire whether this thing is white or black, because that would pertain to a particular sense, or whether this thing is healthful or harmful, because that would pertain to the

interior sense. It is the ratio of pleasure which is sought, and this is
found to consist in a proportion of equality, a *proportio aequalitatis*,
in the case of each source of delight: the beautiful, the suave, and the
salubrious. But a ratio of equality does not depend upon size, so that
both large things and small can equally produce the ensuing pleasure.
It is not extended by dimensions, does not pass away with transitory
things, nor is it altered by motions.

This is a point where Saint Bonaventure differs from Saint Thomas.
The latter proposes that an element of grandeur is needed for an object
to be considered beautiful. That which is small, in his estimation,
cannot be so. Saint Bonaventure, on the contrary, rejects dimensions
of any kind. The measurement of extension, of succession, of time, of
motion, are all excluded. Proportion abstracts from place, time, and
motion, and thus takes on the attributes of immutability, illimitability,
interminability, and spirituality. Thus by the act of discernment, the
sensible perceptions of pleasure in beauty, suavity, and salubrity
become spiritual concepts of the intellect. Thus through the gates of
the five senses the whole of this world enters the mind.[86]

What sparkles most in all of this for a modern observer is the discovery, in relation to a critical world divided according to the mirror
and the lamp, of an aesthetic based upon the traditional concept of
the *speculum*, yet one which is thoroughly affectively oriented.[87] As
we have seen, an affective bias is everywhere apparent in the Bonaventuran aesthetic. Agostini Gemelli saw that

> the sensitive, artistic nature of St. Francis, his admiration of natural
> beauty and passionate love of music, became in St. Bonaventure con-
> scious and systematic study of beauty and of art. Though he did not
> arrive at a formulation of the problem of aesthetic beauty in the mod-
> ern sense, he established, in a way that no one—not even the Greeks—
> had ever done before, its psychological elements. Firmly maintaining
> the reality of the objective value of beauty, he distinguished and laid
> stress on the subjective moment of appreciation, underlining in the
> subjective moment the emotional elements.[88]

This predominant affective quality serves as a chief distinguishing
feature of the Franciscan art forms which, to a large degree, characterize the great style change of the thirteenth century. In them, an
acute appreciation of "terra, erbe con lor colori, arbori e frutti con
sapori," "sumer . . . wið fugheles song" or, indeed, "windes blast and
weder strong" can readily become a subjective moment of emotional
introspection and spiritual reevaluation.

Ej! ej! what þis nicht is long,
and ich wid wel michel wrong
soregh and murne and faste.[89]

The influence of the Bonaventuran aesthetic on art and architecture has been recognized before.[90] If some have seen that Franciscan
theology borrowed in its structural design from architecture, they have
also seen that architecture was not slow to borrow from theology a
rich supply of content, if not originally the inspiration for the design
itself.[91] Regimus Boving, for example, has pointed out that St. Bonaventure exercised a profound influence over Louis IX and the archi-
tects and builders of his court in the designing of La Sainte Chapelle,
the cathedral of Notre Dame de Paris, as well as those of Rheims,
Rouen, Amiens and others built or completed during the years (1239–
74) when Bonaventure lived or traveled in France. Boving found that
Notre Dame in Paris provided a particularly good opportunity to compare changes in style which occurred between completion of its west
and main façade in the first half of the thirteenth century, the north
façade in the middle of the century, and the south façade in the
second half. The south façade, he discovered, showed a greater accent
on the natural beauty of the human figures; the long parallel lines
and flatness of the figures of the west façade are replaced by rounded
ones, more highly raised, expressive of a treatment which is perhaps
more individual than universal.[92] This, of course, is the same effect
achieved in other plastic arts, notably painting, following the Fran-
ciscan-influenced school of Giotto.[93] Raimond van Marle characterizes
this influence:

> The effect of the Franciscan movement was of a twofold character;
> besides the forms of art created by the enormous . . . popularity of
> the order . . . decoration of churches, in pictures of saints and in the
> painted Crucifix (etc.) . . . one might say that the art of figure painting
> in general was influenced by the teaching of St. Francis and the effect
> produced thereby on the medieval mind.
> While the unrealistic conception of Christ and the saints and the
> *abstract mysticism* of the age had produced the inhuman and sym-
> metrical forms of Byzantine art, St. Francis' conception in which the
> beauty of all things created by God formed so large a part, led people
> once more to observe and admire this creation.[94]

Van Marle goes on to suggest that the effect of the new Franciscan
theories was a direct encouragement to what he calls "the study of

Nature," and the depiction of the central figures of worship as partici-
pating much more freely in the commonest traits of human nature
than their hitherto stylized holiness had permitted. It became possible
for artists to portray these figures without distinction in physical appearance from other men, and even to make them physically ugly.
Comparable trends emerged not only in the other plastic arts, but
also in poetry like that of Jacopone da Todi.[95]

A further dramatic effect of Franciscan theology and spirituality
on the plastic arts was the emergence in thirteenth-century painting
of numerous representations of the crucifixion in which the Savior
was depicted dead on the cross, or in the agonies of physical
death. This idea, Van Marle notes, was carried even further in
Franciscan sermons: "It was not on the death of the Lord but on His
wounds that St. Francis meditated, and in Italy the Savior dead upon
the Cross became the Redeemer of humanity, His body twisted in
agony, His features distorted by suffering . . . ."[96] Painters of Franciscan
orientation often represented Christ not only in physical agony with
eyes closed, confronting death, but with eyes open, appealing to the
onlooker with what Van Marle calls a "plaintive expression." Frequently crucifixes from the mid-thirteenth century of Franciscan type
show at the lateral extremities of the transept arms representations
of the Blessed Virgin on the one hand, John or Mary Magdalene on
the other, which evidence "a power of dramatic action"[97] highly personalizing the plaintive appeal in the manner of the *Meditations on
the Life of Christ*.[98]

The intent to focus on the human nature of Christ partly accounts
for the most notable stylistic feature of the *Meditations* and of most
Franciscan graphic and literary art. There are a very large number of
illustrations to the text of the *Meditations* edited by Ragusa and
Green. The compiler of that manuscript seems to have provided illustrations for every narrative in an unprecedented variety of treatment
which is expressive of the Franciscan love for graphics. But it is in
the character of the illustrations that the Franciscan style most vigorously asserts itself; the humanity of Christ is pointed to repeatedly in
the details of physical suffering and pain presented, in his physical
contact with other people in the narrative, and in the naturalized
detail in the various poses of the key figures, especially the Virgin.
While costumes are conventional for many of the figures, they are
contemporary for secondary ones, such as cripples, midwives, beggars,
soldiers, and ordinary people of both noble and lower classes. Details
of setting are contemporary—chests, tables, trappings of horses, techniques of spinning, carpentry, fishing, and innkeeping. Typically,

animals are introduced often, very well characterized and delineated, and apparently interest the artists more than do devils, which appear only in the Temptations.[99] In all of these details the attention to common life is as relevant as the participatory intent of contemporary guise and setting, characterizing, with the text of the *Meditations on the Life of Christ*, typical Franciscan theological as well as literary concern and method.

Another major Franciscan contribution to art may be found in the great output of didactic hagiographical painting, beginning with St. Francis himself but rapidly spreading beyond the *legenda* to representations of other saints. Here two noteworthy characteristics are manifested: first, the hagiographical representation is as highly articulate in a moral and didactic sense as the written hagiography discussed in chapter two above; second, the favorite subjects of Franciscan graphic iconography are not just the legends of St. Francis, but of other medieval saints who appear almost as often or in some categories more frequently than Francis.[100] Some of these favorite subjects are standard and predictable, such as St. Benedict in the thorn-brake, or St. Nicholas rescuing the sailors. Others, such as St. Margaret in the dragon's mouth and details from the life of St. Catherine, are more peculiar to Franciscan influence, and are worthy of notice for later comparison with the contents of Middle English lyric manuscripts.

Finally, Franciscan art shows the interest of the order in the Apocalypse. Here we can as readily turn to English examples in the graphic arts as Italian. A. G. Little recognized that consistent with their much exercised speculation as to the meaning of Revelation, the Franciscans apparently had a great deal to do with the design and execution of the pictures in illustrated Apocaylpses.[101] Brother William's unique drawing preserved by Matthew Paris was clearly intended for such a series, he says, though it may be the only survivor. In several extant English Apocalypses Franciscans are represented, e.g., in that in MS. Trinity College, Cambridge, 41. Before the middle of the thirteenth century Franciscans are often depicted as standing on the glassy sea, escaping the fall of Babylon, or grouped among the saved at the Last Judgment. Many of the pictures illustrating the *expositio* of the relevant texts contain Franciscan friars. Usually, these are presented as preachers against Antichrist, and in one particularly good one a very truculent-looking friar is about to hit Antichrist on the head with a cross.[102] In the Douce Apocalypse (ca. 1270), the "Two Witnesses" of chapter 11 ("Enoch and Elijah according to medieval tradition . . . typifying preacher and prophet") are represented as laybrothers of the Franciscan Order, and in a later Apocalypse as regular

Franciscan friars.[103] One particularly intriguing example is the Last
Judgment scene from the wall painting in St. John's, Winchester.
Portrayed is the figure of a Franciscan leading the blessed naked into
Paradise; obliterated is a section which apparently showed a mon-
strous devil leading away the damned to Hell. Below, in the border,
are bands of people rising from their coffins at the last day, and near
the scene of judgment stands one of the Four Daughters of God,
extending the lash of penance. This touch is obviously consistent with
the function of the painting in general, and is typical of Franciscan
interest in eliciting a contritional response.

The nature of Franciscan influence on the plastic arts, in conjunction with what we have already observed about Franciscan aesthetic
theory, leads us toward a working hypothesis. The major emphases of
Franciscan theology and aesthetics, even if not all original with the
Friars Minor, tend to repeat themselves in fairly consistent constella-
tions in a variety of Franciscan-inspired enterprises. The concern with
nature, the tendency to "humanize," the focus on the moment of
the Passion and its psychologically compelling appeal, a desire for
contrition, the use of the Virgin as an emotional focus for this appeal,
an increased development of a morally instructive hagiography, and
even the orientation toward Apocalypse and judgment—all of these
have not only been recognized in Franciscan plastic art, but are indeed
its prominent features, just as they achieve unusual proportion in the
theology and aesthetic from which they come. The primary distinguishing characteristics of Franciscan affective theology, infused with
its peculiarly intense spirituality, conditioned by an evangelically
oriented exegesis, and informed by the "Franciscan aesthetic," express themselves naturally and consistently in Franciscan art. We
should expect to find these same features in Franciscan poetry.

Notes

1. Chap. 2, pp. 43–7. Evelyn Underhill, *Jacopone*, p. 143, cogently objects to excessively far-ranging conclusions drawn from Jacopone's *Lauda* XXXI, "Mal vedemmo Parisci/ c'hane destrutto Ascisi."

2. Beryl Smalley in *English Friars and Antiquity* demonstrates the extent of Dominican and Franciscan educational enterprises.

3. The translated excerpt is from Cuthbert Gumbinger, "*Prediche Volgari*," p. 19.

4. It should be noted that at least one Dominican work is listed, "prima pars sancti Thomae."

5. The catalogue is fully recounted in G. Mazzatinti, "La biblioteca di S. Francesco in Rimini," in *Scritti vari di filologia in onore a Monaci* (Rome: Forzani, 1901), pp. 345 ff.

6. For example, Boccaccio's *Genealogia Deorum*, the commentary on Virgil, Bartholomaeus Anglicus' *De proprietatibus rerum*, etc.

7. Hilarin Felder, *Geschichte*, p. 316. For a full study see his chapter 4, "Das General studium zu Oxford und die Entwicklung der Englischen Ordensschulen."

8. A. G. Little, *The Grey Friars in Oxford* (Oxford: Clarendon Press, 1892), pp. 55–60; see also F. M. Powicke, *The Medieval Books of Merton College* (Oxford: Clarendon Press, 1931); and Decima L. Douie, *Pecham*, p. 276. Many of the Digby MSS were acquired by Thomas Allen from the Greyfriars' Oxford holdings. See also M. R. James, "The Library of the Grey Friars of Hereford," in *Collectanea Franciscana*, vol. 1, ed. A. G. Little et al. (BSFS 5; Aberdeen: Univ. of Aberdeen Press, 1915), pp. 114–23; and H. M. Bannister, "A Short Notice of Some Manuscripts of the Cambridge Friars," in *Collectanea Franciscana*, vol. 1, pp. 124–40.

9. R. A. B. Mynors, "The Latin Classics Known to Bolton of Bury, F.S.," in *Fritz Saxl, 1890–1948: A Volume of Memorial Essays from His Friends in England*, ed. D. J. Gordon (London: Nelson, 1957), pp. 199–217.

10. Clement Schmitt, "Manuscrits de la 'Franciscan Library' de Killiney," *Archivum Franciscanum Historicum* 57 (1964):165–90. The sermons of St. Bernardino are those published in the Quaracchi (1950) series 1:3–532; 2:5–470. Schmitt notes that at folio 398, and following "Filoli, agnoscatis, eam vulgari reservabo vobis," occurs an "hymne italien que le saint croyait être de Jacopone da Todi (cf. S. Bernardino *Opera Omnia* II, 470, n. 2, texte ibid. 470–1) mais qui est attribué à Ugo Panziera, O.F.M.": see in V. de Benedetto Ugo Panziera, 63–5, *Lauda* VIII, supra 171, n. 6 'Quomodo vulneratus fuit beatus Fr. in hac pugna celesti.' Incip 'In fuoco l'amor mi misse' (ter.), Explin.—di Jesus memorato. Hora son facto capace. Sempre lo ho in cor portato. Trinitati uni Deo sit laus. Amen' " (p. 176).

11. S. J. P. Van Dijk, "Some Manuscripts of the Earliest Franciscan Liturgy," *Franciscan Studies* 14 (1954):225–64; 16 (1956):60–99. M. R. James, "The Austin Friars' Library at York," in *Fasciculus Ioanni Willis Clark Dicatus* (Canterbury: Typis academicus impressus, 1909), pp. 16 ff,. pub-

lished the remains of the York Austin catalogue, 646 volumes listed, among which are many Franciscan works including writings of St. Bonaventure, Robert Grosseteste, Bartholomaeus Anglicus, the *Mirror of the Life of Christ,* etc.

12. *Verb. Admon.,* 7, cited: in Ray C. Petry, *Francis of Assisi: Apostle of Poverty* (Durham, North Carolina: Duke Univ. Press, 1941), p. 72.

13. *I Celano* 80; *Epist. ad fidelis* 9.

14. To this must be added the Franciscan attitude toward the Scriptures which related them to a chronological pattern of God's ordination; focusing on Christ at a point in time, and seeing that which came after as relating to the cross in much the same way as that which came before (see chap. 2 above). This is hinted in Francis' conviction that God's word spoke especially to the Friars so that they might give special witness to the Word (*I Regula* 9); in his equating the "least ones" of Matt. 25:40 with the Friars Minor there is something of both the historiographical consciousness and "moraliter" (*II Celano* 71; *Speculum perfectionis* 26). But the idea of the Friars Minor as a group within the Church specially called, through Divine Scriptures, for peculiarly divine ends, remained strong (e.g., *Leggende Antoniane,* p. 98b).

15. See below pp. 88 and 94–5.

16. Henri de Lubac, *Exégèse médiévale: Les quatre sens de l'Écriture,* 4 vols. (Paris: Aubier, 1959), 1:328–41.

17. See chap. 2, pp. 69–71 above; also de Lubac, 3:437 ff.

18. De Lubac, 3:287 ff.; esp. p. 317.

19. See de Lubac, 4:344–67.

20. E.g., Gregorian pastoral spirituality, Benedictine contemplative spirituality, Celtic asceticism, or even the spirituality of the twelfth-century schoolmen. See Leclercq, *Learning,* chap. 1; also pp. 162 ff.; 187 ff.

21. *Breviloquium* 2. 9, 3, trans. in Tavard, *Transiency and Permanence,* p. 81.

22. "Quod licet *unum* sit secundum intellectum *litteralem,* est tamen *triplex* secundum sensum *mysticium* et spiritualem. In omnibus enim sacrae Scripturae libris praeter *litteralem* sensum, quem exterius verba sonant, concipitur triplex sensus *spiritualis,* scilicet *allegoricus,* quo docemur, quid sit credendum de Divinitate et humanitate; *moralis,* quo docemur, quomodo vivendum sit; et *anagogicus,* quo docemur qualiter est Deo adhaerendum. Unde tota sacra Scriptura haec tria docet, scilicet Christi aeternam generationem et incarnationem, vivendi ordinem et Dei et animae unionem. Primum respicit *fidem,* secundum *mores,* tertium *finem utriusque.* Circa primum insudare debet studium doctorum circa secundum studium praedicatorum, circa tertium studium contemplativorum" (*Reductione artium,* p. 46).

23. Fr. Roger Bacon organized his *Opus majus* on the lines of St. Bonaventure's *Reductione artium* to show the relationship of all creation, arts, and sciences to the Scriptures. Typically, Bacon is concerned with literal understanding of the text: see P. T. Witzel, "De Fr. Rogero Bacon eiusque

sententia de rebus biblicus," *Archivum Franciscanum Historicum* 3 (1910):1–22; 185–213. Fr. Nicholas of Lyra asserted the literal level to be even more important than the spiritual levels: he explains the fourfold interpretation in the first prologue to his *Postilla super quattor evangelistas* (Mantua, 1477), and in the second emphasizes the need for first understanding the literal level. This position was disputed and defended, within and without the order; the final defense of Nicholas was by fellow-Franciscan Matthew Doering (end of 1477, in Mantua).

24. *Reductione artium*, p. 46.

25. Ibid.

26. "Deus est subiectum theologiae radicale, Christus est subiectum integrale, res et signa sunt subiectum universale sive etiam credible, prout transit in rationem intelligibilis . . . . Nam subiectum, ad quod omnia reducuntur ut ad *principium*, est ipse *Deus*.

"Subiectum quoque, ad quod omnia reducuntur, quae determinantur in hoc libro, ut ad *totum integrum*, est *Christus*, prout comprehendit naturam divinam et humanam sive creatum et increatum . . ." (*Commentarium in sententiarum*, 1. proem. 1 [Quaracchi, 1:7]).

27. A. G. Little, *Franciscan Papers, Lists, and Documents* (Manchester: Univ. of Manchester Press, 1943), p. 109 (hereafter cited as Little, *Documents*). Henri de Lubac (*Exégèse*) has forcefully made the point that tropology is the medieval spiritual sense *par excellence*; but Franciscans like Nicholas Bozon and the compiler of the *Gesta Romanorum* could write to the moral point to the entire exclusion of the other spiritual senses.

28. Rohr, *Sermons*, p. 64.

29. See pp. 49 and 66–8 above.

30. See Tavard, *Transiency and Permanence*, p. 42.

31. Rohr, *Sermons*, pp. 37; 38–39. The heretical doctrines Rohr refers to here are those of the Cathars and Patarines. See Steven Runciman, *Manichee*, pp. 148 ff.; Christine Thouzellier, *Catharisme et Valdéisme en Languedoc à la fin du xiie et au début du xiiie siècle* . . . (Paris: Presses universitaires de France, 1966).

32. Rohr, *Sermons*, p. 37. Cf. chap. 2, n. 11.

33. Mary Eunice Raisen, *Evidences of Romanticism in the Poetry of Medieval England* (Louisville: Univ. of Kentucky Press, 1929), pp. 3–87, makes this sort of mistaken assumption. Her book does recognize the affective psychological basis of Franciscan devotion however (pp. 103 ff.), and is an early study of nature in Middle English poetry.

34. *St. Francis of Assisi* (New York: George H. Doran, 1924), pp. 126–29. Although St. Francis himself may have been more simply spontaneous in his approach to nature, it is important to stress the more systematic Augustinian theologizing of his followers. Cf. Paul Sabatier, *Études inédites sur Saint François d'Assise*, ed. Arnold Goffin (Paris: Librarie Fischbacher, 1932), pp. 63 ff. It is possible to be much more precise than to say "Ces idées étaient du reste dans l'air" (p. 64).

35. *Commentarium in sententiarum*, I, d. I, i (Quaracchi, 1:27): "Omnis doctrina est de rebus vel de signa" and section ff.; see also n. 26 above.

36. Augustine, *De doctrina Christiana* 2. 2, in *PL* 34: 19.

37. Lombard, *Libri IV sententiarum*, d. 1.

38. *Commentarium in sententiarum*, I, d. 3, p. 1, q. 3, ad 2 (Quaracchi, 1:73).

39. "Si ergo Deus non est magis gloriosus post conditionem rerum quam ante, si faceret res principaliter propter gloriam suam, faceret frustra: quodsi non frustra facit, non producit ergo principaliter propter gloriam suam, sed propter utilitatem alienam," *Commentarium in sententiarum* II d. 1, p. 2, a. 2, q. 1, ad 3 (Quaracchi, 2:44).

40. See Robertson, *Preface*, pp. 310–16. It is my conviction that the exegetical and aesthetic principles of many medieval Franciscan writers differ somewhat from the mainstream tradition in the Middle Ages which Professor Robertson has described. The differences, appearing in part in the discussion here, are apparently not so much in approach as in emphasis. I should like to have explored this variance and some of its more immediate implications in a chapter dealing with English Franciscan commentaries and symbolic dictionaries, particularly those of Ridewall and Bartholomaeus Anglicus. Though such an investigation is outside the immediate context of this study, it is certainly worthy of further interest. At this moment an edition of Trevisa's translation of Bartholomew's *De proprietatibus rerum* based on B.L. MS. Addit. 27944 is being prepared under the general direction of M. C. Seymour.

41. ". . . in qualibet enim creatura est refulgentia quadeam divini exemplaris, sed cum tenebra permixta. Item, est via, ut fenestra: in hac enim creatura sic, in illa sic; radius aeternus in viis suis ostendit se ut radius per vitrum coloratum: sicut enim radius ex multis coloribus vitri multipliciter coloratur, sic radius divinus in proprietates. Item, est vestigium vel simulacrum sapientiae Dei, sculptile quiddam. Ex iis omnibus est quidam liber *scriptus foris*. Quando ergo anima videt hoc, videtur sibi semper quod deberet transire de umbra ad lucem, a via ad terminum, a vestigio ad veritatem, a libro ad veram scientiam" (*In Hexaëmeron* 12. 14–15 [Quaracchi, 5: 386b]). An excellent guide to St. Bonaventure's idea of reading the Book of Nature, with references to passages additional to those cited, may be found in Tavard, *Transiency and Permanence*, pp. 56–79.

42. Published by Servius Gieben in "Traces of God in Nature according to Robert Grosseteste," *Franciscan Studies* 24 (1964):144–58. (All quotations from *Dictum* 60 are from this article.)

43. *Dictum* 48, MS. Gonville and Caius College, 380, fol. 39v; and *Sermo* 19, BL. MS. Royal 7. F. II, fol. 52 rb: "Mundi machina manifestissime loquitur aeternam artem per quam facta est sicut vox exterior assumpta a verbo interiori eius signum illius artis et invisibilis Verbi visibile verbum."

44. "All the world's creatures are as a book and picture—a mirror to us in which our life, our death, our circumstances and our destiny are faith-

fully signified" (printed in *Psalterium profanum*, ed. and trans. Josef Eberle [Zurich: Manesse Verlag, 1962], p. 126).

45. See A. Ampe, "Exemplarisme," in *Dictionnaire de spiritualité* (Paris, 1961), 4. 2. 1870–78.

46. *Dictum* 60 (Gieben, "Robert Grosseteste," p. 153).

47. Also: "Etsi enim res omnis secundum sui totalitatem sit Creatoris vestigium, non tamen possible est ut ipsa sit vestigium totalitatis Ipsius . . . nec etiam totam simul creaturam existimo esse vestigium, imitationem et enarrationem completam totalitatis ipsius infinitissimae et simplicissimae Deitatis unitatis et trinitatis. Non enim potest creatura factori suo comparari nec cum Eo in aliquo univocari; potest tamen per modum aliquem imitari" (*In Hexaëmeron* 7. 1), etc.

48. *Dictum* 60 (Gieben, "Robert Grosseteste," pp. 155–56.

49. *In Hexaëmeron* 8. 4.

50. *In Hexaëmeron* 17. 25. "Figura" is an interesting word here. John Ridewall, the Franciscan who wrote *Fulgentius metaforalis*, speaks of poetic representations as "poetica pictura," "secundum poeticam imaginem," and "pingitur a poetis," but not "figura." See Smalley, *English Friars*, p. 112. Bacon, however, uses it; e.g., "Queritur cui debet attribui assimilato in figura" (*Opera* 10:222).

51. *Dictum* 60 (Gieben, "Robert Grosseteste," p. 157): "Nor sunt haec distortiones in Deo, sed in animae tuae distorto speculo."

52. The preceding argument runs as follows: "Nam communicacio operis infallibile signum est communicacionis cordis. Homo autem maxime se communicando maxime fit bonus, quia sui ad salutem participantium communicacio est universalis boni diffinicio, ac per hos patet quod maxime debet homo moveri ad aliena onera supportanda. Et ad hanc quidem communicacionem invitat hominem omnis creatura. Quelibet enim creatura alii se communicat tota communicacione sibi possibili, ut patet primo in corporibus supercelestibus que indesinenter ideo moventur ut effectum sue bonitatis creaturis inferioribus communicent. Ita est de creaturis aliis. Nam terra omnibus se communicat per supportacionem: aqua per suas proprietates—na[ta] bilitatem, potabilitatem et labilitatem et ceteras, aer etiam per suas, scilicet inspirabilitatem, exspirabilitatem, transparenciam et continenciam et ceteras; ignis quoque per suas, scilicet per proprietatem splendificativam, calefactivam et ceteras innumeras: sicque ordinatur omnia in universo quod illa pars universi que magis est necessaria ceteris magis se communicat" (Little, *Documents*, p. 113).

53. MS. Riccardian Library, Codex 1264, Part II, fol. 23 (Sermon XXV).

54. See Giovanni Getto, *Francesco d'Assisi e il cantico di frate sole* (Turin: Universita di Torino, 1956).

55. *Meditations*, p. 42; also p. 329.

56. Gieben, "Robert Grosseteste," p. 158.

57. See L. Baur, *Die philosophischen Werke des Robert Grossetestes* (Münster in Westphalen: Aschendorff, 1912), pp. 141–42.

58. Gieben, "Robert Grosseteste," p. 145, n. 6. "Ipsa rerum universitas fit scale ad ascendendum in Deum" (*Itinerarium mentis in Deum*, c. 1, 2 [Quaracchi, 5:297]). Similarly, an inscription in the Franciscan glass and carving program of S. Maria in Venice instructs the viewer:

Nam Deus est quod imago docet: sed non est Deus ipsa.
Hanc videas, sed mente colas quod noscis in ipsa.

59. *Lauda* LIX, in *Jacopone da Todi, Laudi*, ed. Franca Ageno (Florence: Le Monnier, 1953; hereafter cited as Ageno), p. 235. This is a modernized edition.

60. Medieval Irish lyrics certainly express a delight in nature of this order, but because of their date and provenance they can in no way be considered as a formative influence on the Middle English lyric.

61. *EL XIII*, no. 6; Brook, no. 23.

62. *Reductione artium*, p. 46.

63. "Per hunc modum est reperire in illuminatione *artis mechanicae*, cuius tota intentio versatur circa *artificialium productionem*. In qua ista tria possumus intueri, scilicet *Verbi generationem* et *incarnationem, vivendi ordinem* et *Dei et animae foederationem*. Et hoc, si consideremus *egressum, effectum* et *fructum*; vel sic: *artem operandi, qualitatem effecti artificii* et *utilitatem fructus eliciti*" (*Reductione artium*, p. 52).

64. The study of exemplarism has a twofold objective: "Sicut exemplar secundum proprietatem vocabuli dicit expressionem per modum activi . . . , sic et contrario imago per modum passivi; et dicitur imago quod alterum exprimit et imitatur" (*Commentarium in sententiarum* I, d. 31 [Quaracchi, 1:540]); and what Bonaventure suggests is that art in like dual sense participates in creation.

65. "Si consideremus *egressum*, videbimus, quod effectus artificialis exit ab artifice, mediante similitudine existente in mente; per quam artifex excogitat, antequam producat, et inde producit, sicut disposuit. Producit autem artifex exterius opus assimilatum exemplari interiori eatenus, qua potest melius . . ." (*Reductione artium*, p. 52).

66. E.g., Gabriel Marcel, in *La Dignité humaine et ses assises existentielles* (Paris: Aubier, 1964); Nikolai A. Berdiaev, in *The Divine and the Human*, trans. R. M. French (London: G. Bles, 1949).

67. "Si vero consideremus *effectum*, intuebimur *vivendi ordinem*. Omnis enim artifex intendit producere opus pulcrum et utile et stabile; et tunc est carum et acceptabile opus, cum habet istas tres conditiones. —Iuxta haec tria necesse est reperiri tria in ordine vivendi, scilicet "*scire, velle* et impermutabiliter sive *perseveranter operari*." *Scientia* reddit opus pulcrum, *voluntas* reddit utile, *perseverantia* reddit stabile. Primum est in rationali, secundum in concupiscibili, tertium in irascibili" (*Reductione artium*, p. 54).

68. "Si consideremus *fructum*, inveniemus *Dei et animae unionem*. Omnis enim artifex, qui aliquod opus facit, aut facit, ut per illud laudetur, aut ut per illud sibi aliquid *operetur* vel lucretur, aut ut in illo *delectetur*, secundum tria, quae sunt in appetibilibus, scilicet bonum *honestum, conferens* et *delect-*

abile. —Propter haec tria fecit Deus animam rationalem, ut ipsa eum *laudaret,* ut ipsa illi *serviret,* ut ipsa in eo *delectaretur* et quiesceret; et hoc est per caritatem . . ." (*Reductione artium,* p. 54).

69. 'Si autem est in *utriusque adminiculum,* hoc est dupliciter: aut *defectum supplendo,* et sic est *navigatio,* sub qua continetur omnis *mercatio* sive pertinentium ad operimentum, sive ad alimentum; aut *removendo imped-imentum* et nocumentum, et sic est *medicina,* sive consistat in confectione electuariorum, sive potionum, sive unguentorum, sive curatione vulnerum, sive decisione membrorum, sicut est chirurgia. —Theatrica autem est unica. Et sic patet sufficientia" (*Reductione artium,* p. 40).

70. *Didascalicon,* chap. 3. See the translation by Jerome Taylor (New York: Columbia Univ. Press, 1961), pp. 83 ff.

71. *Reductione artium,* p. 83.

72. "—Quarum *sufficientia* sic accipitur. Quoniam omnis ars mechanica aut est ad *solatium,* aut ad *commodum;* sive aut est ad excludendam *tristi-tiam,* aut *indigentiam;* sive aut *prodest,* aut *delectat,* secundum illud Horatii:

Aut prodesse volunt, aut delectare poetae.

Et iterum:

Omne tulit punctum qui miscuit utile dulci.

Si est ad *solatium* et delectationem, sic est *theatrica,* quae est ars ludorum, omnem modum ludendi continens, sive in cantibus, sive in organis, sive in figmentis, sive in gesticulationibus corporis" (*Reductione artium,* pp. 38–40).

73. *Reductione artium,* p. 50. Similarly, Alexander of Hales describes all exterior senses as an avenue toward union with God, and sees music and song as of chief value in such a movement. He cites Augustine and Gregory on the value of music for moving the heart to confession of sin, e.g., from Augustine, *Confessiones:* "Cum cantus quam id quod canitur amplius me moveat, poenaliter me peccasse confiteor . . ." in *Glossa,* III, dist. 32. 8; 33, 1 (Quaracchi, 1954), pp. 392, 396.

74. *Reductione artium,* p. 54.

75. Ibid., p. 48.

76. Ibid., pp. 48–50.

77. "Omnis enim sensus suum sensibile conveniens quaerit cum desiderio, invenit cum gaudio, repetit sine fastidio, quia *non satiatur oculus visu, nec auris auditu impletur.*—Per hunc etiam modum sensus *cordis* nostri sive pulcrum, sive consonum, sive odoriferum, sive dulce, sive mulcebre debet desideranter quaerere, gaudenter invenire, incessanter repetere.—Ecce, quo-modo in cognitione sensitiva continetur occulte divina sapientia, et quam mira est contemplatio quinque sensuum spiritualium secundum conformitatem ad sensus corporales" (*Reductione artium,* p. 50).

78. "Ad illud quod obiicitur, quod ordo pendet ex partibus; dicendum, quod sicut aliqua contigentia in se habent esse absolutum contingens, sed ordinem necessarium; sic et in proposito intelligendum, quod quamvis aliquod non sit optimum in se, tamen optime ordinatur. Et exemplum huius patet in partibus corporis et in re artificiali, in qua est consonantia et har-

monia, sicut in cithara. Quamvis enim nobilior sit situs oculi quam pedis, tamen si consideremus utrumque secundum suum officium, tam oculus quam pes optime situati sunt in toto, ita quod nec oculus melius pede, nec e conservo. Et ita dicit Augustinus super Ioannem (Cap. i, 3 tract. 1, 13), quod sicut angelus optime in caelo, ita vermiculus optime in imo, sicut in terra. Et similiter apparet in cithara: possunt enim omnes chordae ita proportionari, quod si aliqua tendatur, ut detur ei melior sonum, nunquam remanebit consonantia. Similiter dictiones possunt ordinari ad faciendum versum, ita quod ex illis dictionibus impossibile est fieri versum melius ordinatum; sic in propositio intelligendum" *Commentarium in sententiarum*, I, xliv, I, 3 (Quaracchi, 1: 756–57). This same idea was an expressed ideal of the *trobar clus*, the poetic academy of Provençal poets—see Leo Pollmann, "*Trobar Clus.*"

79. Henri Pouillon, "La Beauté, propriété transcendentale chez les scholastiques (1120–1270)," *Archives d'histoire littéraire et doctrinale du Moyen Âge* 15 (1946):314.

80. M. M. Gorce, *L'Essor de la pensée au Moyen Âge: Albert le Grand–Thomas d'Aquin* (Paris: Letouzey et Ané, 1933), p. 128; see esp. pp. 127–37.

81. See Leclercq, Vandenbroucke, and Bouyer, *Christian Spirituality*, 2:331 ff.

82. E. J. M. Spargo, *The Category of the Aesthetic in the Philosophy of St. Bonaventure* (St. Bonaventure, New York: Franciscan Institute, 1953), pp. 14 ff.

83. See here also the article by E. Lutz, "Die Asthetik Bonaventuras nach den Quellen dargestellt," in Festgabe Baeumker, *Beiträge zur Geschichte der Philosophie des Mittelalters*, Supplement, vol. 1 (Münster in Westphalen: Aschendorff, 1913), pp. 202 ff., which does more than Spargo's chapter to relate the Bonaventuran aesthetic to Augustinian and Neo-platonic models.

84. See Harry B. Gutman, "The rebirth of the Fine Arts and Franciscan Thought," *Franciscan Studies* 25 (1945):225; Clement M. O'Donnell, *The Psychology of St. Bonaventure and St. Thomas Aquinas* (Washington: Catholic University of America Press, 1937), p. 100.

85. Spargo, *The Aesthetic*, p. 15.

86. Ibid., pp. 45–46. The idea of proportion, order, and symmetry as keys to the beautiful is at root classical and Augustinian; the emphasis on the avenue of the five senses is typically Franciscan. See Jacopone da Todi, *Lauda* V, "Cinque sensi mess'on pegno." Cf. *Lauda* VII.

87. See Meyer Abrams, *The Mirror and the Lamp* (New York: Norton, 1953), p. 14. Abrams suggests that beginning with post-Renaissance critics like Sidney the mimetic mode was being oriented to pragmatic theories in an affective, or audience-oriented way. Actually, the aesthetic developed by St. Bonaventure, who must rank as one of the great theoretical critics having an influence on Western art and literature, shows that this tendency was already fully articulated by the mid-thirteenth century.

88. Agostini Gemelli, *The Franciscan Message to the World*, trans. H. L. Hughes (London: Burns, Oates, and Washbourne, 1934), p. 56.

89. *EL XIII*, no. 7; see the discussion of St. Francis' poem and Jacopone da Todi's "Quanto e nel mondo m'invita ad amare," p. 152 below; also "Terra, erbe con lor coluri," p. 95–6 above.

90. See Gutman, "Rebirth," and notes following below.

91. Thomas Plassman, "The Pointed Arch in Franciscan Theology," *Franciscan Studies* 25 (1945):97–114. Plassman notes that Bonaventure, like his master Alexander, differs from Lombard and St. Thomas in placing his treatise "De gratiae" not before, but after "De Verbo Incarnato," which organization Plassman says is theologically significant, bespeaking "his leaning toward the affirmative side of the *motivum finale Incarnationis* and consequently to the opinion that all grace is *Gratia Christi*." In this way, says Plassman, Bonaventure's "unequalled *Breviloquium* . . . assumes the shape of a graceful heptagon. The Incarnate Word is sheltered in the central hall, surrounded by the other six in harmonious symmetry" (p. 100). The seven divisions of the *Breviloquium* (Quaracchi, 5:199–291) are as follows: I, de trinitate Dei; II, de creatura mundi; III, de corruptela peccati; IV, de incarnatione Verbi; V, de gratia Spiritus sancti; VI, de medicina sacramentali; VII, de state finalis judicii.

92. P. Regimus Boving, *Bonaventura und die französische Hochgotik* (Werl in Westphalen: Franziskus-Druckerei, 1930), pp. 17 ff., 49–54.

93. Harry B. Gutman, "The Rebirth of the Fine Arts and Franciscan Thought [Part 2]," *Franciscan Studies* 26 (1946):3–29; cf. Millard Meiss, *Giotto and Assisi* (New York, 1960): Emile Mâle, *L'Art religieux*. See Lynn White, Jr., "Natural Science and Naturalistic Art in the Middle Ages," *American Historical Review* 52 (1947): 421–35.

94. Raimond van Marle, *Italian Schools*, 1:258.

95. See pp. 143–44 below.

96. Van Marle, *Italian Schools*, 1:260.

97. Ibid., 1:308–9.

98. In painting, Giunta of Pisa is the artist whom van Marle cites as best demonstrating the Franciscan conception of the crucifix. See also P. Thoby, *Les Croix limousines de la fin du XIIe siècle* (Paris, 1953), chap. 1.

99. *Meditations*, Introduction, p. xxxiv.

100. Van Marle, *Italian Schools*, 1:260, 318, 333–48. See also Tancred Borenius, "Some Franciscan Subjects in Italian Art," in *St. Francis of Assisi: 1226–1926: Essays in Commemoration*, ed. Walter Warren Seton (London: Univ. of London Press, 1926), pp. 3–12.

101. Little, *English Medieval Art*, esp. pp. 39–40.

102. On the other hand, association of Franciscans with the Apocalypse was what we might today call a politically polarizing issue. On the continent, especially in France, following William of St. Amour and Jean de Meun it was popular to show friars as "Antichrist's men," just the reverse of what we have been noting for thirteenth-century England. In the fourteenth-century Apocalypse mystery, *Jour de Jugement*, Antichrist himself is dressed as a Franciscan.

103. Little, *English Medieval Art*, p. 40, n. 1, reveals that in one MS the two *false* prophets are garbed as Dominicans.

The Earliest Lyrics in Italy

Most studies of medieval poetry have concentrated on that now larger canon of verbal artistry which derives from an essentially aristocratic cultural experience.[1] But verbal creativity hardly ever has been the exclusive preserve of gentility; in certain countries, such as Italy, a vernacular literary tradition was in fact first developed in the popular culture. Still, non-courtly poetry has usually received only a distant secondary consideration by critics, partly because the extant materials often come later in time, and partly because popular literature does not come off very well when judged according to literary standards developed for courtly genres. This is not to say that one can pretend literary value which is not there; many medieval lyrics, for example, are nearly destitute of literary quality, even when given the most liberal of assessments. It is to say, however, that it is proper to seek to define a genre according to its own announced purpose, if that can be found, and then to judge poetry of the genre in terms of what that genre sets out to do. Knowledge of the context and application of the medieval lyric is essential to a just appreciation of it.

I have already noted that the early thirteenth century was far from tranquil in northern and central Italy. In addition to the spiritual upheavals within the Church discussed in chapter one, external forces such as the political rivalries between cities which were constantly at war, rivalries between emperors like Fredrick II and the Pope, and recurrences of the plague added to a remarkable social turmoil. Of all these events the plague had the most general effect, with so many hundreds of thousands dying that the church bells were silenced lest the sick should panic. Then, with the wailing of people in the streets that signaled the advent of the Flagellants, there arose remarkable religious revivals. All classes of men in great processions, moan-

118

ing 'godly songs of praise' while lashing each other with scourges of leather and iron, staggered through the cities bleeding, and out onto country roads. Salimbene records that if any man would not be scourged he was held worse than the Devil, all pointed their finger at him as at a limb of Satan, and in a short time he would fall into some misfortune and die. Hermits multiplied—Augustinians, hermits of William of Monte Vergine, hermits of John the Good. Others founded strange sects and religions, and taught the people unusual songs. Despite the short respite of peace in the year of the Great Alleluia (1233), renewed tales of visions of Antichrist and the burgeoning of new orders (in defiance of the Fourth Lateran decree) continued with redoubled vigor. Often renegade Franciscans were the instigators of wild observances, such as that of the Friars of the Sack, who took certain words of Salimbene's friend Hugh de Digne literally and ran off to the woods to live on roots in the face of the immanent Tribulation.[2] Thousands of other visionaries in 1233 climbed to the top of a mountain to await the moment of rapture, only to perish there in a violent storm. Francis himself was horrified by a vision that Antichrist was to spring from the ranks of his own order.[3] Heretical groups like the Patarini and Cathari, with their dualistic doctrines and occult rites, began to spread again as if there had never been an Albigensian crusade, and in their new expansion they claimed poets of rank like Guittone d'Arezzo.[4] Distinction between many groups affianced to the new spiritual fervor must have been difficult: when Brother Pacifico and his laud-singing group of friars first arrived in France they were confused with "Albigenses" by the native population, and encountered unwelcome difficulties.[5]

That there should have been such confusion between the early friars and other spiritual groups is not really so surprising. Indications of organized laud-singing are sporadic until the rise of the Flagellants, who began to exert their maximum influence in this way by the middle of the thirteenth century.[6] Some of the groups were instigated by Raineri Fasani, an Umbrian hermit who once had some connection with the Franciscans,[7] but afterwards with the roving bands of *disciplinati de Gesu Cristo*, who began to weave their way in penitential snake dances through the streets of Italy, scourging each other's shoulders raw with thongs, and at the same time, singing "laudes divinas ad honorem Dei et Beatae Virginis, quas cantabunt dum, se verberando, incedebant."[8] Some of the contemporary accounts offer truly striking insights into commonly shared psychological, spiritual, and particularly penitential features of these grotesque rituals,[9] by means of which people gave vent to their contrite sorrow, hoping fer-

vently that through their anguished tears they might see Christ's passion in their own flesh, imploring pitifully the mercy of God and aid
of the Virgin that in their individual case, as with innumerable other
penitent sinners, they might be forgiven their sins. By day and by
night, in all sorts of weather, preceded by crosses and standards they
stumbled through the streets and into the churches of their cities,
prostrating themselves before the altars. It is said that villages, castles,
and the very fields and mountains rang with their cries, and with the
sound of their musical instruments and songs.

One of the most remarkable things about this phenomenon is that
it did not quickly die out, as the disparate objectives and the geographical isolation of the participants would have seemed to warrant.
Far in the north in Germany and in Scandinavia penitential songs
were being sung by flagellants in the streets up to the time of the
Great Plague of 1349.[10] The persistence more particularly of penitential songs, without the physical scourging itself (which became increasingly rare and eventually disappeared after 1350), suggests a
broader base of encouragement for the songs, and their increasing
preservation a more generally organized support. Favoring this probability is some very interesting evidence that the Franciscans openly
encouraged and sought to guide the *disciplinati* movement. Vincenzo
de Bartholomaeis writes that the Seraphic Order without doubt had
favored the flagellant movement from the beginning, organizing it
into stable companies—"bastera ricordare San Bonaventura." The
minstrels of the Lord, he writes, were not able to regard without sympathy anything which strengthened religious sentiment among the
people, and it is to their influence that he attributes preservation of
the lyric and dramatic manuscripts of Abruzzi.[11] And among the earliest of Franciscan songs are the two *laude* used by the flagellants in
Umbria who sang the praises of "San Francesco glorioso" as they
flailed each other through the dusty streets of Perugia.[12]

It seems evident, then, that although many spiritual and heretical
groups other than the Franciscans employed popular song in their
proselytizing activities, a chief reason for the survival of the lyrics is
the reclamation of much of this variegated tradition under the cloaks
of the Friars Minor.[13] It is in this perspective, too, that we should
evaluate the loose connection between the movement of St. Francis
and the rise of Italian vernacular poetry which has been asserted before
now: the following statement is typical of many which make St.
Francis midwife at the nativity of such poetry without considering
possible consequences of that fact for interpretation of the poetry. It
suggests, however, a point of enterprise:

Italian poetry in its beginnings does not offer much originality. The first great literary movement to define itself is religious, the Franciscan movement. The example of the sweet saint of Assisi gave birth to a lively enthusiasm, and his fiery songs of universal love became the model for a new literary genre which flourished all over Italy. This art form is naturally enough in its early stages unpolished. The oldest lyrics, as well as the most crude, are Umbrian. Along with St. Francis himself, it is necessary to cite the virulent Jacopone da Todi. But the majority of the lyrics which remain to us are anonymous.[14]

The effective anonymity of the Umbrian Franciscan poets to whom Henry Chazel here alludes has been one reason that comparatively little has been written about the purposes and method of early Franciscan poetry. Another reason, related to the "anonymity," is that most of the early Franciscan poets were apparently among the *spirituali*, the die-hard observers of the original Rule most of whose records have disappeared. Because of increasingly bitter disagreement between the observant Spirituals and the more lax Conventuals among the Franciscans, the Chapter at Paris in 1266 published a decree that all legends previous to Bonaventure's *Life* of St. Francis were to be destroyed. The Spirituals had based much of their literal interpretation of the Rule on certain injunctions by St. Francis recorded in earlier biographies, and presumably many of the lacunae in the Spirituals' history are due to the ordered suppression.[15]

At first, and for a long time, the *spirituali* were merely zealots opposed to affluence and to papal relaxation of the Rule and model of St. Francis. Their hopes for reformation were crushed by the deposition of the sympathetic John of Parma. Generally speaking, only after 1266 did theological differences, heresy, and real tribulation begin, with extreme persecution of the Spirituals until 1289, when with the election of Raymond Gaufridi as Minister General there followed a brief respite. But after the ascension of Clement V many Spirituals were put to torture under the name of Lombard heretics of the sect of Dolcino,[16] and though many individual Franciscans continued to prefer the ideal of a stricter observance the organizational strength of the zealot movement rapidly dissipated.[17]

Comparatively recently, however, some of the early Spirituals' writings have come to light. The most notable of these documents is the *Speculum perfectionis*, an early biography of St. Francis which Sabatier and others claim to be the earliest legend.[18] It is in this account that we get some idea of how St. Francis himself may have viewed the role of poetry and song within the order. Upon completing his own "Praise of Creatures," and teaching the brothers to sing it,

. . . his spirit was then in so great consolation and sweetness that he
wished to send for Brother Pacifico, who in the world used to be
called the King of Verses, and was a truly courteous teacher of singers,
and he wished some friars to be given to him that they should go
together with him through the world preaching and singing praises of
the Lord. For he said that he wished that he who knew how to preach
best among them should first preach to the people, and after the
preaching they should all sing together the praises of the Lord like
minstrels of the Lord.

But when the praises were finished, he wished that the preacher
should say to the people, "We are the minstrels of the Lord, and for
these things we wish to be paid by you, that is, that you should remain
in true penitence."[19]

Here are revealed a number of intriguing points. First, the Saint himself in at least one notable instance had directed the organization of
poetic means as an aid to the Franciscan ministry; second, he specified
its use in conjunction with preaching, each friar to attend to preaching or singing as his abilities suited; third, the songs were to be an
adjunct to the preaching or an expression of devotion; and fourth,
the songs should be consistent with the Friars' object of moving their
hearers toward penitence. In a consideration of their methodology,
this explicit wish of St. Francis for the brothers' use of poetry presents
a promising beginning.

Brother Pacifico, the poet delegated by St. Francis, is an intriguing
figure about whom too little is known. Born in Ascoli, he is identified
by some as William of Lisciano, who before becoming a Friar Minor
had been poet laureate at the court of Fredrick II in Sicily.[20] There
he was known as an "inventor canticum," and "princeps cantantium
lascivia," one who in songs of worldly love could "trop ben violar et
trobar et cantar."[21] It is perhaps significant that Pacifico was crowned
for his prowess in lyric verse; unlike his colleagues who were lauded
for "un'*orasione panegirica*," his crown was for "un 'carme' italiano
o sia cantico economastico, recitato dal nostro *Vuillielmo* poi Pacifico
poeta, quale nella sua eta avenzata fu frate e disceplo di S. Francesco."[22]
It has been suggested that he employed lyric techniques of the Provençal tradition, and that many early Italian poets who are cited as
of the "school of William" were his disciples. Eventually, he became
provincial minister of the Order in France.[23] But none of these things
interest us as much as his skill in the lyric (as opposed to other kinds
of verse), and his foray into France with Agnellus and other companions, presumably to employ this poetic form in spreading the

Franciscan message. There is certainly good evidence that the lyric form of the Italian confraternity poems made its way at this time into France; and in fact, it is lyric verse forms which seem everywhere in these areas to have been employed by Franciscan and confederate spiritual groups.[24] Yet Pacifico stands in shadows, a symbolic figure who evades substantial contact.

Beyond the injunction of St. Francis, his own poems, and incomplete information about Brother Pacifico, from the first thirty years of the history of the Order we have only fragmentary and circumstantial evidence to suggest the nature of Franciscan employment of lyric verse, and little of the verse itself. The trail begins to become much stronger only as we approach that period of chaos between the Great Alleluia of 1233 and the rise of the *disciplinati* in 1258, but then strong enough to raise the possibility of restoring a composite of Franciscan "literary" activity in the early years.

It was Sabatier who first suspected that the relationship between the Franciscans and other less orthodox spiritual groups was in some way related to a foundational confraternal movement, the Third Order of St. Francis,[25] though he did not develop his idea. Only recently, Professor Arnaldo Fortini has devoted an entire chapter of his book to tracing the many evidences for Franciscan presence in and control of many segments of the *disciplinati* movement.[26] His investigations have unearthed much information about the relationship of the Friars Minor to confraternity life in thirteenth-century Italy, and it is to his discoveries that the following paragraphs most owe their development.

When the Fourth Lateran Council forbade the formation of new religious orders in 1215, a tremendous multiplication of lay brotherhoods resulted.[27] Most of these centered their spiritual activity on worship and penance, and often the singing of religious songs was a particular object of their convocation. Fortini shows that the confraternities at Assisi with which he deals were notable for their activity in continuing the tradition of transferring vulgar lauds into vernacular sacred lauds in the manner begun earlier by Franciscans, but now with such prolixity as to give the process real impetus. In the case of the Assisan confraternities which he examines, verse-making and singing were the major functions of each group.[28] Elsewhere the pattern is the same. The confraternities grew rapidly. Margarita of Cortona, a Franciscan Tertiary, founded on the model of the Third Order the company of "Laudesi di Santa Maria in San Francesco" and the Fraternity of Saint Mary of Mercy, both of which were run by the Friars Minor. At Prato the Franciscans instituted the Confraternity of the

Holy Cross, which actually met in the friary, and similarly at Florence "La Societas laudum Sanctae Crucis." Later on, in 1325, the
"Fraternita e disciplina del beato sancto Francesco" was begun at
Orvieto by one Friar John of Pustierla, a Spiritual Franciscan. Fortini
lists more examples than are practical to record here.[29] While the specific details of Franciscan participation in the development of confraternities is more often apparent by implication than by detailed demonstration in the original records, the overall picture shows the unmistakable persistence of Franciscan influence, and notably in the contexts suggested by the Third Order Rule, which in certain cases is
the direct basis for a foundation of a confraternity. An example of
this is the mother and head church of the Order, San Francesco of
Assisi, where an association of Tertiaries who had secured themselves
some notice toward the end of 1304 transformed themselves into a
true confraternity which felt no need of founding itself on new statutes, but simply followed the rule of the Third Order.[30]

The confraternity of S. Stephano illustrates the way in which one
confraternity developed. Its genesis dates back to 1260, at the height
of *disciplinati* fervor, when it seems to have been itself functioning
as perhaps one of the oldest companies of *disciplinati* under Franciscan
influence, and concerned with typical *laudesi* activity. In the late
thirteenth century a reorganization took place, in which continuance
of the same interests was specified: "raccogliersi nell' oratorio per dis-
ciplinarsi, celebrare la Passione di Nostro Signore, ecc."[31] A notable
difference was the slightly more outward-looking attitude reflected in
the development of hospitals; the texts of their prayers show this
broadened concern as well. But the emphasis still remained the spiritual life, and particularly evangelical concern for those in mortal sin.

The concern of the confraternity with penitence is also emphasized
in their recorded prayer life, and consistently echoed in their poetry.[32]
Strangely enough, in the particular case of S. Stephano, some of the
earliest poetry is in Latin, though showing "il contenuto, i caratteri,
il ritmo . . . di esse con le più antiche laude in volgare." Exemplary
is an early Passion poem attributed to the confraternity.[33] The expression of confraternal spirituality in similar poems, mostly vernacular,
is virtually universal, and follows the typical emphases of Franciscan
spiritual influence. It is interesting that one Franciscan-organized
confraternity, that of S. Antonio, in explicitly commanding its members to write poetry went so far as to stipulate that all communication
should be in the medium of verse.[34] But the main focus of the verse
turned outward: "True *ioculatores Domini*, they were fully successful
in a program of adaptation and utilization of secular poetic forms
for their purpose of propaganda for the salvation of souls." The adap-

tation of popular songs to religious purposes was directed towards evangelical ends, and in the vigorous pursuit of poetry as means, "Questo della poesia era come un commandamento della regola, al quale tutti obbedivano, dal Generale fino all'ultimo laico."[35]

There remains a group of Franciscan lauds which apparently were directed to meditation and devotion, and which were calculated for less intense uses of worship than most of the penitentially motivated lyrics. The meditational style generally characterizes the famous Cortonese lauds, which, while they have been known for some time as *disciplinati* songs, have not generally been credited with Franciscan authorship. However, the codex of the poems belonged to the Franciscan friary at Cortona, and dates from the time of its foundation by Brother Elias, whose particular influence as a poet-singer has been suggested as formative for the Cortonese manuscripts.[36] Internal evidence also points convincingly to Franciscan authorship.[37] Fernando Liuzzi, in his *La Lauda e i primordi della melodia italiana*, characterizes the particular attention paid to the beauty of the musical effect intended by the authors of the Cortonese lyrics:

> With a free and clear modulation in voice as if for an idyll, in love with its own pristine juvenescence . . . the melody of the lauds often rises in a slow wave, full and solemn, heavy with voices gathered in magnificent unison, and the sober rhythm, the vigorous scansion, the solemn intonation and the flowing of the notes closes like a circle round the thought, which intensifies itself and ascends to heaven.[38]

Professor Liuzzi finds the Cortona lyrics profoundly meditative, not liturgical, but completely filled with mystic adoration, and he sees in such songs a clear index of the lyrical tension which appealed to and was produced by the religious consciousness of the confraternities. He also thinks that in them may be discovered what he calls "individual feeling." While his "sentimento individuale" might be a slightly romantic projection, it is nevertheless true that many of the poems show a marked tendency to concern themselves with inner rather than objective reality, to be brief, earthy, and direct, and to evince a strongly emotional rather than purely intellectual response. As much as in anything else, this focus reveals itself in a remarkable force of direction, one which is asserted in increasing degrees of intensity. Following are some examples from the Cortonese meditational lauds.

> Ben è crudele e spietoso
> ki non si move a gran dolare
> de la pena del salvatore
> che di noi fo sì amoroso.

Amoroso veramente
fo di noi cum gram pietanca,
poi ke d'alt' onnipotente
discese ad nostra semblanca.

Or non fo grande disianca
per noi prender humanitate
et darsi in altrui podestade
quei k'è sovr' ogne poderoso?

(Liuzzi, 1: 351–52)

[Really cruel and merciless is he who would not be moved to great anguish for the pain of the Savior, who loved us so completely. He truly loved us with such great compassion that he who was all-powerful lowered himself to our likeness. Wasn't that a great love-longing, to take on himself our human nature and to yield himself to human power, he who is the most powerful of all?]

Spirito sancto da servire
dann'al core de te sentire.

Spiritu di veritade
e fontana de bonitade
per la tua benignitade
la tua via ne fa seguire.

(Liuzzi, 1: 387)

[Holy Spirit, for your service grant our hearts to feel your presence. Spirit of Truth and Fountain of Goodness, for the sake of your bounty make us to follow your way.]

These examples are much more tranquil than some of the appeals to penance we shall examine, and reflect a more devotional intention. Thus the burden of one Cortonese Franciscan carol.

Venite a laudare, per amore cantare
l'amorosa vergine Maria,[39]

[Come to praise, to sing your love for the Virgin Mary]

is a more gentle invocation than that in some Franciscan lyrics which seek radical identification in the dramatic spectacle where

De la crudel morte de Cristo
on' hom pianga amaramente.

(Liuzzi, 1:355)

[For the cruel death of Christ let everyone weep bitterly.]

Yet both are registers of the same Franciscan poetic voice, and both ultimately turn to one objective. The poem "Venite a laudare" subtly but surely indicates the ultimate aim of the *pietosa vergine:*

> Cortese ke fai grandi doni,
> l'amor tuo mai non ci abandoni:
> pregán-te che tu ne perdoni
> tutta la nostra villania.
>
> Villania peccatori semo stati
> amando la carne e li peccati:
> viden ke n'à 'l mondo engannati:
> defendane la tua gran bailia.

(Liuzzi, 1:258)

[Courteous lady so bounteous, may your love never abandon us; we pray you forgive us all our villainy. We have been most hardened sinners, loving the sins of the flesh: we see that the world has taken us in; may your power preserve us.]

In any number of examples one might care to examine simple evangelical purposes prevail. Whether accomplished by stark, raw dramatic confrontation with the crucifixion, or evoked through more subtly aroused emotional and psychological identification with the scene of the Passion, the evident object of Franciscan poets is to produce a contritional response in preparation for penance. The performance context of the lauds solidly supports the content of the lyrics and demonstrates that the commandment of St. Francis to his followers was indeed obeyed.

The early Franciscan and confraternity lauds were sung not only in flagellant processions, but were used for worship, for private devotion, for joyous celebration, and probably in certain cases were even sung as lullabies.[40] But the indications are that their most important use was the one which St. Francis initially commanded—as an aid to preaching. This is strongly suggested by a number of considerations. In record after record, friars who are listed as good singers and composers are noted also as good preachers, in such a way as to make the talents appear compatible and mutually useful. Salimbene in his *Chronica* lists many of his friends who excelled in both achievements, mostly fellow-Italians, Spirituals, and often Joachites—but also one foreigner, Brother Walter, an Englishman, devout, well-mannered, and learned.[41] Ugo Panziera di Prato, the most important Italian Franciscan poet after Jacopone da Todi, also had established his reputation as a preacher.[42] Another of Salimbene's friends conveniently illustrates the readiness with which a talented Franciscan preacher might seize upon an opportunity: Brother Henry of Pisa was

> a great preacher of great weight and favor with both clergy and people . . . skilled to write music, to compose the most sweet and delightful songs, both in harmony and in plainsong. He was a marvellous singer . . . devoted to God and the Blessed Virgin . . . . Having heard a certain maid-servant tripping through the cathedral church of Pisa and singing in the vulgar tongue,

> > "Es tu[d] no cure de me,
> > e no curaro de te,"

> he then made, after the pattern of that song, words and music of this hymn following:

> > "Christe Deus, Christe meus
> > Christe rex et domine."[43]

And the adaptations were most often put to use by the preacher-singers, or in many cases, by Franciscan preachers who employed singing brothers when their own talent was lacking, as an aid to their preaching.

Franciscan preachers like St. Bernardino of Siena were immensely successful in directing their sermons toward moral instruction, popular devotion, and penitence. Theological obscurities were not very popular with the friars or their audiences. Like Chaucer's Parson, St. Bernardino avers that his audience should not be surprised if he does not always speak about the letter of the Gospel, which is like the rind outside the fruit; it is sufficient, he says, for his audience to have the marrow and whatever is inside.[44] In other words, his concern was with the "sentence" of Scripture. Yet in order to hold the attention of his listeners as he expounded on the "marrow," Bernardino was given to ingenious and novel devices. Contemporary biographers describe his powers of dramatization as marvelous. We have descriptions of him arm-waving, play-acting, and singing, mimicking personal foibles and even the sounds and behavior of chickens and pigs.[45] More to our interest, he employed vernacular lyrics as preaching aids. In one manuscript of his sermons, MS. Ashburham 150, are quoted numerous verses attributed to Jacopone da Todi, including

Amor de caritate,
Perché m à sĩ ferito?
Yhesu sperancia mya
Ormay ucidemy in amore.[46]

[Charitable love, why have you wounded me so? Jesus my hope, now
slay me with love.]

In concluding the last sermon, "De Amore Dei" (fol. 376v), Bernardino
says, "Ultimo oro ut sim vobiscum ligatus et vos mecum cum cantena
sincere caritas in Christo Ihesu . . . ." Other preachers would employ
the services of a singer like Brother Vita, who had his own range of
special effects[47] which, together with the appeal of his song in general,
was sufficient on one occasion to cause a nun "to throw herself from
a window that she might follow him; but this might not be, for she
broke her leg with the fall."[48] Salimbene, to his credit as a practical
critic, seems to have had considerable appreciation for the potency of
his friend's talent.

The general effect of the Franciscan preaching style was remarkable. Even if St. Bernardino of Siena is a somewhat extraordinary
example because of his spectacular popularity, he nevertheless reflects
the effect that Franciscan preachers in general tended to have on their
audiences. Moving from town to town in one, two, or sometimes six-
week stands, he would preach penitential and moral sermons to crowds
which could number in excess of sixty thousand people.[49] Similar
followings are recorded for other Franciscan preachers, such as St.
Anthony and Berthold von Regensburg. As a result of his appeals
great bonfires crackled, created to burn playing cards, dice, ornaments,
hairpieces, and other means and symbols of vice. New laws would
often go into effect while a sermon course was still in progress, legis-
lating against blasphemy, sodomy, card-playing, excessive dowries—
even against silk dresses or over-lengthy hoods for men—and in one
town every citizen under fifty years of age was required to find employment. Everywhere the Franciscan preachers traveled, thousands upon
thousands were persuaded to contrition and repentance.[50]

In view of St. Francis' original injunction in the *Speculum perfectionis* we might expect to discover on this path some poems and
songs reflective of the style and concerns of Franciscan preaching. As
we shall see in the rest of this chapter, that reasonable expectation
is not to be disappointed. Very many songs which would be entirely
appropriate to provoking a contritional attitude or sealing a penitential response to a sermon are to be found in Franciscan manuscripts in Italy. Often the appeal is forthright:

Et però tuctu pecchaturj,
retornatj, de bun core,
ad Jhesu nostro criatorj.
Chiascheun sia deliberato.

Et a chiascheun sia palese
che aparve nel contà d'Asese
Christo, che in croce se stese.
Ne faccia el core humiliato!

(Fortini, p. 38)

[Therefore, all you sinners, go back with willing heart to Jesus our
creator. Let everybody be firm in his own mind. Let it be perfectly
clear that Christ who stretched himself to the cross showed himself
in the region of Assisi. Let this cause our hearts to be humble.]

Here the exemplarism so soon applied to the hagiography of St. Francis
is already part of the penitential song. In other cases, the poem may
extend to a simple, practical recommendation:

Madonna Santa Maria
mercé de noi peccatori;
faite prego al dolce Cristo
ke ne degia perdonare.

....

Peccatori abhominati,
pensiam li nostri peccati:
taupinelli, andate al padre
metteteve 'n suo iudicare.

....

Penetentia penetentia
domandâla con reverentia:
omgn'om pensi la sententia
ke non se dia mai revocare.[51]

[Holy Mother Mary, have mercy on us sinners; pray to the sweet
Christ that he will forgive us. . . . Abominable sinners, let's think about
our sins; wretched that you are, go to the priest, put yourself under
his rule. . . . Penance, penance, let us ask for it with reverence; everyone consider the sentence which can never be revoked.]

Such a lyric might serve as a basis for a penitential sermon in itself,
or, as in an interesting sermon of the most famous popular preacher
in Germany, Franciscan Friar Berthold von Regensburg (d. 1272),[52] the
homiletical springboard might be a devotional laud. Berthold's ser-

mons present an interesting parallel to Bernardino's. In one of them he introduces the following piece,

> Nû biten wir den heilegen geist
> umbe den rehten glouben, aller meist,
> daz er uns behuete wol am ende,
> so wir heim suln varn von disem ellende.

Kyrie eleyson; des helfe uns der vater und der sun und der heilige geist,[53]

and then in another sermon develops his entire discourse around it as framework.

Berthold demonstrates in more than one instance that the injunction of St. Francis was taken seriously fairly early by Franciscan preachers, and elsewhere than in Italy. In the middle of a sermon in which he has built upon the history, legend, and romance of Alexander to support his theological points, he sets out to provide his hearers with criteria by which they can discern heretical from orthodox preachers, so as not to be deceived. Someone in the audience appears to have found the elaborated distinctions confusing, and wished simpler guides whereby truth might be known from falsehood. Berthold's response was to formulate "test words," or doctrines: "Mark these words," he says, "I wish indeed that songs were sung about them. If there are any composers here who can sing new songs about them, take heed of these words exactly and make the songs. And you will be doing well thereby. Make them short and easily understandable so that any child can learn them well. For thus can the people learn and have less trouble remembering."[54] If Berthold's cry for help sounds like something a Waldensian preacher might have said seventy-five years earlier, it is also completely in accord with the expressed wishes of St. Francis, and in fact, in this instance, was directed toward countering German equivalents of the Waldensians and Italian spiritual groups who likewise were employing songs very effectively in a proselytizing campaign—the *Geissler*.[55]

The picture of a Franciscan preacher and his assistants standing on a street corner or market square and gustily singing vernacular religious lyrics to popular tunes in order to attract crowds for a penitential sermon is not the only one which we get from the early records. For example, it is clear that the composers, performers, and preachers did not always sing alone and that frequently the audience might be invited to join in. This was particularly true of those lauds which

were part of confraternity celebrations. One document of an early
confraternity in Assisi reveals the following procedure. After a few
prayers, the brothers assist in singing the lesson, which ends with an
extended *pater noster*, and at intervals between phrases—e.g., "Lead
us not into temptation; but deliver us from evil"—might have responsory pauses in which the brothers could rise to sing a popular or
vernacular song of praise. The text is worth a full citation in the
original:

> . . . statim minister cum disciplina omnium fratrum absolute dicat:
> Pater noster. Et ne nos inducas in tentazionem. R/. Sed libera nos a
> malo, quo dicto in silentium ad signum campanelle vel aliud signum
> disciplina quiescat et immediate surgat debens laudes vulgares cantare,
> qui cantando illas ex devotione moveat corda fratrum ad planctum
> et lacrimas intendentium magis ad verba quam ad vocem. Laudes
> autem huiusmodi tali ordine disponantur quia diebus veneris vel
> aliis quibus de paxione ageretur vel dispositis passioni, cantentur
> laudes de paxione Salvatoris nostri Yesus, et mestissime matris eius.
> Sed diebus dominicalibus et festivis et quocumque alio tempore can-
> tentur laudes diei vel festi si de festo agitur disciplina vel alias secun-
> dum diei devotionem vel solemnitatis festi et temporis dispositionem
> et in cantu cuiuslibet stantie seu versus, si disciplina nunc agitur in
> vestibus sacci, finita stantia sive versu fiat disciplina, sed dum cantor
> cantaverit laudes, ad sonum campanelle vel aliud signum surgens,
> disciplina quiescat et sic prosequatur et fiat donec laudes predicte
> complete fuerint per cantorem. Laudibus vero completis cantor ipsarum
> ad suum locum revertatur et disciplina fiat spatio unius pater noster in
> silentio dicendi per omnes.[56]

Here are revealed, in fact, a number of interesting features. First, the
song in question occurred as part of a larger worship ceremony; second, its function is openly stated to be the moving of the hearts of
the brothers "ad planctum et lacrimas"; third, the lauds involved deal
principally with the Passion of Christ and the attitude of the Virgin to
effect this response; fourth, the songs are said to be used on a variety
of occasions. But most interesting of all is the manner in which the
songs were performed. The *cantor* intones the *stantia* and the others
respond by singing what is called the *versus,* and then the process is
repeated. If the bell sounds, there is a brief silence, then the song
resumes in the alternating verse/stanza routine as before.

Now this routine is fascinating in view of the preponderant carol
stanza form of early Franciscan poetry which we have commented
on before. This stanza, known in Italy as the *ballata*, is usually com-

posed of a two-line burden, $X\ X$, and several four-line stanzas, rhymed
$a\ a\ a\ b$ or $a\ a\ a\ X$, etc. Deriving from Provençal and perhaps ultimately
Arabic verse forms,[57] it plays the prominent part in Italian vernacular
lyric poetry, is the prevalent verse form in Italian Franciscan poetry,[58]
and is, interestingly enough for our purposes, a dominant verse form
among Middle English lyrics.[59] The most important species of this
particular form, usually called "carol" by English scholars, has been
frequently associated with the ring-dance, in which cantor and followers would sing stanza and burden *(versus)* in much the same alternating manner as described in the directions to the confraternity at
Assisi. Richard Greene has given particular attention to the dance-
connections of the carol form in his edition of Middle English carols,[60]
but to this point, no one seems to have discovered any record of
carol performance which would indicate the relationship of supposed
popular folk-dance ritual to the performance context of religious
lyrics adapted from its tunes. It is my belief that the performance
record of the Franciscan confraternity at Assisi offers an indication
that in at least some instances the verse form was preserved integrally
with the singing customs associated wtih it. Moreover, the pedagogical
and psychological potential of such a performance manner for the
vernacular lyrics is highly compatible with the purposes to which we
have seen it to be directed.

In fact, the indications are that the popular dance to which a
majority of lauds owed their form and tunes may have contributed
its physical movements to some performances of the lauds as well.
It is worth remembering that in the Middle Ages the dance was still
a part of the liturgy, and dancing around the altar as a liturgical
exercise was not unknown.[61] A positive distinction was made between
the sensual dance, and that of the spirit, the new dance, which was
associated with biblical precedents like that of David dancing for
spiritual joy around the Ark of the Covenant. In the early biographies
of the Franciscan movement we also find this distinction.[62] The verb
used to indicate the dancing is *salire,* which signifies the movement
of the dance. The same verb is used to describe certain actions of
Francis when preaching before the Pope and cardinals. On this occasion, Celano reports, the Saint was so filled with the love of God that
his words turned to poetry, and as he spoke he began to dance the
divine dance: "Pedes quasi saliendo movebat, non ut lasciviens, sed
ut igne divini amoris ardens."[63] The close relationship of the popular
song forms employed by Franciscans to the dance calls forth the possibility that the distinction between worldly and divine kinds of
dancing, as with worldly and spiritual songs, may have related to

content and purpose and not to the forms in themselves; it also suggests that, if we had more actual records of performance, we might in fact find the actions of the dance as easily adapted to religious use as its tunes. Another hint in this direction comes from recent studies of the *Tripudanti*, a confraternity who seem to have frequently engaged in mass spiritual dancing through the streets, much in the same fashion as the *disciplinati* and Franciscan confraternities would parade through the streets, singing lauds.[64] It is certain that at least one Franciscan, Englishman Roger Bacon, argued forcefully that dancing, like music and singing, was a legitimate and valuable instrument for inculcating the faith.[65] As to the music, Professor Liuzzi has seen strong connections between the melodies of lyrics in the Cortona codex and dance songs.[66] One fascinating thirteenth-century lyric set to a dance tune (though not in the more popular *X X, a a a X* measure) is prefaced "D'alquanti spirituali li quali in fervore di spirito dancaro":

> Nollo pensai giamai
> Jesu   di dançare alla dança
> ma lla tua innamoranca
> Jesu   ci farà giocondare.
>
> Nollo arei pensato
> ch'adivenir potesse
> d'essere si 'nfiammato
> ch'io mi ci aprendesse;
> ma ll'amor del beato
> si mmi sforcò et disse
> ch'io non mi sottraesse
> di dançare alla dança:
> nella tua innamoranca
> Giesu   ci farai giocondare.
>
> Non vi maravigliate
> se alla dança dançai;
> colli dolci mie' frati
> si mmi mossi e andai,
> poi dissi: "Innamorati,
> non dancate ora mai"—
> Gia non mi ricordai
> s'i' fu' entrato alla dança:
> tanto sentì' allegrança
> Jesu   non si potria contare.
>
> Non si poria contare
> lo diletto di mente;

lo figlio di Maria
sì llo dà certamente.
Homo non ne saria
sança saggio credente:
et pero tutta gente
pregar voglio per Deo
che col dolce amor meo
Jesu   lingua nol puo parlare.

O voi che riprendete
di dançare alla dança,
per Dio or vi prendete
ancor vi sia pesança:
et poi assaggerete
quant'e l'amorosanca
che vien da Cristo amança.
Quell' amoroso gioco
che cci s'aprend'a un foco,
Jesu   che tutti ci faccia infiammare.

O Christo mio cortese,
tu che se' gioa compita,
dalle gravose offese
si nne scanpa e aita
che vengnamo alle prese
della superna vita,
dove is truova unita
dancan per li beati:
tanto sono infiammati
Jesu   lingua nol quo parlare.

(Liuzzi, 1: 215)

[I never thought, Jesus, to dance in the Dance; but your loving, Jesus, will make us go rejoicing. I would never have thought that it would be possible to be so enflamed that I would catch fire; but the love of the blessed ravished me utterly and said that I shouldn't hold back from dancing in the Dance. In your loving, Jesus, you will make us go rejoicing. Don't be surprised if I dance the Dance; with my sweet *frati* I began, I joined in and I said: "Lovers, stop dancing now!" I didn't even remember that I had joined the Dance; so happy I felt, Jesus, that I couldn't express it. It would be impossible to tell the mind's delight; (but) certainly the Son of Mary gives it. One wouldn't believe this without proof. And therefore I want to beg everybody for God's sake that they will let me dance this way with my sweet lover Jesus. O you who criticize dancing in the Dance, for God's sake, join hand in hand—even if it displeases you—and then you will taste how much is the loving which comes from Christ's love. May that loving

play which catches us all up as one flame set us all on fire—Jesus! O my
Christ *courtois*, you who are complete joy, from egregious offense save
and help us when we come to the point of the life beyond, where one
finds the unified dance of the blessed who are so enflamed, Jesus,
that no tongue can express it.]

Here there is no absolute distinction between physical and spiritual,
temporal and eternal experience. The dance in which the *frati* participate is only the beginning of the Dance of Dances, which reaches its
climax in the Dance of the Blessed around the Throne in the New
Jerusalem. This, one is reminded, accords with what St. Bernardino
later said about earthly and divine canticles, that earthly singing
should be a preparation for the songs of the blessed in Paradise,[67]
and to be invited to enter upon the new dance is to be invited to
the new spiritual life which is eternal: the dance is the Dance of Life.
Jacopone da Todi writes that whoever enters upon this dance finds
love and, even for those who increase the dancers' "humility," pardon
in abundance:

> Chi vole entrare en questa danza,
> trova amore d'esmesuranza:
> cento dì de perdonanza
> a chi li dice villania.[68]

[He who wants to join this dance will find love beyond measure: one
hundred days of indulgence to those who insult him.]

In the "nollo pensai" lyric above there is a clear distinction drawn
between two dances. One is tempted to think of the Dance of Death
or *danse macabre* in these contexts, and not without cause. In the
Cortona MS. 91 occurs a poem: "La Morte," which has already been
seen by one little-heeded scholar as pertinent to the history of the
Dance of Death.[69] In dance-carol form, it reveals a striking similarity
to *danse macabre* themes and verses discussed by James M. Clark.[70]
The poem, to which there are parallels in English, runs as follows,

> Chi vuol lo mondo disprecare
> sempre la morte de' pensare.
>
> La morte e fiera et dura e forte,
> rompe mura e passa porte;
> ell' e si comune sorte
> che verun ne puo campare.

Tutta gente in gran tremore
vive sempre con timore
inpercio che son sicure
di passar per questo mare.

Papa co imperadori,
cardinali et gran signori,
giusti et sancti et peccatori
fa la morte raguagliare.

La morte viene come furone
spoglia l'uomo come ladrone,
satolli et freschi fa digiuni
et la pelle rimutare.

Non riceve donamenti,
le ricche ce à per neente,
amici non vuole ne parenti
quando viene al separare.

Contra lei non vale forteça
sapientia né belleçça
torri et palagi et grandeça
tutte le fa abandonare.

A l'om ch'è ricco e bene asciato,
a l'usurier, che mal fo nato,
molto è amaro questo dettato,
chi non se vole emendare.

A li giusti è gran sollaccio,
quando vien la morte vaccio:
remane 'n terra el corpo marcio,
l'anima con Dio va a stare.

Peccatori, or ritornate,
li peccati abbandonate,
della morte ripensate,
che non vi trovi folleggiare.

A te, segnore accomandata
l'anima ch'e trapassata
e la vergine beata
a te la deggia apresentare.[71]

[He who wishes to despise the world must always think of death. Death is fierce, wicked, and grievous, shatters the walls and smashes the doors; she is such a common fate that no one can escape her. Everybody, trembling, lives always in great terror because they are sure that they will have to pass by these waters. Pope and emperor, cardinals and great seigneurs, just and holy ones and sinners too, Death levels them all. Death comes as a thief, robs everybody like a burglar, starves the well-fed and shrivels their skin. She is not bought off; she considers riches as nothing; friends and relations are of no use when the time of separation comes. Against her, strength is useless: neither wisdom, nor beauty, towers, palaces, nor high status—she makes all to be abandoned. What I have said is very bitter for the man who is rich and well off and for the wretched usurer who doesn't want to mend his ways. To the just it is great solace when Death comes nigh: the rotten body remains on the earth while the soul goes to live with God. Sinners, now come back; abandon your sins; think about Death so that she won't find you (living it up).]

In the same manuscript, to which Liuzzi assigns a compilation date between 1260 and 1297,[72] is an interesting illumination which, though it is not itself a Dance of Death, may relate to the development of the Dance of Death sensibility—which begins much earlier than the early fifteenth century suggested by Clark.[73] One of the three major illuminations in MS. Cortona 91, it is situated at the beginning of the laud just quoted, and shows the confrontation of three young nobles on horseback with a friar who is pointing to three corpses, in open coffins, in progressively more advanced states of corruption (Plate 5).[74] This, of course, is a reference to the familiar legend of "The three living and the three dead."[75] *La Morte*, notably, is in the $X X, a a a X$ form, as is the great and vivid death poem of Jacopone da Todi, "Quando t'aliegri" (*Lauda* XXV), which makes the same point in its burden:

> Quando t'aliegri, omo de altura,
> va' pone mente a la sepultura.

[When you rejoice, haughty man, go and think about the grave.]

We do know that the Franciscans had a great deal to do with the Dance of Death tradition. The *Danse macabre* of the Innocents, the *Bello della morte*, the *Augsburg Dance of Death* and most other expressions of this theme evidence Franciscan authorship and/or provenance.[76] In the Dance portrayed in the cloisters of the Innocents at Paris, Franciscans are the *predicateurs* who draw the moral both in the picture and in the verses underneath, and Death is made to be the mouthpiece of the Franciscan friar. The use to which the poems might be put by the Franciscans and others of compatible spiritual style is clear both from the poems themselves, and from the accounts. For example:

Plate 5. The Three Living and the Three Dead; "Chi vuol lo mondo" (MS. Cortona 91)

in 1429 . . . Friar Richard of the Franciscan Order preached at the Innocents on a high platform, with his back turned to the charnel houses . . . "at the place of the *Danse macabre.*" The sermons of Friar Richard were apocalyptic. He announced the approaching coming of Antichrist and the end of the world. Five or six thousand people are said to have flocked to hear him; gaming tables, cards, and women's finery were cast into the flames.[77]

Here we have another St. Bernardino: the point of the Franciscan's style was, as in the *Danza de la muerte*, "Since the friar has preached to you/ That you should all go to do penance."[78] The Cortona poem clearly had the same object, related in the same way to the spiritual dances, and would readily fit into Franciscan penitential programs.

In short the spiritual aspect of the dance, both as metaphor and as practice, is a highlight of late medieval spirituality. Johann Bischoff, a Viennese Franciscan writing in the year 1400, states that at Easter dancing was very popular among all classes of people; in beginning a list of twenty dances he says: "The first is that in which Christ leads his elect to eternal life, who have kept the Ten Commandments. The second dance is that of the Devil, who leads his own to eternal suffering, who have been transgressors of the Ten Commandments."[79] Unfortunately Bischoff never got to the other eighteen; if he had, I think that we might have discovered some very interesting things about medieval carols and dances. In any case, in the distinction between the new and the old dances, parallel to that between the new and the old songs, no one could lay claim with the Franciscans to having done so much to turn the old dance and old song of flesh and death to lyric formulations expressing the new harmony of spirit and life.

> O novo canto,   c'hai morto el pianto
> de l'omo enfermato,

[O new song, which has quelled the plaint of fallen man]

sings Jacopone da Todi,[80] and the singers of Cortona, in one of their many references to the new song, reply in tripartite harmony:

> Canto novello e versi co laudore
> cantiam di puro core   a l'amorose
> di Cristo spose   vergine beate.[81]

[A new song and verses of praise let us sing with pure heart, blessed virgins, to the loving bride of Christ.]

In similar vein, one pointed lyric speaks of spiritual dancing and points in evangelical terms to the ever-present pragmatic considerations involved in the theme of such songs:

cioe Cristo, cui tengno nelle braccia,
per contemplar m'avaccia ad dansare.
Ad dansare m'infiammo tutto quanto
com'io in questo canto vo' mostrare;
ch'i' ballo, canto et rido con gran pianto,
tutto quanto mi sento trasformare;
quando il dilecto soprabbonda tanto
che per amor fa canto rinnovare,
tant'e 'l mio core nell'amore eterno
non posse dello 'nferno dubitare.

(Liuzzi, 1: 216–17)

[He who I hold in my arms is Christ. In order to look at him I am urged to dance—to dance, I am all inflamed, as I want to show in this song. So I dance, sing, and laugh with great weeping, completely transformed in my feelings; as the delight overflows so much that the song is renewed by love, my heart is so plunged in eternal love that it is not able to doubt hell fire (either).]

The concern of the fraternal poets seems to be persistently with the inner spiritual life of hearers of their songs—and, for that matter, with that of the singers as well. For example, in one long piece entitled "l'Anima parlare con la Ragione," an invitation to those who wish to sing along is interposed:

Chi vole audire o legere o cantare
tucto lo core se debbia renovare,
nullo amor carnale in se lassare;
poi venga ad audire securamente.[82]

[He who wants to listen, read, or sing must renew all his heart and put away from himself carnal love. Then let him come and he will truly hear.]

The song to which the singer is invited is clearly not only the literal song being sung, but also the spiritual New Song as opposed to the Old Song of sin and death, the song of divine rather than cupiditous love.[83] If a man wishes to sing he ought to renew his whole heart, since only when carnal love is extirpated may one hear clearly. The hearing involved is spiritual, akin to the spiritual seeing which is the motif of the Franciscan poem about the miracle of Oliva,[84] and gives rationale to the choice of the adverb *securamente*. No one who remains tone-deaf through addiction to carnal love may sing his part in the new harmony.[85]

In respect of all of this evidence from the annals of the Italian Order, the value which Franciscan friars placed upon the lyric as a devotional and evangelical tool can hardly be overemphasized. The nature of their valuation is manifest in the content of the lyrics, in the historical contexts of lyric performance, and in their use of song as a metaphor for the whole Franciscan evangelical endeavor. St. Anthony of Padua, commenting upon the text of Isaiah 23:16, was unwittingly consistent with the Franciscan program for the adaptation of popular song. His text read: "Take a harp, go about the city . . . sing well, sing many a song, that you may be remembered." St. Anthony adapted the text as follows:

> *Take a harp*, that is confession; *go about the city*, that is in your mind go about your life so that you turn over everything; *sing well* accusing yourself, *many songs* charging yourself, weeping, *so that you may be remembered* in the sight of God.[86]

In their setting the words of Isaiah refer to the restoration of Tyre; St. Anthony, however, fitted them into his theme of examination of conscience and confession of sin. The spirit of his exegesis was entirely appropriate to the methodology of his Franciscan brothers, who went through the streets of the city, singing many a song, urging the people to join in,

> Et da novo, con gran voce,
> ad Ihesu Cristo, che era in croce,
> tucte gridavano più feroce:
> "Misericordia del pecchare!"
>
> (Fortini, p. 29)

[And again, in a loud voice, to Jesus Christ who was on the cross, like everyone who was there the more fervently cry, "Have mercy on our sin!"]

Most of the medieval Italian lyric poets, like most Middle English poets, remain anonymous. In the case of the Italian Franciscans we have seen that part of this may be explained by their Spiritual leanings, and hence the shortage of records. But more applicable still is the conclusion of Professor Fortini that in the context of their work and mission, personal recognition for a lyric was relatively unimportant outside of the most immediate circles.[87] In fact, adaptation of popular song, as we have seen, could almost become the *opus die* of a given confraternal rule. A lack of concern for individual recognition is suggested by the facts that though we know the names of many Franciscan poets from Salimbene, he gives us none of their poems, and that for those very few poems of which we know the author, such as the *Paradiso e Inferno* by Giacomo da Verona, we know the poet's name only because it happens to occur in the poem.[88]

The most notable exception to this general rule is Jacopone da Todi, whose remarkably prolific talent and stubborn struggle with Pope Boniface won him mention in several contemporary accounts. Even here, however, one gets the impression that the writers looked upon Jacopone not as a poet, but as an austere moralist, model Spiritual, and observant of the Primitive Rule. Only one account, that of Bartholomew of Pisa, connects Jacopone with his songs.[89]

Jacopone's was an unusual spiritual autobiography, and he did not become a regular Franciscan in the usual way. For the first ten years after his celebrated conversion and before being admitted to the Order, he wore the habit of the Franciscan Tertiaries. One luminous (and humorous) detail from the records asserts that he had never washed or changed that original cloak, and that it was probably only by virtue of his poetry that he was admitted to the Order.[90] His early poems are associated with confraternity life, and "were probably sung by him in the course of his preaching"; many of his lauds are found in confraternity laudarios of the fourteenth century.[91] Though some of his poetry campaigns for *spirituali* causes (e.g., *Laude* **XXX, XXXII, LI, LII, LIX, LX**), a majority of his vernacular poems are more representative of what we might expect in a Franciscan poet. Out of these may be constituted two general groupings, the first representing his evangelical concern with penitence, the second appearing often as sermons or rhymed tracts on the Christian life and special Franciscan virtues. His poems proclaim a powerful emotional fervor, but also reveal an acute theological sensibility that is often more intellectually articulated than in more "popular" Italian Franciscan poetry of the thirteenth century.[92] He probably knew the works of Richard of St. Victor, St. Bernard, and particularly those of St. Bonaventure. At one time he lived in Assisi, and wrote there, and thus would have been directly influenced by the tradition of Assisan laud-makers.[93] He wrote frequently in the *ballata*, or carol form.[94] He was one of the most imitated poets of the Middle Ages. In short, though he actually wrote in two different styles—the one professional in the manner of the courtly Sicilian school, the other popular[95]—he is, by virtue of his associations as well as his reputation, useful for the purposes of illustrating something of the range and focus of Franciscan poetry in the thirteenth century.

As we have seen, one very dominant Franciscan concern is repentance, with emphasis on contrition and conformity to the Suffered-Christ.[96] We do not need to re-read the entire *Stabat mater* or the *Donna de Paradiso* (*Lauda* XCIII) of Jacopone to assure ourselves that he did not differ from other Franciscan poets in this respect; a brief recollection of one stanza from the *Stabat* can sustain comparative analysis with a number of other passages from his vernacular poetry. In the *Stabat* we read:

> Fac ut portem Christi mortem
> passionis eius sortem
>   et plagas recolere.
> Fac me plagis vulnerari,
> cruce fac inebriari,
>   in amore filii.[97]

[Make me to bear the death of Christ, his lot and passion, and renew in me his injuries. Cause me to be wounded with the wounds, the cross, and make me drunk with the love of your son.]

This cry for radical sharing in the Savior's passion occurs also in Jacopone's *Lauda* LXXXIII, "De l'amore de Cristo in Croce, e como l'anima desidera de morir con lui":

> O dolze amore,   c 'hai morto l'Amore
> prego che m'occide d'Amore.
> ....
> O croce, eo m'appico   e a te m'afficco,
> ch'eo gusti morendo la vita: . . . .[98]

[O sweet love, by which love was killed, I beg you to kill me with love. . . . O cross, I hang myself from you and affix myself to you in order that in dying I might taste life.]

The extension of this attitude to contrition is easily recognized in his *Lauda* XI, "De l'anima contrita de l'offesa di Dio," where the persona cries:

> Meglio è si tu me occide,
> che tu, Segnore, si offeso,

> ch'eo non m'emendo, già 'l vide;
> 'nante a far male so acceso;
> condanna ormai questo appeso
> ché so caduto nel banno![99]

[It is better if you kill me than for you to be offended, Lord. I have already realized that I am not amending myself; I am so prone to do evil. Condemn now this guilty sinner, who I know has been exiled.]

Jacopone also illustrates the Franciscan emphasis on the Savior's humanity, through which identification with Christ is made possible. It is thus that he shares with us in our predicament, and that we have double joy in his Incarnation:

> Fiorito è Cristo nelle carne pura
> or se ralegri l'umana natura.
>
> (*Lauda* C)

[Christ has blossomed in mere flesh; now let human nature rejoice.]

The fact of the Divinity's subjection to frail human nature is a source for amazement, but also a point of sympathetic contact:

> Accurrite, accurrite,   gente, co non venite?
> Vita etterna vedite   co la fascia legata.[100]

[Hurry, hurry! People, why don't you come? Look at eternal life wrapped up in swaddling clothes.]

> O dolce garzoncello,   en cor t'ho conceputo
> ed en braccia tenuto,   però sì grido: "Amore!"[101]

[O sweet little boy, in my body I have conceived you, and held you in my arms; that is why I cry "Love!"]

One confraternity poem, too long to be reproduced here, functions to identify Christ with wretched humanity, contrasting his human experience to the divine kingship which makes his suffering efficacious; like Jacopone's "Fac ut portem," it urges the reader/hearer to become so closely involved with the scene of the sacrifice that he will become drunk (*ennibrare*) with the Passion.[102]

We saw earlier that Friar John in his *Meditations* distinguished between two heights of mind, the intellectual and the affectual.[103] The intellect must be purged, he said, so that a man may understand, the affection so that he may will. Both are necessary for salvation, and both are illuminated in the person of Christ. In the same Italian Franciscan confraternity poem referred to above, the poet concludes:

Poi ke l'entelliecto è preso
de la grande esmesuranca,
l'amore vola ad exteso,
va montando in desianca;
adbraçando l'abundança,
l'amirança el fa piglare.[104]

[When the intellect is caught in the infinite, love flies to the limit; it
mounts in desire, embracing the fullness of things. Adoration makes
(the intellect) able to go beyond itself.]

But of the two heights of mind, the affectual is the harmonizing principle. So also with Jacopone:

Scienzia acquisita   assai pò contemplare
non pò l'affetto trare   ad essere ordenato;*
scienzia enfusa,   puoi che n'hai a gustare,
tutto te fa enfiammare   a essere ennamorato;
con Deo te fa ordenato,*   'l prossimo edificando
e te vilificando   a tenerte en veretate.[105]

[Acquired knowledge can contemplate a great deal (but) can't recom-
pose the emotions (italics mine). Knowledge granted by the Spirit,
once you have tasted it, will completely ignite you to be in love; it
puts you in harmony with God, edifying your neighbor, villifying yourself, and keeping you in the truth.]

When both intellect and affection are purged, the will is totally con-
quered by the Divine Love, which opens the way to a total response of
"mind, soul, and heart":

La Bontate enfinita   vol enfinito amore,
mente, senno e core   lo tempo e l'esser dato: . . . .[106]

[The infinite bounty wants infinite love, soul, mind, and heart, time
and dedication . . . .]

Or, as Jacopone puts it elsewhere:

Destenguese l'amore en terzo stato:
bono, meglio, summo sullimato;
lo summo sì vole essere amato
senza compagnia.[107]

---

* Ordenato in these two instances is a difficult word to translate. It implies, in
theological definition, a state of possession of the cardinal and theological virtues
(Ageno, p. 122, n.), but more simply it means a state of personal organization
of "right relationship" or "harmony with God."

[Love has three steps: good, better, and best. The Supreme Love must be loved exclusively.]

Here "lo summo" is both the feeling of love and its spiritual object: God is Love.

As we might expect, Italian Franciscans and their confrères wrote numerous poems reflecting on themes of the Apocalypse, anticipating its nearness.[108] But the point of most such poems, whether by Jacopone or by other Franciscan poets, seems to have been to express the urgency of repentance, and so apocalyptic themes are never far removed from the centrality of the Passion. A reasonably typical poem from the Cortona manuscript, which begins as follows,

> Troppo perde 'l tempo ki ben non t'ama
> dolè amor, Iesù, sovr'ogn'amore,[109]

[He who doesn't love you properly, above all other loves, wastes too much time, sweet love, Jesus]

finds relatives in Jacopone's own poems. But in one of these Jacopone moves easily from a sense of the end of all things to a participatory memory of the cross. In the voice of Christ:

> Ne lo sesto perdio el sonno,
> tenebroso vidde el monno:
> furome nimici entorno,
> volserme far desperare.
>
> La memoria m'adiutòne
> e de Deo me recordòne:
> lo mio cor se confortòne,
> e la croce volse abbracciare.[110]

[In the sixth hour I regained consciousness. I saw darkness in the world. I was surrounded by enemies who wanted me to despair. Memory aided me and reminded me of God; my heart was comforted and it wanted to embrace the cross.]

Other poems are directed at the conversion of heretics.[111] All of these correspond to the Franciscan evangelical and moral emphasis which is also their overriding spiritual and exegetical objective.

As we noted in chapter three, instruction in practical doctrine was a strong secondary concern of the Franciscans. Outstanding examples of poems which would fit conveniently into a program of doc-

trinal instruction and general spiritual edification are Jacopone's
laude on the Seven Deadly Sins (XIV, "La superbia de l'altura"), on
Chastity (XXVIII, "O castitate, fiore"), on the Lord's Prayer (XLIV,
"En sette modi"),[112] on the Cardinal Virtues (XX, "Alte quattro
virtute"); his allegory "L'omo fo creato virtuoso" (*Lauda* XLIII);
and the two poems on the Incarnation beginning "O Cristo onnipotente" (*Laude* XL, XLI).[113] Two very effective lauds champion the
sacraments of confession and eucharist.[114] More than any other
group of Jacopone's poems, those given to doctrinal instruction employ allegorical techniques and invite a more tutored exegesis or exfo-
liation. The same is true of this type in other Franciscan and confraternal poems. Some even elaborate specific doctrine, as in the following
praise of the Trinity from MS. Cortona 91, which reads as though it
were a poetic translation of Robert Grosseteste's *Dictum* 60:

> Alta trinita beata
> da noi sempre si' adorata.
>
> ....
>
> Quando vidde tre figure
> adorò un creatore;
> e 'mpercio da te, segnore,
> la so fe' fo confirmata.
>
> En tutte le creature
> Sì reluce 'l tuo splendore
> come dicon le scripture
> et è verita provata.
>
> La potença in creando,
> sapienca in ordinando,
> bonità in gubernando
> ogne cosa tutta fiata—
>
> Tu padre celestiale
> per lor guardar d'ogne male
> o filioli a te uguale
> mandast' a la gente insanata.
>
> (Liuzzi, 1: 391–92)

[Most blessed Trinity, by us always so much adored. . . . When (Abraham) saw the *figura* he worshipped a creator; and therefore by you,
Lord, his faith was confirmed. So in all creatures may your splendor
be reflected, as the scriptures say, and true experience proves: the
power in creation, the wisdom in ordering, the goodness in governing,
everything complete— You, celestial father, sent to demented men the
Son in your own likeness to protect them from every evil.]

Such poems of doctrinal instruction fit into the category urged by Berthold von Regensburg,[115] and are supplemented by other poems which lend themselves to a more strictly homiletic usage. The doctrinal category is to be found in Franciscan manuscripts everywhere, along with poetic aids to moral preaching closely corresponding to the following sermonette on watchfulness over the senses:

> Guarda che non caggi, amico,
>   guarda!
>
> Or te guarda dal Nemico,
> che se mostra esser amico,
> no gli credere a l'inico:
>   guarda!
>
> Guarda 'l viso dal veduto,
> ca'l coragio n'è fèruto,
> c'a gran briga n'e guaruto:
>   guarda!
>
> Non udir le vanetate,
> che te traga a su' amistate:
> più che vesco appicciarate:
>   guarda!
>
> Pon a lo tuo gusto un frino,
> ca 'l soperchio gli è venino;
> a lussuria è sentino:
>   guarda!
>
> ....
>
> Guardate dal toccamento,
> lo qual a Deo è spiacemento,
> al tuo corpo è strugimento:
>   guarda!
>
> ....
>
> Guardate dal mal pensire,
> che la mente fo firire,
> la tua alma emmalsanire:
>   guarda![116]

[Watch that you don't fall, friend, watch it! Now keep yourself from the Enemy who advertizes himself a friend; don't believe the Evil One—watch it! Guard your eyes from what you see which would wound your heart, for it can be healed only at great cost—watch it! Don't listen to vanities which would draw you into his (the Devil's) company. They would stick (to you) like pitch—watch it! Control your gluttony because excess is poison and the companion of lust—watch it! . . . Keep your-

self from sensual pleasure which displeases God and is destruction for
your body—watch it! . . . Keep yourself from bad thoughts which will
damage your mind and corrupt your soul—watch it!]

This poem by Jacopone and others like it are representative of
lyrics characteristically found in a special class of Franciscan manuscripts—a tradition which derives from the earliest Franciscan relationship of poetry and homiletics. An example of such an Italian
manuscript is Co. 656 of the Biblioteca Communale in Assisi, which
contains extracts from the Fathers, sermons, meditations, and other
miscellaneous materials which are collected together as a "fascicolo"
for the use of preachers. The manuscript begins: "Incipit liber de
doctrina proficiendi ad honorem Christi Crucifixi et ad utilitatem
hominis religiosi." Following are three orations "ad crucem metrice
descriptam"; three prayers; a "tractatus de laudibus beate sacratissime
crucis Christi"; a meditation on the Passion, "ante sacrificium hostie
salutaris"; another meditation on the cross, and a short piece on the
significance of sacred ornaments and furnishings, all in Latin. At fol.
105 the lauds in Italian begin, the first of which is the dialogue debate
between the Soul and Reason concerning the love of God which has
been quoted in part here (p. 141 above). At fol. 108 occurs a moving
lyric of Jacopone, or perhaps of an imitator: "O derrata, esguarda lo
preco."[117] There are numerous other such Italian Franciscan codices
containing poems—compilations in the manner of the Middle English manuscripts discussed in the next chapter. Most of them contain
sermon notes, *exempla*, poems on the Seven Deadly Sins, moral verses,
versified Ten Commandments and other mendicant preachers' tools.[118]
At least one of the Italian manuscripts of this kind found its way to
England;[119] probably others did so as well.

Finally, the Franciscan emphasis on nature and on sensual perception found in the writings of Friar John, in the early Franciscan
biographies, and in Franciscan theology obtains a sharp articulation in
Italian Franciscan poetry. St. Bonaventure's remarkable ascription of
insight into the Divine through the five senses[120] is very precisely
echoed in Jacopone's *Lauda* LXXXII, of which the title is "Como
l'anima trova Dio in tutte creature per mezzo de sensi." This poem
succinctly affirms Bonaventure's doctrines of nature and the senses
as revelatory of God, and is particularly worthy of attention. One
stanza reads:

> Da cinque parte veio   che m'hai assidiato:
> audito, viso, gusto,   tatto ed odorato;
> si esco, so pigliato, non me to pò occultare.[121]

[From five sides I see that you have beseiged me: hearing, sight, taste, touch, and smell; if I try to break loose I am caught, I can't hide myself from you.]

But, as the poems on death and apocalypse remind us, Nature, her gifts, and all of the senses must themselves eventually vanish away. Only God himself, to whom all creation points, remains eternal.

> Anema mia, tu si etterna,
>   etterno vòi delettamento;
> li sensi e lor delettanza
>   vide senza duramento;
> a Deo fa' tu salimento,
>   esso sol te pò empire:
> loco el ben non sa finire,
>   ch'è etterno el delettare.[122]

[My soul, you are eternal; I want eternal delight. I saw that the senses and their pleasure pass away. Go up to God, he alone can fulfill you. There goodness knows no boundaries because that delight is eternal.]

While life lasts Nature remains a valuable guide and exemplar, and a love of Nature for her beauties teaches a Greater Love, preparing the human mind to contemplate its chief expression. In one of the best of the carols of Cortona the burden turns to address the singers and listeners with the voice of the Virgin Mary, saying,

> Voi ch'amate lo criatore
> ponete mente a lo meo dolore.
>   (Liuzzi, 1: 351–52)

[You who love the Creator, place your mind on my sorrows.]

The movement here is typical. Early followers of St. Francis knew Nature as the experience of God's creative love, a natural and progressive channel to the redemptive, recreative, and consummate experience of the Love of Christ. It is this progression, after all, which is apparent in St. Francis's own *Laudes creaturarum*.[123] Francis praises God through His creation, from the sun, which suggests Christ; to the moon, the Virgin; to the stars, the saints; to the wind, the Holy Spirit; to the four elements, characteristic of God's attributes; to those who share the Love of Christ and finally that Love itself. And the theme is amplified readily in other friars' poems, even in the form of a borrowed secular love song:

> Quanto è nel mondo m'invita ad amare,
> Bestie ed uccelli e pesci entro il mare,
> Cio c' è sotto all' abisso e sopra al are,
> Tutti fan versi davanto al mio Amore.
>
> Voglio invitare tutto il mondo ad amare,
> Le valli e i monti e la gente a cantare,
> L'abisso e i cieli e tutt' acque del mare,
> Che faccian versi davanti al mio Amore.
>
> [All that is in the world calls me to love,
> The beasts and birds and fishes in the sea,
> What's in the depths below, the air above;
> Before my Love they all make melody.
>
> And I will call on all the world to love;
> Valleys and mountains and the folk must sing.
> The depths, the waters, and the skies above;
> Before my Love let their sweet voices ring.]124

Here the "Amore" referred to may encompass the figure of the Blessed Virgin, or the fullest expression of Love, the person of Christ himself. The most intense consummation of this progressive experience in early Franciscan poetry is probably that in the lengthy "Cantico dell'amore," a long meditative piece traditionally ascribed to St. Francis. Here, "Per comperare l'amore tutto ho data/ Lo mondo," the poet's rhetorical beginning is to "deny" the experience of God's creation:

> Gia piu non posso veder creatura
> Al Creator gridda tutta mia mente,
> Cielo ne terra non mi da dolzura,
> Per Cristo amore tutto m'e fetente.

[Now I can't look at any creature; my whole mind cries out to the Creator. Neither sky nor earth give me pleasure; because of the love of Christ everything else puts me off.]

He learns however, that:

> Tutte le cose, che aggio create
> Con numero son fatte e con misura.
> Ed al lor fine son tutte ordinate:
> Conservasi per ordin tal valura:
> E molto piu ancora caritate
> E ordinata in la sua natura.

[Everything that I have created is made with number and measure, and all of them are ordered according to their purpose. This arrangement is kept by my order. The nature of charity is even more ordinate.]

And as the poem moves forward from its acknowledgement of creation (cf. Wisdom 11:21) through love of creature to love of Creator, the acceptance of the progression grows subjectively inward, to wonder, recognition, and ultimately to an ecstatic and frenzied crescendo, a passionate expression of contrite love for the Crucified:

> Amore! di Gesu desideroso
> Amor, voglio morire te abbracciando.
> Amor, amor, dolce Gesu mio sposo,
> Amor, amor, la morte ti domando;
> Amor, amor, Gesu siimi pietoso,
> Tu me t'arrendi in te me transformande
> Pensa, ch'io vo spasmando
> Non so dov' io mi sia,
> Gesu speranza mia
> Abissami in amore.[125]

[Love! desiring Jesus, love, I want to die embracing you. Love, love, sweet Jesus my spouse; love, love, I am asking you for death. Love, love, Jesus have pity on me; you make me surrender to you, transforming me in yourself. Think—I am in agony, I don't know where I am; Jesus my hope, immerse me in love.]

In the mirror of nature we learn to read that all creatures, like all words of Scripture, point to God[126]—not just by a process of intellectual abstraction in which nature itself remains externalized, but by a direct physical apprehension of his love, found by faith to be exemplified in each of creation's details. And from the experience of God's expression of his *creative* love Franciscan spirituality always arrives at the experience of his *recreative* love in personal confrontation with the Passion. This drama proves to be the most sublime entertainment of all.

Aesthetically and spiritually the approach of the Franciscan friar was to begin with that supreme standard of beauty made flesh and experienced in the physical world—the crucified Christ—and to move outward from that point. In the more articulate Augustinianism of Bonaventure, one could extend his exegetical system from Scripture to nature to discover divine revelation, and further apply the same system to the arts. Similarly, all roads led back, inevitably, in growing refulgence to the light of the cross.

Most of the poems cited in this chapter, besides those of St. Francis, derive from only three major sources—Jacopone da Todi, MS. Cortona 91, and a few poems from the Assisan codex. Many more examples of Italian Franciscan poetry could be adduced to show conformity with the theological, spiritual, and aesthetic principles of the most central Franciscan thinkers. And, obviously, much more could be said about the few examples already drawn. But it is with the medieval English poets of the Friars Minor that this study must consummate its intention.

Notes

1. D. W. Robertson, Jr., in his *Preface to Chaucer*, p. 15, argues that the mainstream intellectual tradition of medieval poetry bypassed the devotional poetry written under Franciscan influence. See note 40 (to Chapter 3) above.

2. Salimbene, p. 254, pp. 464–65; É. Gebhart, *Mystics and Heretics*, pp. 194–97; G. G. Coulton, *From St. Francis to Dante*, p. 21.

3. See Bartholomew of Pisa, in *Analecta Francescana*, 4:437; J. R. H. Moorman, *A New Fioretti*, p. 86.

4. Achille Pellizzari, *La Vita e le opera di Guittone d'Arezzo* (Pisa: 1905), describes the strong influence of the Patarines on Guittone, as well as the influence of what he calls "Joachite" and Franciscan poets. Guittone uses the *plazer* and *l'envoy* form of Provence, and also notably the X X, a a a X measure. In later life he converted and entered the cure of a "priore di Camaldoli" (pp. 19–25).

5. E. Gurney-Salter, trans., "Chronicle of Brother Jordan of Saxony," in *Friars Minor*, pp. 133–34.

6. See Vincenzo de Bartholomaeis, *Le Origini della poesia drammatica in Italia* (Bologna: N. Zanichelli, 1924), pp. 218–37.

7. Gebhart, *Mystics and Heretics*, p. 226; also M. D. Lambert, *Franciscan Poverty: The Doctrine of the Absolute Poverty of Christ and the Apostles in the Franciscan Order, 1220–1323* (London: SPCK, 1961), p. 114.

8. Salimbene, p. 239. See *Origini del teatro in Italiano* (Turin: E. Loescher, 1891), p. 112, where d'Ancona notes that Salimbene uses *componebant*, which verb he says supports the idea of an improvization—"laudes divinas . . . quas cantabant dum, se verberando, incedebant . . . et eas nudi processionaliter . . . devoti cantabant."

9. "Nell'anno 1260 . . . una commozione subita e nuova occupo dapprima i Perugini, indi i Romani, di poi quasi tutte le popolazioni italiane, cui per modo sopravvenne il timor di Dio, che, nobili ed ignobili, vecchi e giovani, e perfino fanciulli di cinqu' anni, per le piazze della citta, nudi e sol coperti le parti vergognose, posto giu ogni ritegno, processionalmente incedevano, tenendo ciascuno in mano un flagello di cuoio con gemiti o pianti acremente frustandosi sulle spalle fino ad effusione di sangue." The continuation is also worthy of note: "Dato libero sfogo alle lagrime, come se cogli occhi stessi del corpo vedessero la passione del Salvatore, imploravano piangendo la misericordia di Dio e l'ajunto della sua Genitrice, supplicando che, come ad altri innumerevoli peccatori, cosi a loro, penitenti, perdonate fossero le peccata. E non solo nel giorno, ma nella notte ancora, con ceri accesi, durante un freddo asprissimo, a centinaja, a migliaja, a decine di migliaja andavano attorno per le chiese delle citta, e si prostravano umilmente innanzi agli altari, preceduti da sacerdoti con croci e stendardi. Altrettanto facevasi nelle ville e ne' castelli, sicche delle voci de' gridanti a Dio sembravano risuonare egualmente i campi ed i monti. Tacquero allora

i musici strumenti e le amorose cantilene; il solo lugubre canto de' penitenti d' ogni parte si udiva, tanto nelle citta, quanto nel contado: alla cui flebile modulazione i cuori piu duri s'ammansivano, e gli occhi de' piu ostinati non potevano trattenersi dalle lagrime" (Alessandro d'Ancona, *Origini del teatro*, pp. 106–7).

10. For example, the *Geisslerlieder*, fourteenth-century German penitential songs of a slightly heretical flagellant group, who were similar in many other respects to the Waldensians though active particularly in 1329. They are published by Paul Runge, *Die Lieder und Melodien der Geissler des Jahres 1349* . . . (Leipzig: Breitkopf and Härtel, 1900). Many readers will recall certain scenes from Ingmar Bergman's *Seventh Seal* which are based upon the spread of flagellant activity to the north.

11. "Che l'ordine Serafico abbia favorito il movimento flagellante, dapprima, il costituirsi delle Compagnie stabili, poi, è cosa indubbià: bastera ricordare san Bonaventura. La 'giulleria del Signore' non poteva riguardare se non con simpatia quel rinvigorirsi che il sentimento religioso veniva facendo presso le motitudini, mediante un esercizio che tanto aveva del giullaresco" (*Poesia drammatica*, p. 371). See also the *laude* in praise of the Stigmata in *Miscellanea Franciscana* 16 (1915): 161–68.

12. O. Grifoni, *Saggio di poesie et canti popolari religiosi di alcuni poesi Umbri*, 2nd ed. (Foligno, 1911), p. 79.

13. See pp. 29–30 above.

14. Trans. from Henry R. Chazel, ed. and trans., *Les Poètes mineurs italiens des xiiie et xive siècles* (Paris: La Renaissance du livre, 1926), pp. 8–9.

15. David S. Muzzey, *The Spiritual Franciscans* (New York: Columbia Univ. Thesis, 1907), pp. 4–16. Some idea of what may have happened to the records is indicated by A. G. Little in discussing the chronicle of Salimbene: "Fate has dealt hardly with Salimbene: he was a prolific writer but only one of his works remains, and that in a single MS. The MS of the chronicle now in the Vatican was actually written by Salimbene's own hand, but it is in a sadly mutilated condition; the first 200 leaves are lost: the end is missing: and in the body of the work leaves have been deliberately cut out apparently by some censor who objected to the contents. The fragment which we possess (some 280 leaves of manuscript) begins *ca.* 1170 and ends in 1288" (in "Chronicles," p. 91).

16. See Eugenio Anagnine, *Dolcino e il movimento ereticale all' inizio del Trecento* (Florence: Nuova Italia, 1964).

17. Muzzey, *Franciscans*, pp. 16, 17–22. M. D. Lambert in *Franciscan Poverty* suggests that the consistent distinguishing feature of the Spiritual Franciscans was their insistence on absolute poverty; it was poverty which was finally most severely condemned. But the early writings reveal that as important to them was their historiographical consciousness.

18. Muzzey, *Franciscans*, Appendix III; A. G. Little, "The Sources of the History of St. Francis of Assisi: A Review of Recent Researches," *English Historical Review* 17 (1902):622.

19. "Nam spiritus ejus erat tunc in tanta consolatione et dulcedine quod volebat mittere pro frate Pacifico qui in saeculo vocabatur rex versuum et fuit valde curialis doctor cantorum et volebat dare sibi aliquos fratres ut irent simul cum eo per mundum praedicando et cantando Laudes Domini. Dicebat enim quod volebat ut ille qui sciret praedicare melius inter illos prius praedicaret populo, et post praedicationem omnes cantarent simul Laudes Domini tanquam joculatores Domini.

"Finitis autem laudibus volebat quod praedicator diceret populo: 'Nos sumus joculatores Domini et pro hic volumus remunerari a vobis, videlicet ut stetis in vera paenitentia.' [The source continues:] Et ait: 'Quid edim sunt servi Dei nisi quidam joculatores ejus qui corda hominum erigere debent et movere ad laetitiam spiritualem?'

"Et specialiter hoc dicebat de fratribus Minoribus qui dati sunt populo Die pro ejus salute" (*Speculum perfectionis*, ed. Paul Sabatier, pp. 197–98).

20. L. Lancetti, *Memorie interno ai poeti laureati* (Milan, 1839), pp. 82–86. It is strange that of such a figure we should have no more than the sketchiest of records; Italian scholars have long found it odd that "Di frate Pacifico . . . ho scritto nel testo . . . non un verso, non un parola ci rimane," and there is no record even of where or how he died. See Umberto Cosmo, "Frate Pacifico: Rex Versuum," *Giornate storico della letteratura italiana* 38 (Turin, 1901):23, 27. Pacifico was a Spiritual.

21. Alessandro d'Ancona, "Musica e poesia nell'antico comune di Perugia," *N. Antologia* 29 (1875):61 ff.; also Raynouard, ed., *Choix des poésies.* 5:278. Celano, 3:66, 76, records that Pacifico "feurat in sæculo citharista."

22. Cosmo, "Frate Pacifico," p. 29.

23. A. F. Ozanam, *Les Poètes franciscains*, p. 85; also Cosmo, "Frate Pacifico,' p. 31.

24. After the death of Francis, Pacifico left for France with singers. Liuzzi, *I musicisti italiana in Francia* (Rome: Edizioni d'arte Danesi, 1946) attributes to his work in the north of France the making of religious lyrics in the vernacular "per facilitarne la propogazione tra il popolo, sia in omaggio al desiderio di S. Francesco" (p. 37). As in England, there begin to appear in France about 1240 *canti religiosi* in the new style, vernacular, and of a type not known before. Noting that the bulk of writings in Italy were from confraternities, he says that one can see from that group as whole chief features of the style "cioè di liriche spirituali in lingua volgare e in forma di ballata, con melodie intonate, per lo piu, in parte da un solista e in parte dal coro all'unisono (dal solsista la ≪ stanza ≫, dal coro la ≪ ripressa ≫ che constituiva l'ornamento precipuo dei loro raduni. Sorte poco dopo confraternite tra i francesi a somiglianza di argomenti e strutture poetiche e di motivi musicali, dato il lavoro in comune e la destinazione in fede, tra l'altro, il fatto che anche oggi qualche traccia di simili canti sussiste tra il lavatori d'arte muraria, ad esempio, in Brettagna, tramanduta, con la tenacia propria delle tradizioni popolari, di generazione" (p. 38). See also A. Gastoué, *Le Cantique populaire en France* (Lyon: Janin frères, 1924), pp. 77–78.

There are one or two exceptions: for example, the *Paradiso* and *Inferno* of Giacomo da Verona, ed. Luigi Malagoli (Pisa, 1951), which while stylistically characteristic of Franciscan spirituality, are narrative (340 and 280 lines), and are in the Veronese dialect. They act as a progression, from Babylon the Great to the New Jerusalem.

25. Paul Sabatier, *Études*, pp. 190–91.

26. Arnaldo Fortini, *La Lauda in Assisi e le origini del teatro italiano* (Assisi: Edizioni Assisi, 1961; hereafter cited as Fortini), chap. 2.

27. Muzzey, *Franciscans*, p. 54; see his list.

28. Cf. Fortini, pp. 11–12.

29. Ibid., pp. 152–53 and notes.

30. "Ne abbiamo un luminoso esempio nella stessa chiesa che è considerata come madre e capo dell'Ordine, in San Francesco di Assisi, dove una associazione di Terziari, du cui si ha sicura notizia fino dall'anno 1304, si transforma in una vera e propria confraternita, che non ha bisogno di fondare la sua esistenza su di un particolare statuto, ma segue puramente la regola del Terz'Ordine" (Fortini, p. 150).

31. Fortini, pp. 97–99.

32. "Anchi per tucte quelle persone che sonno en peccato mortale o ennalcuna tenebra o scuritade de peccato, che esso dolcissimo et pietoso Sengnore per sua santa misericordia gli reduca allume de veretade et dia 'ro conesscemento et voluntate et pentemento verace che reconoscendose peccaturi facciamo con cor contriti et humiliati verace penetentia per vera comfessione, cuntritione et satissfatione d'opere, facendo sempre la volontà de Dio, elle suoie sant comandamenta servando en questa presente vita che ultimamente esso edio no dingne cuncedere vita eterna. *Amen*" (Fortini, p. 135).

33. Fortini, p. 157. Later, the statutes like the poems are recorded in the vernacular rather than in Latin.

34. Fortini, p. 84: "Anche di questa compagnia si conservano gli statuti, redatti in latino nel 1330, come è spiegato in fine: *Iste est liber disciplinatorum sancti Antonii. Iste liber completus est anno millesimo trecentesimo trigesimo.*

"Ma come è vero che tutti i confratelli sembravano vivere in stato di grazia con la Poesia, per cui non potevano pensare ed agire ed esprimere i loro sentimenti, anche i più modesti, se non in versi!

"Tutti, perfino gli amanuensi, come ci dimostra tal Ghino scritturale che, se aveva il bernoccolo del poeta, non aveva però buona vocazione di disciplinato; sì che, avendo avuto l'incarico di ricopiare con bella calligrafia questi statuti di Sant'Antonio, lo fece con tanto malgarbo e con tale clamorosa impazienza che non si peritò alla fine del lavoro, a documentare nei secoli la molta noia e la nessuna edificazione, di postillare con un metro latino che non era quello delle laude:

"Ghinum scriptorem, cui det Christus honorem
Et lucrum donet, post hoc suo regno coronet.

Laus sit tibi, Christe, quoniam liber explicit iste.
Scriptor huius libri requiem habeat paradisi. Amen, amen."

35. "Veri *ioculatores Domini*, erano pienamente riustici ad attuare il programma dell' adattamento e dell'assorbimento delle forme poetiche profane a scopo di propaganda per la salvezza delle anime" (Fortini, pp. 18–19, also pp. 196–208). Immediate physical concerns like the pestilence are remarkably infrequent in the songs; of first importance was the penitence of their own souls, then that of others.

36. See G. Brunacci, "Il Codice e l'oratorio dei laudesi," *Polimnia, Bollettino dell' Accademia Etrusca di Cortona* 8 (1931): pt. 1, pp. 873; 879–80. Salimbene records that Elias had in his company one Giovanni de Laudibus, a lay-brother, "hard and keen, a torturer and most evil butcher," who at Elias' bidding would scourge the brethren without mercy (p. 157). Presumably this is the same man as the Giovanni delle Laude who seems to have been one of the laud-makers who followed Elias in the Cortona school (see Fortini, p. 222).

37. "Che il manoscritto provenga dai Francescani non si può mettere in dubbio. La scrittura musicale è quella della notazione romana, di cui fecero efficace propaganda i Frati minori i quali, avendola adottatata, ottenero da papa Niccolò III (1277–1280) che i loro libri di canto liturgico fossero proposti a modello presso le chiese di Roma" (Fortini, p. 220).

38. "A un modular libero e chiaro in voce quasi d'idillio, che c'innamora della sua intatta giovinezza, il manoscritto cortonese pone a contrasto saggi d'una disciplina spirituale capace di affermarsi potente anche nel canto. Spesso la melodia della lauda s'alza in un'onda lenta, ampia e grave, densa di vocalità collettiva raccolta in unisoni grandiosi; il ritmo sobrio, la scansione rigorosa, l'intonazione solenne, il periodo a blocchi, stringono le note, come un cerchio compatto, intorno al pensiero che si concentra e s'inalza al cielo." The continuation is worthy of note: "Non penitenziale ma profondamente meditativo, non liturgico ma tuttavia pieno di mistica adorazione, un tal canto è indice della tensione lirica a cui si spinge la coscienza religiosa del popolo; della rigorosa compostezza con cui codesta tensione si risolve in forme estranee al repertorio ecclesiastico, materiate di linguaggio poetico e melodico perfettamente volgare. Canto di fraternità, di comunanza in affetti e contemplazioni millenarie, e insieme patrimonio munvo di parole e di note, conquista recente di un' espressione in cui si versa e s'appaga appieno il sentimento individuale" (Liuzzi, 1:49).

39. Liuzzi, 1:257. Cf. text by Gianfranco Contini, *Poeti del Duecento* (Milan, Naples: Riccardo Ricciardi, 1960; hereafter cited as Contini), 2:12. This is the burden in a traditional carol form. The music is styled *andante*, and even in this piece one of the later stanzas turns toward thoughts of penance (p. 258).

40. Fortini, pp. 47–48, colorfully describes the tone of the *laude* in this character: "Vecchi canti popolari soffusi di gentilezza affettuosa, che le donne appresero allora ai loro bambini, che i padri ripeterono prostrati nei vasti templi durante le pause delle feroci battaglie."

"Maria, eterno sorriso luminoso di amore alle anime angosciate:
    Tu sey nave del gran mare
    per lo popolo salvare,
    tu sey via del nostro andare
    alla gloria biata.

        Per te, matre, el paradiso,
        ove è l'angelico viso,
        alegrecca, giocho e riso,
        requie eterna ce sia data.

    ....

        Maria, chiara stella,
        Maria, tu sey quella
        rosa relucente e bella,
        solo da Dio desiderata."

41. Salimbene, pp. 550 ff., also pp. 54, 300, 315, etc. Salimbene wrote poetry himself—one poem in imitation of Gerardo Patechio (p. 54). He liked drinking songs, and includes one in his *Chronica* (p. 219).

42. Fortini, p. 228. Panziera was born early in the second half of the thirteenth century, and died in 1330.

43. Salimbene, p. 181. Here is yet another illustration that behind the Latin religious lyrics of the period lies the form of popular song.

44. Ciro Cannarozzi, *Le Prediche volgari di San Bernardino da Siena* (Pistoia, 1934), 1:xv.

45. See Bernardino Mazzarella, "St. Bernardine of Siena, a Model Preacher," *Franciscan Studies* 25 (1944):309–28, esp. p. 318.

46. Fols. 272–74r. This version differs in a number of respects from that printed in Ageno's edition, pp. 366–78. At fol. 345rv occurs, in another sermon, the laud "In fuocho d'amore me misse Lo hyo sposo novello/ . . . Sempre l'o in cor formato De Christo consolato./ In fuocho . . . ," etc. A bad edition of this MS occurs in Giovanni de la Haye, *Sancti Bernardini Senensis opera omnia* (Venice, 1745), 3:146–362. This MS has not yet been included in the new Quaracchi edition.

47. Fortini, p. 226: ". . . cedebat isti, si cantare volebat et ascultabat eum diligenter nec movebatur de loco, et postmodum resumebat cantum suum, et sic alternatim cantando voces delectabiles et suaves resonabant ab eis."

48. Salimbene, p. 181; translated in Coulton, *From St. Francis to Dante*, p. 100.

49. Paul Thureau-Dangin, trans. Baroness G. von Hügel, *The Life of St. Bernardino of Siena* (London: Dent, 1906), p. 22.

50. Cuthbert Gumbinger, "*Prediche Volgari*," pp. 11–12, 25; Thureau-Dangin, *St. Bernardino*, pp. 148–52.

51. Liuzzi, 1:271–72. These examples conform neatly to what Sabatier has to say about response to the Passion in general: "Ramené par la pensée du Christ crucifié à toutes les souffrances que celui-ci avait endurées, il voulut

le suivre de plus près et s'imposer toutes les privations que la bon prêtre avait voulu lui épargner" (*Études*, p. 183).

52. See Otto Ursprung, *Die katholische Kirchenmusik*, in *Handbuch der Musikwissenschaft* 10, ed. Ernst Bücken (Potsdam: Akademische verlags Gesellschaft Athenaion, 1928–34): 102; also Coulton, *From St. Francis to Dante*, pp. 32–33, where he records that Berthold "expounded the Apocalypse after the manner of Joachim," and had "a special grace of preaching," with power of lungs to be heard by the crowds of sixty to one hundred thousand that would gather to hear him.

53. *Berthold von Regensburg: Vollständige Ausgabe seiner Predigten*, ed. Franz Pfeifer, 2 vols. (1862–80; rep. Berlin: De Gruyter, 1965), 2:63 and 1:29–47; Anton E. Schönbach (*Sitzungsberichte der Kaiserlichen Akadamie der Wissenschaften*, vols. 142, 148, 151, 152, 154, 155 [ca. 1900–08]) has shown that these sermons were probably adapted by another Franciscan for use in a convent. This probably explains the relative shortage of practical delivery aids, such as poems, in their present form.

54. "Dâ von hüetet iuch vor in mit allem flîze unde mit allen iuwern sinnen. "Bruoder Bertholt, wie sülle wire uns cor in behüeten, sô lange daz sie guoten liuten sô gar gliche sint?' Seht daz wil ich iuch leren, den worten daz ir iuch iemer mere deste baz gehüeten künnet. Ir sult sie halt ouch an siben worten erkenen. Von swem unde swenne ir der siben worte einz erhoeret, vor dem sült ir iuch hüeten, wan der ist ein rehter ketzer, und ir sült den pfarrer an sie wîsen oder ander gelêrte liute. Unde merket mir disiu wort gar eben unde behaltet sie iemer mêr unze an iuwern tôt. Ich wolte halt gerne daz man lieder dâ von sünge. Ist iht guoter meister hie, daz sie niuwen sanc da von singen, die merken mir disiu siben wort gar eben unde machen lieder dâ von: dâ tuot ir gar wol an; unde machet sie kurze unde ringe unde daz sie kindegelich wol gelernen mügen; wan so gelernent sie die liute alle gemeine diu selben dinc unde vergezzent ir deste minner. Ez was ein verworhter ketzer der machte lieder von ketzerîe unde lêrte sie diu kint an der straze, daz der liute deste mer in ketzerîe vielen. Unde dar umbe sæhe ich gerne, daz man diu lieder von in sünge. Nu merket alle samt! Daz êrste: swer da sprichet, ez müge . . ." (*Predigten*, 1:405–6). Ursprung notes: "Was uns aus diesen Worten entgegenklingt, ist ein Bekenntnis zum schlichten Volksgesang und kundet von einem pedagogisch seinen Erfassen der höhen Bedeutung und der weitausgreifenden Wirkung, die dem einfachen Volksgesang viel mehr innewohnt als dem Kunstlied der Minnesänger" (*Kirchenmusik*, p. 102). Cf. Franciscan friar James Ryman of England who espoused the same ideal, and related it to missionary responsibilities:

> For cause alle men shall vnderstonde
> My lordes preceptes iuste and right,
> He hath me made to euery londe
> In theire owne speech them to endite
> And in this fourme them for to wright.
> Therfore take hede bothe sume and alle
> To his preceptis, bothe grete and small.

(Here follow eighteen quatrains of poetic doctrinal instruction; Zupitza, pp. 269–72).

55. Ursprung, *Kirchenmusik*, p. 103; also *Lexikon für Theologie und Kirche*, 2:229. From 1262–63 Berthold worked in Hungary where he denounced the excesses of the *Geissler*. See n. 10 above. Cf. the note on David von Augsburg, chap. 1, n. 43, above.

56. Fortini, p. 274. My translation follows: ". . . immediately let the celebrant together with the order of all the brothers say, in its entirety, 'Our Father. And lead us not into temptation. Response. But deliver us from evil.' This said, let the group fall silent at the sign of a bell or some other sign and immediately let one rise who has the duty of singing vernacular lauds, so that by singing these worshipfully he may turn the hearts of the brothers to lamentation and tears as they concentrate on the words rather than the voice. But let such lauds be so ordered that they are sung on Fridays or on other days which deal with the Passion or are given over to singing lauds of the Passion of our Savior Jesus and of his most sorrowful mother. But on Sundays and festivals and at any other time let there be sung the lauds of the day or of the festival, if the order is observing a festival, or at other times according to the devotion of the day or of the celebration of the festival and the arrangement of the time; and in the singing of any stanza or verse, if the group is at this time dressed in sackcloth, at the end of the stanza the verse is sung [*fiat*] by the brothers, but when the cantor is singing the lauds, rising at the sound of the bell or some other sign, let the group keep silent and so continue until the aforementioned lauds have been completed by the cantor. When they have completed let their cantor return to his place and let the order keep silence for the space of one 'Our Father,' to be said by them all."

57. Robert Briffault, *The Troubadours*, pp. 24–38, shows that the most prevalent verse form among Mozarab poets was the *murabba'* form, *a a, b b b a* (or *X X, a a a X*, etc.), composed with a view to accompaniment, that after its adaptation into Spanish poetry it became the dominant verse form of developing Provençal lyric poetry, and then spread to Italy as the Procençal poets began to influence early Italian poets including St. Francis and Jacopone da Todi. He does note the dominance of this form in "a whole class of lyrical poetry," and says that Chaucer uses it only once because Chaucer was influenced primarily by French sources.

58. The *X X, a a a X* form is, for example, the form of the majority of the Cortonese lauds edited by Liuzzi.

59. See *SL XIV–XV*, p. xlix. The number of responsory lyrics increases from the thirteenth century, with only a small number, to the fifteenth century, where the carol and *ballade* outnumber all others. See Beatrice H. N. Geary, "A Study of Fifteenth-Century English Lyric Verses . . . with Special Reference to Metrical Form" (Thesis, Bodleian Library, 1932).

60. *EEC*, pp. xxix ff.

61. See Renée Foatelli, *Les Danses religieuses dans le christianisme* (Paris:

Éditions Spes, 1938); L. Gougaud, "La Danse dans les églises," *Revue d'histoire ecclesiastique* 15 (1914):5–22.

62. Arnaldo Fortini, *Nova vita di San Francesco*, 5 vols. (Assisi: Porziuncula, 1959), 1:170–71.

63. II Celano *Analecta franciscana* 10. 27, p. 54, n. 73. Dante said (*Vulgaria Eloquentia*, ed. Pio Rajna [Florence: G. C. Sansoni, 1897], pp. 45–46) that the *ballate* do not rank as high as *canzoni* because they require the assistance of the performers for whom they are written, *plausoribus*, who clap their hands and stamp their feet.

64. Fortini, *Nova vita*, 2:121–22.

65. Bacon, like Bonaventure, explicitly associates music with the contents and objectives of theology. In his *Opus tertium* (ed. J. S. Brewer, Rolls Series, 1859), he discusses the spiritual values of "musicae predicatorum" (chap. 73, p. 298) for devotion and moral instruction; he discusses its uses in reference to Scripture, "Si igitur rerum omnium proprietates requiruntur sciendae propter sensum literalem, ut per convenientes adaptationes eliciantur sensus spirituales, secundum quod sancti docent et omnes sapientes, et videmus quod ipsa expositio Scripturae hoc requirit"; he relates the function of singing to "sciat elicere sensus spirituales" (chap. 60, p. 233)—precisely the context of the Franciscan lyrics as they are discussed in the present and following chapters. Significantly, Bacon points out that the *dance* also is part of this music, "Praeter vero has partes musicae, quae sunt circa sonum, sunt aliae, quae sunt circa visibile, quod est gestus, qui comprehendit exultationes et omnes flexus corporis. Nam conformantur gestus cantui . . . motibus consimilibus et configurationibus competentibus . . . Nos enim videmus quod ars instrumentorum, et cantus, et metri, et rhythmi, non vadit in plenam delectationem sensibilem, nisi simul adsint gestus, et exultationes, et flexus corporales . . . apud duos sensus. . . . gestus est radix musicae, sicut metrum et sicut melos, id est, cantus. Et Augustinus dicit hoc secundo Musicae" (chap. 59, p. 232). See also *Opus majus*, ed. J. H. Bridges (Oxford: Clarendon Press, 1897), 1:236 ff., for more on the relation of music to theology.

66. Liuzzi, 1:195.

67. S. Bernardini Senensis, *Opera omnia* (Quaracchi, 1950–67), 2:447 ff.

68. *Lauda* LXXXIV, Ageno, p. 342; cf. Contini, 2:73–74.

69. P. Vigo, *La Danze Macabre in Italia* (Bergamo, 1901), p. 100.

70. *The Dance of Death in the Middle Ages and Renaissance* (Glasgow: Jackson, 1950).

71. Liuzzi, 2:401–2, stanzas 7–9 from Contini, 2:53. (One of the interesting aspects of this poem is the word *furone* in stanza four, which may in the Cortonese dialect have signified "furious dance.") To stanzas 1, 2, 5 and 6 compare the speech of Death to the Friar Minor in Lydgate's poem translating the *Danse macabre* from the Innocents (EETS OS 181, ed. F. Warren [London: Oxford Univ. Press, 1931], p. 68):

> . . . yn ȝowre prechynge hau ful ofte tawght
> How þat I am most gastful for to drede,
> Al-be that folke take ther of none hede

> ȝitte is ther noon so stronge ne so hardi
> But dethe dar reste and lette for no mede
> For dethe eche owre is present & redy.

The Friar's reply:

> What mai this be, that yn this world no man
> Here to a-bide mai haue no seuerte;
> Strength richesse ne what so that he can,
> Worldly wisdom al is but vanyte;
> In grete astate ne yn pouerte
> Is no thynge founde that mai fro dethe defende.

La Morte is equally reminiscent of the best known of Dunbar's poems, *The Lament for the Makaris*, especially stanzas 3 and 4:

> Onto the ded gois all Estatis,
> Princis, Prelatis, and Potestatis,
> Baith riche and pur of all degre,
> *Timor mortis conturbat me.*

72. Liuzzi, 1:30.

73. Clark, *Dance of Death*, p. 5. See also R. Woolf, *English Religious Lyric*, pp. 347–55.

74. Plate in Liuzzi, 1:74. The illustration is, of course, later than the composition of the poem, but not likely so late as the fifteenth-century French poem cited by Clark. See the painting of St. Francis and the skeleton Death, which he is introducing, reproduced in Fortini, fig. 75.

75. Clark (*Dance of Death*, p. 95) says that the first representation of the three nobles mounted is a late fifteenth-century poem. His statement needs revision in light of the Cortona illustration, probably of the late thirteenth century, and the fourteenth-century English de Lille Psalter (Arundel MS. 83), which in a rich program of illustrations corresponding to the Lambeth Constitutions of Archbishop Pecham includes an illustration of the Three Living and the Three Dead, with inscriptions in English. See the description by M. Rickert, *Painting in Britain: The Middle Ages* (London and Baltimore: Penguin Books, 1954), pp. 147–48.

76. Clark, *Dance of Death*, pp. 104 ff.

77. Ibid., p. 23.

78. Quoted from Okey's translation, by Clark, p. 103.

79. Vienna Nationalbibliothek MS. 2827, fol. 252r, quoted by Clark, pp. 110–11.

80. *Lauda* LXIV, Ageno, p. 261.

81. Liuzzi, 2:391.

82. Ed. from Assisan codex by Fortini, p. 198.

83. See Robertson, *Preface*, pp. 127–32, where he discusses the connection between Old Song and New Song and their respective Dances in late medieval art and literature.

84. Fortini, pp. 34–38.

85. Most of the Cortona lauds, like others which have spaces provided for musical annotation, are written in three-part harmonies, usually calling

for tenor, counter-tenor, and baritone voices. A minimal amount of plain-song occurs in the Cortona MSS in particular. The performance of this type of score has been illuminated by Higini Anglès, *La Música de las Cantigas de Santa Maria del Rey Alphonso el Sabio* (Barcelona, 1943), pp. 11–12, who reads the scores to show that very rich non-polyphonics are involved in certain situations, as well as ternary and binary combined monody.

86. "*Sume citharam,* idest confessionem, *circui civitatem,* idest mentem vel vitam tuam, ut omnia revolvas, ne aliquid te lateat; *bene cane* teipsum accusando, *frequenta canticum* tibi imputando, te plangendo *ut memoria tui sit* in conspectu Dei" (*In festo S. Stephani protomartyris* 3. 757a).

87. Fortini, pp. 18–19. Cf. the similar "anonymity" of English medieval religious lyrics, for which essentially the same reason is advanced by Rosemary Woolf (*English Religious Lyric,* pp. 4–6).

88. For more on Giacomo, see n. 24 above.

89. Underhill, *Jacopone,* pp. 160, 165.

90. Ibid., pp. 14, 112–13. Jacopone writes: "Lo desprezare piaceme/ e de gir mal vestito" (*Lauda* XXXVIII). These tendencies may account for the name given to the street where many of London's friars resided in the fourteenth century—"Stynkyng Lane."

91. Ibid., pp. 216, 219.

92. Ibid., pp. 126, 145.

93. Fortini, pp. 157–65; Underhill, *Jacopone,* p. 230.

94. Jacopone wrote in both *ballata maggiore* and *ballata-lauda* forms. The *ballata maggiore* has an eight-line stanza with four-line *ripresa,* or burden; the *lauda* has a four-line stanza and two-line burden, in the X X, *a a a* X pattern already discussed. Both are dance-derived forms. Good examples of the *lauda* form in Jacopone's poems are *Laude* XXV, "Quando t'alegri"; LIII, "Piange la Ecclesia"; and LXXV, "Fuggo la croce." Johann Schmitt, *La Metrica da Fra Jacopone,* in *Studii medievali,* vol. 1, no. 4 (1905), pp. 515 ff., points out that the *lauda* form is the more vulgar and popular of the two. Jacopone's work embraces two traditions, "la tradizione popolare, quasi empre orale . . . e la tradizione letteraria." Two metrical developments in his verse are first, the development of the caesura in his popular verse, accenting 4/-4, as distinct from the latinate and Ovidian metrics in the more urbane verse forms, and second, his characteristic ordinance of metric patterns with meaning and the emotive surge of his lines (Schmitt, pp. 536–37, 559 ff.). See note 57 above.

95. Underhill, *Jacopone,* p. 212.

96. See above, p. 53 ff.

97. Raby, p. 440. Cf. the following lines by English Franciscan James Ryman:

> And we, whiche be on the roode tree
> *Tuo redempti sanguine,*
> For the day of thy natiuitie
> A new songe we do singe to the.

> (Zupitza, p. 194)

An interesting variety of the on-the-Cross appeal is the sort of lyric in which the pattern of Christ as judge, Mary as advocate, forms the framework. Fortini describes one such early confraternity laud: "Del resto è questo il solito motivo delle laude delle confraternite: Gesù sdegnato che vuole far giustizia dei peccatori, la Vergine che intercede misericordiosa per questi che si raccomandano al suo aiuto. Esso ritorna anche nei dipinti dell'epoca, dove si scorgono questi incappati biancovestiti, assistiti dai Santi cui le diverse compagnie sono dedicate e dai protettori della città, specialmente San Francesco e Santa Chiara, inginocchiati ai piedi della Madre di Dio, che supplice si volge a Gesù" (p. 41). This sort of lyric usually ends up with Mary comforting the postulant:

> Pecatore, or me entendete,
> per vuy prego, nol sapete?
> el mio figliol nol cognoscete
> e non avete en luy amore.

> Prega el nostro Signor altissimo
> almo figliol tanto carissimo
> che dal iudicio crudelissimo
> ve retraga e de dollore.
>
> (Fortini, pp. 45–46)

98. Ageno, pp. 339–40; cf. Contini, 2:116–18.

99. Ageno, p. 36; see also *Laude* LXIX; XCII:
> Spogliare se vol l'om d'onnecovelle,
> cioe en questo stato . . . (p. 394).

100. *Lauda* II, ibid., p. 8

101. *Lauda* LXV, ibid., p. 273.

102. See Fortini, pp. 166–70. This metaphor became a popular one in Franciscan poetry, as in the following medieval Dutch example:
> O siele cristi heilicht mij
> O licham cristi behoet mij
> O bloet cristi suvert mi van alle mynen sonden
> O passie cristi sterct my in een deuchsaam leven.

See Wolfgang Schmitz, *Het Aandel der Minderbroeders in Onze Middeleeuwse Literatuur* (Utrecht, 1936) p. 131; see also his interesting translation of Jacopone's *Stabat mater*, p. 136.

103. See p. 50 above.

104. Fortini, p. 170.

105. *Lauda* XXXIV, Ageno, p. 122. It is not likely that a Dominican would have written such a poem.

106. *Lauda* LXXIX, Ageno, p. 325. Similarly, *Lauda* LXXIV (Ageno, p. 310):
> L'Affetto, puoi gusta el cibo
> de la grazia gratis data,
> lo 'ntelletto e la memoria
> tutta sì l'ha renovata,

e la volontà ha mutata;
piagne con gran desianza
la preterita offensanza,
e nullo consol se vol dare.

107. *Lauda* LXXX, Ageno, p. 328. These lines strike an interesting comparison with the thrust of the *Vita* of *Piers Plowman*.

108. See, for example, *Lauda* L (Ageno, pp. 199–200):

Tutto lo monno veio conquassato,
e precipitanno va en ruina:
como l'omo che è enfrenetecato,
al quale non pò om dar medecina,
li medeci sì l' hanno desperato,
ché non ce iova encanto né dottrina,
vedemolo en estremo lavorare.

109. Liuzzi, 1:397; see also 1:411.

110. *Lauda* LXIX, Ageno, p. 288.

111. For example, Liuzzi, 1:407 ff. See also p. 131 above.

112. Cf. Berthold von Regensburg, pp. 130–31 above. We shall discuss this poem of Jacopone later.

113. Cf. poem in Liuzzi, 1:334. One interesting Cortonese poem in praise of Augustine reflects the nature of his preeminence in the Franciscan mind. Archbishop Pecham would have liked it:

Sancto Agostin doctore,
confessor et pastore
et pien di sapientia, si laudato.

Luminatore   et doctore,
della fe' divina
difenditor e   guar datore,
colla sancta doctrina
distrugitore,   d'ogne errore
facesti gran ruina;
tutti di sì gram sancto
novel or facciam canto,
ché nn' è sie degno   et àlo ben meritato.
....
la tua molta scriptura
sanctissima et pura
che tutto 'l mondo n'era alluminato.

O glorioso   amoroso
noi ti vogliam pregare . . . .

(Liuzzi, 3:296)

114. *Lauda* IV, "O Alta penitenza," and *Lauda* XLVI, "Con gli occhi ch'agio nel capo."

115. Cf. n. 54 above.

116. Lauda VI, Ageno, pp. 20–21. Cf. Contini, 2:71; Rosanna Bettarini, *Jacopone e il Laudario Urbinate* (Florence: Sansoni, 1969), pp. 602–3.

117. See the account by Fortini, pp. 165–66. I have not yet had the opportunity to examine this codex. Fortini describes other similar MSS containing Latin sermon materials, prayers, and vernacular religious verse. Some, such as the codex Angelica CCXIII, contain the same sort of materials plus treatises by St. Anselm, St. Bernard, and St. Bonaventure. There are other similar codices, however, which Fortini does not describe.

118. See, for example, Paolo Guerrini, "Due Codici Francescani Bresciani," *Archivum Franciscanum Historicum* 30 (1937):229–34.

119. B. L. MS. Addit. 22557, fourteenth century, beginning "Lo libor de multi belli miraculi e de liuicij," the first part of which treats of the Seven Deadly Sins, the heavenly city of the Apocalypse, the Lord's Prayer, Apostle's Creed, etc., and which includes *exempla* in the manner and arrangement of English collections such as the *Fasciculus morum*. MS. Addit. 22557 has been described and partially edited by J. Ulrich in *Romania* 13 (1884):29–59.

120. See p. 102 above.

121. Ageno, p. 337.

122. "Cinque sensi mess'ò el pegno," *Lauda* V, Ageno, p. 19.

123. Ed. in Sabatier, *Life of St. Francis*, p. 305—with translation, after Assisan MS. 338.

124. Ed. Tressati, *Iacopone da Todi* (Venice, 1613), p. 34; trans. from V. D. Scudder, *The Franciscan Adventure* (London and Toronto: Dent, 1931), p. 346. The poem has been mistakenly ascribed to Jacopone; see d'Ancona, *Jacopone da Todi* (Todi: Casa editrice "Atanor," 1914), p. 63 n.

125. Ed. in Le Monnier, *Nuova istoria* (Assisi, 1895), pp. 433–43. Like the equally famous *In foco l'amor mi mise* it cannot, at least in its present form, be certainly attributed to Francis. Both of these pieces derive from sermons of St. Bernardino of Siena, whence Wadding gets his texts. See Sabatier, *Life of St. Francis*, p. 358 n.

126. Cf. the Cortonese laud, edited by Liuzzi, 1:262; also the poem "Alta trinita beata," cited above.

5

Ioculatores Dei in England

"This same year, O grief, and more than grief! O savage pest, the Friars minor came to England."[1]

ON 10 September 1224, during the same week in which St. Francis received the stigmata, Fra Agnello of Pisa landed at Dover. Though Agnello and his eight companions left the largest part of their group (including Brother Pacifico) behind in France, within six months they had established friaries at the three centers—ecclesiastical, civil, and intellectual—of national life (Canterbury, London, and Oxford), as well as at Northampton. Within five years a dozen more houses were added in major English towns and by 1240, thirty-four strategic-ally located friaries, extending past the Scottish border, and several hundred friars offered a testimony to the spiritual blitzkrieg effected by the first British Franciscans.[2] Writing to Pope Gregory in 1238, Bishop Grosseteste could say:

> They illuminate our whole country with the bright light of their preaching and teaching. Their most holy conversation gives a power-ful impetus to contempt of the world and to voluntary poverty, to humility even among those in high places, to entire obedience to prelates and the head of the Church, to patience in tribulation, to abstinence in the midst of plenty, in short, to every virtue. Oh that Your Holiness could see how devoutly and humbly the people run to hear from the word of life, to confess their sins, to be instructed in the rules of living, and what advance the clergy and religious have made by imitating them; you would indeed say that "to those that sit in the valley of the shadow of death the light hath shined."[3]

169

Down through the thirteenth century the bishops of England welcomed, encouraged, and protected the Franciscans, and valued them especially for their work as preachers and confessors.[4] Still, it is probably significant that the first to welcome the Friars into the country were not kings or bishops, but merchants and citizens such as Sir William Joyner (Lord Mayor of London in 1239) and Sir Henry de Wales (Lord Mayor three times between 1273 and 1299). (Henry of Wales was also one of the founders of the poetic confraternity of the Pui.)[5] It is true that Franciscan influence on the population moved upwards to the noble classes in time, outward to distant parts of the realm, and into political life, so that within a few years it would have been difficult to find a significant portion of England's population who at one time or another had not come under Franciscan influence.[6] The main focus of their activity, however, as in Italy, remained the town, village, and country peoples to whom they directed their vernacular sermons.[7]

The hagiography and general mystique of St. Francis and the first twelve also came to England with Agnellus and his followers. Dom Roger of Wendover in his *Flores historiarum* reports of the Minorites (and Minoresses) without comment in 1225, suggests that the legend of St. Francis preaching to the birds was well known in England by 1227, and describes the Franciscans "going through the towns and in the parochial churches, and even among the field labourers [where] they planted the roots of virtue, and offered to the Lord abundance of fruit . . . ."[8] Matthew Paris, who succeeded Roger of Wendover as historian of the Abbey St. Alban's, copies his account of St. Francis and the birds almost verbatim, except that he makes certain tell-tale additions which exactly follow Celano's *Legenda prima* (at *I Celano* 1.21), showing that at least this one among the early biographies was known in England by 1235.[9] An abridgement of *I Celano* in hexameter verse had appeared by 1230, attributed (though possibly erroneously) to John of Kent.[10] And in the chronicles of Matthew Paris appear apocalyptic drawings by Brother William of England, one of Francis' early companions.[11] (See Plate 6.)

It has been noted that "with the exception of St. Bonaventure—and he was taught by Alexander of Hales—all the greatest and most original Franciscan scholars of the Middle Ages were natives of Britain," and that the English province was heralded for its adherence to poverty and the Rule—that is, for its Spiritual leanings.[12] One of the first friars to come across the channel with Agnellus was an Englishman, Brother Henry of Burford, who had been "cantor fratrum

Plate 6. Brother William of England (MS. C.C.C. Cambridge, 16)

Parisius." He wrote the following poem, recorded by Eccleston, which
underscores the observant spirit of the English province:

> Laugh not, thou who Minor art, better tears befit thy part.
> Minor thou in name, then see that thy name and acts agree.
> Toils endure, let patience bring low thy proud imagining.
> Thou dost hate the lowly, say? Patience clears such dregs away.
> He who chides thee knows thy needs, hates not thee, but thy misdeeds.
> What avail thy vesture poor, squalid food, and couch of boor?
> Each is naught if deeds belie what thy habit would imply.
> He is but a Minor's ghost who seeks the name without the cost.[13]

English Brother Haymo, who wrote an apocalyptic commentary on
Isaiah, and was particularly noted for his abilities at preaching
contrition, was chiefly instrumental in obtaining the downfall of the
lax Brother Elias.[14] Salimbene testifies, on the basis of evidence from
his acquaintance, Brother Stephen the Englishman, to strict observance
of the Rule in the English province.[15] Eccleston tells of southern European brothers coming to position in England who were given to some
of the more extreme forms of self-mortification.[16] All of these things
suggest an English province whose community life-style and spirituality developed along lines similar to those of the parent Italian
movement, with a characteristic shaping of Augustinian theology and
doctrine by vigorous and strongly-rooted devotional observances.
There is ample evidence in English Franciscan records to confirm
this suggestion, and to show that both in content and methodology
the evangelical message carried by English Franciscans was the same
as that of their Italian brother friars.

After the Italian example, there is reason to take a special interest
in the musical and homiletical context of extant Middle English
lyrics. As we have seen, St. Francis conceived of his *ioculatores Dei* as
preachers who would sing men into the kingdom of Heaven, drawing
and focusing their attention on the crucified Christ. When sermon
and song are thus closely connected, even perhaps interdependent, it
is only natural that there should be some obvious manifestation of
this relationship in the manuscript sources.

In the last chapter we observed that there were two principal
kinds of manuscript in which Franciscan poetry is found in Italy:
the *laudario,* such as MS. Cortona 91, and the homiletic handbook
such as Codex Biblioteca Communale 656. In England, much the
same is true, and for Middle English lyric poetry in general. R. H.

Robbins in the introduction to his *Secular Lyrics of the XIVth and XVth Centuries* lists ten varieties of manuscript source for Middle English lyrics. Of these, what he calls "Minstrel Collections," "Aureate Collections," "Song Books," and even "Closet Hymns"[17] (like the manuscripts of Franciscans Ryman's and Herebert's poems) are usually varieties of what in Italy might have been called *laudario*. MS. Cortona 91, for example, has attributes of the Closet Hymn collection and the Aureate collection. This kind of Middle English lyric manuscript has already been discussed by English scholars with some thoroughness;[18] the large number of religious "song-book" manuscripts, however, is worthy of some further comment.

Besides showing that the religious carol and lyric in the vernacular had for transcription purposes somehow achieved greater popularity than secular poetry, these manuscripts, many of which have musical notation, remind us that the early English lyric, like its Italian counterpart, had very much to do with song. Most of the musically scored pieces occur in *laudario*-type manuscripts. Examples of this type include British Library MS. Additional 5666 (fols. 2–83 passim), which is a small collection of carols for three voices or plain song written by John Brackley, Friar Minor of Norwich in the fourteenth century;[19] British Library MS. Egerton 3307 (see Plate 7);[20] MS. Sloane 2593; MS. Bodleian 29734; and MS. St. John's Coll. Camb. 259, all of the early fifteenth century. The exception to the general *laudario* pattern, where there are far more vernacular than Latin lyrics, is MS. Egerton 274, in which (fols. 305–6b passim) are found many secular songs, liturgical pieces, and typically Franciscan poems in Latin. The author to whom this thirteenth-century collection is ascribed is none other than Henry of Pisa,[21] the enterprising Franciscan poet-friend of Salimbene whose lyric gifts proved too much for the unfortunate nun.[22]

It has been said that the musical scores do not appear with similar poems in preachers' books.[23] This is not true.[24] Actually, several of the extant musically scored lyrics occur in manuscripts which are intended for the use of preachers. A fine example to the point is early fourteenth-century MS. Royal 12.E.i, a miscellaneous collection of prayers, saints' lives, and practical theology, which concludes with a "narratio Roberti Grosseteste, episcopi Lincolniensis pro collectione elemosine." This manuscript is the source of several Middle English lyrics of the thirteenth century, including the well-known "Stond wel, moder, vnder rode," which here is set to music. This most famous English *stabat mater* poem is an excellent example of the various contexts in which the Middle English lyric may be found: in its four

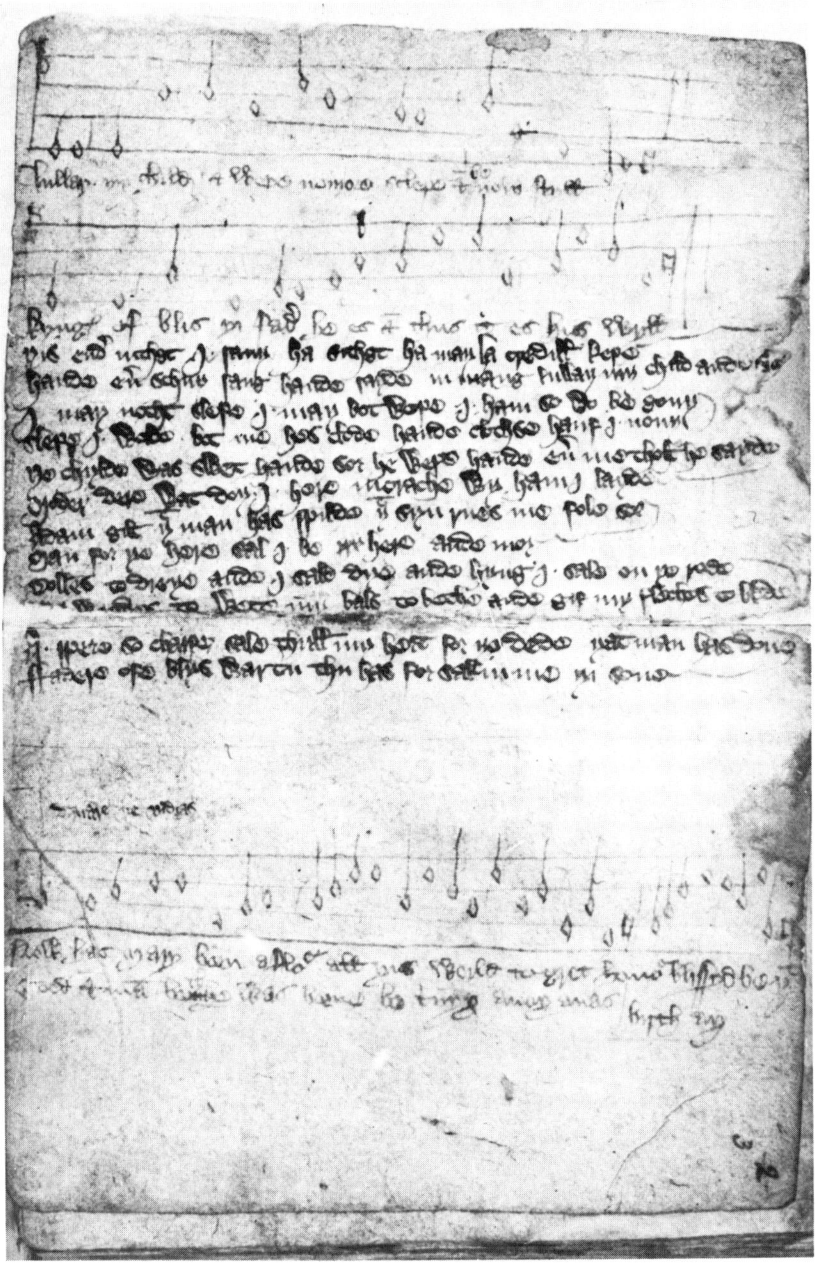

Plate 7. "Kyng of blis" (MS. Egerton 3307)

appearances it occurs in two collections of pastoralia with music, and in one Friar Miscellany and one sermon without music.[25] MS. Arundel 248, a late thirteenth-century collection of theological and moral pieces for preaching use, also includes musical notation for one of its many typically Franciscan-styled lyrics: "Jesu cristes milde moder/ stud, biheld hire son o rode."[26] Other examples of lyrics with music are MS. Harley 5396 (fols. 273b, 280b), MS. Harley 275 (fol. 146b), and possibly the thirteenth-century MS. Harley 322, where at fol. 74b occurs the poem "Seinte Marie, virgine moder" with musical notation.[27] I have printed a separate tune, or musical exercise, from a manuscript of Franciscan friar Nicholas Philipp's sermons in Appendix II.

On the other hand, the absence of musical settings does not indicate that a lyric was not meant to be sung. Nicholas Philipp, though he lived in the fifteenth century, interlarded his sermons with dozens of tag-rhymes and short poems in the manner suggested by thirteenth- and fourteenth-century preachers' compilations of the kind just mentioned, and those which we are presently to explore in greater depth. Some of the songs are for ornament or attraction, others are more integral to the sermon and can form critical steps in the argument. At the close of his Easter sermon he seems to have sung the following song, introducing it thus:

sic secure domino clames dicens sibi sic. Et cantes deuote in corde:

> Ihesu þat woldist for manys sake
> Suffrest þin bonys to crake,
> us from synn fre þu make.
> Comen ffrom heuen to oure wendynge
> & bere þe corounne þat was pynnyng
> & brynge us alle to good endynge.

Istam melodium si feceris ore mundo & corde puro. dominus supra domine tu exaudiet & tecum manebit & post vitam istam in gloria celesta te videbat . . . .[28]

Homer C. Pfander, in noticing this poem, has rightly observed that while a spoken poem was often called a song, it was far from customary to use the word *melodia* of verses which were spoken.[29] While

---

sic secure . . . corde, Thus to the Lord we cry in confidence. And sing with devoted hearts; *pynnyng,* torturous; *Istam . . . videbat,* This melody is to be made with a clean voice and pure heart. Lord of lords, hear us and abide with us and let us after this life in heavenly glory behold you.

Friar Nicholas gives here only the burden and one stanza of the song (the stanza occurring above the burden, physically reversing the *X X, a a a X* form), a song in the carol form undoubtedly would have had more verses in the actual performances. As with all popular lyric poetry where transmission is largely oral, the whole could be adequately signaled in a written text merely by a key stanza and burden, or often by the refrain alone. This particular song occurs in Nicholas' dilation of his fourth principle, "& loke he hafe good mynstralcye." He probably refers to actual singing, since in his brief development of the principle he speaks of the delight, *oblectamentum*, physical and spiritual, emanating from melody and musical instruments.[30] Two more things can be said about this delight: while Friar Nicholas is probably talking about the actual singing as well,[31] the fourth principle he elaborates nicely conforms to Bonaventure's injunctions concerning the mechanical arts which come under *theatrica*,[32] and further, involves the same *oblectamentum* which Bonaventure gives as the utility of the arts, that ultimate delight to which St. Francis also in the *Speculum perfectionis* and St. Anthony[33] addressed the medium of song.

Franciscan friars, we have noted, were sometimes mistaken for minstrels and not always happily. It has been popular among historians and anthologists to note condemnations of minstrels and popular singers in the time, and to assume a general clerical opposition to dabblings in popular song.[34] A familiar example and the most famous of such condemnations is contained in the manual of Thomas de Chabham, written about 1230 in Salisbury. It is not so frequently noted concerning this piece, however, that Chabham makes a particular exception of "ioculatores qui cantant gesta principium et vitas sanctorum."[35] Franciscan friar Thomas Docking also makes such a ritual condemnation of *hystrionibus* which "provocent homines ad ocium vel lasciviam," based in all probability on Chabham, but which expands on Chabham's qualification to say that if the minstrels or singers evidence that their purpose is spiritual benefit, then they are to be received as the "poor of Christ," a term reserved for fellow Friars Minor.[36] One fourteenth-century poet of undetermined religious connections illustrates the distinction Docking was getting at, when after decrying those who indulge "in vanis fabulis et turpiloquiis scurilitatibus ociosis et luxuriosis verbis," he writes:

> And techeþ vs goode vertues euene
> That bryngen vs to þe blisse of heuene.
> Of such þyng men shulde her matere take
> That writen rymes and hem can make,

> As of oure lady and of hire sone
> And of seyntis þat wiþ hem wone,
> Of holywrit þe examplis loke
> And holy myraclis writen in boke.
> Ffor what bote is it to sette trauaile
> Vppon þyng þat may nouȝt auaile,
> That nys but fantom of þis werld
> As ȝee han often seen and herd;
> ffor by þe fruyt men may see
> Of what vertue is ilk a tree.[37]

Presumably this exception was a large enough umbrella for poets of the Franciscan and kindred fraternal spirits. Certainly its injunction is honored by the thirteenth-century "Love Ron" of Thomas de Hales, "de ordine fratrum Minorum"—itself a fair précis of St. Francis' ideal for preaching, covering typically Franciscan points— which concludes with a statement of purpose which might speak for all of Franciscan poetry:

> þis rym, mayde, ich þe sende
>   open and wiþ-vte sel;
> Bidde ic þat þu hit vntrende
>   & leorny bute bok vych del;
> Her-of þat þu beo swiþe hende
>   & tech hit oþer maydenes wel.
> Hwo-so cuþe hit to þan ende,
>   hit wolde him stonde muchel stel.
>
> Hwenne þu sittest in longynge,
>   drauh þe forþ þis ilke wryt;
> Mid swete stephne þu hit singe,
>   & do al so hit þe byt . . . .[38]

As lengthy as the poem is, it should be noted, Thomas says that it may be sung.

It is not always recognized that poems "sung" in the Middle Ages may not have sounded very much like lyric poems sung after the Renaissance. In early medieval troubadour music there is no fixed meter, as in later lyrics. Unlike the later forms, where polyphonic music was emphasized often at the expense of the poems, in early lyrics the poem itself was central, and recent studies show that

---

bote, profit.

vntrende, unroll; *leorny,* learn; *bute,* without; *hende,* courteous; *ilke,* same; *wryt,* writing; *stephne,* voice.

accompanying music closely followed the declamatory rhythm of the poetry, rather than the other way around, especially in non-carol forms. The declamatory chant style turns out to be, at least in troubadour and trouvère poetry, the musical style most associated with poems in non-ballad or carol form, and it is especially prevalent in the *a b a b x x x . . . a* form and its variants[39]—a kind found in English in MS. Harley 2253 for example ("Iesu, for þi muchele miht"). This suggests one way of "singing" for lyrics appropriate to preaching, or even private devotion, and another, the more metrical measure which we better understand, probably to be associated with group singing and probably in *X X, a a a X* carol form. A further idea of this, at least in a general way, may be obtained from imagining the performance of the Annunciation lyric in the Wakefield Cycle—very likely chanted or sung to provide a contrast with the regular speech of the play, as opposed to the song of the shepherds in the *Second Shepherd's Play* of that cycle, which is specifically to be in measured three-part harmony.[40]

Because, despite the substantial number of song texts, a relatively small percentage of medieval English lyrics survive with their music, some scholars (e.g., Rosemary Woolf) have underestimated the relationship of the Middle English lyrics to song. But there are fairly simple reasons for the relative shortage of manuscripts with musical notation. First of all, to judge from the kinds of variations among poems of multiple texts, most of the poems were conveyed orally, and transcribed by memory or from recitation. We should not assume that the "author" or compiler of a preacher's handbook, for example, would have composed all or even many of the poems he transcribes. Rather, he may have heard them, been impressed, and copied them into his book, as the friar who owned it before him probably had done as well. Presumably a knowledge of the melodies of the poems was also a matter of aural retention—as it was in church hymnals and ballad books until fairly recently; and because the music was more easily memorized and required a much more specialized skill to transcribe, it was seldom written down. We should be wary of the temptation to draw too specific an inference here from contemporary cultures where the written vocabulary of music was much better distributed, and where, naturally enough, a solid majority of lyrics are preserved with their music; for example, in northern France over fourteen hundred (of two thousand) trouvère lyrics have been preserved with their musical accompaniment. But even there, in cases where there are multiple copies of a text, the music shows the same kinds of discrepancies, attributable to aural error, as does the poetry

There are in English manuscripts a number of instances of dance songs converted to sermon use, which fact suggests a lively flexibility for adaptation of popular materials to religious purposes among English Franciscans. A song from MS. Bodley 26 is one case in point. It occurs in a series of Franciscan sermon outlines dated before 1350.[41] The sermon notes themselves are in Latin, with the English phrases and rhyme tags interspersed. Beginning at folio 201b is an exposition of the four locks by which the heart of the sinner is closed, of the several keys which will open these locks, and then of the banquet to which Christ invites all those who will open the door to him:

> . . . pro 3° panes . . . 3^m farculum gaudiorum omnium plenitudinem & iocunditatem & hoc est cena de qua in apoc. xix. 9 beati qui ad cenam agni vocati sunt; ad quam cenam specialiter vocat deus 3^a hominum genera sicud alibi, &c.

Honnd by honnd we schulle ous take,
& ioye & blisse schulle we make,
for þe deuel of elle man haȝt for-sake,
& godes sone ys maked oure make.

A child is boren a-monges man,
& in þat child was no wam.
þat child ys god, þat child is man,
& in þat child oure lif bygan.
  Honnd by honnd þanne schulle ous take, &c.

Senful man be bliþe and glad,
for your mariage þy peys ys grad,
  wan crist was boren:
com to crist, þy peis ys grad,
for þe was hys blod ysched,
  þat were for-loren.
    Honnd by honnd þanne schulle ous take
    & ioye & blisse schulle we make, &c.

Senful man be bliþe & bold,
for euene ys boþe boȝt & sold,
  euereche fote:
com to crist, þy pes ys told,
for þe he ȝahf a hondre fold,
  hys lif to bote.
Honnd by honnd, &c.[42]

. . . from three loaves . . . three dishes of joy, of all plenty and mirth, and this is that meal spoken of in Apocalypse 19:9 of the blessed who are invited to the feast of the lamb; to this special feast God invites three kinds of men . . . .

maked, made; *make*, companion; *wam*, stain; *grad*, prepared; *euereche fote*, in full measure; *ȝahf*, gave.

Plate 8. Friars and Nuns at Song and Dance (B.M. Royal 2.B.vii)

Words written alongside the last stanza and below it, "secundum primos thema tristicia vestra convertetur in gaudium Joh. 16: Verba ista sunt Christi ad discipulos . . . ," show the way in which this poem was worked into the sermon. The refrain is clearly adapted from that of a popular ring-dance in just the manner suggested by Italian Franciscan examples, and with the same spiritual overtones of Old and New Dance-song appropriate to its understanding. A manuscript illustration which shows Franciscans garbed like minstrels and cheerfully ring-dancing "honnd by honnd" (Plate 8) may even suggest that such poems, like certain of the Italian lyrics, could on occasion be performed in this way.[43] There are other examples of dance-songs being so employed in the course of sermon notes. One occurs in a sermon collection of undetermined provenance, MS. Worcester Cathedral F. 126, fol. 28; here the song is "Gay, gay þou ert yhent." This, too, has been given religious words, though the part of the burden and the form indicate the existence of its secular version.

Popular songs also are employed in sermons simply as auxiliary texts. For example, in the sermon manuscript of Nicholas Philipp there is another poem, a three-stanza secular song, apparently unaltered, which is made the basis for an extended and sober moralization.[44] In Trinity Coll. Camb. MS. 43 another sermon begins with a quotation from a popular song:

> Atte wrastling mi lemman i ches
> and atte ston kasting i him for-les.

After quoting his biblical texts (from Matthew 12 and 1 Corinthians 9) in Latin, and uttering his invocation, the friar says:

> Mi leue frend, wilde wimmen & gol men i mi contereie wan he gon o
> þe ring, among manie oþere songis þat litil ben wort þat tei singin
> so sein þei þus: Atte wrastling mi leman, etc.

Here is a sample of the "exegesis" he makes from the lines of the song refrain:

ches, chose.

gol, lustful.

Atte wrastlinge, *ut supra*. Nu mon we understondin i þeise wordis to manere of folk. þe ton is þat bleþeliche & mid suet herte herin godis word & mid bisinesse ben abutin to chesin ihu crist here saule lemman, þat dere had a-bout here loue mid blodi wondis & mid deth on rode, and chesin him atte wrastlings as i er seide.

Wrastlinge is a manere of feiteinge. & sikirlike ne comid no man to his loue ne to his blisse but he be god champiun & manlike feite again hise 3 fomen. þo ben þe deuel of helle, his owene sinfule fles, and tre þe cuuenant to world. & he þat tus don mouen sein þe forme word of ure songe, "Atte wrastlinge."[45]

The subsequent portion of the sermon proceeds in the same vein and concludes with a plangent petition to Christ to give all men responsive and loving hearts. Thus we can see that the popular song, unaltered, might be incorporated into a sermon bodily and so given association, for the congregation at least, forever after with the message of the sermon—a touch of pedagogical genius. Here again fraternal history could offer a model: St. Francis himself once took a couplet from an Italian secular song as the text for a sermon,[46] though his adaptation seems somewhat smoother than that of "Atte wrastling" or the songs used by Nicholas Philipp.

On the whole, when we consider that the form and nature of preaching collections usually dictated an abbreviated version of a poem if it was to be included at all, the many preaching manuscripts which do contain poems and songs acquire extra significance. The general admonition of St. Francis to his *ioculatores* was to preach for the "utility and edification of the people, announcing to them vices and virtues, punishment and glory, with brevity of speech, because the Lord made His words short upon the earth" (*Regula*, chap. 9). This injunction plus the added suggestion for employing songs in the *Speculum perfectionis* basically characterize the content and methodology of preaching which St. Francis suggested to the early brethren of the Order. Their interests were typically pragmatic. For homiletical style, we have the sparkling eyewitness testimony of a bemused Thomas of Spolanto that St. Francis preached "not according to the rules, but like a tub-thumper."[47] His followers, like Bernardino of Siena and Friar Richard,[48] were prone to employ a similar vigor. Where extras are included the purpose is utilitarian. Berthold von Regensburg, like the Friar preaching at the cloister of the Innocents one hundred and sixty years later, will seem only for a moment more wastefully elaborate in being attentive even to staging details in his

bisinesse, devotion; *lemman*, beloved; *rode*, cross; *cuuenant*, covenant.

preaching environment: Salimbene tells us how for one sermon he had his pulpit set up over against a gibbet whereon gently swung the decomposing bodies of several thieves.[49]

The great importance which the Franciscans attached to preaching is characterized by St. Bernardino of Siena, who held attendance at sermons even more important than attendance at the Mass: "If of those two things you can only do one—either hear the mass or hear the sermon—you should let the mass go rather than the sermon."[50] When Eccleston reports that Grosseteste instructed the first English Franciscan friars "both in scholastic discussions and in the subtle moralities suitable for preaching," he indicates the consistent relationship of Franciscan theological principles to the concrete practical job of evangelism. In short, there is little room for doubting that the expressed principles of the Franciscan theologians are relevant guides to the practice and methodology of Franciscan preachers. Even the rigorously academic *Dicta* of Grosseteste discussed in chapter three above are referred directly to the use of preachers, who are invited to invent examples of their own to illustrate the theological points discussed.[51]

Yet if we attempt to obtain a firsthand knowledge of the English Franciscans' preaching we are met, strangely enough, by some difficulty in finding textually complete sermons.[52] There are plenty of Franciscan chronicles, but few if any sermons. In considering this problem, A. G. Little writes:

> Now, if we consider first the works relating expressly to the history of either of the two Orders, one contrast at once strikes us. Such histories are fairly numerous among the Franciscans, rare among the Dominicans . . . . What is the explanation of this remarkable contrast? It does not seem to be that Dominican chronicles have been lost: the Friars Preachers have preserved their *records* much better than the Friars Minor.

Little reasons that the Franciscan concern with the preservation of chronicles—in Latin—rather than with the recording of vernacular sermons owes to the apocalyptic self-view of the historiologically sensitive Order, and secondly to the fierce struggle between the Conventuals and Spirituals which forced the latter in particular to appeal to history for support.[53] If we add to this the general principle that vernacular sermons of any kind were apparently not often considered worthy of transcribing in the period, we may appreciate that there are reasons for the lack of complete English Franciscan sermons at our disposal.[54]

Besides the sermon of Nicholas Philipp already cited, however, there
are a few Franciscan sermons containing poetry, and quite a number
of preachers' handbooks—collections for the use of preachers like the
ones referred to above—which are of Franciscan provenance and which
together with the few sermons can give a sufficent idea of the performance context of certain varieties of Middle English lyric.

It has been recognized for some time that wandering friars were
the first in England to use vernacular verse in their sermons,[55] and
various preachers' compilations in addition to those already mentioned
suggest the continued employment of English lyrics in the course of
evangelical sermonizing.[56] Indeed, Wyclif in his denunciation of the
friars makes it plain that even in his day they continued to embellish
their preaching by the use of poetry:

> For freres in her prechinge fordon prechinge of Crist, and prechen
> lesyngus and japes plesynge to þe peple; . . . . For þei docken Goddis
> word, and tateren it bi þer rimes, þat þe fowrme þat Crist ȝaf it is
> hidde by ypocrisie.[57]

Not all Middle English lyrics were formally set to music, obviously,
and almost certainly not all of those set originally to a tune were
always sung when used. The Franciscan preacher could employ a
lyric poem in such a way that music was hardly essential to his
purpose. But, as in one Rood poem from MS. Harley 913 (the Kildare
MS. of Franciscan verse), the friar in either case seldom leaves much
doubt as to the functional value accorded to the lyric, poem or song.
At folio 28 we read:

> Respice in faciem Christi tui etc. Augustinus. Pendens nudatum pec-
> tus, rubet sanguineum latus, regia pallent ora, decora languent
> lumina, crura pendent marmorea, rigat terebratos pedes sanguinis
> unda. De istis auctoritatibus anglicum:
>
>> Behold to þi lord, man, whare he hangiþ on rode,
>> And weep, if þou miȝt, teris al of blode,
>> And loke to is heued wiþ þornis al bewende
>> And to is felle so bispette and to þe sper is wnde.[58]

Respice . . . anglicum, Consider yourself in the presence of Christ—[in the manner
suggested by St.] Augustine—hanging with naked breast, dripping with red blood,
regality fading, eyes faintly shining, marble-like legs hanging, pierced feet wet
with streams of blood. Adduce the testimony of this English poem.

bewende, wreathed; *felle,* skin; *bispette,* bespat

The poem continues for another twelve lines, describing vividly the anguish of Christ on the cross, then adds a note for the preacher's interjection: "Dilexit nos et lauit nos peccatis nostris in sanguine suo, etc." [He loved us and washed us from our sins in his blood . . . .] Following a final couplet there appears at the top of the next page further notation to the preacher for drawing the point of his sermon:

Quid misericordius ualet intelligi ipsi peccatori eternis tormentis dampnato et, vnde se redimat, non habenti quam ut dicat deus ipse peccatori. Dicit enim deus pater: "Accipe vnigenitum meum et da [tum] pro te." Et ille filius: "Tolle me et redime te." Anglicum expone.

[What more merciful thing can be heard by the sinner himself, condemned to eternal torments and unable to redeem himself, than that God himself should speak to the sinner? For God the father says, "Receive my only-begotten son, given for you." And the son says (to the sinner), "Take me up and redeem yourself." Set it forth in English.]

Two quatrains of another poem turn this toward the perspective of the hearer (more, it is indicated, were sung in the performance), and begin vigorously to pound home the traditional Franciscan theme of identification with the Passion of Christ which produces contrition. The preacher at this point sums up dramatically (his notes in Latin again), then plunges into a dramatic monologue of the "Christ-from-the Cross" type:

Man, bihold what ich for þe
þolid up þe rode tre.
Ne mai no kinnes wo be mare
þan min was, þo ich henge þare.
Hire me, man, to þe gredind,
For loue of þe biter deiend;
Loke my pinis biter and strang,
Wan ich was nailed þroჳ fot and hond.
For þe ich ad hard stundes,
Dintes grete and sore wondes;
For þe biter drink ich dronk,
And þou cunnest me no þonk.
Wiþ vte ich was ipinid sore,
Wiþ in ich was mochil more.
For þou nelt þonk me
þe poue þat ich schowid þe, *etc.*

þolid, suffered; *kinnes,* peoples'; *Hire,* hear; *gredind,* crying out; *deiend,* dying; *pinis,* torments; *stundes,* hours; *Dintes,* blows; *cunnest,* acknowledge; *ipinid,* tortured; *mochil,* much; *nelt,* would not.

The outline of the rest of the sermon follows, beginning with this
note: "Preparandum est cor hominis tamquam domus ad magnam
hospitem suscipiendum, Christum sanctum dominum" (MS. fol. 29).
It would be difficult to find a clearer indication that English Franciscans (here an Anglo-Irish Franciscan) used vernacular poetry in
the way commanded by St. Francis in *Speculum perfectionis,* or one
which better illustrates the appropriation of the poetic medium to
Passion-centered, contrition-minded Franciscan theology and spirituality as it also follows from Italian models to English Franciscan
sermons.[59]

Like the Italian Franciscan poems, such English Crucifixion poems
can focus attention on the physical agonies of Christ, or on the sorrows of Mary (as in "Stabat mater ounder rode"). One poem from
Franciscan friar John Grimestone's Commonplace book, in the traditional *X X, a a a X* form also, is an alternating dialogue, stanza and
refrain, between Mary and Christ—pointing to the Virgin's new relationship to the Christian as exemplified in the disciple John:

> Womman, Ion I take to þe
> Instede of me þi sone to be.
>
> Allas! we sal myn herte slaken?
> To Ion I am towarde taken;
> Mi blisful Sone me hat forsaken,
>   And I haue no mo.
>
> Womman, Ion I take to þe
> Instede of me þi sone to be.
>
> Wel may I mone and murning maken,
> And wepen til myn eyne aken,
> For wane of wele my wo is waken,
>   Was neuere wif so wo!
>   Womman, Ion I take to þe
>   Instede of me þi sone to be.[60]

The poem calls to mind both the relevant passage from the *Meditations on the Life of Christ* (chap. 79) and Italian Franciscan poems
on the subject,[61] revealing that the English Franciscans retained the
affective spiritual orientation to the Passion characteristic of Franciscan theology and Italian Franciscan poetry.

The employment of such songs in sermons could turn toward
specific objects of the liturgy or symbols of worship in an effort to

we, when; *slaken,* be set free; *wane,* loss; *wele,* joy.

make the same theological points. In the following instance the preacher appears to take apt advantage of the presence of the crucifix:

> Sires, beholde before you the figure of oure redemptour Ihesu Crist, as he honge in þe crosse in þe same fourme þat he suffered deþ in and brouȝt mankynde fro the peynes of helle. Wherfore he cryeþ and seiþ to vs yche day in syche wordes:

> > Lystne, man, lystne to me,
> > Byholde what I thole for the.
> > To the, man, well lowde I crye;
> > For thy loue þou seest I dye.
> > Byholde my body how I am swongyn;
> > Se þe nayles howe I am þrouȝ stongyn,
> > My body withoute is betyn sore,
> > My peynes with-in ben wel more.
> > All this I haue thelyd for the
> > As þou schalt at Domysday se.[62]

The last line provides a transition device from the crucifixion scene to the Last Judgment,[63] which is the substance of the balance of the sermon, and which in typically Franciscan fashion proceeds to contrast the mercy and love evidenced in the Passion with the inevitable justice of the Last Judgment.[64]

Though other manuscripts of actual Franciscan sermons which employ verse could be cited,[65] one or two further illustrations from these relatively scarce sources will be sufficient to show the kinds of uses to which the vernacular lyric might be put in a sermon. In one sermon on the Passion, preserved in three manuscripts from about 1390–1440, are many short poems in English. Four of these are designated as prayers in the manner of the following example:

> > Facies sibi istam oracionem,
> > lord blyssyd be þi name;
> > for me þu suffered despyte & schame;
> > for as þu ert full of grace,
> > þe to serfe gyfe me space.[66]

As we have seen, this is the sort of moral doctrinal poem which Berthold von Regensburg employed in his sermons, and which is represented in the works of Jacopone da Todi.

thole, suffer; *swongyn*, scourged; *thelyd*, suffered.

Another poem, from Bodleian MS. 1871, from which comes also "Honnd by honnd we schulle ous take" quoted above, is one whose burden,

> My doȝter, my darlynnge,
> Herkne my lore, y-se my thechyng,[67]

is repeated several times in the text, and then at fol. 193b is placed together with the following stanza:

> How mankende furst bygan,
> In what manschepe now ys man,
> What wykednesse man hat y-do,
> What ioye and blisse man ys y-broȝt.[68]

With its enclosing sermon, this last verse is exemplary of the Franciscan poetic and particularly preaching ideal as stated in chapter 9 of the *Rule*.

In England, as in Italy, such poems are generally found in manuscripts of pastoralia rather than in sermons. Even if the relative scarcity of extant Franciscan sermons leaves our understanding of the friars' homiletical use of vernacular lyrics somewhat incomplete, the great number of such lyrics in general pastoral collections written and used by Franciscans establishes the pattern of their use beyond doubt. And such collections are far from scarce; the end of the thirteenth century in England appears to have witnessed a considerable proliferation of preaching manuals, which may reasonably be assumed to relate to an official rededication to preaching in which the Franciscans were centrally involved. Grosseteste, like Pecham forty years later (1271), drew attention to this concern by ordering parish preaching on a list of subjects. His list serves to identify the subject matter the friars might expound upon, and to which parish priests or seculars were invited to give their attention.[69] It includes the Articles of the Creed, the Ten Commandments, the Seven Sacraments, Seven Works of Mercy, Seven Virtues, and Seven Vices. Although none of the thirty-eight manuscripts of Pecham's *Lambeth constitutiones* are earlier than the fourteenth century, there is ample evidence to show that a number of manuals owing to its influence sprang up in the thirteenth century, and the authors of these compilations appear for the most part to have been Franciscans. The title

thechyng, teaching.

manschepe, human condition.

of one such collection (not an English one) illustrates the practical function of the preaching handbook: "Dormi secure"—in other words, don't worry about your sermon tomorrow, all you will need is in this little book.[70]

Notable among early collections of this kind is the *Liber exemplorum*, compiled by an English Franciscan about 1275, but in Ireland. Only one manuscript, which has been edited by A. G. Little, exists.[71] In the same manuscript occurs the poem *Stimulis amoris* of Friar Giacomo da Milano, sometimes ascribed to Bonaventure. The *Liber exemplorum* frequently cites Gerald of Wales,[72] the *Vitae Patrum*, the Bible, Gregory the Great, Augustine, the *Summa de vitiis et virtutibus* of Guillelmus Peraldus (in that order of preference), and thirty-seven other authors of rank.[73] It stresses the person of the Virgin, and the usual doctrinal mainsprings. The *Liber* employs some Latin rhyme (chap. 184), and in one place gives explicit directions for concluding an exemplum in verse.[74]

The *Speculum laicorum*, another preaching manual, was compiled toward the end of the thirteenth century, during the archepiscopate of John Pecham, by an English friar who was most probably a Franciscan from East Anglia.[75] Still known and used extensively in the seventeenth century, it addresses itself to the chief subjects of Franciscan theology and spirituality as discussed in chapters two and three above, coming to the traditional applications and conclusions at all points.[76] It centers, as does all of Franciscan theology, practical or academic, on the Passion of Christ. In chapter 63, "De Christi Passione," while stressing that men's attention ought to be turned constantly toward the Passion, the author says:

> Memoranda Christianis est sepius Christi passio propter tria: 1º quia liberat ab exterminatore . . . 2º quia confortat exercitates in labore . . . 3º quia consolidat in amore.[77]

At every stage up to this point several *exempla* have been adduced for the selection of the friar or preacher using the manual: at this point, curiously, there are only two stories suggested (one the stigmatization of St. Francis), and a space left, presumably for use at the preacher's discretion.[78]

Les Contes moralisés de Nicole Bozon, Frère Mineur, were compiled in French by an English Franciscan soon after 1320,[79] and were intended to be used in a similar way to the other collections cited. Bozon's poetry is in vernacular Anglo-French and has become much better known than most of the English collections.

The *Fasciculus morum* is a very important preacher's collection

which is not so well known. It exists in at least twenty-one manuscripts, is ascribed in some of them to a Franciscan named Robert
Silke, or Selk (in one manuscript, John Spiser), and was apparently
written before 1340.[80] It has not been edited, nor is it likely to be
for some time because there are great variations among the manuscripts, with whole sections altered or transposed. The strongest
manuscript tradition which I have been able to determine covers
only a few versions.[81] However, there is a basic structure common
to most of the manuscripts which divides into seven parts, each
treating of a vice with its counteracting virtue.[82] Part V, on *accidia*
and the means by which it can be overcome (Mass, penance, confession, contrition, prayer, alms, faith, etc.), and Part III, which includes
chapters on the life and death of Christ, break down into the greatest
number of sub-chapters and provide the greatest number of variable
inclusions. Significantly Friar Silke (if that was his name) opens with
a reference to Chapter 9 of the *Rule* of St. Francis: "As it is laid
down in the Rule of our blessed Father Francis, we are bound to
preach to the people and announce to them vices and virtues, punishment and glory, with brevity of speech; therefore we will begin with
vices and end with virtues."[83] This did not mean that he would
exclude traditional and scriptural sources however: he cites the Bible,
Augustine, Gregory, Jerome, and other Fathers, saints' lives, Aristotle,
Ovid, Virgil, Martial, Valerius, Vegetius, Seneca, Pliny, Boethius,
Isidore, Rabanus Maurus, Alexander Neckham, John of Salisbury,
William of Malmesbury, Robert Grosseteste, Matthew Paris, Vincent
of Beauvais, St. Bonaventure, the *Meditations on the Life of Christ,*
and St. Bernard's Sermons on Advent.[84] In other words, he had
available to him a library as extensive as the Franciscan libraries
discussed at the outset of chapter three. It is especially remarkable
that he is careful to confine himself to passages and ideas which
could be easily understood by less literate people.[85]

What makes the *Fasciculus morum* most interesting is that like
manuscripts as diverse as MSS. Royal 12 E. i, Arundel 248, Bodley
26 and others noted above, it includes poems for the use of the
preacher.[86] As the *Fasciculus* was the most widely used collection
expressly designed as a preaching aid in its time, it presents highly
creditable evidence of a Franciscan attempt to augment the program
of lay instruction with vernacular English verse. It should be noted
that not all manuscripts have the same poems, indicating that
favorites of each subsequent transcriber could be included at his
own will, or others excluded at his whim; not all of the poems which
I shall cite have to my knowledge been printed before.

The Passion, naturally enough, is central also to the *Fasciculus morum*, and crucifixion lyrics are suggested to the preacher. One, in MS. Rawlinson C. 670, is of the familiar "dialogue" type; in this case, Christ addresses the sinner from the cross:

> Behold myne woundes how sore y am dyȝth;
> ffor all þe wele þat þu hast y wun hit in fyȝt.
> I am sore wondet: behold on my skyn;
> leuie lyf for my leuie let me comen yn.[87]

The rest of the song is not included, but the direct nature of the appeal is already explicit. It follows the usual theme of "Behold, see how much Christ has suffered for you, and thus how much he loves you. Therefore forsake worldly loves and return the love of Christ." Two poems from another manuscript of the *Fasciculus morum* turn to the third person admonition to speak to this point.

> Loue god, thou man that loueth the;
> Ffor the he sufferd dethe vp on a tree
> And brought the oute of helle.
> Loue hym with herte soule & thouȝte
> Which he hathe derer boughte
> Than any tonge can telle.[88]

> Treweloue among men þat most ye of let,
> In hatte and in hoode hit ys þe bet.
> Treweloue in herbis sprinketh in may,
> But trewe loue in herte gaweth a way.

There follows a short exposition of these lines in Latin on the order of the "Atte Wrastlinge" poem discussed above, and then the ubiquitous injunction "sic dicite in anglice":

> Loue god þu man ouer all thinge
> sythen thy self with [outyn] sinnyng,
> synthen thy frynde as kynde the tech,
> afterward þy foo with outyn any wreth.[89]

Evidently what we have here is an exposition based on the exegesis of either fragments of a poetic homily, or possibly a song which addresses itself to the problem of the "kinds of love." While at first glance we might not expect it to be sung in the context provided,

dyȝth, dealt with; *fyȝt*, fighting; *leuie*, beloved.

let, learn; *bet*, better; *sprinketh*, springs.

sythen, then; *kynde*, nature; *wreth*, wrath.

the poem resembles a greatly extended multistanzaic poem of this type used by Friar Nicholas and called in the manuscript of his sermons a song, so that it may well be that quatrain versifications of Scripture (the poem above culminates in the Great Commandment) or stanzaic moralizations were also performed in this way as homily, if not as part of the liturgy.[90] Certainly whole versified sermons were sung, and in some cases their music has been preserved.[91]

The Rawlinson C. 670 manuscript of the *Fasciculus morum* also contains a fragment of a Christ-from-the-cross song; the scribe had perhaps forgotten the poem in its entirety, yet he works tantalizing snatches of it into his section "de contricione et elemosma":

> Ffyre wat waynd & lond
> y wilne to haue in my honde.
>
> ....
>
> Byd fast and y come.
> sone yf þow sorow þe cut þy bone
>
> ....
>
> Whyle þu bydde redy y am,
> When þu lenyst y go þe fram.
>
> ....
>
> & Anglice sic:
> I helpe anon forsake,
> gladly y fyȝt þe maystry to take.[92]

The application of this poem, even from the few lines given, is quite apparent.

In the same manuscript occurs a poem, typical of the "orison" lyric, following from an ordered discussion of man's sinful state, Christ's sacrifice, the propriety of contrition, and the necessity of grace. It is in an imperfect carol form:

> Mary moder of grace we cry en to þe,
> moder of mercy & of pyte,
> Wyte us fro þe fendes fondyng
> And helpe us at oure last endynge.
>
> & to þy sone oure pes þu make
> þat he on us no wrethe take.
> Alle þe halewen þat aren in heuen
> to ȝow I cry with mylde steuene.
> Helpe þat cryst my gult forȝene
> And I wol hym serue whyl þat I leue.[93]

Ffyre, fire; *waynd*, air; *wilne*, wish; *lenyst*, turn away.

pyte, compassion; *fendes fondyng*, devils' tempting; *halewen*, saints; *steuene*, voice; *forȝene*, forgive.

While poem scraps,[94] or unfollowed "dice in anglice" headings abound throughout the manuscripts' contents, indicating that songs might be brought to bear on the preachers' materials anywhere, the heaviest concentration of longer quotations occurs in those sections which apply themselves to the reasons for repentance: the Passion of Christ, and man's inevitable death. Thus, in the section of pride versus humility there is a subsection entitled "de fragilitate vite," and in it, Friar Silke attacks "þe syne of pride"; "Superbia cordis unde Anglios":

> Wrecche man wy artou proud
> þat art of herth ymaked
> hydr ne browtestou no schroud
> bot pore you come & naked.
> Wen þi soule is faren out
> þi body with erthe y raked
> þat body þat was so rouk and loued
> of alle men is hated.[95]

The sense of fleeting time is very apparent, and inevitably there is a play on time with respect to repentance. Sometimes it is gentle:

> Now is tyme to sle ant tyme to hele,
> tyme to gedder ant tyme to dele . . . .[96]

"Ecce nunc tempus," the preacher says, for you to become contrite and repent, for (here another note): "dicite in anglois, ende narrat de quodum,"

> Who so woll noȝt when he may,
> he schall noȝt when he wolt.
> When þon þy lyfe upholdyste,
> þenke wan þu arte coldyste
> and do gode at þe ȝate;
> When þu with deth unholdest
> ffor þan is al to late.[97]

Of course, on occasion the message could be considerably blunted, as in the following popular ditty, of which we have in one manuscript of the *Fasciculus morum* three grisly stanzas and a stark refrain:

herth, earth; *browtestou,* brought you; *faren,* gone; *rouk,* cherished.

upholdyste, consider; *ȝate,* gate; *unholdest,* conjure.

> Whenne þe hed quaketh
> and þe lippis blakyth
> and þe nose sharpyth
> and þe synwys starkyþ,
>
> and þe brest pantyþ
> and þe breþ wantyþ
> Whane þe teyþ ratellyth
> & þe þrote rotelyþ.
>
> Thenne þe sowle fro þe body ys fet
> And þe body þan clout fast ys y knet,
> And a noyn after buryd yn a pit
> And with erthe fast ys det,
>
> Then a noyn be hyt so he reke,
> Body & sowle ys clene forȝete.[98]

A song inserted by the compiler of one manuscript has a nearly illegible refrain which is likewise bluntly pointed, but allows itself in the quoted stanza a pleasing bit of vernal (and biblical) imagery:

> þe flesches lust may þu nouȝt olyne—better quenche
> Bote after þy deth [which] þu beȝ euer more be þenche.
>
> Mon ibere of women he lyueth but a stonde;
> In wrechednes and in wo ben his dayes.
> Woude he sprynges out as blossome & some falles to gronde
> And wondes away as schadewe þat ne wey is ifonde.[99]

Yet there is no flagging in the purpose of either sermon or song, and in lines reminiscent of certain quatrains from the Italian MS. Cortona 91, the preacher could sing or say:

> He þat hem kuyth he ruyt ful sore
> Amende thi life an synnomore
> Lest he ofte so riue þe;
> þat þou be war y rede the.[100]

The perspective of the question of repentance, ordered along the temporal plane, looks toward the Final Judgment, where ("nocent tunc placebunt Anglios sic"):

sharpyth, sharpens; synwys starkyþ, muscles atrophy; rotelyþ,? fet, freed; a noyn, immediately; det, covered; reke, stinks.

slyne, slay; stonde, hour.

kuyth, knew; ruyt, grieves; riue, chasten; rede, warn.

an schal stynt þat now is kyd,
an shal seme þat now is hid,
an shal deie þat now likyth,
an shal like þat now swikith.[101]

Yet not all of the conjurations of death and the grave in Franciscan pastoralia collections are so gloomy. The compiler of MS. Laud Miscellany 111 adds another kind of sometimes ill-wrought verse; for example:

Who so speket ofte of þyng þat is vnwrest,
þou hit seme soft wen he speketh mest,
he schal hyt heryn on left wen he weynth lof
Bet to let thy tunge rest, and þe schal nouȝt reu,
                    quod hendynge.[102]

This homely saw is useful to show a tendency in the tone of the collection, which is not all so dark as some of the poems might project. In fact, it is typical of the *Fasciculus morum* that its compilers do not over-stress material on the Last Judgment, but in the typically moralizing Franciscan fashion turn from poems and tags like the lines just quoted to discourse on the practical and more immediate evils of gossip, backbiting, and nagging wives.[103]

Life is, however, a transient thing, and few poems are far from the theme of the necessity of contrition and repentance while there is time. In the section "de Avaricia" occurs another poem which has somehow missed being indexed by Brown and Robbins. In MS. Bod. 187 it is prefaced with an attribution to an author—the same man whose name appears in the poem—"fit illo Wulfrido ioculatore . . . ." It warns of Dame Fortune:

The mantel þat þe kyng to Wulfryde lent
Wt haþ hyt com : & wt haþ hyt went.
The lady dam fortune ys boþe frende & foo,
of pore she makyth riche & of ryche pore al so;
she turnyþ wele to wo & wo to wele al so;
Tryst nat þu on: for hyt ys sone a go.[104]

(Obviously the term "ioculatore" could be somewhat loosely applied, or else Wulfrid's poem came to the *Fasciculus* compiler in a mutilated

stynt, cease; *kyd,* active; *seme,* be known; *likyth,* pleases; *like,* please; *swikith,* displeases.

vnwrest, wicked.

condition.) The idea of the fickleness of Fortune works well, of course, with the general idea of the impermanence of life to undergird the Franciscan preachers' contention that it would be better to repent and confess now than to risk putting it off for a later hour which might not arrive. Another example follows: a moralizing poem in first person dialogue, its couplet separated by lines of Latin exposition, it shows that time and Fortune are no respecters of persons:

> Kyng y sitt and loke aboute,
> tomorue y may be wtout.
>
> ....
>
> Wo is me, a kyng y was;
> is world y loued & hit y lasse.
>
> ....
>
> Rowȝt longe agone ywas ful riche,
> but nou is riche and pore y liche.
>
> ....
>
> y schallbe kyng þat me schall see,
> But as a wreche y shal ded bee.[105]

The examples thus far given from the *Fasciculus morum* and other homiletic handbooks suggest a number of ways in which Middle English lyrics and carols might have been used. Obviously, some could simply be injected into the sermon as an illustration, such as Wulfrid's poem about his erstwhile coat. Others, such as "Loue god thou man" and "Mary moder of grace" might be sung; perhaps the latter might be sung responsively, the preacher or another friar acting as *cantor*. "Dramatic" poems, such as the ones in which Christ speaks from the cross, could call for some minor role-playing by the preacher, and poems in which a dialogue occurs, such as the one above, open the possibility of more definite play-acting.[106]

But there are other interesting uses of English lines which suggest that parts of the homiletical narrative may even have been carried in the form of a poem or song or at least rhyming English lines. Thus, in MS. Rawlinson C. 670 of the *Fasciculus,* in an unbroken flow of sense from Latin to English under the heading "de Avaricia" occur the following two lines:

> The ryche ne rychesse god ne hatyth
> But who so for rychesse god forsakyth,

Rowȝt, I reckon; *y liche*, alike.

continued in the Latin to the effect that "then Christ will forsake him," and so on. And in the section "de elemosina" of another manuscript there is a discourse on the parable of the prodigal son after which appear the following lines among the Latin commentary:

> y spende þat y hadde;
> that y ȝaf, þat y haue;
> That y kepte, þat y lost,[107]

and then the Latin resumes as if there had not been any transposition. Rosemary Woolf's point that Middle English lyrics are often incomplete, and that knowledge of an "enclosing story" is presupposed,[108] is amply justified in the light of Franciscan handbooks and preaching manuals. The examples given are similar to tag-ends found elsewhere in medieval sermons intended for vernacular delivery, but in certain instances, like these two, the continuous flow of sense suggests that it may have been possible to use at such junctures verse-sermons of the kind existing in the Franciscan Kildare manuscript, or the seventh tabula of the *Speculum Christiani*.[109]

Versification of the Ten Commandments was common among Franciscans and considerable variation prevails among even the manuscripts of the *Fasciculus morum*. The version in one of the manuscripts runs:

> Tak uno god bot on in heuen;
> Neme noght hys neme in ydel stenyn;
> Kepe ryght wel þyn holyday;
> þi fadur þi modur þu worchyp ay;
> Loke þu be no man sleuer,
> Of fals wettnes no berer;
> þu schalte do no lychory
> ne no thefft of felany;
> thy neyburs gode ne þu wyll
> Ne wyffe ne doghter ne mayden moue for to spul.[110]

The manuscripts of the *Fasciculus morum* contain more poems and many more scraps or key lines to poems than can be included here. There are poems which might be styled as political[111] as well as theological and moral. One poem even troubles itself to condemn certain kinds of avant-garde dancing.[112] The general tone of the poems runs from plaintive to laudatory, from thoughtful to what we

stenyn, speech.

might think morbid, and from pensive to fiery. But it is not all hellfire and brimstone, gloom and doom, despite the inevitable and typical apocalyptic tone of some passages. A touch of nonsense and laughter runs through the compilation as well—as in the following lines:

> Here is comon þat no man wot,
> þe deuol in þy eye & rew forth þe boot.[113]

Nor did Satan threaten overmuch:

> The fende our fo ne may us dere
> bot ȝif we bowen to hym for fere.
> he is a lyon bot þu wiht stonde
> and ferde as flyȝe yf þou ne wonde.[114]

Though the world was full of cupidity and doubt, there was an appeal open to truth and righteousness through God's great gift of love:

> Sithen that this world was ful of honde
> Trewth and loue has leyn in bonde.
> Wherefore thou, Lord, that ar aboue,
> Little that honde and send us loue. Amen.[115]

Friar Robert Silke is consistent when he claims that "de amato per que intelligo laude" is the force by which move the instruments of faith.[116]

We shall return to the *Fasciculus morum* in the next chapter, when we come to discuss the case for widening the Franciscan poetic canon. For the moment, one more example of the medieval English Franciscans' preaching handbook should confirm the patterns observed in the Franciscan preaching guides already discussed. In many ways the *Speculum Christiani*[117] is the best example of the Franciscan preaching manual which was organized to fulfill both the preaching ideal of St. Francis and the orders of the Franciscan Archbishop of Canterbury. Pecham's *Lambeth constitutiones* are in fact the basis upon which the prologue and first four tabulae of the *Speculum Christiani* are organized. In other places in the *Speculum* are quota-

---

comon, come; *wot*, knows; *deuol*, devil; *rew*, row; *boot*, boat.

dere, harm; *ferde as flyȝe*, flies in fear; *wonde*, cease.

honde, possessions; *Little*, lessen.

tions from the Council of Lambeth in 1281.[118] It is the most elaborate
and careful of such compilations—a contrast to the haphazard *Fasciculus morum*. In its introduction the *Speculum* says that its purpose is
to furnish materials that the priest can use four times a year—that is,
there is enough in the manual for a full quarter—in instructing the
people in matters necessary for the salvation of their souls, such as:

> The articles of the fayth, The ten commaundmentes, The two preceptys
> of the gospel. The seuen werkys of pyte, The seuen dedly synnes wyth
> ther braunches, The seuen principal vertuse, and The seuen sacraments of grace.[119]

Neither is there any question about the purpose of this endeavor.
Just before the lines quoted above, the fourteenth-century author of
the *Speculum* quotes the apostle James to his purpose: "He that
maketh a synner to be conuertyde from errour of hys wey schal saue
hys soule fro deth, and coueres or excuses the gretnes or the multitude
of synnes."

The *Speculum* also uses poems to illustrate or expound doctrinal
and credal points, or to effect devotion and contrition. In fact, the
entire seventh tabula is in verse and may have been intended to
function as a verse sermon. It dwells upon sin, especially the sin of
coveting worldly riches, and is briefly interspersed with lines of commentary from the Bible and the Fathers.[120] The eighth tabula begins
with a prose prayer to the Sacrament, and then has a long "Oracio
ad virginem Mariam" which is highly typical of the many Middle
English poems of that type. In the sixty-six odd manuscripts of the
Speculum there are, of course, a great number of variations in the
poems, in the choice of poems included, and in the actual chapters
themselves, though not so many as in the *Fasciculus*. In the "Ten
Commandments" poem, for example, the poems in three major manuscripts differ notably from each other.[121] In the English manuscript
(Harley 6580) used by Gustaf Holmstedt for his text, the commandments are arranged as ten quatrains, one for each commandment,
prefaced by a two-line burden:

> In heuene schal dwelle al cristen men
> þat knowen and kepe goddes byddynges ten.[122]

After each commandment stanza follows a lengthy commentary and
exposition covering much the same ground as the material preceding

and following the shorter Ten Commandments lyric in the *Fasciculus morum*. The treatment of the Vices in the *Speculum* is much the same, with the interesting addition that each Vice has its own quatrain of verse through which it "addresses" the audience in the first person.[123]

The poem on the Virgin from the eighth tabula has in the version of MS. Ashmolean 61 this preface:

> Herkyns, serys, þat standes a bowte,
> I will ȝow tell with gode entente,
> how ȝe to god schuld kne & lowte
> Iff ȝe wyll kepe his commandment.[124]

The initial lines, it seems to me, show that on at least this occasion the long Mary poem was delivered out-of-doors, perhaps at a market place, and that it formed the basis of the friar's sermon to the people who were standing "a bowte." This, I think, illustrates a key to one of the real values of the poems and songs employed by the Franciscans: they enabled the friar to draw and hold his audience in public places where a "straight" and schooled sermon might have been cheerfully ignored by milling crowds and noisy vendors.

The *Speculum Christiani*, like all of the other Franciscan compilations we have discussed, is clearly designed as a tool for evangelism. All of these preaching collections show themselves, despite the ostensibly "secular" orientation of the *Lambeth constitutiones*, to be designed primarily for the advantage of the mendicant evangelist.[125] The central focus of them all is contrition and repentance, and they strive to achieve the objective of St. Francis, Archbishop Pecham, and St. James.

The sermons of Nicholas Philipp (or more likely, of Franciscan Friar William Melton, transcribed and used by Philipp)[126] provide an excellent illustration of the way in which the poems worked their way from preaching collections into the actual sermon delivery of a friar. In two sermons concerned with repentance and the Passion, after already employing popular songs, religious verse, and moral tags, Friar Nicholas begins his final argument by reminding us of the impermanence of the world and all of its possessions and associations. He reads or sings the following lyric, of which only two stanzas are preserved in the manuscript.

lowte, make obeisance.

Werdys lowe lestyth but a qwyȝle;
In worldly loue is al wey gyȝle.
leue may comen ant lofe may goon,
But trost lofe is of noon but oon.

Deth bringith down lowe þat ben belde;
Deth takyth ȝoung as well as helde.
þe more stowt þu art ant more gay,
paraventure þe nere þine endyng day.[127]

Again he points to the cross of Christ, which stands in the way of transience, false love, and death, if man will but listen. "Stand & behold þu man ȝif þere be any swilk sorowe," he says, and then points to the inevitability of judgment and Apocalypse: "I sawe a boke þat was all wrotyn, bothe with in & with oute" (fol. 121r)—he quotes the vision of John, and proclaims that in that apocalyptic day the sorrow of Christ will be triumphant. Perhaps taking advantage of the standard, if he was inside a church, he sings:

Now begynnys to go þe bannere of oure Lord þe kynge
now & un spryng wide þe crose tokenynge
god þat made man & euir thynge
Is hongid on þe rode tre for oure giltis & syninge.[128]

(fol. 121r)

He seeks a contrite response:

Werkes of gret on ryȝte,
þyngys of so rweful pyȝte,
worde of luf to kingge of gret myȝt.

(fol. 122v)

He stresses the humility of Christ in accepting human form and suffering at human hands. "How lowe & meke crist for to suffyr shame for þi pride," he reminds his audience, and how appropriate their contrition since their sin was the cause of "his hurtynge." Think of Christ's death on the cross, he argues, but remember also that he is no longer dead: "But if he ware dede, so þat be his own word shall dye & be falle to dye" (fol. 124r). As Christ is eternal, so is his Word. Remember, he says in another place,

qwyȝle, while; *belde*, bold; *helde*, old.

þat þi broþir in heuene is mayster & Kyng;
þi rustere is maister of all þinge.
he þat þat shal deme þe at þe dome,
he is þi felaw & þi grome.

(fol. 174v)

There are two kinds of law, the law of Moses and the law of Grace
through Christ's sacrifice. Only the fool would say:

To moyses lawe a peel I make,
þe law of Kynde I will forsake.

The wise man will ask:

Telle me now quate is þi rede;
Thorgh moises law I am but dede,

recognizing that unless "of manys/ He haue þe maistrie," men will
continue in a state of doom (fol. 124r). Thus all of the standard
concepts of Franciscan penitential theology are ordered through the
audience's knowledge of the reflective and transient world to a focus
on the Passion, wherein lies the reason for contrition. Nicholas ends
one sermon with an expounded version of the song quoted earlier
(p. 175), which is perhaps not atypical of a Franciscan concluding
hymn:

Jesu, þat woldes for mannys sake—
Jesu! mankynd þu woldes take—
Suffreste þi bonys for to quake
We, from synne, fre yow make.

Comen from heune to oure wendynge,
us to helpe from synnyng,
& bere þe crowne þat was pynnyng,
And bryng us alle to good endynge. Amen.

(fol. 173r)

In its vernacular lyric formulation, it is a characteristically Franciscan
nunc dimittis. Collectively these examples offer us, I think, a reasonably accurate sense of the place of Franciscan poetry in medieval English homiletics.

rustere, rooster; *deme*, judge; *dome*, judgment; *grome*, servant.
wendynge, changefulness; *pynnyng*, torturous.

As I observed in the Introduction, the ubiquity of Franciscan lyric poets in medieval England was first noted by that most eminent of Middle English lyric textual scholars, R. H. Robbins. Recording his tentative observations on the influence of the Franciscans, he estimated that up to two-thirds of all Middle English short verse written before 1350 was produced by members of the Order of Friars Minor.[129] In another place, Robbins described the sources of Middle English lyric verse, and drew attention to six major "Friar Miscellanies," three of which he ascribed to Franciscan sources, two to Dominican, and one, which contained friars' songs, to monastic provenance.[130] This evaluation alone suggests the large role played by Franciscans in the development of the Middle English lyric. But the Dominican attributions, if justified, form a major collection rivaling recognized Franciscan manuscripts of the thirteenth century. Since these attributions would tend to constitute in the *Ordo praedicatorum* a reasonable if not critical challenge to a theory of Franciscan dominance in vernacular poetry, and also since the supposed Dominican poems treat of the same subjects in basically the same way—indeed are often the same poems as those in some Franciscan manuscripts— it seems appropriate to examine the evidence for their provenance here.

A general consideration of the two major mendicant orders in England reveals that they not only differed in certain points of theology, as we saw earlier, but that they tended to play different roles in English society, and consequently differed in their respective approaches to their ministries. One historian of the English Dominicans has remarked that "on the whole, the Franciscans were the more democratic and popular; for the political, ecclesiastical, and social advantage of the Dominicans led them to be regarded as 'climbers' by the mass of the people."[131] In moving their ministry more or less away from the common peasant and toward courtly and landed audiences, the Dominicans would not, it seems, have been as likely to require a popular vernacular poetic medium to assist them in their preaching and counseling. Unlike the spectacular productions of Franciscan preachers, Dominican sermons were characterized by restraint, minimal use of *exempla*, relatively infrequent allusion to Scripture, and no notable use of vernacular verse.[132] If they were to have interested themselves in poetic media at all, they would probably more often than not have employed poetic genres based on French literary models. Also, since we know from already established provenance that the preponderance of early popular poetic endeavor was undertaken by Franciscans, it seems unlikely, in view of the considerable early dissension between the two orders, that the Dominicans would have deliberately copied the example of a group whose method and theology they felt to be unsophisticated and perhaps naive.[133]

If we go back to Italian sources, we find general agreement that the relatively much smaller body of poetry produced by the Dominicans in that country was "una poesia sopratutto a un carattere di riflessione teologica e scientifica"[134]—that is, in the mode of the theology of Albert and Aquinas above all philosophical and "scientific"—while the poetry of the Franciscans followed the devotional and theological modes discussed earlier in a simple (even simplistic) and occasionally irrational and fantastic fashion. Moreover, while on the continent there had been one or two compilations of sermon *exempla* by Dominicans (e.g., that of Stephen of Bourbon, ca. 1261), there is nothing to evidence a thorough-going program of such works comparable to that conducted under Franciscan auspices, and in England there are no notable example collections of Dominican provenance or authorship.[135] In fact, while some Dominicans certainly would have written poems, and many more must have used them, the more important attributions made to them are very much open to question.[136] And it would seem that even the Austin friars, who were generally closest in spirit to the Franciscans in England, did not make much use of verse in their sermons,[137] though probably more so than the Dominicans.

While it will not be within the scope of the present study to discuss Franciscan Latin poetry, even a superficial observation reveals that it conforms to the subject matter of Franciscan songs in the vernacular, and parallels it in basic approach to its audience. A significant difference in content and technique has been noted for Dominican Latin poetry as opposed to representations of the Franciscan school by Walter J. Ong, whose distinctions were invoked in the Introduction to this book. "Generally speaking," he writes, "the poetry of this other tradition [Franciscan] is simply uninterested in the complexity of the Adamic-Thomistic style."[138] Comparing four lines of the "Adoro te Deuote" of St. Thomas with an exactly parallel treatment of the same subject by Jacopone da Todi in eight lines, Ong discovers that the Franciscan short-circuits the philosophical confrontation of Thomas, avoids, for example, entering into the theology of the Logos, and while accepting the basic doctrine, even depending upon it, makes no attempt to explore or explain it as a doctrine. And it is significant, it seems to me, that while Dominicans like Nicholas Trivet were working toward developing exegetical apparatus for the understanding of the *dictorum poeticorum* in the writings of the Fathers,[139] Franciscans like Nicholas Bozon, the compilers of the *Gesta Romanorum, Fasciculus morum, Speculum laicorum,* and other *exempla* collections were busy adding vernacular poetic expressions which could be applied to the popular understanding of Scripture. Finally, while the Franciscans were often in political opposition to other religious organizations, such as the Benedictines and Cistercians,[140] with the Dominicans they were in conscious social and theological opposition as well.[141]

This is not to say that Franciscans did not influence other orders with their spirituality and poetic techniques: Salimbene had several friends who found their way into Cistercian and Benedictine houses; one, Brother Vita, changed back and forth regularly.[142] Ubertino da Casale, the mystic and Spiritual Franciscan, is reported to have become a Carthusian as a result of his persecution as a member of the *zelanti,* and at one point he received permission from Pope John XXII to become a Benedictine.[143] His principles, revealed in his *Arbor vitae crucifixus Iesu,* and in the Latin cross poem from it (printed in Appendix A), show that he did not waver in his Spiritual Franciscan ideas despite changes of address. And while the official history of the Carthusian Order in England mentions only two poets or instances of poetic activity, one of these is the translation in 1400 by Nicholas Love, Carthusian prior of Mountgrace, of the *Mirror of the Life of Christ,* then still attributed to the Franciscan St. Bonaventure.[144] But of similar commerce between Franciscans and Dominicans we do not appear to have any record, and from such historical and ideological considerations as those suggested above, it does not seem likely that much interchange would have taken place.

There is conjectural reason, therefore, to question Robbins' attribution of thirteenth-century "Friar Miscellany" MSS. Digby 86 and Trinity Coll. Camb. 323 to Dominican sources. If we look at Digby 86, we see that besides containing several songs strikingly characteristic of Franciscan spirituality,[145] it shares at least three of thirteen lyrics with manuscripts of known Franciscan provenance: "Domes-dai" and "þene latemeste dai" with MS. Jesus Coll. Oxford 29, and the "XV Signs of Judgment" with MS. Harley 913, the Kildare MS.[146] While these three poems are no clear proof of Franciscan provenance for a whole manuscript, their approach to evangelical methodology and the doctrine of the Last Judgment suggests a spirituality characteristically Franciscan, one which a Dominican would probably have found slightly distasteful, and would hardly have included in his collection of verse. Further, the book belonged in the early seventeenth century to Thomas Allen, who acquired a large proportion of his manuscripts from the Grey Friars at Oxford, and the contents of the manuscript are typical of Franciscan interests in the period. A large part of the materials is in French. Of these, several poems and short treatises cover exactly the same ground as the preaching compilations spawned by Grosseteste's and Pecham's injunctions. Thus, the first poem in MS. Digby 86 is a "Distinctio peccatorum," a treatment of the Seven Deadly Sins; the second (fol. 5) is "Les X. commaundemens"; third (fol. 6b), "De septem sacramentis"; and so on—mostly in Anglo-Norman. Further, there is a list of prayers and orisons to St. Francis, the Blessed Virgin, and all three persons of the Trinity, and a "Commendatio animae in manus Domini" in English (fol. 206), all characteristic of the popular preachers' guidebooks. Other hints of Franciscan provenance are the Latin prophecies of Daniel with commentary which appear at fol. 34b,[147] and the prophetic French verses based upon it at fol. 41; the Latin treatise on the "Quindecim signa quindecim dierum ante diem judiciii" (fol. 48), and the English poem titled in French "Les XV signes de domesdai" (fol. 120b); the "Les diz de seint Bernard" (fol. 125b); the poem "De vn pecheur ki se repenti" (fol. 110); and finally "Des iiii files Deu" of Robert Grosseteste, spiritual father to the English Franciscans, whose poem on the Four Daughters of God begins,

> Vn rois estoit de grant pouer,
> De bon valour, de grant sauer.[148]

(fol. 116b)

Finally, at folio 26 appears an "oreisoun" in French verse "fist seint franceis" which, if not likely by Francis, is typical, beginning "Ave ihesu crist ki pour nous de cel venistes."[149] Since there are no comparable hints of distinctive Dominican theology, spirituality, or hagiography in the contents of the manuscript, it seems that not only is the case for Dominican attribution seriously weakened by these considerations, but that all reasonable indications point toward Franciscan authorship or provenance for MS. Digby 86.

The ascription by Robbins of the second major thirteenth-century Friar Miscellany to the Dominicans is similarly doubtful. MS. Trinity Coll. Camb. 323 shares even more of its poems (seven) with manuscripts of Franciscan provenance. Five poems, the "Proverbes of Alfred," "Of one that is so fair and bright" (*EL XIII*, no. 17), "Domesdai," "þene Latemeste dai," and "A Prayer of Penitence" (*EL XIII*, no. 32) are found also in the slightly later (1275) MS. Jesus Coll. Oxford 29 (the last three in MS. Cotton Calig. A.ix as well). The poem on the "Ten Commandments" (*EL XIII*, no. 23) is a version shared with Franciscan friar John Grimestone's Commonplace Book, MS. Advocates 18.7.21; and "Wose seye on rode" (*EL XIII*, no. 34) is also found in MS. Harley 7322, a manuscript of the *Speculum Christiani* discussed above.[150] In this case, the greater number of sharings is not conclusive since Trinity Coll. Camb. 323 is the earliest of the manuscripts, even earlier than Jesus Coll. 29. But notable here is that the unique poems of the Trinity manuscript are redolent of Franciscan theology and spirituality, and one (*EL XIII*, no. 14) is based upon a story that occurs first in a sermon of Franciscan Berthold von Regensburg, and then is first recorded in England in the *Speculum laicorum*, one of the early Franciscan preachers' books discussed above.[151] Another poem (*EL XIII*, no. 33) translates a portion from St. Bernard, a figure who, as we have seen, was particularly influential in Franciscan theology and thought, and most commonly translated by Franciscans. The other contents of MS. Trinity Coll. Camb. 323 also suggest Franciscan rather than Dominican provenance: a number of pieces particularly designed for the instruction of laymen, among them a Life of St. Margaret, and also a homily for the anniversary of St. Nicholas (in which reference is made to a "pleye" which is to follow). St. Margaret and St. Nicholas were foremost subjects of Franciscan hagiography.[152] Two final items of note: a Latin Distich from the Trinity manuscript is translated into English in the *Fasciculus morum*;[153] and if we accept MS. Digby 86 as a likely Franciscan compilation it will be interesting to note that it also shares three poems with Trinity 323.[154] All of these things considered, it seems that MS. Trinity Coll. Camb. 323 must be taken out of the "Dominican" column and listed as very much "leaning toward" Franciscan provenance.

If the foregoing arguments are accepted, it would mean that of the great Friar Miscellanies of the thirteenth century we would count three as definitely Franciscan (MSS. Digby 2, Jesus Coll. Oxford 29 and its sister Cotton Calig. A.ix, and Harley 913—already agreed to by Robbins),[155] and two more as almost certainly Franciscan or certainly incorporating a very substantial body of Franciscan materials (MSS. Digby 86 and Trinity Coll. Camb 323). One is left.

MS. Harley 2253, although in the past thought to have been compiled by monks of Leominster,[156] "clearly contains work by friars, since half its poems are duplicated in manuscripts belonging to friars."[157] It shares eight poems with MS. Digby 86; one with MS. Digby 2; one with MS. Trinity Coll. Camb. 323; one with apparently Franciscan MS. Egerton 613 (*EL XIII*, no. 55); one (*EL XIII*, no. 49)

with Digby 86, St. John's Coll. Camb. 111, and MS. Royal 12.E.i;
three with Digby 86 and MS. Auchinleck 19.2.1; two with MS. English
Poet. E.6; and one with MS. Royal 2.F.viii. Of these poems, then, the
majority are of Franciscan derivation, and in fact, the spirituality
reflected even in the unique pieces of MS. Harley 2253 nicely conforms
to the basic tenets of Franciscan theological and methodological practice. Harley 2253 gives all evidence of being compiled from diverse
sources, perhaps from many live performances, and while the transcribing of the manuscript itself cannot be given to the Franciscans,
it seems more than likely that the bulk of its songs were either originally written by them, or derived a great deal from their influence.[158]

This sort of argument for extending the English Franciscan poetic
canon could be continued for some pages, but to little added profit,
as the remaining manuscripts of English lyric poetry of the thirteenth
and fourteenth centuries are either already of proven Franciscan
provenance, or so small in their number of contributions as to affect
the total picture negligibly. MS. Arundel 248, for example, could be
argued as Franciscan on the basis of internal evidence and its sharings
with Digby 86;[159] the sermon MS. Maidstone A.13 can be shown to
share three poems with MS. Jesus Coll. Oxford 29, one with the
Gesta Romanorum, one with MS. Harley 7322, and another with
Grimestone's Commonplace Book;[160] and MS. Harley 2316 shares a
poem (*RL XIV*, no. 61) with Grimestone and MS. Harley 7322. But
arguments for the provenance of such manuscripts would be difficult,
in many cases inconclusive, and the number of new poems affected
extremely small.

A few of the lesser collections can be treated in passing, however,
in a consideration of the relationship between preachers' handbooks
and the Miscellany manuscripts. It is evident that the Franciscan
handbooks related to one another: in theological material, in quotations, in arrangement of subject material and use of *exempla* they
shared both content and technique. This is why it is often difficult
to distinguish one preaching compilation from another, and it may
be the reason there seems to be no agreement even as to the number
of manuscripts of the *Fasciculus morum*, for example.[161] There is a
good reason for this lack of definitive originality, of course, if the
majority of the works in question were Franciscan-inspired treatises
designed to effect the regulations for preaching embodied in the
decrees of Grosseteste and in Pecham's *Lambeth constitutiones:* collections of this kind would not naturally arise independently of one
another, but would tend to relate to and overlap upon the materials
and methodology of the Franciscan friars, who in any case seem to

have been largely the ones who put the preaching collections to work. It should not surprise us that poems too are shared between manuscripts which have become known as "Miscellanies" and the more prosaic of the preaching compilations. Thus, for example, the first four lines of a poem printed in full in MS. Rawlinson Poet. 175,

> Man, þus on rode I hyng for þe,
> For-sake þe syn for luf of me,
> Sen I swilk luf þe bede;
> Man, I luf þe ouer all thing . . . ,
>
> (*RL XIV*, no. 47)

are given to indicate the use of the same poem in at least three manuscripts of the *Fasciculus morum*, though the entire text does not occur in any.[162] Another four-line piece quoted above (p. 191) from the *Fasciculus* appears in stanza four of "Lollai, lollai, litil child," from MS. Harley 913, the Kildare MS. (*RL XIV*, no. 28). It occurs similarly in Cambridge Univ. MS. Oo.7.32, a sister compilation to Harley 913 which also shares materials with the *Fasciculus morum*.[163] The *Fasciculus* shares a number of poems with MS. Harley 7322 of the *Speculum Christiani*, among them "When þi hed whakeþ," "Kinge i sitte & loke a bowte," and "Ffyre wat waynd & lond"; the first poem also occurs in MS. Trinity Coll. Camb. 43, the manuscript of the "Atte wrastling" poem sermon discussed above (pp. 181–82). MS. Harley 7322, which like Digby 86 and Harley 2253 contains "versus rudiores Anglici et Gallici," contains also two poems (*RL XIV*, nos. 61 and 75) in common with Grimestone's collection, Advocates 18.7.21—which really should be regarded more as a preaching manual than as a "Commonplace Book," since it resembles more the former—one with MS. Arundel 292, one with MS. Jesus Coll. Oxford 29, one with MS. Harley 7333 of the *Gesta Romanorum*, and, as we have seen, one with MS. Trinity Coll. Camb. 323 (*EL XIII*, nos. 11, 13, 34)—at fol. 7a. The interchange among these manuscripts of poetic and other materials, plus their correspondence in general character, seem to me to indicate that manuscripts such as Harley 913 and Advocates 18.7.21 functioned in the same way as designated preaching collections. The Kildare collection contains precisely the materials recommended by Pecham's *Constitutiones* and is organized to provide homiletical as well as poetical material for the preacher's use, grouped around credal and dog-

---

bede, offer.

matic touchstones in exactly the manner of preachers' handbooks such
as the *Speculum Christiani* or the *Fasciculus morum*—with both of
which it shares material. The compilation owned by Grimestone and
"Nicholas de Roma" is somewhat differently organized: its poetical
and homiletical source materials are topically organized under 143
separate headings, each of which lends itself to the structuring of a
sermon. The hermeneutical interests and doctrinal contents of Grimestone's work are, however, virtually the same as those of the other
collections.

This still leaves the question of less obviously preaching-oriented
"laudario" or miscellany manuscripts such as MSS. Jesus Coll. Oxford
29 and Harley 2253.[164] The former has a list of contents which shows
a greater flexibility than some of the other collections. The portion
of the manuscript which dates from the thirteenth century (ca. 1275)
begins at fol. 144, with the words in Anglo-French "Ici comence la
passyun Jesu Crist en Engleys": the *Passion of Our Lord*, a shorter
adaptation in the manner of the pseudo-Bonaventuran *Mirror of the
Life of Christ*.[165] The adaptability of this piece as a lengthy narrative
scriptural lesson is obvious. Following, at fol. 156, is the poem *The
Owl and the Nightingale*, presumably dating from the late twelfth
century in composition.[166] Its inclusion suggests that the manuscript
may have been directed more to educated and clerical audiences than
was the usual case for Franciscan Miscellanies, and this notion is
strengthened by the fact that the manuscript was evidently compiled
by an Anglo-Norman friar: many of the headings, even of the English
poems, are in French, and there are several French pieces included,
beginning at fol. 195b with the story of Tobias versified, "Les unze
peynes de enfern les queus seynt Pool wyt," a "Doctrinal" (fols. 201–
207b)—a versified statement of basic doctrines and creed given in the
form of a doctrinal sermon—and three *legenda*—the Seven Sleepers of
Ephesus (fol. 207b), St. Josaphat (fol. 223), and "Le petyt ple entre le
Juvencel e le veylard" (fol. 244b). Complimentary verses at the end
of two of the pieces provide added evidence of its educated and clerical
audience, and remind us that on occasion the friars performed for
monks and clergy: the Middle English "Passyun" closes with a salu-
tation to

> Magister Johan eu greteþ of Guldeuorde þo
> And lendeþ eu te seggen þat synge nul he no,
> Ne on þise wise he wille endy his song:
> God Louerd of heuene beo us alle among,

                                                                    (fol. 155)

and the Anglo-Norman history of Tobias interrupts its opening lines
to promise

> Le prior Gwilleyme me prie
> De la eglyse seinte Marie
> De Kenylleworthe en Arderne.

(fol. 195b)

Finally, Thomas of Hales, the Friar Minor who wrote the famous
"Love Ron" which appears at fol. 187a (*EL XIII*, no. 43) was a personal friend of Adam Marsh (or Marisco), the notable Franciscan
theologian who came to England with Agnellus and became the
fast friend of powerful and influential Robert Grosseteste at Oxford.[167]
Those considerations would suggest that the contents of MS. Jesus
Coll. Oxford 29 may have circulated in more prestigious and educated company than some other Franciscan collections, but not, however, exclusively.

In addition to the longer pieces already cited, there are a number
of purely homiletical English poems, such as the lyrics "Domes-dai,"
"þene latemest dai," "The Ten Abuses," and "Sinners Beware"; and
the so-called "Poema Morale." This last item is actually a written
treatise structured for delivery in place of the sermon (see its final
lines); it is of a piece with the short verse-sermon on Adam's fall
beginning "Herkne alle gode men and stylle sitteþ a-dun," and with
the poem "Hwi ne serue we crist, and secheþ his sauht." Also included
is the "Signs of Death" lyric which appears as well in manuscripts of
the *Fasciculus morum* and *Speculum Christiani*.[168] All of these are
fairly good indications that MS. Jesus Coll. Oxford 29 was probably
used by mendicant Franciscan preachers who addressed themselves to
the peasantry as well as to landed classes.[169] As such, it relates very
much to the preaching manuscripts, while including superior poetry
like the pre-Franciscan *Owl and the Nightingale* which is not so obviously suitable for homiletic purposes. It is my conviction that these
collections, chiefly of verse, probably served as an adjunct to Franciscan preaching missions in the same way as more limited materials
would within the confines of sermon-notes, but providing a greater
repertoire, and one which had inclusions for a greater variety of
occasions. MS. Harley 913, it will be remembered, includes even
whole sermons in verse dedicated to special occasions.

Two of the other Friar Miscellanies of the thirteenth century—
MSS. Digby 86 and Trinity Coll. Camb. 323—have, as we have seen,
the same composition, and can be considered part of the same Franciscan source-book or "pastoralia" tradition.[170] The last major col-

lection of the period, MS. Harley 2253, corresponds to the style of manuscript of which we noted MS. Cortona 91 as a foremost Italian example. Like the Cortona codex, Harley 2253 is a deliberate collection, an anthology of songs. Like some of the lesser Italian collections however (e.g., the Assisan codices), it does not have music. It also has the distinction of having three languages represented—a response to the peculiarities of English history, and a fairly good indication that it was intended for a more sophisticated audience than some of the other collections.

Further, the quality of these poems is very high. As Sabino Casieri has shown, of all Middle English lyrics of the early period, the ones from MS. Harley 2253 most clearly have affinities with that brand of courtly poetry, directed to an audience of knights, merchants, and "landed gentry," which was produced by the troubadour poets of Provence.[171] The more subtle and sophisticated indirection of the better religious lyrics from this manuscript (e.g., "Wynter," "Lenten ys come with loue to toune," "When y se blosmes springe"—a spring song on the Passion) suggests that if this book was used by itinerant friars there may have been some differences in evangelical methods used among the noble as opposed to the peasant classes (though there still are some typical pieces: "Stond wel moder," "I syke when y singe"). For one thing, the quality of the poetry in MS. Harley 2253 is more "meditative," and often creates the devotional tone of a book of hours rather than the emotional fervor of a public sermon. Some of the poems were not likely sung at all, and some of those which have the carol form may or may not have been sung by their knightly audience; we have no certain way of knowing. The Harley book seems to contain a mixture of poems, some lyrical in the modern, and some in the medieval sense.

Finally, Harley 2253 has a good selection of apparently secular songs. We have already seen, however, that secular songs were adopted to spiritual exegesis at the hands of Franciscan preachers so readily that their inclusion should not be easily regarded as a "non-Franciscan," or "non-religious" addition to the corpus of Middle English lyrics. For example, at fol. 128a of the manuscript occur in succession two well-known poems, usually titled respectively "The Way of Christ's Love" and "The Way of Woman's Love." The poems are clearly parallel in structure, sharing the same stanza form and refrain, and the same key words and lines. Brown's notes (*EL XIII*, nos. 90, 91) observe the direct relationship and argue that the "Christ" poem is a religious adaptation of the "Woman" poem, which he assumes to have been a secular lyric. Now it is very possible that a secular lyric of some kind lies behind these poems, as the independent attempts at adaptation in MS. Caius Coll. Camb. 512 suggest, but "The Way of Woman's Love" is not, in its Harley form, a "secular" song. What is surprising is that Brown, whose excellent detective work discovered a parallel to the second poem in MS. Egerton 613, fol. 2v—clearly intending the Blessed Virgin as the "swete leuedi" and having a French piece above it which calls her "Mun tres duz amy"—should not have seen that "The Way of Woman's Love" is, in all likelihood, really a devotional poem to the Virgin:

> "ffayrest fode vpo loft,
>   my gode luef, y þe grééte
> ase fele syþe & oft
> as dewes dropes beþ wééte,
> ase sterres beþ in welkne, ant grases sour ant suete."
> Whose loueþ vntrewe, his herte is selde sééte.
>
> Euer & oo, for my leof icham in grete þohte,
> y þenche on hire þat y ne seo nout ofte.

> *(EL XIII, no. 91)*

The celebration here is similar to that of the troubadour poets, and it is in this sense that the "Woman" poem parallels the "Christ" poem. Both can be "religious" lyrics. It would seem that a critical division of the Harley lyrics into camps of the worldly and the divine is of scant value, and in specific cases clearly open to question. The poems, like some of the poets themselves, appear to have been subject to a continual process of redemption, of the conversion, revision, and completion of love:

> No more ne willi wiked be,
> Forsake ich wille þis world-is fe,
> þis wildis wedis, þis folen gle;
> ich wul be mild of chere,
> of cnottis scal mi girdil be,
> becomen ich wil frere.
>
> Frer menur i wil me make,
> and lecherie i wille asake;
> to ihesu crist ich wil me take
> and serue in holi churche,
> al in mi ouris for to wake,
> goddis wille to wurche.

Frer menur, Friar Minor.

Wurche i wille þis workes gode,
for him þat boyht us in þe rode;
fram his side ran þe blode,
so dere he gan vs bie—
for sothe i tel him more þan wode
þat hantit licherie.

(*EL XIII*, no. 66)

The influence of the Franciscan friars' preaching mission upon the development of Middle English religious verse is clearly pervasive. As a result of the arguments for provenance advanced here with respect to various thirteenth-century collections, and with the addition of Franciscan Friar William Herebert's poems from MS. Phillipps 8336, another great Friar Miscellany of the early fourteenth century,[172] it is now possible to ascribe not only sixty-six per cent of Middle English lyrics before the Black Death to the Franciscans, but probably somewhere between eighty-five and ninety per cent. When the difficulty of ensuring provenance for the remaining manuscripts is considered, it will be realized that this is an overwhelmingly decisive figure. To go on *ad infinitum* ferreting out evidences for Franciscan influence in the balance of the Middle English poetic corpus to 1350 would be both redundant and nugatory.[173] Altogether, the profession of *ioculatore Dei* seems to have remained largely a Franciscan vocation, and the lyric productions of the *ioculatores* to have continued to relate in one way or another to the perennial Franciscan propensity for devotion and contrition. Whether in songs of praise or petitions to the Blessed Virgin, poems of the cross or reflections upon time and decay, the Franciscan poet looked toward the moment when his audience could sing as one:

Swete Ihesu criste to the
I a synfulle wreche ȝelde me . . . .[174]

Though the modern critic who hopes in the Middle English lyric for some harbinger of Wordsworth may not celebrate the fact, the typical poem favored by his medieval ancestor seems to have been a gospel song.

Notes

1. From the Middle English *Peterburgh Chronicle*, ed. Jos. Sparke in *Historiae Anglicanae scriptores varii* (London, 1723), 3:102.

2. David Knowles, *The Religious Orders in England*, 2 vols. (Cambridge: Cambridge Univ. Press, 1948–59), 1:127–45.

3. "Illuminat enim totam nostram regionem praeclara luce praedicationis et doctrinae. Sua sanctissima conversatio vehementer accendit ad mundi contemptum et spontaneam paupertatem, ad humilitatem tenendam etiam in dignitate et potestate, ad praestandam omnimodam obedientiam praelatis et capiti ecclesiae, ad patientiam in tribulatione, ad abstinentiam in abundantia, et ut ad unum dicam, ad omnium virtutum opera. O si vederet vestra sanctitas quam devote et humiliter accurrit populus ut audiat ab illis verbum vitae, ut confiteatur peccata, ut instruatur in regulis vitae agendae, quantumque ex eorum imitatione profectum suscepit clerus et religio, diceret profecto quod *habitantibus in regione umbraemortis lux orta est eis!*' (in a letter to Pope Gregory IX, in 1238, *Epistolae*, vol. 25 in *Rerum Brittannicarum medii aevi scriptores* [1861], p. 180). See also the letter following, to Cardinal Raynald, afterwards Pope Alexander, opposing Brother Elias. Grosseteste's sympathies, like that of the English province in general, tended towards Spiritual observance of the Rule.

4. V. G. Green, *The Franciscans in Medieval English Life (1224–1348)*, *Franciscan Studies* 20 (Patterson, New Jersey: St. Anthony Guild Press, 1939), pp. 26 ff., adduces a considerable body of evidence on this point.

5. See Eccleston, *De adventu fratrum minorum*, ed. Little, p. 21; D. W. Robertson, Jr., *Chaucer's London* (New York: John Wiley & Sons, 1968), pp. 87–88. For a brief sketch of Henry's career see G. A. Williams, *Medieval London from Commune to Capital* (London: Univ. of London Press, 1963), pp. 333–35.

6. See for example the incident narrated by the author of the *Chronicon de Lanercost: 1201–1346*, ed. J. Stevenson (Edinburgh, 1839), p. 31. The Franciscans were very active, for example, in the dispute between Llewellyn (who dates one of his letters "in crastino B. Francisci") and Richard; see Green, *Franciscans*, p. 146, and sources cited; also Stevenson, ed., p. 29.

7. J. R. H. Moorman writes: "Most of the friars were, therefore, part of the wayfaring life of the country, that restless crowd of merchants and pedlars, minstrels and jugglers, outlaws and fugitives, friars and preachers, pilgrims and messengers who were constantly moving up and down the roads of this island, meeting in the inns and alehouses, arguing, joking, gossiping, and, incidentally, acting as the main channel through which news was spread about the country." (*The Grey Friars in Cambridge, 1225–1538* [Cambridge: Cambridge Univ. Press, 1952], p. 77.) See also Jack Straw's confessions, in Walsingham, *Historia Anglicana* 2. 10 (Rolls Series), and Green, *Franciscans*, pp. 25 ff. In Ireland the Friars Minor came under fire from their English superiors for making so much of the Irish language; see A. G. Little and E. B. Fitzmaurice, *Materials for the History of the Franciscan Province of*

Ireland: 1239–1450 (Manchester: Univ. of Manchester Press, 1920), p. 53. The educated also were affected: by the end of the thirteenth century, thirty thousand students had attended the lectures of Franciscan John Duns Scotus (C. E. Mallet, *A History of the University of Oxford*, vol. 1, [London: Methuen, 1924] chap. 6).

8. *Flores historiarum*, ed. H. R. Luard (Rolls Series, vol. 95, 1890), 2. 189, 222. Dom Roger elsewhere *(Flores 2.* 218) commends the Franciscans for preaching against the Patarines.

9. See Little, *Documents*, pp. 16–17. Little notes that certain of Paris's drawings—e.g., of the seraph—also show Celano's influence. In the bird drawing the four classic kinds of fowl are represented, as in Chaucer's *Parliament of Foules*; the drawings are probably not by Paris but by Franciscan friar William (Little, pp. 18 ff.), on whom see note 11 below.

10. Edited by Christofani, *Il Più antico poema della vita di S. Franceso* (Prato, 1882).

11. Little, *Documents*, p. 19, describes the *Liber additamentum* of Paris' *Chronica*, now in Brit Lib. MS. Cotton Nero D. I, where at fol. 156 Paris gives again the Franciscan Rule, opposite which is a full-length drawing in ink, with washes of color, of the apocalyptic Christ, or vision of the Son of Man in Chapter 1 of the Apocalypse. Little surmises that this is probably the sole survivor of a series of illuminations for an Apocalypse. Both Bartholomew of Pisa and the *Fioretti* (chap. 2) make Friar William of England the twelfth companion of St. Francis; see Little, *Collectanea Franciscana*, vol. 1, pp. 4–8, 74. The *Chronica of the XXIV Generals* makes him a layman, but by the time he appears in the *Chronica majora* he has a tonsure. See also F. Gilbert, *B. Agnellus*, pp. 18–19.

12. Gilbert, *B. Agnellus*, p. 57. See Smalley, *English Friars*, passim. John of Parma, Minister-General of the Order (1247–57), particularly valued the English province for these qualities; see Gilbert, p. 68; cf. his note 4b.

13.   "Qui minor es, noli ridere, tibi quia soli
               Convenit ut plores; iungas cum nomine mores.
               Nomine tu minor es, minor actibus esto, labores
               Perfer, et ingentem minuat patientia mentem.
               Nempe cor obiurgat parvam, patientia purgat,
               Si quicquam faecis est; si quis te corripit, is est
               Qui te custodit; non te, sed quod facis, odit.
               Quid tibi cum vili veste, cibove cubili
               Porcorum? Certe, tu singula perdis aperte,
               Si mentitus eris factis, quod vetse fateris.
               Umbra minoris erit, qui nomen re sine quaerit."
                    (Little, ed, *De adventu fratrum minorum,* p. 31)
The translation is that of E. Gurney-Salter, in *Friars Minor,* p. 44.

14. Little, ed., *De adventu fratrum minorum,* pp. 27–29.

15. Salimbene, pp. 324–26.

16. Little, ed., *De adventu fratrum minorum,* pp. 10, 19, 32–33.

17. *SL XIV–XV*, pp. xvii–xxxi.

18. Cf. R. H. Robbins, "The Earliest Carols and the Franciscans," *MLN* 53 (1938):245.

19. Songs in this MS include "Lullay my childe & wepe no more"; "Puer natus in bethlehem"; "Now has Mary born a flour"; "I saw a swete semely sight."

20. Gwyn S. McPeek, *The British Museum Manuscript Egerton 3307* (London and Chapel Hill: Univ. of London Press, 1963)—music and Latin pieces. English pieces edited by John Edgar Stevens, *Medieval Carols* (London: Steiner and Bell, 1952), with music. The tri-part arrangements in this MS show remarkable similarities to some of those in MS. Cortona 91.

21. Ascription in the *Catalogue of Manuscripts and Music in the British Museum*, 1:423–24 (hereafter cited as *Cat. Mus. MSS*). Both liturgical pieces and secular songs occur in this collection. The Latin pieces have typically Franciscan subjects: "Ave gloriosa virginum regina" (fol. 3), "Homo, vide que pro te patior" (fol. 20), "Homo natus ad laborem" (fol. 42), "Omens cogita" (fol. 20b), "Homo, considera" (fol. 22b), etc.

22. See p. 128 above.

23. Robbins, "Earliest Carols," pp. 244–45. Rosemary Woolf seems to me to underestimate the importance of musical setting for the Middle English lyric in her study, forgetting, perhaps, that the carol and ballad stanzas are preponderant among Middle English lyric verse forms, and that we have music for other forms as well (see her introduction, pp. 1–3).

24. In addition to the examples to the contrary cited below, the word "song" is used to describe a poem and its employment in MS. Bod. 11247, at fol. 69a, a MS of the *Speculum sacerdotale*; see Appendix B.

25. *EL XIII*, no. 49B; it also occurs in MS. Digby 86, without music, but with music in early thirteenth-century MS. St. John's Coll. Cambridge III, fol. 106v. Extracts occur in a Latin sermon dated about 1300, MS. Royal 8.F.ii, flyleaf, without music.

26. *EL XIII*, no. 47. Note the other poems edited by Brown from Arundel MS. 248—nos. 44, 45, 46.

27. Certain MSS of Middle English cycle plays also have musical settings for songs, for example, three songs in "the Weffers" play (no. 46) in the York Cycle; and there are notes to "Gloria in excelsis Deo" in the seventh play of the Chester cycle. See *Cat. Mus. MSS* 1:243.

28. MS. Bodleian Lat. Th. d. i, fol. 175v.

29. *Popular Sermon*, p. 48.

30. MS. Bod. Lat. Th. d. i, fol. 173r.

31. This is what Pfander (*Popular Sermon*, pp. 48–49) believes. Franciscan William Melton, in a sermon published by Little (*Documents*, p. 248), develops an interesting theme: "Dolar iste siue passio potest assimilari bene:

a man of ple and motyng,

a boke of scripture and wrytyng,

a harpe of melodye makyng."

Robert de Brunne records the following lines concerning Robert Grosseteste, from the *Manuel des péchés*:

> Y shall yeu tell as I have herd
> Of the bysshop seynt Roberd;
> His toname is Grosteste
> Of Lyncolne, so seyth the geste.
> He lovede moche to here the harpe,
> For mans witte yt makyth sharpe;
> Next hys chamber, besyde his study,
> Hys harpers chamber was fast the by.
> Many tymes, by nightes and dayes,
> He hadd solace of notes and layes.
> One askede hem the resun why
> He hadde delyte in mynstrelsy:
> He answerde hym on thys manere
> Why he helde the harpe so dere:
> The virtu of the harpe, thurgh "skyle and ryght
> Wyll destrye the fendys myght;
> And to the cros by gode skeyl
> Ys the harpe lykened weyl, &c."

32. See pp. 100–1 above.

33. See pp. 121–22 above.

34. Underhill, *Jacopone*, p. 101, writes: "The popular appeal, the ardour and directness of these minnesingers of the Holy Ghost threw the unconvincing ministrations of the professional clergy into unpleasant relief; and it seemed best to class them with other minstrels as 'ballad-singers and vagrants'. This feeling was particularly strong among the Conventual friars, who regarded the continuance and success of these primitive Franciscan methods as an implied reproach."

35. See Helen F. Rubel, "Chabham's *Penitential* and Its Influence on the Thirteenth Century," *PMLA* 40(1925):233.

36. It is worthwhile to note what sort of "hystrionibus" Docking urges to be eschewed: "De hystrionibus sciendum est quod histriones dicunter quasi hystoriones, eo quod corporum suorum gesticulacione representant hystorias aliquas turpas sive confictas sive factas, sicut olim fecerunt tragedi et comedi in theatris, et hodie fit in turpibus spectaculis et turpibus ludis, in quibus denudantur corpora vel induuntur larve, ut fiant turpes saltus vel alii turpes gestus: et tales magis sunt puniendi et prohibendi quam ad aliquod beneficium recipiendi, eo quod provocant homines ad turpia.—De mimis autem cuiusmodi sunt cithariste et viellatores et alii utentes instrumentis musicis: si hac intencione utuntur labore et officio suo ut provocent homines ad ocium vel lasciviam, repellendi sunt et prohibendi a beneficio: si autem indigentes sunt et utuntur talibus pro victu suo adhipiscendo hac intencione ut faciant hominibus solacium contra iram, tristiciam, tedium et accidiam, vel contra infirmitates corporales, tanquam pauperes Christi ad beneficia sunt recipiendi" (Little, *Documents*, p. 108).

Some further idea of the sort of dancing opposed may be had from the following remarkable account in the *Lanercost Chronicle:* "Insuper hoc tempore apud Invirchethin, in hebdomada paschæ [Mar. 29–Apr. 5] sacerdos parochialis, nomine Johannes, Priapi prophana parans, congregatis ex villa puellulis, cogebat eas, choreis factis, Libero patri circuire; ut ille feminas in exercitu habuit, sic iste, procacitatis causa, membra humana virtuti semi- nariæ servientia super asserem artificiata ante talem choream præferebat, et ipse tripudians cum cantantibus motu mimico omnes inspectantes et verbo impudico ad luxuriam incitabat. Hi qui honesto matrimonio honorem deferbant, tam insolenti officio, licet reverentur personam, scandalizabant propter gradus eminentiam. Si quis ei seorsum ex amore correptionis ser- monem inferret, fiebat deterior, et conviciis eos impetebat. Et quorundam hominum peccata manifesta sunt præcedentia ad judicium, sub ejusdem anni circulo cum parochiani sui ad ecclesiam in hebdomada pœnosa [Mar. 29–28] ad matutinum in crepusculo, ut moris est, convenirent, in hora disciplinarum instaret ac suo documento [ut] quidam aculeis pungerent denudatos ad pœnitentiam. Burgenses, contumeliam sibi factam dedignantes, in auctorem retorquent; et ille, dum opus nefarium defendit ut auctor, in eodem cœme- terio ecclesiæ, ubi choream inceperat, cultro perfossus ipsa nocte occubuit, Deo ei pro scelere reddente quod meruit" (p. 109).

37. MS. Ashmolean Oxford 60, fols. 6a–6b; also printed in Pfander, *Popular Sermon*, p. 21.

38. *EL XIII*, no. 43, lines 193–204.

39. I am indebted for this information to Professor Hendrik van der Werf, medieval musicologist at the Eastman School of Music; his book *The Chansons of the Troubadours and Trovères: A Study of the Melodies and Their Relation to the Poems* (Utrecht: A. Oosthoek, 1972) offers a compre- hensive study of the music of troubadour and *trouvère* poetry in the early Middle Ages.

40. Ed. A. C. Cawley, *The Wakefield Pageants in the Towneley Cycle* (Manchester: Univ. of Manchester Press, 1958), pp. 48, 60.

41. *RL XIV*, p. 272.

42. *RL XIV*, no. 88. Brown notes (p. 272) that the poem also occurs in another Latin homily of the fourteenth century.

43. An excellent example of the sort of dance song apparently adapted by the Franciscans is "When the nyhtegale singes," a carol from MS. Harley 2253; it is edited by Brook, p. 63. Little (*English Medieval Art*, p. 47) notes two particularly fascinating illustrations: one shows four people, a Franciscan friar and nun and a Dominican friar and nun dancing hand in hand—an apparently idealized conception; the second (chap. 4, pl. 20) shows two figures, a minoress with a psaltry, and a Franciscan friar with a mandolin. Little indicates that this MS illustration "may well represent actual happenings" (p. 47): he adduces evidence of the Franciscans' having played for Benedic- tines and receiving payment. The occasion was Epiphany, or Twelfth Night, and the payment was for "disgysyng."

44. Printed in Pfander, *Popular Sermon*, p. 49. The stanzas in the MS are separated by about fifty words of commentary.

45. Brown edits this fraternal sermon in "Texts and the Man," *Modern Humanities Research Association* 2, no. 5 (1928):106–7. Brown's reason for ascribing it to the Dominicans is that in the same MS occurs a Latin treatise on the Rule of St. Augustine. This is hardly conclusive, since some of the MSS of the recognized Franciscan *Fasciculus morum* (see below) have non-Franciscan rules—in one case, MS. Laud Misc. 111, a "Rule of Richarde de Hampole." See the arguments for provenance advanced below.

46. See Paul Sabatier, *Vie de St. François d'Assise* (Paris, 1894), p. 195.

47. "Non modum praedicantis tenuit sed quasi contionantis," quoted by J. R. H. Moorman in *Sources*, pp. 56–57.

48. See p. 140 above.

49. Salimbene, pp. 559 ff.

50. See A. G. Ferrers Howell, *St. Bernardino of Siena*, p. 219—cited in Little, *Studies*, p. 133.

51. "In hoc libello sunt capitula 147, quorum quaedam sunt brevia verba quae, dum in scholis morabar, scripsi breviter et incomposito sermone ad memoriam. Nec sunt de una materia nec ad invicem continuata. Quorum titulos posui ut facilius quae vellet lector possit invenire. Spondentque plerumque plus aliquo titulo quam solvant capitula lectori. Quaedam vero sunt sermones, quos eodem tempore ad clerum vel al populum feci . . ." (MS. Bod. 798, fol. 121r).

52. Little, at the time of his *Studies* (1917), thought that there were none at all (pp. 135–36).

53. "Chronicles of the Mendicant Friars," *BSFS ES* 3 (1932): 85–103. The Dominicans, on the other hand, were more interested in universal history than in recording their own experiences or the history of their Order (p. 98). An amusing contrast is provided by the Franciscan writer in the *Lanercost Chronicle*, who slips out of decorum to interject a vernacular couplet:

Wille Gris, Wille Gris,
Thinche twat you was, and quat you es!

though he claims it "et confirmatur hoc factum per sancti Gregorii dictum, 'Tunc bene possimus servare quod sumus si nunquam negligimus pensare quod fuimus.'" For Franciscan authorship and provenance of the *Lanercost Chronicle* see Little's articles in *English Historical Review* 31 (1916): 269; 32 (1917):48.

54. For reasons why more sermons have not been preserved see G. R. Owst, *Preaching in Medieval England* (Cambridge: Cambridge Univ. Press, 1926), pp. 223–27; also Green, *Franciscans*, p. 31, and Little, *Grey Friars*, pp. 91–92.

55. Owst, *Preaching*, pp. 231 n., 272, etc.; also *RL XIV*, passim. See Knowles, *Religious Orders*, 1:127–45.

56. E.g., MS. Harley 7322, a manuscript of the *Speculum Christiani*, discussed below; also MS. Bod. 649.

57. Wyclif, *Opus minorum*, Wyclif Society (London: Trübner, 1884), p. 331; *Sermones* 1:xvii; 4: 266; also *John Wiclif's Polemical Works in Latin*, ed. R. Buddensieg, Wyclif Society (London: Trübner, 1883), 1:41. Wyclif's first complaint, however, is hardly supported by the various Franciscan preaching handbooks and sermons now extant, many of which are discussed in this chapter.

58. Ed. W. Heuser, "Die Kildare Gedichte," *Bonner Beiträge zur Anglistik* 14 (1904):128–29. All further quotations are from this edition.

59. A good example is Thomas of York's sermon on the Passion, where Thomas explains why we look on the physical/spiritual Passion of Christ in a human sense, and how the resulting contritional response is necessary to salvation, and then proceeds to discuss the necessity of radical identification with Christ. See the edition of J. P. Reilly, Jr., in *Franciscan Studies* 24 (1964):205–22.

60. This poem has been edited by Robbins in "Earliest Carols," pp. 243–44.

61. E.g., Jacopone da Todi, in whose "Donna del Paradiso" (*Lauda* XCIII, Ageno, pp. 400–401) we read:

Mamma col core afflitto, entro le man te mitto
de Ioanne, mio eletto: sia el tuo figlio apellato . . . .

62. From *Speculum sacerdotale*, ed. Edward H. Weatherly, EETS OS 200 (London: Oxford Univ. Press, 1936), p. 112.

63. See the discussion by Stephen Manning, *Wisdom and Number*, pp. 44–45.

64. The *Speculum sacerdotale* is a sermon collection, largely penitential, which uses vernacular verse. While its authorship has not been established, in view of certain internal considerations it seems most likely to have been written by a friar, e.g., the sections describing how "prelates" are to be shriven (pp. 86 ff). In any case, it has strong fraternal bias.

65. For example, in the Franciscan sermons of MS. Rawl. C. 534, fol. 7 ff.; there is also a sermon by the Franciscan friar Lawrence Briton, lector of Oxford (ca. 1340), in Latin and English with considerable English verse, collected in Bishop Sheppey's fourteenth-century sermon anthology in MS. Merton Coll. Oxford 248, fols. 131a–132b. One of the poems is in Anglo-French. Also, the sermons of the fourteenth-century Austin preacher John Waldeby, in MS. Laud Misc. 77, have a collection of *exempla* at the end and dozens of English verses along the margins with indications for insertion. Some of the lyrics have been revised. Also notable are the collections in MSS. Harley 505 and Harley 2316, and a sermon well larded with materials from the *Gesta Romanorum* and two poems about repentance from MS. Royal 18. B. xxiii, ed. W. O. Ross, *Middle English Sermons*, EETS OS 209 (London: Oxford Univ. Press, 1940), pp. 160 ff.

66. This sermon occurs in MSS. Balliol Coll. Oxford 149, fols. 31b–38b, Magdalen Coll. Oxford 93, fols. 136 ff., and Trinity Coll. Dublin 277, a Franciscan book of the fifteenth century.

67. Cf. Thomas of Hales' poem, cited above p. 177.

68. Robbins, "Earliest Carols," p. 243.

69. See G. G. Perry's introduction to *Religious Pieces in Prose and Verse*, EETS OS 26 (London: Trübner, 1867), pp. vii ff. The *Lambeth constitutiones* in particular employ Franciscan standards as models for the secular clergy, for whom Pecham apparently has not overmuch regard; see T. F. Simmons' introduction to *The Lay Folks' Catechism*, EETS OS 118 (London: Kegan Paul, Trench and Trübner, 1901), pp. xii ff.

70. Little, *Studies*, p. 136. Little does not discuss the *Speculum sacerdotale*, *Speculum Christiani*, and some of the unpublished compilations considered here. He does however give brief bibliographical descriptions of the *Liber exemplorum*, *Speculum laicorum*, *Contes moralisés* of Bozon, and the *Fasciculus morum*. The *Gesta Romanorum* he omits, since he believes it was probably put together by a German Franciscan, though from English materials, about 1340; neither is it treated here, since it is not a preaching manual as such, and does not include Middle English lyric poetry. (Beryl Smalley, however, thinks that the author was an English Franciscan, and notes that he drew on Robert Holkot; see *English Friars*, p. 3.)

71. *Liber exemplorum ad usam praedicantium*, BSFS 1 (Aberdeen: Univ. of Aberdeen Press, 1908).

72. Little misses, however, the story from Gerald of Wales' *Gemma ecclesiastica* which occurs on p. 112 of his edition of the *Liber exemplorum*.

73. See Little's listing, p. ix. He notes of the *Liber* MS: "One cannot fail to be struck by the absence of all allusions to Franciscan ideals, legends and literature. A similar peculiarity may be observed in the *Summa* of the Dominican Guillaume Peraud, and it may be due to the fact that these works of the mendicant friars were intended for the use of all kinds of preachers" (p. xiii). The conclusion is most reasonable. In fact, although Peraldus was a Dominican, his *Summa* was used by the Franciscans, and since in many MSS the authorship or provenance is not stated the very similarity of its contents to analogous Franciscan materials occasionally makes it difficult to identify. See Clement Schmitt, "Manuscrits," p. 189.

74. "Quoniam autem non habetur expresse utrum miser iste dampnaretur aut peniteret in extremis et salutem consequeretur, idcirco quibusdam verbis potest concludi narracio, quibus, salve veritate, terror audientibus incuciatur . . . . Anglice dicitur;

> hym were bettre þat he ne were ne neuer boren
> for liif and soule he his forloren.

Hiis verbis aut allis consimilibus potest hiis verbis aut alliis consilimibus potest exemplum memoratum terminari" (ed. Little, chap. 76).

75. Ed. J. Th. Welter, who lists 18 MSS, many of which were used extensively up to the time of the Reformation (p. iv). One copy was owned by Thomas Browne (MS. Univ. Coll. Oxford 29). The author quotes heavily from St. Bernard, and has a high regard for the Sack Friars (final story), something which would not have been very likely in a Dominican.

76. The following table compares on the left some sermons of St. Ber-

nardino (ed. Quarrachi, vols. 1 & 2) with chapter headings of the *Speculum laicorum* on the right.

1.	3.	de eleemosyna	31.	de elemosina
1.	5.	de ultime iudicio	28.	de die judicii
1.	6.	de vera contritione	19.	de contricione
1.	7.	de vera confessione	20.	de confessione
1.	8.	de sacra Religione	22.	de crucis virtute
2.	9.	Contra alearum ludos	40.	de coreatricibus

Other topics are held in common, and often structured proportionately within subgroupings, such as "de honore parentum," and "de passione Christi memoria" (Bernardino's sermon 55 and the *Speculum's* topic 63).

77. Ed. Welter, p. 87. [The Christian's memory focuses on the Passion of Christ on account of three things: one, it liberates at the point of death; two, it comforts those who labor; three, it confirms in love.]

78. At chapter 21 there is a ritual condemnation of song and dance in the manner of Chabham, but with the usual exception noted; see notes 35 and 36 above.

79. Ed. Lucy Toulmin Smith and Paul Meyer for the Société des anciens textes français (1889). There are only three MSS, all of the fourteenth century. Important evidence of Franciscan activity in lyric production could, of course, be drawn from the Anglo-Norman tradition, which is quite strong. Unfortunately, this will be impossible within the scope of the present study. For a few examples of this verse I refer the reader to the Anglo-Norman lyrics of MSS. Harley 2253 and Digby 86, and to MS. Phillipps 8336. For a description of the Anglo-Norman Franciscan poems of MS. Phillipps 8336, see P. Meyer, *Romania* 13 (1884):497–541. Bozon's own typically Franciscan poems are treated in *Histoire littéraire de France* 36 (1937):400–24.

80. See the discussion by Little, *Studies*, pp. 189 ff.

81. This "tradition" includes MSS. Rawl. C. 670, Laud Misc. 111 and 568, and Bod. 332.

82. MS. Laud Misc. 568 is in fact entitled "de vitijs et virtutibus."

83. Trans. Little, *Studies*, p. 141, from MS. Bod. 410.

84. For St. Bernard, see MS. Laud Misc. 111, fol. 173 especially. As in the pseudo-Bonaventuran *Meditations*, the most frequent sources cited for gloss are St. Augustine and St. Bernard, in that order.

85. Little quotes illustrations of this in *Studies*, p. 146.

86. Unlike those MSS, or the sermon MS of Nicholas Philipp from which the lyric with music is edited in Appendix B, the *Fasciculus* does not have, to my knowledge, musical scoring in any of its extant MSS.

87. This poem occurs in the third page of the "de passione" section of the MS, which has to the present no adequate foliation hence the lack of folio numbers in citations of it which follow. Cf. the Kildare poems, ed. Heuser, pp. 128–29.

88. MS. Laud Misc. 111, fol. 90.

89. MS. Laud Misc. 111, fol. 94b.

90. See pp. 200–201 above.

91. "Worldes blis ne last no throwe" (*EL XIII*, no. 46) and "Man mei longe him liues wene" (*EL XIII*, no. 10) have even been performed recently and recorded (Saville Clark, Medieval Heritage Society, #683); cf. chap. 1, n. 1. The second of these is noted by Brown for certain musical affinities with the liturgical sequence. The *Stabat mater dolorosa*, or "Stond wel moder vnder rode" (*EL XIII*, no. 49), also used in the pulpit, in two of its manuscripts has a musical accompaniment, though neither is complete (hear *Medieval English Lyrics*, Argo #ZRG5443). Recently the examination of a thirteenth-century Sarum missal in the Bibliothèque de l'Arsenal, Paris, revealed the same music, note for note with the existing six stanzas of music, and completing the song. This instance does not however appear to suggest a common pattern of the influence of liturgical music on vernacular lyrics. For example, going the other way, Gautier de Coincy (ca. 1200) in Paris borrowed *trouvère* songs regularly for adaptation to liturgical purposes, as did English Franciscans like James Ryman, whose adaptations are discussed below.

92. This poem is also found in MS. Bod. 187, fol. 184r; and in MS. Harley 7322, fol. 155b—a manuscript of the *Speculum Christiani*.

93. See another version in Laud Misc. 111, fols. 59, 60. Robbins has printed a version of this poem from MS. Caius Camb. 71, fol. 17b, in "Popular Prayers in Middle English Verse," *Modern Philology* 36 (1939):345.

94. Often these appear as a couplet of the sort that might be either a tag, or perhaps a carol burden, as:

> Crist þat died upon þe rode
> is our lambe, our ester fode.
>
> (MS. Bod. 332, fol. 190v).

95. MS. Laud Misc. 111, 65r; cf. poem at fol. 51. This poem also occurs in certain MSS of *Erthe upon Erthe*, B version—see Brown and Robbins, *Index of Middle English Verse* (New York: Index Society, Columbia Univ. Press, 1943), no. 4239. (In MS. Bod. 187, at fol. 126, the portion which would have included those poems coming at MS. Laud Misc. 111, fol. 51, has been cut away.)

96. MS. Bod 352, fol. 189v. An example of the way this poem was probably continued comes from Ryman (Zupitza, pp. 253–54), beginning:

> Atte sumtyme mery, at sume tyme sadde;
> At sumtyme wele, at sumtyme woo;
> At sumtyme sory, at sumtyme gladde;
> At sumtyme frende, at sumtyme foo;
> At sumtyme richesse and welthe is hadde,
> At sumtyme it is gone vs froo:
> Truly, he is not wyse, but madde
> That aftur wordly welthe will goo.
>
> As medowe floures of swete odoures
> Vadeth to erthe by theire nature,

> Likewise richesse and grete honoures
> Shall vade fro euery creature;
> Therfore to suffre grete douloures
> I holde it best to do oure cure
> And to forsake castellis and toures,
> So that of blisse we may be sure.

97. Ed. from MS. Rawl. C. 670, under section "de elemosina," corrected by MS. Bod. 187, fol. 187r/b. At this point in MS. Laud Misc. 111 (fol. 67a), the scribe indicates that an example might be given "in gallico."

98. MS. Rawl. C. 670; other versions exist in MSS. Harley 7322, fol. 169r, Trinity Coll. Dublin 312, fol. 152a; Jesus Coll. Oxford 29 (ed. F. J. Furnivall, *Political, Religious, and Love Poems*, EETS OS 15, 2nd ed. [London: Kegan Paul, Trench, and Trübner, 1903], p. 221, cf. pp. 249–50)—all Franciscan MSS. Here it appears to be a tag made into a song.

99. MS. Rawl. C. 670; also MS. Laud Misc. 111, fol. 66v; cf. "Whoso levyth in flescly wylle," at fol. 206r in MS. Bod. 187. "Mon ibore"is a highly accurate translation of Job 14:1–2. I suspect that the rest of the chapter may have been translated in the complete poem.

100. MS. Laud Misc. 111, fol. 50. See pp. 125–26, 130 above.

101. MS. Bod. 332, fol. 183r, corrected by MS. Bod. 187, fol. 210, which has erasures and marginal corrections.

102. MS. Laud Misc. 111, fol. 52r; cf. MS. Rawl. C. 670 at the same point. This piece does not appear in the *Proverbs of Hendynge*, despite the ascription.

103. Interjected throughout the text are a number of homely saws, such as the following marriage counsel for nagging wives:

> see and her & hold ye stylle
> ȝif þou wolt hrne & haue thi wylle.
>
> (MS. Laud Misc. 111, fol. 53)

("Hrne" here means "hasten.") Cf. MS. Trinity Coll. Camb. 323 (*EL XIII*, no. 21), where the counselor (or incubus?) is called "viit in þe brom." At this point in the MS there is in the margin a large figure of the Thau, surrounded by four groups of four dots, with a balance scales hanging from the bottom of the Thau, a Franciscan Cross-symbol (see A. Strong, "St. Francis in Rome," in *St. Francis of Assisi: 1226–1926: Essays in Commemoration*, ed. W. W. Seton [London: Univ. of London Press, 1926], p. 281, for a discussion of this symbol in the Order). On the left of the figure appears the word "signa," below "nostra," on the right "thau." The idea of the scales of judgment hanging from the Cross is discussed by Francis Wormald, "The Crucifix and the Balance," *Journal of the Warburg Institute* 1 (1937):276–80.

104. Also in MS. Laud Misc. 213, where the last line reads "Ne trust not to his word: þe wele lyrn thnn foo," and the poem is interspersed with Latin injunctions for expansion.

105. MS. Laud Misc. 213; also MS. Bod. 187, fol. 162b, and MS. Rawl. C. 670.

106. I will be exploring this subject, with many further examples, in a forthcoming companion volume, *The Early English Drama and Franciscan Spirituality*.

107. MS. Bod. 187. Interestingly, in this MS the lines are said to be inscriptions found on three rings in a sarcophagus.

108. Woolf, *English Religious Lyric*, p. 45.

109. *Speculum Christiani*, ed. Gustaf Holmstedt, EETS OS 182 (London: Oxford Univ. Press, 1933). See Woolf, *English Religious Lyric*, p. 45.

110. MS. Laud Misc. 568, a version of this versification which has not been printed before. I know of none with so inclusive a final line. Another version, in the *De decem preceptis* of English Franciscan friar John Staunton (ed. G. R. Owst, "Some Franciscan Memoirs at Gray's Inn," *Dublin Review* 176 [1925]:278 ff.), adds two lines:

> These ben the hastes of grete mede,
> Wyt hem wel and thu shalt spede.

One of the earliest versified Ten Commandments and *Pater noster* in Middle English occurs in Franciscan MS. Camb. Ff. 6.15 of the thirteenth century. By far the most such poems occur in Franciscan MSS—see the *Index of Middle English Verse*. Cf. MS. Bod. 187, fol. 143r. Note the lengthy exegesis of the Lord's Prayer in the *Fasciculus morum*, which may be found in MS. Laud Misc. 111, fol. 176 ff.

111. MS. Bod. 187, fol. 163rv:

> Syþþen lawe for wyl bygyuinþ to slaken,
> and falshede for slynesse ys ytaken,
> Robbyng & reuyng ys holdyn purchas,
> and wontonnesse ys holdyn solas,
> þen now may Yngelonde synge alas.

112. MSS. Bod. 410, fol. 51r; Bod. 187, fol. 176v:

> Longslepers and over lepers,
> Fore skyppers and over hyppers,
> I hem noght here ne they be myne,
> But ye sone amende ye schul in hell pyne.

(Another possibility is that these lines may refer to slovenly chanters or choir boys.)

113. MS. Rawl. C. 670, under "de trinitate."

114. MS. Laud Misc. 111, fol. 51. These lines translate 1 Peter 5:8.

115. MS. Bod. 410, fol. 17v.

116. MS. Laud Misc. 111, fol. 61.

117. See Holmstedt's edition, pp. clxxix, cxc, cxcv; Holmstedt dates it about 1360.

118. Holmstedt, *Speculum Christiani*, p. clxxx, shows this in detail; see also p. clxxvi, where he points out that some MSS concur in saying that the treatise was "tractatum de uno magistro apud oxoniam."

119. Holmstedt, *Speculum Christiani*, p. 6.

120. Ibid., pp. 148, 150, which resemble Latin/English quotations from

the *Fasciculus morum* (some of whose poems also appear in certain MSS of the *Speculum Christiani*, e.g., MS. Harley 7322); see p. 197 above.

121. MSS. Sidney Sussex 55 (see Holmstedt, *Speculum Christiani*, p. lxxiv), Harley 5396, fol. 2856, which closely resembles the Kildare version (p. cxxiii), and Harley 6580, the text quoted here.

122. Holmstedt, *Speculum Christiani*, p. 16.

123. Ibid., pp. 58–73.

124. Cited in Holmstedt, p. cxviii. Following the regular seventh tabula poem (as printed by Holmstedt) there come a further twelve lines about the necessity of keeping the Ten Commandments.

125. Obviously parish priests were to use them too; that was Pecham's and Grosseteste's idea.

126. One of these is printed in Little, *Documents*, pp. 247–56.

127. MS. Bod. Lat. Th. d. i, fol. 175v. Opposite four of the quatrains, including those quoted, appear in the margins the word "song," in English.

128. Cf. *RL XIV*, no. 13, "þe kynges baneres beth forth y-lad."

129. R. H. Robbins, "The Authors of the Middle English Religious Lyrics," *JEGP* 39 (1940):230–38.

130. *SL XIV–XV*, pp. xvii–xxxi.

131. Beryl E. R. Formoy, *The Dominican Order in England before the Reformation* (London: SPCK, 1925), p. 48.

132. See W. A. Hinnebush. *The Early English Friars Preachers* (Rome: Sabina, 1951), pp. 303–5. He quotes Thomas Waleys to the point: "Tradere vere omnes modos et formas praedicandi, etiam a modernis praedicatoribus observatos, non solum superfluum sed etiam impossibile judicarem, cum vix inveniantur duo, sermones a seipsis compositos praedicantes, qui in forma praedicandi quoad omnia sint conformes."

133. Matthew Paris, *Chronica majora*, pp. 279–83; see also the beginning of chapter 2 above.

134. Fortini, p. 18.

135. Hinnebush, *Friars Preachers*, pp. 300 ff. One possible exception is B. L. Royal MS. 7. D. i (summarized in Herbert's *Catalogue of Romances*, pp. 477–503), but this seems doubtful.

136. E.g., MS. Digby 86, from which comes lyric no. 49 in *EL XIII*. This manuscript will be discussed below.

137. A good example of an Austin sermon in English is MS. Oxford 97, fols. 324–39. It employs no song or poem, and only two or three rough tags, despite being written entirely in English, a fairly unusual thing. In all of the seventy-four sermons in secular prior John Mirk's *Festial*, compiled at the very end of the fourteenth or early fifteenth century, there are only two sermon tags and one poem, the latter a translated antiphone; see the edition of Theodor Erbe, EETS ES 96 (London: Kegan Paul, Trench and Trübner, 1905), pp. 232–33. But cf. n. 65 above.

138. Ong, "Wit and Mystery," p. 323.

139. See Smalley, *English Friars*, p. 62, who quotes Trivet: "Quamquam

autem in omnibus libris istis beatus Augustinus studiosis quibus cumque
utile ac delectabile exercitium prebeat, tamen non nunquam interserendo
gesta quedam, quorum historie sunt minus note, et quedam poetica aliaque
dicta gentilium, precipue in primis decimis libris et in decimo octavo, ut
hostes civitatis Dei ex propriis convincat, sepe exercitatis minus in talibus
prestat offerdiculum continue lectionis. Intentionis nostre est fratrum meorum
[sic] frequenti pulsatus instantia hec impedimenta tollere et obscura huius
lectoribus reddere clariora" (MS. Merton Coll. Oxford 256B, fol. 46).

140. Green, *Franciscans*, pp. 67, 125; see also Derek Whitfield, "Conflicts
of Personality and Principle: The Political and Religious Crisis in the Franciscan Province, 1400–1409," *Franciscan Studies* 17 (1957):321–62, for later
political associations and problems relating not to other orders, but to the
affairs of state.

141. Formoy, *The Dominican Order*, pp. 48 ff.

142. Salimbene, pp. 181, 623.

143. E. Gurney-Salter, "Ubertino da Casale," in *Franciscan Essays*, ed.
A. G. Little (Aberdeen: Univ. of Aberdeen Press, 1912), 2: 118.

144. E. Margaret Thompson, *The Carthusian Order in England* (London:
SPCK, 1930), pp. 339–41.

145. E.g., *EL XIII*, nos. 49, 50, and the so-called "Sayings of St. Bernard."

146. *EL XIII*, nos. 28, 29; Heuser, "Die Kildare Gedichte," p. 100. Robbins himself (*SL XIV–XV*, pp. xvii–xxxi) gives MS. Jesus Coll. 29 to the
Franciscans.

147. See the final portion of chapter 2 above and the section describing
holdings of Franciscan libraries in chapter 3, pp. 84–85.

148. I shall consider the ME translation of Grosseteste's poem in my
forthcoming companion volume on the Middle English drama.

149. Brown, *EL XIII*, pp. xxviii–xxxiii, has noticed the prayer to St.
Francis and a few general indications of Franciscan provenance, but Robbins
apparently ignores this. See the MS at fol. 26b. Though there is a substantial
amount of French verse in Digby 86, it is all in the Anglo-Norman dialect
and less popular in style and genre.

150. Found also in MS. Royal 12.E. i (fol. 194), which shares also with
MSS. Digby 86 and Harley 2253 the "Stond wel moder ounder rode" edited
in *EL XIII*, no. 49.

151. *Speculum laicorum*, ed. Welter, p. 16, which makes Odo or Eode
an English cleric; see *EL XIII*, p. 176, notes. Cod. germ. 354, from Munich,
is a handbook of pastoralia, including short homilies and lyrics, and contains
some of the writings of David von Augsburg.

152. Also in MS. Digby 86 occurs (fols. 150–61) "Les miracles de seint
Nicholas," in Anglo-Norman verse.

153. "Þat he ȝaf," etc., MSS. Laud Misc. 213, fol. 70a, Bod. 187, fol. 167b.

154. "Debate of the Body and Soul," and nos. 28, 29 of *EL XIII*.

155. *SL XIV–XV*, pp. xvii–xxxi.

156. Actually, G. L. Brook, in the introduction to the third edition of

The Harley Lyrics, has pointed out that the ascription to Leominster Priory "rests on no certain evidence" (p. 3).

157. *SL XIV–XV,* p. xvii.

158. One obvious objection to ascribing MS. Harley 2253 to the Franciscans is that it contains a poem, "Mon in þe mone," which has anti-fraternal overtones, specifically, in fact, satirizing sluggardly "ase a grey frere" (*EL XIII,* no. 89, line 19). It should be remembered, however, that the most assuredly Franciscan Kildare MS (Harley 913) contains a much more specific and virulent anti-fraternal satire. The Kildare book has satires on the various orders and on the friars in its *Epistolae principis regionis Gehennalis* (fol. 32b). (The "Land of Cokaygne" was long thought to be an attack on friars, though recently Thomas Jay Garbaty ["Studies in the Franciscan 'The Land of Cokaygne' in the Kildare MS.," *Franziskanische Studien* 45 (1963):139–53], has suggested the possibility that the satire was written by a Franciscan of the Athlone friars [Ath Luain, fol. 1224] and directed against the Cistercians of the neighboring abbey). See also Fitzmaurice and Little, *Materials for the History of the Franciscan Province of Ireland,* p. 121. The friars were not averse to including such items for the spiritual chastisement of their own faults, and the presence of "Mon in þe mone" is not a valid reason for ruling out a Franciscan provenance or influence on this manuscript.

159. *EL XIII* includes four lyrics from MS. Arundel 248, nos. 44–47, of which no. 46, "Worldes blis ne last no throwe," is shared with MS. Digby 86.

160. "Proverbs of Alfred," ed. Richard Morris, *An Old English Miscellany,* EETS OS 49 (London: Trübner, 1872), pp. 102–38; "Death's Wither Clench," *EL XIII,* no. 10, also used by Grimestone (MS. Advocates 18.7.21, fol. 87r) and MS. Laud Misc. 471 (Kentish sermons); "Three Sorrowful Things," *EL XIII,* no. 11; also MS. Harley 7322 and others of that tradition. All are in MS. Jesus Coll. 29.

161. Little, *Studies,* pp. 139 ff., finds 21; Brown counts 29 (*RL XIV,* p. 287, notes); Robbins finds 30 ("Authors," p. 233), and later changes his mind to 22 MSS (*SL XIV–XV,* p. xviii). The problem is that there is a great variance among even those MSS of the *Fasciculus morum* found in the Bodleian Library at Oxford, and if one wished to count the inclusion of large sections of material from the most clear tradition of these MSS (see n. 81 above), the number might grow considerably beyond 30 to include MSS of what are now considered to be corrupt versions of the *Speculum Christiani* (e.g., MS. Harley 7322) and other preachers' compilations. One of these, which I have discovered to draw very heavily on the *Fasciculus,* or to be a "corrupt" version, is MS. Bod. 416.

162. MSS. Laud Misc. 213, fol. 34v; Rawl. C. 670, Bod. 416. This poem relates to the tradition (see also *RL XIV,* no. 46 and notes), and a version of both poems exists in Franciscan Grimestone's collection together (MS. Advocates 18.7.21, fol. 125r).

163. Ed. Heuser, "Die Kildare Gedichte," p. 173; see "The Lady Fortune," p. 195, shared with *Fasciculus morum.*

164. See *SL XIV–XV*, pp. xvii–xxxi.

165. Ed. R. Morris, *Miscellany*, pp. 37–57.

166. Ed. E. G. Stanley (London: Nelson, 1960); cf. the facsimile reproduction, EETS OS 251 (London: Oxford Univ. Press, 1963).

167. See the letter printed by Brewer, *Monumenta Franciscana*, 1 (Rolls Series 4, 1858); 395; also *Roberti Grosseteste . . . Epistolae*, ed. H. R. Luard (Rolls Series 25, 1861), pp. 45, 69, 302, 344, 437, etc.

168. These are edited in Morris, *Miscellany*.

169. To a lesser degree this may be said to be true of its sister MS. Cotton Calig. A. ix.

170. MS. Digby 2 has much the same kinds of material, but other items including one long "Tractatus de Logica," suggest that it may have been the property of a Franciscan friar who was still a student.

171. Sabino Casieri,, *Canti e liriche*, pp. 8–27.

172. F. Herebert died in 1333. See the selection of his poems in *RL XIV*, nos. 12–25; also Robbins' article, "Friar Herebert and the Carol," *Anglia* 75 (1957):194–98. Robbins, however, fails to give sufficient recognition to the derivation of the $a\,a\,a\,X$ stanza in fourteenth-century Latin hymns from popular carol form (see Introduction, on Green, and chap. 6, n. 62, below). Herebert's poems are only a small part of MS. Phillipps 8336; the bulk is composed of poems and moralized tales by his fellow Franciscan friar Nicolas Bozon. Bozon's poems, in Anglo-Norman, are excellent paradigms of Franciscan spirituality, and are often superior to similar poems in Middle English. For a description of the contents of Friar Miscellany MS. Phillipps 8336, see Paul Meyer, "Notice et extraits du MS. 8336 de la Bibliothèque de Sir Thomas Phillipps à Cheltenham," *Romania* 13 (1884):497–541.

173. For example, it could be shown that sermon tags which may or may not be parts of a song eventually become part of a written lyric or carol. Robbins, "Popular Prayers," pp. 337–50, shows for example that this frequently happens, and traces one tag from MS. Copenhagen Royal Library 29264, fol. 325a (and two other MSS) to the second stanza of a carol at fol. 49v of MS. Ee. 1.12 of Cambridge University Library—the carol collection of Franciscan friar James Ryman. The whole carol is edited by R. L. Greene, *A Selection of English Carols* (Oxford: Clarendon Press, 1962), p. 126.

174. Printed in Holmstedt, *Speculum Christiani*, p. xcviii.

Spirituality & Style
in the Early English Lyric

"And alle mine ureondmen þe bet beo nu to-dai
þet ich habbe i-sungen þesne englisce lai."

THE commanding Franciscan influence on our early lyric poetry is
at one level largely a matter of historical and textual record. Its
demonstration has been to some degree augmented here with reference
to style and special content. But so pervasive an association of an entire
literary genre with the life-style and spiritual concerns of one religious
group must surely offer its most pertinent results at the point of critical
interpretation. We should wish, even if briefly, to discover in the
English lyrics any continuity parallel to that developed between
Franciscan theology and aesthetics and early Italian Franciscan poetry,
and to try to appreciate what a corresponding influence on Middle
English popular poetry might now be construed to mean for our
actual reading of these poems. The difference it could make, one hopes,
is a better critical prospect on their organization, performance, and
style.

To deal with some of the latest distinctive pieces first: the catechal
intention of poems on the Seven Sins, the Ten Commandments, and
the Lord's Prayer can hardly escape us.[1] But we can also recognize in
related poetry, such as poems on the five wounds (*RL XIV*, no. 52),
"Man must fight three foes" (*EL XIII*, no. 75), and the "Hours of
the Cross" (*RL XIV*, no. 55), explicit potential for a similar intention,
as well as the presence of discernible Franciscan style and tradition.
Poems of this type can express a considerable liturgical influence. For
example, the "Hours of the Cross" is also found attached to the Horae

231

and in liturgical books for English lay people; in fact, it was largely the friars who, in the thirteenth and fourteenth centuries, were responsible for popularizing lay folk's horae and other vernacular liturgical materials. The natural relationship of their popular translation of liturgical pieces to programs of doctrinal instruction carried out following the Fourth Lateran Council or Pecham's *Constitutiones* is apparent in the contents of many handbooks of pastoralia. The compilation of John Grimestone itself, in its main body so homiletically organized, is prefaced by a special gathering of poems including the "Hours of the Cross," which clearly owes to a liturgical model.[2] One of the advantages of the compiler, however, is selectivity, and the liturgical selections translated tend to lend themselves to the affective nature of Franciscan sprituality, which, as we saw in chapter two, had its roots in the particular articulations of Franciscan theology. We should not be surprised to see the great number of "Christ-from-the-Cross" poems, which amplify the confrontation and personal note of lyrics like the "Stabat mater ounder rode" of MS. Digby 86 and three other manuscripts of the thirteenth century, and reflect the tradition of the *Meditations of the Life of Christ*. In the fourteenth century dozens of poems appear in which Christ appeals directly to man on the basis of His suffering in the manner of the *Fasciculus morum* poem quoted in chapter five (p. 191). Many bear a striking resemblance to Italian Franciscan cross poems of the sort reviewed in chapter four, as well as the Latin cross poems of Jacopone, Ubertino, and St. Bonaventure ("Laudismus de sancta cruce"). These vary in tone from the intensity of "Loke to þi louerd, man" (*RL XIV*, no. 2) to the plaintive cry in Friar Grimestone's book based ultimately on Lamentations 1:12 via the hymn from the office, "O vos omnes qui transitis per viam":[3]

> ȝe þat pasen be þe weyȝe,
> Abidet a litel stounde!
> Be-holdet, al mi felawes,
> ȝef ani me lik is founde.
>
> To þe tre with nailes þre
> Wol fast i hange bounde,
> With a spere al þoru mi ȝide
> To min herte is mad a wounde.
>
> (*RL XIV*, no. 74)

Some of the longer versions dwell on the wounds of Christ in detail (e.g., *RL XIV*, nos. 46, 127), others relate the sufferings of Christ to

stounde, while.

man through examples of his forgiveness (e.g., *RL XIV*, no. 47), several are in the vein of Jacopone da Todi's *Lauda* XXVI, "Omo, de te me lamento, che me vai pure fugenno, ed eo te voglio salvare."[4]

If the corpus of Middle English lyric poetry is rich in examples of Franciscan biblical "translation" and contrition spirituality it also offers examples of their adaptation of the vernacular poetic medium to liturgical and catechal ends in the spirit of Pecham's *Constitutiones* and early Franciscan preaching handbooks. There is not space here to explore in detail the liturgical poems, which in any case have received adequate consideration in Weber's *Theology and Poetry*, but in addition to the instructional poems cited in chapter five and liturgical poems like the one on the Eucharist by Ryman cited below there are a few other Franciscan poems relating to the liturgy which deserve brief mention.

Decima L. Douie, in her biography of Archbishop Pecham, writes:

> . . . Pecham resolutely opposed the movement for shortening the offices in order to provide further time for study. The divine praises were the core of the religious life, and at the Curia the pope and cardinals, in spite of their heavy administrative duties, recited the offices according to the form in the Roman Breviary used by the Friars Minor. Each office had a symbolic significance, for Matins represented the nine orders of Angels, Lauds the different ages of the history of the Church, and the other hours the different stages of Christ's passion: Prime His trial before the high-priest, Terce His condemnation by Pilate, Sext His Crucifixion, None His death, and vespers His burial.[5]

Pecham's well-known Latin poem, *Philomena*, develops the same theme more dramatically. In it the bird is the image of the devout soul, which, after singing all day the various scenes of the Passion, dies in the evening of a broken heart.[6] This poem is similar to a song on the Horae by Jacopone da Todi, and it appears that both were inspirational to the four versions by Middle English poets.[7] Perhaps the best of these is the one in Friar Grimestone's book, which is in long-line carol form. It begins:

> At þe time of matines, lord, þu were i-take,
> & of þine disciples sone were for-sake;
> þe felle Iewes þe token in þat iche stounde,
> & ledden þe to Cayphas, þin handis harde i-bounde.
>> We onuren þe crist & blissen þe with voys,
>> For þu boutest þis werd with þin holi croys.
>> (*RL XIV*, no. 55, lines 1–6)

i-take, taken; *iche stounde,* same hour; *boutest,* redeemed.

Other poems are more specifically applicable to the liturgy, such as
the *rhyme royale* rendition of the Lord's Prayer and the Magnificat by
James Ryman. Its medieval structure readily suggests a musical setting:

> O oure fader, that art in blisse,
> Sanctified thy name mote be.
> Of thy kingdome lete vs not mysse.
> In erthe be done the wille of the,
> As in heuen, in eche degree.
> Oure dayly brede graunt vs this day
> Vnto oure foode, good lorde, we pray.
>
> And forgeue vs oure dette alsoo,
> As we forgeue oure dettours alle,
> And suffre not the fende, oure foo,
> To ouircome and make vs thralle,
> But defende vs, that we not falle
> Into no synne in dede nor wille,
> And deliuer vs fro alle ille.
>
> Hayle, full of grace: Crist is with the;
> Blessed thou be of women alle.
> The frute of the blessed mote be,
> The sonne of god sempiternall,
> With seintis alle to whome thou calle,
> O Marie myelde, meke, chast and pure,
> So that of blisse we may be sure.
>
>   (Zupitza, p. 247)

This kind of lyric shows that the English Franciscan poets, like their
Italian forebears, could and occasionally did adapt vernacular songs
or poems from the liturgy, and then quite possibly for liturgical use.
In England this custom became particularly developed in the years
following 1350.

The Virgin, as we saw in some of the Italian poems discussed in
chapter four, very frequently served as a channel for devotion to the
Passion, as any number of Middle English examples will show. It
is notable that the orisons to Mary which grew out of this devotion
increase in frequency down through the fifteenth century, and find
their most prolific exploitation at the hands of Franciscan friar James
Ryman, who includes some 42 of them in his 163 carols.[8] Some of
these, like number 16, "Come my dere spowse and lady free" are
simply paraphrases of the call of the Bridegroom to the Bride from

the Canticles, and show the considerable influence of St. Bernard; but the best of the Mary poems are often "lessons" in the concordance between the Old and the New Testaments. Though there are very good earlier examples of these,[9] one of Ryman's carols illustrates the instructive powers of a "concordance" laud to Mary more briefly:

> O closed gate of Ezechiel,
> O plentevous mounte of Daniel,
> O Iesse yerde, o Mary myelde,
> For vs thou pray vnto thy childe.
>
> O perfecte trone of Salamon,
> O flore and flese of Gedeon,
> O moder of grace, o Mary myelde,
> For vs thou pray vnto thy childe.
>
> O flamed bushe in alle stature
> Of Moyses, of whome nature
> Ihesus hath take, o Mary mylde
> For vs thou pray vnto thy childe.
>
> O Aaron yerde moost of honoure,
> O moder of oure savioure,
> O gate of lyfe, o Marie myelde,
> For vs thou pray vnto thy childe.
>
> O lanterne of eternall light,
> By whome of Criste we haue a sight,
> O welle of grace, o Marie myelde,
> For vs thou pray vnto thy childe.
>
> O spowse of Criste immaculate
> Assumpte to blisse and coronate,
> O quene of blis, o Marie myelde,
> For vs thou pray vnto thy childe.
>
> Fulfilled is the prophesye
> For why thou has brought furth Messy
> To save mankynde: o Mary myelde,
> For vs thou pray vnto thy childe.
>
> Eternally that we may be
> With thy swete son Ihesus and the
> In heuyn blisse, o Mary myelde,
> For vs thou pray vnto thy childe.

(Zupitza, pp. 173–74)

yerde, rod; flore, floor; flese, fleece.

While much of the inspiration for this sort of Virgin imagery may be
traced to the *Corona B. Mariae Virginis* of St. Bernard ("Ave coeleste
lilium! Ave rosa speciosa!" etc.), and is available in the texts of the
Mass itself, a system of concordance images much further reaching
than Bernard's allusion to the Song of Songs[10] was detailed and appropriated by early Franciscan preachers like St. Anthony of Padua,
who as we noted before were wont to demonstrate Old and New
Testament relationships when they could.[11] It is in fact with respect
to the Virgin that the minimal Franciscan emphasis on allegory is
most developed in English poetry. Foremost among doctrines of the
Blessed Virgin is her virginity, and St. Anthony explains its perpetual
character by a variety of allegories. A propos of the first line of
Ryman's poem, Anthony in his sermons makes use of the classical
text from the prophecy of Ezechiel 44:2, "Porta haec clausa erit, et non
operietur, et vir non transibit per eam; quoniam Dominus Deus Israel
ingressus est per eam, eritque clausa principi," which he explains in
the following way:

> Haec *porta clausa* dicitur, eo quod Beata Maria contra aquilonem,
> meridiem, et occidentem, ut dictum est, *clausa fuit;* et Orienti,
> scilicet Iesu Christo, qui de caelo descendit, humiliter patuit. Unde
> subditur: *Vir non transibit per eam;* idest Ioseph non cognoscet
> eam; eritque *clausa principi,* per quem diabolus huius mundi prin-
> ceps intelligitur, cuius suggestionibus *clausa* fuit quia nulli tenta-
> tioni mens eius patuit, sicut et caro virilem contactum nescivit.[12]

Among other symbols used to represent this doctrine is the mountain
in Daniel 2:34, from which Christ, the little stone, is hewn without
human assistance (line 2 of the Ryman poem above).[13] Mary is also
the "rod out of the root of Jesse" from Isaiah 11:1 (line 3), because of
the typical qualities of the rod: "Nota, quod Beata Maria dicitur
Virga propter quinque proprietates quas habet; est enim longa, recta,
solida, gracilis et flexibilis. Sic Beata Maria 'longa' fuit contempla-
tione; 'recta' iustitiae perfectione; 'solida' mentis stabilitate; 'gracilis'
paupertate; 'flexibilis' humilitate."[14] This rod is traced through Scripture to Aaron as well (stanza 4), from Numbers 17:8, and relates ob-
liquely to the story of Moses' burning bush (stanza 3) in Exodus 3:2. St.
Anthony used both these illustrations, again to indicate the preservation of Mary's virginity in the birth of Christ.[15]

The Virgin's role of mediatrix and petitioner as prefigured in
Queen Esther is typically employed in later English Franciscan poetry:

þou ert hester, þat swete þynge,
And asseuer þe ryche kynge
þe heþ ychose to hys weddynge
      And quene he heþ a-uonge;
For mardocheus, þy derlynge,
      Syre aman was y-honge.

                                    (*RL XIV*, no. 32)

The Esther figure had received popular elaboration at the hands of several important Franciscan theologians. St. Anthony had built on the story of Esther and Assuere a complex of prefiguration for the relationship between Christ and Mary (and between Christ and the Church) in which Esther's finding favor with Assuere (Esther 5:2) foreshadows the way in which God shows favor to Mary.[16] Christ is the Assuere who crowns Esther in Esther 2:15–17, the Blessed Virgin.[17] In the incarnation Mary had crowned Christ with the "diadem of flesh": in the assumption Christ crowned the Blessed Virgin with the diadem of celestial glory.[18] Similarly, St. Bonaventure applies these images to the Virgin, saying that she is like the rising sun without whose "dulce lumen" the incarnate word would have been impossible: her incomparable beauty is foreshadowed by that of Esther, who is her prophecy.[19] And St. Bernardino of Siena's sermons are redolent with the same imagery.[20] While the Franciscan theologians are hardly original in this *concordantia*, with them it enters the mainstream of incarnation imagery, particularly where that imagery extends itself in Augustinian fashion to the sacraments as well:

Ete ye this brede, ete ye this brede
And ete it so, ye be not dede.

This brede geveth eternall lyfe
Bothe vnto man, to chielde and wyfe;
It yeldeth grace and bateth stryfe;
Ete ye it so, ye be not ded.

It semeth white, yet it is rede,
And it is quik and semeth dede,
For it is god in fourme of brede:
Ete ye it so, ye be not ded.

This blessed brede is aungellis foode,
Mannes also perfecte and goode;
Therfore ete ye it with myelde moode:
Ete ye it so, ye be not dede.

a-uonge, received.

This brede fro heven did descende
Vs from alle ille for to defende
And to geve vs lyfe withoute ende:
Ete ye it so, ye be not dede.

In virgyne Mary this brede was bake,
Whenne Criste of her manhoode did take
Fre of all synne mankyende to make:
Ete ye it so, ye be not dede.

Ete ye this brede witthouten synne,
Eternall blis thanne shall ye wynne.
God graunte vs grace to dwell therin.
Ete ye it so, ye be not dede.

                                   (Zupitza, pp. 221–22)

The vivid image of stanza five by which the Virgin's womb becomes an oven in which the body of Christ (or the Host) is baked, from the *Meditations on the Life of Christ*,[21] anticipates how eventually the Eucharist was to prompt a remarkable range of unusual imagery, and become a major subject in Middle English poetry. One does not need a further elaboration of examples to see that the concordance allegorizing here illustrated, especially with reference to the Virgin, conforms to Augustinian and Bonaventuran exegetical techniques and emphases particularly as elaborated by earlier Franciscan thinkers, and surveyed in chapter three above.

Yet in general the texts show that detailed allegorical systems are not the dominant feature of Middle English Franciscan lyric poetry;[22] rather, biblical allegory in Franciscan poetry relates chiefly to the Franciscan interest in the *moraliter* or Scripture. As Franciscan theologians and poets looked for fulfillment of Old Testament prophecy in the New, their search for conformation followed their interest in the moral instruction of biblical authority, in biblical prophecy whose formulae had not been finally realized and whose portent augured for a present or apocalyptic vindication. In MS. Digby 86 occur the famous visions of Daniel with commentary in Latin (fol. 40), followed by a long lyrical poem in Anglo-Norman which translates and expounds the apocalyptic prophecies "le soungnarie Daniel le prophet, si est apele Lunarie" (fols. 41–46). We have already noted the many poems of Judgment, Doomsday, and "Latemestedai" which appear in Middle English Franciscan manuscripts of the thirteenth century. In MS. Merton Coll. 248, which will be discussed more fully in a few pages, is an apocalyptic vision of the returning Christ, succeeding which poem in the manuscript are the following lines based upon the Vision of the Four Horsemen from Apocalypse 6:2–8:

> He rod vpon a whit hors in þet
> þet he be-cam man vor þe.
> He Rod on a red hors in þet
> þet he was i-nayled to þe Rode tre.
> He Rod on a blak hors in þet
> þet he þe deuel ouer cam.
> He rod on a dun hors in þet
> þet þe cloude hym vp nam.

He Rod on a whit hors & hadde a boȝe in his hond
in toknyng þet he was skyluol.
He þet Rod on a Red hors hadde a sverd in his hond
in toknyng þet he was medful.
He þet rod on þe blake hors hadde a weye in his hond
in toknyng þet he was riȝtful.
He þet rod on þe dunne hors hadde Muchel uolk þet hym volwede
in tokning þet he was Miȝtful.[23]

The remarkable juxtaposition of the Christ of the Passion with the Christ of the Second Coming in these lines provides, in typically Franciscan style, both text and commentary at once, and so unites the prognostication of a returning Messiah with the past historic moment of the Passion. It is a juxtaposition also well effected in a poem by Franciscan friar William Herebert (*RL XIV*, no. 25), in this case a paraphrase of Isaiah 63:1–7 used in the *Lectiones* for Holy Week: "What ys he, þys lordling þat cometh vrom þe vyht?"

The point of time on which all biblical prophecy focused was the life of Christ, and poets like Ryman continually refer to the fulfillment of prophecy in reference to the Incarnation:

> The prophecy of Isay
> And prophetes alle and sume
> Now ended is thus finally,
> For god is man become.[24]

Other poems explicitly translated the "procession of prophets," including Daniel, Isaiah, Jeremiah, Habbakuk, David, and others, stanza by stanza.[25]

Perhaps the most interesting way in which the English Franciscans related their interest in Scripture to the lyric was the most obvious—by creating songs which actually translate passages from the Bible.

nam, took; *boȝe,* bow; *skyluol,* victorious; *medful,* vengeful.

In the manner of many Italian examples, from Jacopone and the
Franciscan confraternal poets, it was popular to recall the scene of
the annunciation, as in the thirteenth-century MS. Jesus Coll. Oxford
29, from Luke 1:26–38.[26] Another notable thirteenth-century rendering of a biblical passage is the poem from MS. Harley 2253 which translates the parable of the laborers in the vineyard, Matthew 20:1–16.[27]
It is an excellent poetic translation of the first fifteen verses; for the
sixteenth, "So the last shall be first, and the first last: for many be
called, but few chosen," the poet substitutes an effective exegesis designed to turn the meaning of the biblical passage affectively toward
his audience. In this example, the focus for identification is the singer's
apparent internalizing of the point of the parable, where divine and
human perspectives merge:

> þis world me wurcheþ wo;
> rooles ase þe roo,
>   y sike for vn-sete,
> ant mourne ase men doþ mo
> for doute of foule fo,
>   hou y my sunne may bete.
> þis mon þat Matheu ȝef
> a peny þat wes so bref,
> þis frely folk vnfete,
> ȝet he ȝyrnden more,
> and saide he come well ȝore,
>   ant gonne is loue forlete.

Most of the poems written or collected by Franciscan friar William
Herebert (d. 1333) either depend for their central theme on allusion
to specific scriptural passages or else illustrate the tendency to provide
a concordance of Old Testament and New Testament views of the
Messiah. For example, in one poem, following the *Improperia* of the
Good Friday service, Herebert unites God's historical deliverance of
Israel from bondage and guidance through the wilderness to the
promised land with Christ's lament over Jerusalem (Matthew 23:37;
Luke 13:34).[28]

    Among other Middle English lyrics that translate biblical pas-
sages are Franciscan friar John Grimestone's "Christ's Prayer in Geth-
semane" (*RL XIV*, no. 62) which translates Mark 14:35 and Matthew
26:42; his typical rendering of a collage from the Canticles (*RL XIV*,

---

wurcheþ, does; *rooles*, restless; *roo*, roe; *sike*, sigh; *vn-sete*, disharmony; *bete*, make
amends for; *frely*, proud; *vnfete*, (thought) unfit; *ȝyrnden*, sought after; *forlete*,
forsaken.

no. 68) another "Popule meus quid feci tibi" (Micah 6:3), which coordinates with Matthew 23:37 somewhat more smoothly than Herebert's version (*RL XIV*, no. 72); and his liturgical "O vos omnes qui transitis per viam," the reference to the biblical source of which (Lamentations 1:12) stands at the head of the lines quoted (p. 232) above. Friar James Ryman continues this tradition of translation with his several poems on the annunciation (Zupitza, nos. 3, 112, 113, 114, etc.), his narrative carols which translate the stories of the Shepherds and the Magi (no. 32), and the Flight to Egypt (no. 39), the complete Herod story (no. 61), and the Angel's appearance to Joseph (no. 87), and with his long carol-form poem, perhaps intended for use as a verse-sermon, which translates the Sermon on the Mount from Matthew 5 (Zupitza, no. 97).

Also, phrases or verses from Scripture could be woven into a lyric, providing a key to its sense through programmed allusion. This may be observed in Grimestone's "Merci abid an loke al day" (*RL XIV*, no. 61), which recalls phrases from the Davidic Psalms, and in a later poem from the Vernon MS, "Deus caritas est" (*RL XIV*, no. 98), whose Latin lines in the first four stanzas follow the sequence of 1 John 3:16. But one of the most effective Franciscan uses of Scripture is in the doctrinal and biblical recounting which is made possible through the Christ-Virgin dialogues which form such an important part of Franciscan poetry.[29] Grimestone has a long dialogue carol between Mary and her Child which illustrates the point very well. Prefaced with its refrain "Lullay, lullay, la lullay, Mi dere moder, lullay," it opens with the poet in a dream-vision stance:

> Als i lay vp-on a nith
> Alone in my longging,
> Me þouthe i sau a wonder sith,
> A maiden child rokking.
>
> þe maiden wolde with-outen song
> Hire child o slepe bringge;
> þe child þouthe sche dede him wrong,
> & bad his moder sengge.[30]

The Christ-child finds that his mother sings the story of his birth: of Gabriel, the prophecies, the shepherds, Magi, and so on. Thus, within the affectively powerful frame of reference provided by the tender, humanized relationship between mother and child, the basic elements of the incarnation story are unfolded in a précis of liturgi-

nith, night; *sith*, sight.

cally significant items from the biblical account. And when the Virgin can sing no more, since she has covered the story to the "moment" of telling, the Child offers to foretell the rest of the story:

> "Moder," seide þat suete þing,
> "To singen I sal þe lere
> Wat me fallet to suffring,
> & don wil i am here.
>
> Wanne þe seuene daiȝes ben don,
> Rith as habraham wasce,
> Kot sal i ben with a ston
> In a wol tendre place."
>
> (*RL XIV*, no. 56, lines 61–68)

Following from this point he elaborates the stories of the Magi, of Simeon, of the confrontation in the temple, his baptism, temptation, gathering of disciples, and ultimately the Passion, resurrection, and ascension. It does not require much imagination to infer that the performance of a lyric such as this one would be of great benefit in holding the attention of illiterate people sufficiently to impart the basic elements of the biblical story. For them it was probably more effective than a detailed rendition of the Scripture from the Mass, even if circumstances had made such an authorized "translation" possible.

In most such poems, the engagement of emotional identification at any level can be a preliminary to a contritional treatment of the Passion, and the most effective of Middle English lyrics in this vein are still the Passion dialogues such as "Stond wel moder." In the *stabat mater* or cross poem necessary exegesis and commentary on the biblical Passion scene become interwoven into the text in such a way that the dramatic recreation not only stimulates the reflexes of affective piety but develops toward an informed response of contrition in the reader or hearer of the song. The progression is characteristically realized in two carols which come from thirteenth-century MS. Digby 2. The first begins:

> Hi sike, al wan hi singe,
> for sorue þat hi se
> wan hic wit wepinge
> bi-holde a-pon þe tre.
> hi se ihesu, mi suete,
> his herte blode for-lete
> for þe luue of me.

Rith as habraham, just as Abraham.

his wondis waxin wete—
marie, milde and seete,
þu haf merci of me![31]

Reviewing the details of the passion scene, it focuses its energies on the evangelical motive.

Wel ofte wan hi slepe
wit soru hic ham soit,
wan hi wake and wende
hi þenke in mi þoit,
allas! þat men beit wode,
bi-holdit an þe rode
and silit—hic li noyt—
her souelis in-to sin
for any worlde-his win,
þat was so der hi-boyt.

Following immediately in the manuscript is a lyric which takes up the movement toward contrition with a specific prayer of contrition and repentance:

Hayl mari!
hic am sori,
haf pite of me and merci,
mi leuedi,
to þe i cri.
for me sinnis dred ham hi
wen hi þenke þat hi sal bi
þat hi haf mis hi-don
in worde, in worke, in þoith foli.
leuedi, her mi bon!

Mi bon þu her,
leuedi der,
þat hic aske wit reuful cher.
þu len me her
wil hic am fer,
do penanz in mi praier,
ne let me noth ler þat þu ber.
at min endin-day
þe warlais þai wil be her
forto take þair pray.

(*EL XIII*, no. 65, lines 1–20)

soit, sought; *wode*, insane; *silit*, then; *hic li noyt*, I lie not; *win*, pleasure.
þoith foli, foolish thought; *bon*, prayer; *fer*, far; *warlais*, devils.

The function of these poems is obvious and accords with what we have discovered about Franciscan evangelical theory and methodology in the Italian lyrics and in the Anglo-Irish Franciscan manuscript from Kildare.[32] The often bluntly articulated objective of affective and contritional response is repentance and conversion:

> Reuert, reuert, reuert, reuert:
> O synfull man, geve me thyn hert.[33]

But the Franciscan ideal of total identification with Christ, so often expressed in the more sophisticated poems of Jacopone da Todi, is not left unsung in the best of Middle English Franciscan poetry:

> Gold & al þis werdis wyn
> is nouth but christis rode:
> I wolde ben clad in christes skyn,
> þat ran so longe on blode,
> & gon t'is herte & taken myn In—
> þer is a fulsum fode.
> þan ȝef i litel of kith or kyn,
> For þer is alle gode. Amen.[34]

Grimestone's "metaphysical" image grows out of the Franciscan theological concept of the function of sacramental grace in conforming the individual to the Suffered-Christ. In conceits that look forward to the style of Herbert and Donne, Grimestone puns effectively ("þis werdis wyn") on *world-word* and *wine-joy* to introduce a typical movement toward radical physical identification ("I wolde ben clad in christes skyn") which is metaphysical through the mystery of transubstantiation ("wyn," "blode," "fode," "alle gode") as well. Here transubstantiation becomes the essential transformation by which the poet experiences that the supreme good for man is not worldly joy or even *philia,* but the gold of the cross. It is this gold, or wisdom, which is Friar John's ideal of the supreme good. One could hardly desire, in fact, a more precise statement of the Franciscan ethic. But the poem does not stop there: the multivalence and paradox of the initial word-play develops one more classical Franciscan belief, that of the intimate connection between Christ's incarnation consummated at Calvary, and the possibility of poetry, of essential metaphor, as suggested in the opening statements of the Gospel John, "In the beginning was the Word." A further reading of the poem's first two lines thus becomes: "Wisdom, and all the joy of words/ is nothing except for the cross of Christ," a tacit recognition by the poet, appropriately, of his art, of the profound and mysterious dependency of word or metaphor upon Word or Metaphor, of the intimate relationship between philology and the incarnation. Finally we see in this complex little poem that its various valences and paradoxes all operate simultaneously, cross-tracing it with the manifold implications of sacramental grace. In this way, the poem becomes for both author and hearer a song of transformation, at once a conversion poem and a prayer for spiritual renewal.

Even though the English temperament seems to be less given to extravagance of spirit than Italian Franciscan mysticism, we still find in English Franciscan poems some flashes of that kind of emotion too:

> Loue is sofft, loue is swet, loue is goed sware!
> Loue is muche tene, loue is muchel kare!
> Loue is blissene mest, loue is bot ȝare!
> Loue is wondred and wo, wiþ for to fare!
>
> Loue is hap, wo hit haueþ; loue is god hele!
> Loue is lecher and les, and lef for to tele!
> Loue is douti in þe world, wiþ for to dele!
> Loue makeþ in þe lond moni hounlele!³⁵

The resemblance of these lines to Jacopone da Todi's *Laude* LXXVII, LXXI, and parts of XCIX and the last of XC, and even to Francis's "Cantico dell' amore," is striking.

The note of urgency in many Middle English lyrics is relevant both to the Apocalypse, as we have noted, and to the transiency of human life. Any number of lyrics play on the second theme. This is as true of poems on the "Signs of Death" (cf. Jacopone, *Lauda* XXV)³⁶ as it is of the Middle English translations of Jacopone's "Cur Mundus Militat,"³⁷ of poems on the "Signs of the Times,"³⁸ as of poems which point toward Judgment and Doomsday.³⁹ It is this general category that contains some of the best of Middle English Franciscan poetry, as we might expect from the natural relationship between Franciscan methodology and traditional English feeling for the "lif is laene" theme. There is a real constancy of feeling between the earliest known Middle English lyric, with which this study began, (sometimes called "Now comes the blast of Winter"), and the "Three Sorrowful Tidings" of fifty years later.

---

sware, speech; *tene*, suffering; *blissene mest*, the greatest of blessings; *bot ȝare*, quick medicine; *wondred*, misery; *hap*, fortune; *lecher*, lecherous; *les*, false; *tele*, entrap; *douti*, doughty; *wiþ for to dele*, to deal with; *hounlele*, unhappy.

Mirie it is while sumer ilast
wið fugheles song,
oc nu necheð windes blast
and weder strong.
Ej! ej! what þis nicht is long,
and ich wid wel michel wrong
soregh and murne and fast.[40]

Vche day me cumeþ tydinges þreo,
For wel swiþe sore beoþ heo:
þe on is þat ich schul heonne,
þat oþer þat ich noth hwenne;
þe þridde is my meste kare,
þat ich not hwider ich scal fare.[41]

Although such poems call up visions of an old debate in Witan as
quickly as images of active Franciscan spirituality, we may recognize
in their conformity to sibling voices in the Franciscan manuscripts
a likely part in the evangelistic program of the Friars Minor.

But the point of a poem like Grimestone's "Gold and al þis
werdis wyn" is that it would be a mistake to see in these lyrics only
the emotional side of their spirituality. It will be remembered that
the Franciscans saw themselves as erstwhile champions of the Augustinian tradition, and that Archbishop Pecham was not alone in seeking
to evoke and defend a consciously Augustinian theology. The Kildare
manuscript which refers to Augustine at every major doctrinal point
concerning the Passion is typical of Franciscan preachers' compilations, which cite him everywhere.[42] And even the intense and urgent
quality of Franciscan spirituality itself has its deep paternal kinship
to the St. Augustine of the *Confessions*. Among the many evangelical
warnings against procrastination in Middle English poetry is the
following paraphrase of a portion of that work:

Louerd, þu clepedest me
an ich nagt ne ansuarded þe
Bute wordes scloe and sclepie:
"þole yet! þole a litel!"
Bute "yiet" and "yiet" was endelis,
and "þole a litel" a long wey is.[43]

þreo, three; *wel swiþe sore beoþ heo*, exceedingly grievous are they; *heonne*, go
hence; *noth*, know not.

clepedest, called; *scloe*, slow; *sclepie*, sleepy; *þole*, wait.

Typically, the poem picks up an Augustinian theme that Franciscan preachers were wont to employ in their penitential appeal: in putting off repentance a man in effect not only ignores the sufferings of Christ, but spiritually speaking permits its "continuance," effectively crucifying Christ afresh. It is a recurrent notion, and the reason for favoring Augustine as a model in such cases is that this side of his work corresponds to the crucial importance of Christ's suffering in Franciscan theology and preaching. It is natural then, that theological perspectives adapted from Augustine and championed by early Franciscan thinkers such as Alexander of Hales and Robert Grosseteste should also receive elaboration at the hands of English Franciscan poets.

We have noted explicitly theological lyrics among the Italian Franciscan poems discussed in chapter four, and have discussed in chapter two that theological doctrine central to many of them, the question "Si Adam non peccasset."[44] This doctrine, treated according to the principles of Hales and Grosseteste, is the substance of poems from four notable Franciscan manuscripts: Trinity Coll. Camb. 323 (ed. *EL XIII*, no. 24), Advocates 18.1.21 (Grimstone—ed. *RL XIV*, no. 65), Cambridge MS. Ee. 1.12 (Ryman—ed. Zupitza, no. 65), and Harley 913, the Kildare book (ed. Heuser, p. 106). The last is the most complete exposition of the doctrine, being set out in the form of a verse sermon or quasi-theological history of the subject. After his invocation and prayer for guidance the poet says (or sings), in the Kildare version:

> Al þat god suffrid of pine,
> Hit nas noȝt for is owen gilt,
> Ok hit was, man, for sin þine
> þat wer for sin in helle ipilt.

Lucifer's fall started the whole unfortunate predicament, he urges, but man's culpability arises from his forsaking of his reason for the lower flesh, and resigning his will to Eve:

> Skil, resun and eke miȝt
> He ȝef Adam in his mode
> To be stidfast wiþ al riȝt
> And leue þe harme and do gode.

> God ȝaf him a gret maistri
> Of al þat was in watir and londe,
> Of paradis al þe balye,
> Whan him likid to is honde.

pine, pain; *ipilt*, thrust.

Foules, bestis and þe frute—
Saf o tre he him forbede,
Of paradis þe grete dute,
And ӡit he sinied þroӡ iuil red.

To him þe deuil had envie
þat he in is stid schold be broӡte;
A serpent he com þroӡ felonie
And makid Eue chonge hir þoӡt.

Whi com he raþer to Eue
þan he com to Adam?
Ichul ӡou telle, sires, beleue,
For womman is lef euer to man.

Womman mai turne man is wille,
Whare ӡho wol pilt hir to;
þat is þe resun and skille
þat þe deuil com hir first to.

Ette, he seid, of þis appil,
If þat þou wolt witti be
þe worþ at witti of miӡt and wille
As god him silf in trinite.

(lines 37–64)

So ended Paradise. But God still intends redemption. The chain of prophets is recounted to the annunciation by Gabriel, the life of Christ is swiftly described to the time of the capture and Passion, and then again each detail is noted with care. Man's sin caused this terrible suffering, notes the poet. Yet there is a remedy for despair:

þroӡ is deþ he ouercam,
As he is manhed siwed,
As profetis prechid in his name,
So þat he deþ suffrid.

þo he rose fram deþ to liue,
As telliþ Daui þe king,
Is godhed he gan to kiþe;
Holi boke telliþ is uprising.

Iesus was sikir inoӡ
þat seid erlich "ich wol riӡt me"
And answard wiþ vt wo
"After þat deþ ouercom be."

(lines 193–204)

mode, mind; *balye,* authority; *honde,* disposal; *dute,* pleasure; *red,* counsel; *pilt,* hurry.

siwed, pursued; *sikir inoӡ,* confident enough.

Original sin has been countered, the wrong has been redressed which otherwise would have been fatal, and through which, *o felix culpa,* the atonement was performed. This is the wonderful paradox of Christian theology, firmly embedded as the root paradox of English poetry of meditation for another three hundred years. In a playful rendition from the fifteenth century it reads:

> Adam lay i-bounde,
>   Bounden in a bond;
> Foure thousand wynter
>   Thoughte he not to longe.
> And al was for an appel,
>   An eppel that he took,
> As clerkes fynden writen
>   In here book.
>
> Ne hadde the appel take ben,
>   The appel take ben,
> Ne hadde nevere oure lady
>   A ben hevenes quene.
> Blessed by the tyme
>   That appel take was—
> Ther-fore we mowen synge
>   *"Deo gracias."*
>
>   (Stevick, no. 53)

Alexander of Hales would have been pleased with both poems.

One of the splendid images which occurs in that theologian's treatment of the Passion pictures Christ as a champion-knight, who struggles on the cross against the terrible adversary.[45] The image of Christ as knight is an old one, in English poetry alone going back for its inspiration at least to the Dream of the Rood.[46] But the Franciscans show a particular interest in the chivalric association and lend it particular prominence and development. The words of Christ "I haue þe wonnen in fith" are a commonplace in English Franciscan poetry,[47] and root themselves in a Franciscan tradition which both saw Christ as supreme knight, and saw the friars themselves as knights of Christ in the world. St. Francis said of his followers, "Isti sunt fratres mei milites tabulae rotundae" (*Speculum perfectionis,* chap. 72), and chivalric imagery is sometimes associated with the Friars Minor even in graphic art.[48] Franciscan poets like James Ryman could write:

O good Fraunces, of oure kynghthoode
Currus et auriga,
To thy brethren, where they aboode,
Vexit te quadriga,
As clerly nowe itte dothe appere
To feith full men bothe farre and nere.

(Zupitza, p. 318)

This image helps explain a problem raised by Carleton Brown with respect to a sermon in the anthology of John Sheppey, a Benedictine of Oxford, most of whose collection (in MS Merton Coll. 248) as Brown perhaps did not know, came from Franciscan sources.[49] Noting that these sermons contain several verses similar to sections of the York-Towneley cycles, Brown prints one of the tags in question, and the following expansion note:

> primo dico he sent fro aboue a ouercummyer mythiest & sic consequenter similiter in illo sermone de rotunda tabula ibi nam querens causam a primis parentibus quare prohibuit deus ne comedent de ligno paradysi & ille respondente ne forte mor [iamur—Cf. Gen. 3.5] statim dixit dyabolus:
>
> > In thys tre [MS ys thre] es alle hys myth
> > bot þer he ley and sayd nowth ryth . . . .[50]

Brown is fascinated by the reference to the "sermo de rotunda tabula," but can offer no explanation for such a reference. My suggestion is that it is a reference to the Christ-knight and chivalric metaphor cultivated by the Franciscans. Certainly the poems from this sermon are Franciscan in tone and theme (fols. 166 ff.—See *RL XIV*, nos. 39–41) and at least one of the sermons of Sheppey's collection is of explicit Franciscan authorship.[51] In one manuscript containing materials from the *Fasciculus morum* occurs the following poem which ties together the doctrine of the "sermo de rotunda tabula," which relates to "Si Adam non pecasset." The first part of it reads:

Fadur & sone & holi gost, o god in trinite,
To þe y make my mone, pouȝ y unworþi be;
I am but myn one, & fomen haue y þre—
þe fend, þe world, myn owne flesh—him mai y not fle.

þe fend me tempteþ dai & nyȝt,
he wol me reue heuene briȝt,
þat he les þorw his pride;

Currus et auriga, chariot and charioteer; *Vexit te quadriga,* raise your standard.

swete ihesu, y am þi knyȝt,
aȝenus him y take þe fiȝt,
   stifli him to abide.

At þe y mot myn armes borwe,
Mi sheld shal be þe swerd of sorwe,
   marie þat stong to þe herte;
þe holi cros my baner biforn,
myn helm þi garlond of sharpe þorn,
   Mi swerd þi scourges smerte.

Mi plates shullen þi nailes be,
myn acotoun þat spere tre,
   þat stong þi swete syde.
Now y am armed þus wel,
nel y him fle neuere a del,
   tyde what bi-tyde!

þe worlde me haþ long lif bihet,
and biddeþ me murie make;
whanne i am olde and of unmyȝt
to penaunce forte take:
it haþ be shewed to oure syȝt,
þenne is al to late;

he haþ deseyued king and knyȝt,
& many man brouȝt to wrake.
swete ihesu, ful of myȝt,
þou here my bone & do me riȝt,
him here to forsake.

Holi fadur, y herie þe
for þe loue þat þou hast shewed me,
   siþ þat þou furst bigan;
for loue þou came from heuene blisse,
& madest for loue to þi liknes,
   oure fadur adam:
he as unwise þyn heste brak,
whanne he of þat appel at,
   In sorwe to mony man.[52]

The old idea of the three foes of man, the world, the flesh, and the devil, will be recognized as harmonizing with the concept of chivalric battle, and the armor recalls the spiritual arming of the Christian knight for battle in Ephesians 6:11–18. We are on our way to that beautiful sixteenth-century lyric vision of Christ as knight:

stifli, sternly; *borwe,* redeem; *acotoun,* tunic; *wrake,* ruin; *heste,* commandment.

Lully, lulley; lully, lulley;
The fawcon hath born my mak away.

He bare hym up, he bare hym down;
He bare hym into an orchard brown.

In that orchard ther was an hall,
That was hangid with purpill and pall.

And in that hall ther was a bede;
Hit was hangid with golde so rede.

And yn that bed ther lythe a knyght,
His wowndes bledyng day and nyght.

By that bedes side ther kneleth a may,
And she wepeth both nyght and day.

And by that beddes side ther stondith a ston,
"Corpus Christi" wretyn theron.[53]

Here, with each couplet we move closer to the real object of the quest—from lullaby and romance to autumn orchard and a splendid hall where an ever-dying knight and his mourning lady engage their mysterious reciprocity of flowing tears and flowing blood. At the very last comes the most surprising discovery of all—the Word: *Corpus Christi*. Here is *reductione artium*, from words to Word, yet as mysterious (and as compelling) as before.

In chapter three we noted of Franciscan exegesis that it tended to emphasize the literal level for its inherent dramatic qualities. This we can see is borne out in the Middle English lyrics at large. As songs, most of them do not submit themselves naturally to multi-level interpretations; especially is this true of the homiletical poems. Instead, the popular Franciscan song tends toward simple moralization. Allegory plays a lesser role, being brought into play by the English Franciscan poets when they wished to illustrate the relationship between Old and New Testaments as a *concordantia* pointed toward personal history. This balance largely accounts for the reduction *poeticum ad Scripturam* of the Franciscans. But as St. Bonaventure had shown, nature too could be read like the Scriptures to reveal the Divine mind. The treatment of nature by English medieval poets (like that by the Italian Franciscans) follows the same pattern of priorities. In English Franciscan poetry, there is an unfeigned interest in the literal level of the Book of Nature, in nature almost for its own sake. The beautiful opening lines of "Somer is comen with loue to toune" from MS. Digby 86 (*EL XIII*, no. 52) are adapted to a shorter version in MS. Harley 2253:

Lenten ys come wiþ loue to toune,
wiþ blosmen ant wiþ briddes roune,
    þat al þis blisse bryngeþ.
Dayeseȝes in þis dales,
notes suete of nyhtegales,
    vch foul song singeþ.
þe þrestelcoc him þreteþ oo;
away is huere wynter wo
    when woderoue springeþ.
þis foules singeþ ferly fele,
ant wlyteþ on huere wynne wele,
    þat al þe wode ryngeþ.

þe rose rayleþ hire rode,
þe leues on þe lyhte wode
    waxen al wiþ wille.
þe mone mandeþ hire bleo,
þe lilie is lossom to seo,
    þe fenyl ant þe fille.
Wowes þis wilde drakes;
miles murgeþ huere makes,
    ase strem þat strikeþ stille.
Mody meneþ, so doþ mo;
ichot ycham on of þo,
    for loue þat likes ille.

þe mone mandeþ hire lyht;
so doþ þe semly sonne bryht,
    when briddes singeþ breme.
Deawes donkeþ þe dounes;
deores wiþ huere derne rounes,
    domes forte deme;
wormes woweþ vnder cloude,
wymmen waxeþ wounder proude,
    so wel hit wol hem seme.
ȝef me shal wonte wille of on
þis wunne weole y wole forgon
    ant wyht in wode be fleme.

                            (Brook, no. 11)

briddes roune, birds' song; þrestelcoc, song thrush; þreteþ, warbles; woderoue, woodruff; ferly fele, wonderfully; wlyteþ, chirp; wele, happiness; rayleþ, arrays; rode, complexion; mandeþ, sends forth; bleo, radiance; fenyl, fennel; fille, wild thyme; Wowes, woos; miles, animals; murgeþ, gladden; Mody meneþ, high-spirited man complains; Deawes donkeþ þe dounes, dew moistens the hillsides; deores wiþ huere derne rounes, deer with their secret voices; domes forte deme, tell their tales; woweþ, make love; wyht in wode be fleme, quickly in woods be fled.

This poem is a proper example of the aesthetic and emotional response to nature which was well within the capacity of English Franciscan poets. The beauties described are real: the light is the real, physical light, soft and bright, of the sun and the moon, there is a real scent to the blossoms, cadence in the clarion notes of the birds "þat al þe wode ryngeþ," and texture to "þe leues on þe lyte wode." At the same time, the season, Lent, and the double meaning conveyed in lines such as "þe rose rayleþ hire rode," or "þe mone mandeþ hire bleo"—both suggestive of the Virgin—involve the possibility of a heavenly love toward which the poet might run from the cupiditous love which he forsakes, "ant wyht in wode be fleme." Another poem from the Harley manuscript shows clearly the direction in which the real physical beauties of nature were inexorably to lead their appreciator:

> When y se blosmes springe
>   ant here foules song,
> a suete loue-longynge
>   myn herte þourhout stong,
> al for a loue newe,
> þat is so suete ant trewe,
>   þat gladieþ al my song;
> ich wot al myd iwisse
> my ioie ant eke my blisse
>   on him is al ylong.
>
> When y miselue stonde
>   ant wiþ myn eȝen seo
> þurled fot ant honde
>   wiþ grete nayles þreo—
> blody wes ys heued,
> on him nes neut bileued
>   þat wes of peynes freo—
> wel wel ohte myn herte
> for his loue to smerte
>   ant sike ant sory beo.

The beauties of nature are luminescent exemplars of that greatest Beauty of all, revealed in the crucified Christ. Tracing the time-honored route "omnis creatura speculum est," the poem then refers the joy of spring back through the crucifixion to Christ's nativity, an evocation of his eternal juvenescence, and creates a prayer for reconciliation:

> Iesu, milde ant suete,
>   y synge þe mi song;
> ofte y þe grete
>   ant preye þe among;
> let me sunnes lete,
> ant in þis lyue bete
>   þat ich haue do wrong;
> at oure lyues ende,
> when we shule wende,
>   Iesu, vs vndefong!
>   Amen.

(Brook, no. 18)

He who has combined the profitable with the pleasing, says Bonaventure quoting Horace, is worthy of universal applause. One could hardly find a better example of the Franciscan lyrical method than this poem.

Another equally beautiful lyric from the Harley manuscript shows the same open-ended response to nature, moving from the emotive effect of its physical reality to the intellectual apprehension of its spiritual message. "Wynter," it seems to me, hardly fits the "secular" categorization to which G. L. Brook assigns it; the ascription perhaps points up a difficulty in many past attempts to show for thirteenth-century English poetry a developed, extant secular tradition. For pedagogical purposes it may help to approach the poem indirectly, since its spiritual content can be effectively compared and contrasted with a much more obviously didactic poem by Ryman:

> Amende we vs, while we haue space,
> For why nowe is the tyme of grace.
>
> That holy clerke, seint Augustyne,
> Seith, now is tyme for to inclyne
> To vertue and synne to resyne,
> For why now is the tyme of grace.
>
> Now, while we lyve, to do penaunce
> It is oure soules to avaunce
> And into blisse for to enhaunce,
> For why now is the tyme of grace.
>
> Are we departe this worlde fro,
> Oure soules we may save fro woo;
> Whenne we be gone, we may not so,
> For why now is the tyme of grace.

vndefong, receive.

Do we so now, while we here be,
In worde and dede, that we may see
Almyghty god in mageste,
For why now is the tyme of grace.

In wille, in dede, in worde and thought
Axe we hym grace, that vs hath bought,
Ayenst his will that we haue wrought,
For why now is the tyme of grace.

Criste, that ay was, shall be and is,
Graunte vs forgueuenes of oure mys
And graunte vs grace to dwell in blis,
For why now is the tyme of grace.

(Zupitza, no. 49)

It would be a dull fellow who missed the point: "Let us amend ourselves, while we have opportunity, for now is the time of grace." While Ryman's poetic abilities seem to suggest a general deterioration in the artistic quality of religious lyric poetry from the thirteenth to the fifteenth centuries, his poem serves to show us much. Here we have the popular *X X, a a a X* carol form developed in Provence and adopted by the earliest Franciscans to sing the Gospel characteristically expressing the urgency of repentance—not merely by recounting the traditional doctrinal reasons, but by a reiterated emphasis on the prime Franciscan motivation to penance: the immanent foreclosure of human opportunity. What is stated with more than usual traditional explicitness are the reasons for repentance which arise naturally from the nature of man's sin against God's "wille," and from the enabling grace purchased in Christ's atoning death which alone makes penance effective (stanza 5). The well-known Augustinian idea of the six ages of man, of which the sixth and final age of grace began with the atonement, is invoked by the reference to "that holy clerke" in the first line of the song. The great "lif is laene" theme of medieval poetry is sounded in the first lines of stanzas two, three, and four, and together with the reiterating message of the two-line burden or refrain, the song receives a unifying emphasis in the urgency of repentance in the face of fleeting "tyme." The first line of stanza five underscores the totality of commitment involved in the prayer for grace: it is an action of *wille* foremost, followed by *dede, worde,* and *thought.* Thus both the aspect of works consistent with faith introduced in the preceding stanza, and the aspect of grace amplified in the last stanza are compactly stated in the penultimate verse. In addition, the factor of free human will is introduced in the same sentence as God's will, in terms of which it chooses. There is much theology here in little space; in fact the fifth stanza encapsulates the message of the poem. But the sixth and final stanza is not then anti-climactic. This last verse, again in an apt first line, strikes the note which prevents Christian despair over the transitoriness of human existence: it is Christ, whose eternality guarantees that our true "blis," toward which we are called to travel, is not the sort that moth or rust may corrupt.

No one could miss the obvious doctrinal nature of such a poem, or fail to infer its pragmatic value, even if he did not know its ancestry and use. But in earlier poems like the Harley lyric "Wynter," just as much a part of the Franciscan tradition, superior artistic skill may for the modern reader cloud the nature of an equally "evangelical" intent.

> Wynter wakeneþ al my care,
> nou þis leues waxeþ bare;
> ofte y sike ant mourne sare
>   when hit comeþ in my þoht
>   of þis worldes ioie hou hit geþ al to noht.
>
> Nou hit is ant nou hit nys,
> also hit ner nere ywys.
> Þat moni mon seiþ soþ hit ys:
>   al goþ bote Godes wille,
>   alle we shule deye þah vs like ylle.
>
> Al þat grein me graueþ grene,
> nou hit faleweþ al bydene;
> Iesu, help þat hit be sene,
>   ant shild vs from helle,
>   for y not whider y shal ne hou longe her duelle.[54]

If the beautiful, haunting tone, the deft strokes of vernal imagery, and the semi-alliterative whisper of its cadence seem to obscure the doctrine, look closer; it is still there. "Wynter" is very much like the song of a century earlier which began this book.[55] Like "Mirie it is while sumer i-last" it moves without effort from an acute apprehension of physical reality to a personal reflection which is metaphysical and ultimately theological. Both poems in a few swift strokes develop strong emotional involvement at the most basic level. We all die. And in response to that, both poems urge, in the same style, repentance

---

wakeneþ, wakens; *waxeþ*, wax; *sike*, sigh; *sare*, sorrowfully; *ioie*, joy; *soþ*, true; *grein*, grain; *graueþ grene*, bury green; *faleweþ*, withers; *al bydene*, already.

and spiritual preparation for participation in a metaphysical reality
which never changes. For winter is the time of old age, of barrenness,
and the remembrance of misspent summers. The season has a solidly
marked traditional iconography from earliest Christian times.[56] Both
in the visual and literary arts, it is associated with old age and sin,
which in turn is identified with St. Paul's "old man" (Ephesians
4:22). This motif, coupled with the reiterated idea of the utter
impermanence of temporal, tangible things in the fifth, sixth, seventh,
and tenth lines, are contrasted to the poet's starkly effective realization
at the exact center of the poem: "What many men say—truth it is:
all goes but God's will." (Note that the same concept is pivotal in
Ryman's poem.) The lines are uttered in a dramatically perfect
sigh of self-perception: as the leaves of life begin to fall, there is no
use thinking that the earth will not receive its own. There is no surety
in things deciduous. But as every medieval person knew from a
common image in parish sermons and other religious songs, that
which was ever green was a symbol of the eternality of the resurrected
Christ, the perpetual spring of Paradise, and Christ's own resurrection
which is reflected in the greenness of springtime.[57] As this saving note
is sounded at the beginning of the third stanza, another reference is
directly called forth by its first two lines. "All that seed I bury unripe,
now it withers already: Jesus help that it be seen." The source idea
has been recognized[58] as John 12:24, 25: "Verily, verily, I say unto
you, Except a corn of wheat fall into the ground and die, it abideth
alone: but if it die, it bringeth forth much fruit. He that loveth his
life shall lose it; and he that hateth his life in this world shall keep
it unto life eternal." This also is a popular passage with medieval
commentators, who use it to point up the very theme of both these
poems, that man's proper movement is not toward the things of this
life, but toward the love of the New Jerusalem which is to come
(Augustine *De civitate Dei* 14.28).[59] He that loves his life more than
he loves God is guilty of the self-love which leads to destruction and
death. But as St. Augustine and scores of later medieval writers
were wont to stress, he who loves with *caritas,* the crucial virtue of
Christian character (without which St. Paul says all other of life's
efforts are irrelevant), despises the cupiditous desires of his temporal
body that he may achieve eternal life.

Here again, as in Ryman's poem, the poet's goal is to move his
hearers toward the love of God rather than self, emphasizing the dire
urgency of repentance before the seasons of this life conclude their
course. Thus, he too does not close on the note of comfort at the
first of his final stanza, and lacking a two-line "burden" to re-

emphasize his theme, employs another technique. Referring to the "grain" (seed) again, he says "Jesus, help that it be seen," that is, he prays that Christ may notice that he has become "dead to the things of this world," and has laid down his life so that he might not ultimately lose it. The implication is clear: winter is not the usual time for planting seeds, and perhaps Christ might not be looking for grain committed so late. The poet's final lines therefore combine beautifully both the urgency of his belated plea and the poignant air of insecurity he shares with all who are not new men, renewed in the grace which is of Christ:

> ant shild vs from helle,
> for y not whider y shal ne hou longe her duelle.

In Middle English poetry of the Franciscan school, the realm of nature produces an immediate effect, one which is unquestionably emotional, but not indefinitely mysterious or wondrously pantheistic. Emotional response is encouraged and then utilized, coordinated with an implicit and immediate acceptance of the fact that the Book of God's Works, like the Book of God's Word, means something. Almost imperceptibly emotion combines itself with the action of intellect, and will. And in that moment the realms of Scripture, Nature, and Art are finally one. The Exemplar is exemplified.

There is not space in this study to broaden the scope of materials under examination to include the poems of Englishmen such as Robert of Brunne and Richard Rolle, so obviously under the influence of Franciscan spirituality, and to show the relevance of the consideration elaborated here to later poets, such as Scottish Dunbar, himself an Observant Franciscan Friar. These and other later figures must here be passed over in reluctant silence. Indeed, I have consciously omitted even to discuss the poems of the English Franciscans who wrote or adapted popular songs into Latin: John Pecham, John Lathbury,[60] Walter Wimbourne,[61] and the famous Bishop of Ossory, Richard Ledrede,[62] to name a few. Nor have I been able to more than mention a few of the poems in the very large body of Anglo-Norman Franciscan poetry which offers so many excellent paradigms of Franciscan lyric method and spirituality, and so often poems which are superior to their sister-poems in English.[63] Finally, there has not been time to relate the lyrics to the exegetical principles propounded by early Franciscans, to the work of later Franciscans like Ridewall and

Bartholomaeus Anglicus, or to the techniques of commentators such as the author of the *Ovide moralisé* and Pierre Bersuire.[64] Here is work for other books.

However, within the limitations of its enterprise this study allows, I believe, an important new perspective on medieval English lyrical poetry. We have seen how the Franciscan Order instigated a regular use of the vernacular lyric as a missionary and devotional tool in Italy, and how their Italian poems expounded the theological persuasions of the early Franciscans in a tone and style springing from the spirituality fomented and promulgated by the Friars Minor. Though we are deprived of an explicit record of the first Franciscans' poetic activity on their arrival into England, the decisive testimony of Middle English lyric provenance and poetic content conforms to extensive evidences of a highly articulated Franciscan program for employing vernacular verse in religious instruction, and conforms in such a way as to establish the formative role of the Friars Minor for the whole popular genre. We may conclude with justification that the English Franciscans continued the traditions of their Italian forebears in employing the popular vernacular lyric as a methodological weapon in an evangelical ministry, that their lyrics functioned similarly as songs of contrition and devotion, but also of theological instruction, and served to impart basic biblical knowledge in the vernacular.

In medieval English lyrics we may distinguish two types: homiletic and reflective. The latter type adapted itself to private devotional uses, and tended to develop more widely in the period following the Black Death; hence it has not been a large interest in the present study. Of the former type we may say that Professor Greene's assessment that the medieval English lyric is popular by destination rather than by origin[65] is here particularly vindicated. The Middle English lyric begins as a gospel song. In its early numbers it should therefore be critically treated as a song, and not as a court or chamber poem.

The Middle English Franciscan poets—who are not abstrusely theological like the Adamic-Thomist Latin poets—are nevertheless entirely successful in transmitting basic dogma infused with their own spirituality into simple simile and metaphor, *exemplum* and lyric, in what is perhaps the most effective missionary use of a popular medium in the history of the Church. That they were able to do so and actually to recreate and vivify a medium of intense popularity is a tribute to early Franciscan zeal and organizing skill. In fact, the results of this study show that the influence of the Franciscans in creating the Middle English religious lyric was so pervasive and complete that it will henceforth be possible to regard the existence of the popular short-verse genre in England before 1350 as a particular phenomenon of that spirituality. The Middle English lyric is, essentially, a Franciscan song.

Heven and erthe, the see alsoo,
Laudans exultat cantico,
And euery þing that therin is
Thyne auctor of birthe, the fader of blis.

And we, whiche be on the roode tree
Tuo redempti sanguine,
For the day of thy natiuitie
A new song we do singe to the.
                                        James Ryman, O.F.M.

Notes

1. Similarly Ryman's carol LXXVII, ed. Zupitza, p. 247; also the translations of the Ten Commandments by Robert Brunne. Cf. D. W. Robertson, Jr., "The Cultural Tradition of Handling Sin," *Speculum* 22 (1947):162–85.

2. *RL XIV*, no. 55; cf. no. 34, also the *Philomena* of John Pecham and Jacopone da Todi (see n. 6 below). There is some sharing of materials between "liturgical" compilations such as *The Lay Folks' Prayer Book* and *The Prymer*, and preaching handbooks (cf. n. 7 below).

3. See the examples drawn from the *Fasciculus morum* in chapter 5 above.

4. Ed. Ageno, p. 96.

5. *Pecham*, pp. 41–42.

6. *Philomena* is edited by G. M. Drèves, *Analecta hymnica*, vol. 1; see esp. lines 602 ff.

7. Ed. F. J. Mone, *Lateinische Hymnen des Mittelalters* (Freiburg: Herder, 1853–55), 1:106. Other ME versions are MS. Cotton Vespas. A. iii (*RL XIV*, pp. 39–44), Vernon MS. (*The Minor Poems of the Vernon MS.*, ed. C. Horstmann, EETS OS 98 [London, 1892], p. 37), and *The Prymer*, ed. Henry Littlehales, EETS OS 105 (London, 1895), p. 15.

8. Ed. Zupitza; see Greene, *A Selection of English Carols*, p. 126.

9. E.g., the one edited by Brown, *RL XIV*, no. 32. Cf. Rosemary Woolf, *English Religious Lyric*, pp. 114 ff.

10. Note however stanza six, above; this body of imagery is eagerly continued and even expanded by the Franciscans.

11. It may be worth noting that the earliest concordance of this kind in the graphic arts is the doors of Santa Sabena in Rome (fifth century), which, besides having the earliest known representation of the crucifixion, are arranged as a concordance of Old Testament/New Testament iconography. The classic visual concordance, however, adorns the thirteenth-century altar of the monastic church at Klösterneuburg, where the Virgin is seen to be prefigured by many Old Testament people. In sermons, poems, and treatises, it is the Franciscans who later take up this tradition and give it most attention. St. Anthony is an excellent example; so is James Ryman.

12. *Sermo in purificatione Sanctae Mariae* 3. 722b. [The Blessed Mary was a *closed door* against north, south, and west, that is to say she *was closed*; and east signifies of course Christ Jesus, who descended from heaven to endure humble birth. And to continue: *No man will go through it*; that is Joseph did not know it; and it will be *shut* to princes, in which the devil is to be understood as the prince of this world, which is the reason it was *closed*, because that spirit tolerated no temptations, just as her flesh was innocent of contamination.]

13. *In Dominica XXII post Pentecosten* 2. 545a: "Hanc statuam contrivit lapis parvus, scilicet Iesus Christus, qui ut subdit Daniel, *abscissus est de monte*, idest natus de Beata Virgine *sine manibus*, idest opere virili."

14. *In nativitate B. Mariae Virginis* 3. 696a.

15. *In Dominica XIII post Pentecosten* 2. 400a: "Mirabile fuit, quando *ignis ardebat, et non comperebatur;* cum virga Aaron sine flora fructus protulit. Rugus et virge est Beata Maria, quae illaeso virginitatis pudore Dei filium parturivit sine dolore." See Ryman's interesting "yerde" poem, no. 20 in Zupitza's edition.

16. *In annuntiatione Sanctae Mariae* 3. 836b: "Assuerus . . . est Deus . . . cuius oculis placuit Regina nostra Esther . . . *virga aurea* caelestis gratia, quam contra eam tunc extendit, cum eam gratia prae ceteris implevit . . . ."

17. *In assumptione S. Mariae Virginis* 3. 732a: "Ista nostra gloriosa *Esther* hodie per manus Angelorum *ducta est ad cubiculum regis Assueri,* idest aethereum thalamum, in quo rex regum beatitudo Angelorum, stellato solio residet Iesus Christus, qui eamden gloriosam Virginem super *omnes mulieres amavit* . . . . Vere omni gratia praestantior fuit Beatae Mariae gratia, quae Filium cum Deo Patre habuit, et ideo hodierna die in caelis coronari meruit. Unde subditur: *Et posuit diadema regni in capite eius.*"

18. Ibid.: "Quia Beata Maria, Dei *Filium coronavit diademate* carnis in die *desponsatione suae,* idest Conceptionis, qua unita est Divina natura, tamquam sponsus, humanae naturae, tamquam sponsae, in thalamo eiusdem Virginis, ideo idem Filius suam Matrem *coronavit* hodierna die *diademate* gloriae caelestis."

19. *De nativitate B. Virginis Mariae,* Sermo II (Quaracchi 9), pp. 708–9.

20. See Bernardino Mazzarella, "St. Bernadine of Siena, a Model Preacher," *Franciscan Studies* 25 (1944):323–24. It may be objected that the same imagery can be found in Rabanus Maurus (see *PL* 112: 1001, 1031, 1041, 1080–81): This is true; in fact Rabanus and Isidore of Seville were the favorite commentators of the early Franciscans after Augustine. The Franciscan here, as in other areas, simply made more of this particular kind of imagery than anyone else after the thirteenth century.

21. *Meditations,* p. 21.

22. In fact, most of the Middle English lyrics which use allegory as a technique come after 1350—Ryman is a case in point—when the lyric in Middle English, by virtue in the change of prestige of that tongue, could begin to direct itself more to educated and cultured audiences. Allegorical techniques of a complex nature would be of little avail in a song, and of no use at all if the song was to be directed to an essentially illiterate audience. See chap. 3 above.

23. Fol. 129r; *RL XIV,* p. 258. Woolf (*English Religious Lyric,* p. 336, n. 3) notes that in graphic art from the fourteenth century on the Fourth Rider of the Apocalypse often appears as a skeleton astride a horse, though such a picture is not clear here.

24. Zupitza, p. 209. See also the poems edited in Zupitza, pp. 173, 175, 176, 207, 208.

25. Ibid., pp. 203, 274.

26. Ed. Morris, *Miscellany,* p. 100. Later poems, in the fourteenth and

fifteenth centuries, show the influence of the innovation in graphic representation of the annunciation scene inaugurated by Simoni Martini in Italy which has the Virgin first recoil in chaste fear at the words of Gabriel, and then subsequently assume the traditional attitude of the obedient "handmaiden of the Lord." This sequence may be observed in the illustration to the relevant passage of the fourteenth-century MS of the *Meditations*, pp. 17–18, and enters into Middle English poetry in several of the annunciation lyrics by Ryman, e.g., those edited by Zupitza, pp. 168, 277, 288–89, 294–95. Cf. Brown, *EL XIII*, p. 75. But cf. the juxtaposition of matins responses and verses for the Feast of the Annunciation—see the *Sarum Breviary* 3. 237; *York Breviary* 2. 237.

27. Ed. Brook, pp. 42–43. This poem is also edited in *EL XIII*, no. 80.

28. "Popule meus quid feci tibi?" in *RL XIV*, no. 15. One other poem of Herebert's translates not a Latin hymn or a passage of Scripture, but an Anglo-Norman poem by fellow Franciscan Nicholas Bozon. It is edited from Phillipps MS. 8336 by Brown in *RL XIV*, pp. 251–53.

29. One of G. G. Coulton's most strenuous objections to Franciscan treatment of Scripture involved, as it may be remembered (see above pp. 47–48), spurious conversations attributed to the Virgin Mary. Commenting on Coulton's remarks I suggested, with illustrations from the *Meditations on the Life of Christ*, that in just such contrivances is frequently revealed the essential strength of Franciscan transmission of biblical knowledge into the vernacular.

30. *RL XIV*, no. 56. This poem should be read in full, though it is too long to reprint here.

31. *EL XIII*, no. 64. The word *sike* carries the same associations when it recurs in "Wynter" (from MS. Harley 2253), the last poem quoted in this chapter.

32. E.g., *EL XIII*, nos. 84, 88—any number of Cross Poems; cf. examples in chap. 5, above, and in MS. Harley 913, ed. Heuser, "Die Kildare Gedichte," p. 128. Ryman writes:

> Thou shalt not, lorde, despise, but know
> A contrite hert and meked lowe:
> Lorde, fro thy face thou me not throw,
> *Fili Marie virginis.*
>
> (Zupitza, p. 216)

33. Ryman, no. 53, in Zupitza, p. 218; this is the burden of a carol. See also the lyric in *RL XIV*, no. 87, where confession is linked to the five senses. It is a version of the contritional-confessional poem from the *Speculum Christiani* quoted in the concluding lines of the last chapter, and is a classic of its kind.

34. *RL XIV*, no. 71. Cf. Jacopone, *Lauda* LXXXIII.

35. MS. Digby 86, fol. 200—also ed. in *EL XIII*, no. 53. Cf. the Italian poem on pp. 152–53 above.

36. Note Ryman's two poems (among his best) edited in Zupitza, pp. 219–20 and pp. 253–54. The first begins:

O man, whiche art the erthe take froo,
Ayene into erthe thou shalt goo.
The wyse man in his lore seith soo:
"*Amittes mundi* prospera."

Bysshop or emperoure though that thou be,
Kinge, prince or duke of high degree,
Emperesse or quene or lady free,
Amittes mundi prospera.

The similiarity of this poem to the "death poem" from MS. Cortona 91 (pp. 136–38 above) is remarkable, both in form and in content.

37. MSS. Trinity Coll. Camb. 181, ed. *RL XIV*, no. 134; Camb. Univ. Lib. MS. 4. 41, fol. 137 rv—ed. Henry A. Person, *Cambridge Middle English Lyrics* (Seattle: Univ. of Washington Press, 1953), pp. 16–19.

38. Heuser, "Die Kildare Gedichte," p. 133—Kildare MS.

39. E.g., "XV Signs of Judgement" et al.; see also *RL XIV*, nos. 5, 6, 9, 10, 23, 53, 106, 116; Brook, no. 23, etc.

40. *EL XIII*, no. 7. The date given to this song, 1225, is one year after the arrival of the Friars Minor in England.

41. MS. Jesus Coll. Oxford 29; also ed. in *EL XIII*, no. 11.

42. See Heuser, "Die Kildare Gedichte," pp. 128 ff.

43. *RL XIV*, no. 5; cf. Manning, *Wisdom and Number*, pp. 36 ff.

44. See p. 53 above.

45. See p. 57 above.

46. See the article by John V. Fleming, " 'The Dream of the Rood' and Anglo-Saxon Monasticism," *Traditio* 22 (1966):43–72. Rosemary Woolf, "The Theme of Christ the Lover-Knight in Medieval English Literature," *Review of English Studies*, n.s. 13 (1962):1–16, discusses *exempla* organized on this theme, a genre which she notes develops from the end of the twelfth century, and of which the three chief English examples she adduces come from the *Fasciculus morum*, MS. Harley 7322, and the *Gesta Romanorum*. The version in the *Fasciculus* contains the four-line poem reference cited on p. 191 above. See here also Jean Leclercq, "Le Sermon sur la royauté du Christ au Moyen Âge," *Archives d'histoire doctrinale et littéraire du Moyen Âge* 18 (1943–45):143–80, who traces the late twelfth and thirteenth-century development of the Christ-as-the-Knight-King-sermon, *Ecce rex*, which however is in this case more a reflection of feudal language and custom than of the *miles* theme.

47. E.g., the last line of a poem by Grimestone, *RL XIV*, no. 66, and the *Fasciculus* poem cited on p. 199 above.

48. Little, *English Medieval Art*, pp. 40–41 and chap. 4, pl. 6.

49. Brown, "Sermons and Miracle Plays," *MLN* 49 (1934):394–96. One sermon, containing much verse, is at fols. 131v–132r, and is signed by Franciscan friar Laurence Briton, who was lector at Oxford about 1340.

50. Ibid., p. 394. [First: . . . follow in the same vein in this sermon of the round table, and then pursuing the cause, to our first parents whom

God forbade to eat of the tree of Paradise and promised in return hard death. . . . At once the devil said . . . .]

51. See n. 49 above. From this clearly marked Franciscan sermon comes Brown's apocalyptic *RL XIV*, no. 36 and 37.

52. *RL XIV*, no. 125, lines 1–42, from MS. Bod. 416.

53. Greene, *Selections*, p. 128, from MS. Balliol Coll. Oxford 354. There is also a fine Anglo-Norman poem by Franciscan friar Nicole de Bozon, from MS. Phillipps 8336, fol. 90v, "Comment le fiz Deu fu armé la croyz," which begins:

> "Seignours, ore escotez haute chivalerye,
> De un noble chivaler qe pur l'amour s'amye
> Tant se myst avaunt qe il dona sa vye
> Pur reyndre sa epouse, g'ele fu forbanye."

54. MS. Harley 2253; ed. Brook, no. 17; *RL XIV*, no. 9. For a corroboration of the reading which follows compare *RL XIV*, no. 10, "An Autumn Song" from the same MS, and also "An Old Man's Prayer," ed. from Harley 2253 by Brook, no. 13.

55. I should acknowledge that I have begun and ended with these two poems partly because they are among the relatively few English lyrics written before 1350 which do *not* come from MSS of almost certain Franciscan provenance. MS. Harley 2253 contains, to be sure, numerous poems which are shared by manuscripts of proven Franciscan provenance, but its certain authorship cannot be positively established. And "Mirie it is" is an incidental fly-leaf poem in a Latin devotional book; its author we almost certainly will never know. Yet, as we have seen, the two poems share—indeed they are fine examples of—the distinctive spirituality and style which infuse the majority of popular English lyrics written from 1225 to 1350. They are perhaps as convincing an illustration as any that the spirituality of St. Francis and the aesthetic of Bonaventure were a pervasive influence during the birth and early development of the English lyric.

56. Aside from the age-old associations with winter, some of the Franciscans favorite Scriptural commentators elaborate particular spiritual associations for the symbols involved. Gregory the Great interprets winter as the present life, and the austerity of the Old Law (*PL* 79: 498); it signifies also *infidelitas*, says Honorarius of Autun, for just as winter fetters men's hearts with ice so infidelity fetters men's hearts with the coldness of sin so that they do not bear the fruit of faith. It is the coming of Christ alone which can banish this winter (*PL* 91: 391–92). On winter and its coldness as images of the Last Judgment and the end of the world see *Allegoriae in sacram scripturam* (*PL* 92: 937, 954), and Rabanus Maurus, *De universo* (*PL* 111, 303). Pierre Bersuire says that the season (December) of the poem is the season of penitence (*Opera omnia* [Cologne, 1730–31], 2:129), and those familiar with the portent of the liturgical year will immediately recall the breviary and sources like St. Bernard's *Sermons on Advent* at this point. Another preaching MS. Halliwell 219 (ed. T. Wright, *Reliquae antiquae*, 1:38–40) refers to

"wynter", as "the olde wone of worldly coveitise that made me cold and hard y-froze as yse."

57. See the poems ed. Greene, *Selections*, pp. 92–95. For a discussion of spring and garden imagery relevant to this concept see D. W. Robertson, Jr., "The Doctrine of Charity in Medieval Literary Gardens," *Speculum* 26 (1951):24–49.

58. Brown, *RL XIV*, p. 245.

59. See also the commentaries of Nicholas of Lyra (Basil, 1502) and the *Glossa ordinaria (PL 64)* on this passage. Robert Grosseteste, in his *Commentarium in Psalmum*, Eton MS. 8, fol. 40b–c, has a *dicta* (p. 97) which so compares the growth and functions of a grain and man: "Frumentum granum tritici hanc habet proprietatem ab omnibus . . . ."

60. Lathbury wrote Latin verses on the Virgin Mary, and his commentary on Lamentations is sprinkled with verse; he even gives a short lecture on versification in connection with a discussion of the meter of Lamentations (see the discussion by Smalley, *English Friars*, pp. 228 ff., 342–43. In his long commentary on Lam. 1:1, "How doth the city sit solitary," he compares the mourning city to the *Mater dolorosa* of the crucifixion scene, with exhaustive comparisons which cause Smalley to call him a "mincing machine." Some of the comparisons are then worked into his verse. Actually Lathbury may have had a specific source for this "mincing," treatment in the Sermons of St. Anthony, *Dominica II in Quadragesima* 1. 91a.

61. Wimbourne was lector to the Cambridge Franciscans, 1233–66. he who wrote poems chiefly in honor of the Virgin, showing the typically Franciscan tender intimacy with the Holy Family—Mary plays with her baby in one poem as Wimbourne watches (MS. Laud Misc. 368, fols. 204r, 207v; other poems published by Drèves, *Analecta hymnica*, vol. 1, nos. 630, 631, 632, 635, 637, 643). According to Smalley (*English Friars*, p. 50) there is an unpublished poem of Wimbourne's which refers to a tavern, MS. Laud Misc. 368, fols. 204r, 205b, 212r, 215v. Wimbourne was also a theologian, but his works are largely lost.

62. See the mention by Greene, *Selections*, pp. 41–42. The same process may be observed in MS. Egerton 274, where (fols. 98–118, 131r) occur songs with music, in Anglo-Norman, of late twelfth- and early thirteenth-century origin. In several cases the original words of the first verses have been erased and sacred Latin words substituted in their place—e.g., at fol. 98 is a carol emended to begin "Kyrie eleison . . . ," which has a second verse, "De tout son cuer . . . ." Even some of the notes have been altered. I do not know if the "revisor" of MS. Egerton 274 was, like Ledrede, a Franciscan, however.

63. E.g., the Anglo-Norman Harley 2253 lyrics, Digby 86 lyrics, and the many striking poems of Nicole de Bozon from MS. Phillips 8336. See my forthcoming edition, with Brian Levy, *The Anglo-Norman Lyrics*.

64. Bersuire spent his formative years as a Franciscan. See the article "Pierre Bersuire," by Charles Samaran, in *Histoire littéraire de la France* 39 (1962):258–450, esp. pp. 263 ff.

65. *EEC*, pp. cvii–cviii.

Appendix A

The *Lamentatio*
Beate Virginis de Cruce
of Ubertino da Casale

I N THE *Arbor vitae crucifixis Iesu* of Ubertino da Casale (Venice, 1485) occurs a version of Ubertino's poem on the lamentation of the Virgin at the foot of the cross. Since the Venice edition is not readily available, and since Ubertino's poem is a classic of Franciscan spirituality, I append it in full here. It occurs at Book 4, chap. 25, "Jesus mattrem afficiens."

Lamentatio beate virginis de cruce

Crux dura quid fecisti [?]
Multum certe praesumpsisti
Christum deum suscepisti
Qui creavit omnia.

Crux redde mihi filium
Iamnon expecto alium
totam meum solatium
Sicut scripture praedicant.

Crux aperte respice
Vide terram tremere
Solem lumen claudere
Haec Christum deum nunciant.

Responsio beate virginis da crucem:

269

Tibi virgo respondeo
quod pro mundo ihsum teneo
Hunc tibi non restituo
Ut munduma morte redimat.

Et est certe lex naturae
Iugum grave geniturae
Omnes vivunt isto iure
Ut mors omnes recipiat.

Mors est quies viatoris
Finis omnis est laboris
Per mortem corpus redemptoris
Oportet quod transeat.

Deus mortum ordinavit
Mundum morti ibiugavit subjugavit?
Propter hoc ipse gustavit
Quod et aliis ordinavit.

Nihil convenientius
Quam Christum dei filius
Patri succurrit penitus
Secum ad coelum prouehat

Virgo tu eue filia
Matrem damnatam libera
Solue serpentis vincula
Mundus te laude serviat.

Et haec mundus te laudabit
Paradisus exultabit
Adam Christum liberavit
Resurrexit die tertia.

Responsio beate virginis da crucem:

Crux tua verba audio
Non trium dolore careo
Iesum pendare video
Inter latrones viliter.

Responsio crucis ad beatam virginem:

In me deus se humiliavit
propter me coelum laetificavit
Et infernium spoliavit
Christum agens humiliter.

Cum scala coeli ordinata
Sum Christum morte consecrata
A deo que praedestinata
Vexillum sum victorie.

Debes ergo tu guadere
Non debes mundo iudere
Si per mortem subvenire
Voluit eis rex gloriae.

Mundus debet hanc amare
Et devote salutare
Se mihi totum inclinare
Pro christi amicicia.

Responsio pacificate virginis cum cruce:

Pacem simul habeamus
Amplius non contendamus
Deo cuncta comittamus
Cui sit lauset gloria.

Mortem iam non timeamus
Cruce omnes diligiamus
Devote deo serviamus
Cum omni reverentia.   Amen.

Appendix B

Music from a
Franciscan Sermon Manuscript

From MS. Lat. Th. D. i, Bodleian Library, fly-leaf (fol. 91) of the Melton-Philipp sermons: a music lesson and exercise tune, possibly for a lyric. The first series A B K Q identifies value for the notes—roughly eighth, quarter, half, and full in that order. The limerick lists Franciscan houses.

Appendix C

The Franciscans after 1350

I<small>N</small> 1348 the Black Death swept England. The date becomes a turning point for English Franciscan history;[1] Franciscan dominance in the Middle English lyric ends at the same time. Robbins notes that following 1350 only about twenty-five per cent of English lyrics can be attributed definitely to the Franciscans.[2] I think that perhaps the number might be enlarged with poems from manuscripts of the *Fasciculus morum* and *Speculum Christiani*, but the resulting figure would not be appreciably larger. The rather sudden decline indicated by Robbins' calculation may owe partially to the plague: J. R. H. Moorman writes that it "hit the friars very hard. Living in the towns, often in unhealthy districts—and the fact that the London Franciscans lived in 'Stynkynglane' is suggestive—the friars suffered perhaps more than the members of other religious orders, most of whom lived in the country."[3] It has been calculated that in the years before the plague there were in England about 2,000 Franciscans, but that after 1350 only 1,150 remained.[4]

The final triumph of the Conventuals in England may or may not have been a factor in the decline of new Franciscan poetry. It is certain that the Spirituals, who in the days of Eccleston, Albert of Pisa, and Adam Marsh had typified the order to John of Parma, were finally crushed. In 1330 the Chronicle of Meaux states as a matter of fact that twenty-five men and eight women of the Spiritual Franciscans were "burned in England, in a certain forest."[5] One effect of the movement away from the Spiritual emphasis on poverty was of immediate significance: the Franciscan parish changed from the poor to the rich and courtly.[6] Moral decline and corruption in the Order multiplied extraordinarily after the Black Death, by which time the

273

original Observant spirit of the English province seems to have flickered out.[7]

About the same time the English language had ceased to be the language of only the common people, and was moving into accepted literary and governmental use. This increased prestige might lead one to expect perhaps that Franciscans would begin to write in English to the tastes of their now courtly audience, but that does not appear to have happened generally. Rather, the poems that continued to be written were either in the popular diction and style, or like many of the songs of Grimestone and Ryman, more suitable for devotion, books of hours, or liturgical settings in the private chapel. The homiletic activities of the truly mendicant Franciscans still continued, and preachers like Nicholas Philipp and William Melton tugged Friar Miscellanies or copies of the *Fasciculus* about the country with them as they preached, but most of these apparently contained for the most part the same old thirteenth-century poems. For a time in the latter part of the fourteenth century the earlier popularity seems to have revived; during that period Franciscans figure strongly in wills and bequests from all classes.[8] But the revival did not last. The heyday of Franciscan influence in medieval England was over before the Peasants' Revolt of 1381.

In evaluating Robbins' twenty-five per cent, however, we should also consider that the total number of lyrics written between 1350 and 1500 was perhaps ten times greater than that written between 1225 and 1350—or at least that much more of the writing of the later period remains. Those who heretofore might have composed in Latin or Anglo-French now might turn naturally to English. If the number of Franciscans was only half of what it had been before the Black Death, it is perhaps remarkable that they contributed as much as they did in the later period.

One final factor to be considered may be the lack of confraternities. We saw that in Italy the major portion of Franciscan literary output flowed from the confraternities they fostered and guided. In England, there is not a comparable chapter in Franciscan history. In France confraternities like that of the Puy served to continue the early poetic traditions, and to conserve some of the spirituality of southern Europe in the thirteenth century.[9] The Puy, noted like many of the Italian Franciscan confraternities for their poetic functions, founded a chapter in London with its own chapel in 1237, but the organization did not last.[10]

Yet there is substantial evidence that the Franciscans in England did have considerable influence over lay groups that were less clearly defined than the confraternities. It has been observed that "no religious order was so closely connected with the medieval guilds as were the Franciscans."[11] In England the evidence for such a connection is still largely conjectural: a listing of Franciscan provinces and foundations of 1385 assigns four Tertiary congregations to England and three to Scotland, but there is no significant information left about any of them.[12] Green discovered that the English Franciscans enrolled many Tertiaries, but seldom organized them into fraternities, even though many prominent citizens were buried with the cord.[13] And, in addition to the lack of letters of confraternity, the English copy we have of the Third Order Rule is somewhat late.[14]

It would seem that the Third Order organizations in England and Ireland warrant further study, even though little extant evidence of the nature of their activity has so far come to light.[15] Certainly, one of the most striking characteristics of Eccleston's chronicle of the first years is the prominence given to lay brothers of the order. Many of these apparently later joined the order. Some were tradesmen, others knights.[16] Eccleston seems to set a high value on the spirituality even of those who remained as lay brothers.[17] And it is true that continental organizations of a more extreme Franciscan spirituality comparable to the Italian confraternities were received and encouraged by the Franciscans if they came to England.[18] What the significance of English Franciscan confraternal activity might be remains unclear. But it is not impossible that the lay brothers may have served as a significant point of contact between the English Franciscans and medieval English fraternal organizations. The relationship between confraternities and guilds will be studied carefully in the forthcoming companion volume to this book, *Early English Drama and Franciscan Spirituality.*

Notes

1. Thus V. G. Green's title, *The Franciscans in Medieval English Life (1224–1348)*.
2. "The Authors of the Middle English Lyrics," pp. 230–38.
3. *The Grey Friars in Cambridge*, p. 79.
4. J. C. Russel, "Clerical Population of Medieval England," *Traditio* 2 (1944):209. Yet at Oxford during this time numbers seem actually to have increased; see Little, *Studies*, p. 72.
5. Quoted in G. G. Coulton, "The Failure of the Friars," *Hibbert Journal* 5 (1907):296–308.
6. Green, *Franciscans*, chap. 4, gives extensive documentation.
7. Patrick Cowley, *Franciscan Rise and Fall*, pp. 196 ff. Heribert Holzapfel, *Handbuch der Geschichte des Franziskanerordens* (Freiburg in Breisgau: Herder, 1909), p. 82, agrees with Luke Wadding (*Annales minorum* 8. 22) in attributing great importance to the Black Death as a destroyer of religious fervor and observance of the Rule.
8. See C. L. Kingsford, *The Grey Friars of London*, BSFS 6 (Aberdeen: Univ. of Aberdeen Press, 1915), p. 18; A. G. Little, *Grey Friars in Oxford*, pp. 100 ff., 239; *Wills and Inventories* (London: Surtees Society, 1835), 2:6, 32, etc.
9. See É. P. Du Méril, ed., "La Confrèrie des clercs Parisiens" pp. 1–93; also H. J. Chaytor, *The Troubadours and England*, pp. 30 ff.
10. Chaytor, *The Troubadours*, pp. 29–30, 98. The records of the London Puy are in the archives of the London Guild Hall, *Munimenta Gildhallae Londensis* (Rolls Series), vol. 2, pt. 1, pp. 216 ff.
11. Holzapfel, *Handbuch*, p. 236.
12. Green, *Franciscans*, p. 37.
13. Ibid., pp. 37–38.
14. *Two Fifteenth-Century Franciscan Rules*, ed. W. W. Seton, EETS OS 148 (London: Kegan Paul, Trench, and Trübner, 1914), pp. 25–32.
15. D. W. Whitfield, "The Third Order of St. Francis in Medieval England," *Franciscan Studies* 13 (1953):50–59.
16. Little, ed., *De adventu fratrum minorum*, pp. 14, 18–19, 71, 89.
17. E.g., "Iste Ricardus veniens in Angliam narravit in capitulo Oxoniae, quod, cum unus frater Parisius extasi staret, visum erat ei quod frater Aegidius laicus sed contemplativus sedit in cathedra legens authenticas septem petitiones Dominicae Orationis, cuius omnes auditores erant tantum fratres in ordine lectores. Intrans autem sanctus Franciscus primo siluit et postea sic clamavit: 'O quam verecundum est vobis quod talis frater laicus excedit vestra merita sursum in coelo' " (ibid., pp. 51–52).
18. E.g., the Sack Friars; ibid., pp. 129–31 and notes.

Selected Bibliography

THEOLOGY AND SPIRITUALITY

Texts

Alexander of Hales. *Magistri Alexandri de Hales, Glossa in quatuor libros sententiarum Petri Lombardi.* Bibliotheca Franciscana Scholastical Medii Aevi, 15. Vol. 4. Quaracchi, Florence: Coll. S. Bonaventurae, 1957.

Anthony of Padua, Saint. *S. Pat. Thaumaturgi Ineliti Sermones Dominicales et in Solemnitatibus.* Ed. Locatelli. Patavii: Societas Universalis Sancti Antonnii Patavini Edit., 1895.

———. *Leggende Antoniane.* Ed. Roberto Cessi. Milan: Società editrice "vitea pensiero," 1936.

Aquinas, Thomas, Saint. *Nature and Grace, Selections from the Summa Theologica of St. Thomas Aquinas.* Ed. and trans. A. M. Fairweather, London: S. C. M. Press, 1954.

Bacon, Roger. *The Opus Majus of Roger Bacon.* Ed. J. H. Bridges. 3 vols. Oxford: Clarendon Press, 1897–1900.

Bernardino da Siena, Saint. *Sancti Bernardini Senensis Opera omnia.* Ed. Giovanni de la Haye. 5 vols. Venice, 1745.

———. *Le Prediche volgari di San Bernardino da Siena.* Ed. Ciro Cannarozzi. 2 vols. Pistoia, 1934.

Bersuire, Pierre. *Opera omnia.* 6 vols. Cologne: J. W. Huisch, 1730–31.

Berthold von Regensburg. *Berthold von Regensburg: Vollständige Ausgabe seiner Predigten.* Ed. Franz Pfeiffer. 2 vols. Vienna, 1862–80; rpt. Berlin: De Gruyter, 1965.

Bonaventure, Saint, Cardinal. *De reductione artium ad theologiam.* Ed. and trans. Emma Thérèse Healy. 2nd ed. St. Bonaventure, N.Y.: Franciscan Institute, 1955.

———. *Opera omnia.* Ed. F. Fanna and I. Jelier. 10 vols. Quaracchi, Florence: Coll. S. Bonaventurae, 1883–1902.

Brewer, J. S., and Richard Howlett, eds. *Monumenta Franciscana.* 2 vols. Rolls Series 4. London: Longmans, Green, 1858.

Caulibus, Joannes. *Meditations on the Life of Christ: An Illustrated Manuscript of the Fourteenth Century.* Ed. and trans. Isa Ragusa and Rosalie B. Green. Princeton: Princeton University Press, 1961.

277

Francis of Assisi, Saint. *The Little Flowers of St. Francis.* Trans. Damian J. Blaher. New York: Dutton, 1951.

———. *Speculum perfectionis.* Ed. Paul Sabatier. Paris: Fischbacher, 1898.

Furnivall, Frederick J., ed. *The Life of St. Alexius* .... EETS OS 69. London: Trübner, 1878.

Grosseteste, Robert. *Roberti Grosseteste Episcopi quondam Lincolniensis Epistoliae.* Ed. Henry R. Luard. Rolls Series 25. London: Longman, Green, Longman, and Roberts, 1861.

Holmstedt, Gustaf, ed. *Speculum Christiani.* EETS OS 182. London: Oxford University Press, 1933.

Hugh of St. Victor. *Didascalicon.* Trans. Jerome Taylor. New York: Columbia University Press, 1961.

Joachim de Fiore. *L'Évangile éternel.* Trans. Emmanuel Aegerter. 2 vols. Des Textes du Christianisme 3–4. Paris: Rieder, 1928.

Legenda trium sociorum. Analecta Bollandiana 19, fasc. 2. Brussels: Societé des Bollandistes, 1900, pp. 119–97.

Little, A. G., ed. *Liber exemplorum ad usam praedicantum.* BSFS 1. Aberdeen: University of Aberdeen Press, 1908.

Love, Nicholas. *The Mirrour of the Blessed Lyf of Jesu Christ.* Ed. Lawrence F. Powell. London, 1908.

Meditations on the Supper of Our Lord, and the hours of the passion .... *Drawn into English verse by Robert Manning of Brunne.* Ed. J. Meadows Cowper. EETS OS 60. London: Trübner, 1875.

Nicholas of Lyra. *Postilla super quattor Evangelistas.* Mantua, 1477.

Ross, Woodburn O., ed. *Middle English Sermons.* EETS OS 209. London: Oxford University Press, 1940.

Simmons, T. F., and H. E. Nolloth, eds. *The Lay Folk's Catechism.* EETS OS 118. London: Kegan Paul, Trench, and Trübner, 1901.

Weatherly, Edward H., ed. *Speculum sacerdotale.* EETS OS 200. London: Oxford University Press, 1936.

Welter, J. Théodore, ed. *Le Speculum laicorum.* Paris: A. Picard, 1914.

Wyclif, John. *Opus minorum.* Wyclif Society. London: Trübner, 1884.

———. *John Wiclif's Polemical Works in Latin.* Ed. Rudolf Buddensieg. English ed. 2 vols. Wyclif Society. London: Trübner, 1883.

Scholarship

Alençon, P. Ubald d'. "La Spiritualité franciscaine." *Études franciscaines* 39 (1927): 276–95, 338–57, 449–71; 40 (1928): 81–89.

Ampe, A. "Exemplarisme." In *Dictionnaire de spiritualité* (Paris, 1961), IV, 2, 1870–78.

Arenzano, Rodolfo d'. "La Bibbia della tradizione monastica alla spiritualità Francescana." In *Bibbia e spirtualità* (Rome: Ediz. Paoloni, 1967), pp.245–330.

Baur, Ludwig. *Die philosophischen Werke des Robert Grossetestes.* Münster in Westphalen: Aschendorff, 1912.

Benz, Ernst. *Ecclesia Spiritualis: Kirchenidee und Geschichtstheologie der Franziskanischen Reformation.* Stuttgart: W. Kohlhammer, 1934.

Bondatti, P. Guido. *Gioachinismo e Francescanesimo nel dugento.* S. Maria degli Angeli: Porziuncula, 1924.

Bonnefoy, Jean. "La Question hypothétique: Utrum si Adam non pecasset . . .au xiiiᵉ siècle." *Revista española de teologia* 14 (1954): 327–68.

Chenu, M. D. "La Première Diffusion du Thomisme à Oxford." *Archives d'histoire doctrinale et littéraire du Moyen Âge* 3 (1928):185–200.

Dales, Richard C., and Servus Gieben. "The Prooemium to Robert Grosseteste's *Hexaemeron.*" *Speculum* 43 (1968):451–61.

Da Milano, Ilario. "Ispirazione e autorità in S. Francesco d'Assisi." *Italia Francescana* 42 (1967):74–84.

Daniel, E. Randolph. "A Re-Examination of the Origins of Franciscan Joachitism." *Speculum* 43 (1968):671–76.

Deanesley, M. "The Gospel Harmony of John of Caulibus or St. Bonaventure." In *Collectanea Franciscana,* vol. 2, ed. C. L. Kingsford et al. BSFS 10; Manchester: University of Manchester Press, 1922.

Felder, Hilarin. *Geschichte der wissenschaftlichen Studien im Franziskanerorden.* Freiburg in Breisgau: Herder, 1904.

Fournier, Paul E. L. *Études sur Joachim de Flore et ses doctrines.* Paris: A. Picard, 1909.

Gemelli, Agostini. *The Franciscan Message to the World.* Trans. H. L. Hughes. London: Burns, Oates, and Washbourne, 1934.

Gieben, Servus. "Traces of God in Nature according to Robert Grosseteste." *Franciscan Studies* 24 (1964): 144–58.

Gilson, J. P. "Friar Alexander and His Historical Interpretation of the Apocalypse." In *Collectanea Franciscana,* vol. 2, ed. C. L. Kingsford et al. BSFS 10: Manchester: University of Manchester Press, 1922.

Gorce, M. M. *L'Essor de la pensée au Moyen Âge: Albert le Grand–Thomas d'Aquin.* Paris: Letouzey et Ané, 1933.

Grundmann, Herbert. *Religiöse Bewegungen im Mittelalter.* Berlin: Verlag der Emil Ebering, 1935.

Gumbinger, Cuthbert. "St. Bernadine's Unedited *Prediche Volgari.*" *Franciscan Studies* 25 (1944): 7–33.

Hayes, Zachary. *The General Doctrine of Creation in the Thirteenth Century, with Special Emphasis on Matthew of Aquasparta.* Munich: Ferdinand Schoningh, 1964.

Huber, Raphael M. *The Portiuncula Indulgence. Franciscan Studies* 19. New York: Wagner, 1938.

Leclercq, Jean. "Le Sermon sur la royauté du Crist au Moyen Âge." *Archives d'histoire doctrinale et littéraire du Moyen Âge* 18 (1943–45):143–80.

———. *The Love of Learning and the Desire for God: A Study of Monastic Culture.* Trans. Catherine Misrahi. New York: Fordham University Press, 1961.

———. "L'Écriture sainte dans l'hagiographie monastique du haut Moyen

Âge." In *La Bibbia nell' alto medioeve, settimone di studio del centro italiano di studi sull' alto meioev o* 10 (Spolento, 1963).

Leclercq, Jean, F. Vandenbroucke, and L. Bouyer. *The Spirituality of the Middle Ages.* Vol. 2 of *A History of Christian Spirituality,* 3 vols. Newly trans. and ed. London: Burns and Oates, 1968–69.

Lubac, Henri de. *Exégèse médiévale: Les quatre sens de l'Écriture.* 4 vols. Paris: Aubier, 1959.

Lynch, K. F. "The Doctrine of Alexander of Hales on the Nature of Sacramental Grace." *Franciscan Studies* 19 (1959):334–83.

———. "The Sacramental Grace of Confirmation in Thirteenth-century Theology." *Franciscan Studies* 22 (1962):32–149; 172–300.

McAodha, Loman. "The Nature and Efficacy of Preaching According to St. Bernardine of Siena." *Franciscan Studies* 27 (1967):221–47.

Mazzarella, Bernardino. "St. Bernadine of Siena, a Model Preacher." *Franciscan Studies* 25 (1944):309–28.

O'Donnell, Clement M. *The Psychology of St. Bonaventure and St. Thomas Aquinas.* Washington: The Catholic University of America Press, 1937.

Oisy, P. Eugène d'. "François et la Bible." *Études franciscaines* 39 (1927): 498–592, 646–56; 40 (1928):69–80.

Owst, G. R. *Literature and Pulpit in Medieval England.* 2nd ed. 1961; rpt. Oxford: Blackwell, 1966.

———. *Preaching in Medieval England.* Cambridge: Cambridge University Press, 1926.

Petry, Ray C. "Medieval Eschatology and St. Francis of Assisi." *Church History* 9 (1940):54–69.

———. "Medieval Eschatology and Social Responsibility in Bernard of Morval's *De Contemptu Mundi.*" *Speculum* 24 (1949):207–17.

Pfander, H. G. *The Popular Sermon of the Medieval Friar in England.* New York: New York University Press, 1937.

Pourrat, Pierre. *La Spiritualité chrétienne.* 4 vols. Paris: J. Gabalda et fils, 1927–31.

Reeves, Marjorie. *The Influence of of Prophecy in the Later Middle Ages: A Study of Joachimism.* Oxford: Oxford University Press, 1969.

Reilly, J. P., Jr. "Thomas of York: A Sermon on the Passion." *Franciscan Studies* 24 (1964):205–22.

Rohr, Louis F. *The Use of Sacred Scripture in the Sermons of St. Anthony of Padua.* Washington: Catholic University of America Press, 1948.

Rubel, Helen F. "Chabham's *Penitential* and Its Influence in the Thirteenth Century." *PMLA* 40 (1925):225–39.

Sabatier, Paul. *Études inédites sur Saint François d'Assise.* Ed. Arnold Goffin. Paris: Fischbacher, 1932.

Schmucki, Ottaviano. "Saggio sulla spiritualità di San Francesco." *Italia Francescana* 43 (1967):101–14, 336–50.

Smalley, Beryl. *The Study of the Bible in the Middle Ages.* South Bend, Ind.: University of Notre Dame Press, 1954.

Strack, Bonifatius. "Das Leiden Christi im Denken des hl. Bonaventura." *Franziskanische Studien* 41 (1959):129–62.

Tavard, G. H. *Transiency and Permanence: The Nature of Theology According to St. Bonaventure.* St. Bonaventure, New York: Franciscan Institute, 1954.

Unger, D. J. "Robert Grosseteste . . . on the Reasons for the Incarnation." *Franciscan Studies* 16 (1956): 1–37.

Wakefield, Walter L. "Notes on Some Antiheretical Writings of the Thirteenth Century." *Franciscan Studies* 27 (1967):285–321.

Witzel, P. T. "De Fr. Rogero Bacon eiusque sententia de rebus biblicus." *Archivum Franciscanum Historicum* 3 (1910): 1–22, 185–213.

Aesthetics

Borenius, Tancred. "Some Franciscan Subjects in Italian Art." In *St. Francis of Assisi: 1226–1926: Essays in Commemoration,* ed. Walter Warren Seton (London: University of London Press, 1926), pp. 3–12.

Boving, P. Regimus. *Bonaventure und die französische Hochgotik.* Werl in Westphalen: Franziskus-Druckerei, 1930.

Chenu, M. D. "Nature and Man: The Renaissance of the Twelfth Cenutry." In *Nature, Man, and Society in the Twelfth Century,* ed. and trans. Jerome Taylor and Lester K. Little (Chicago: University of Chicago Press, 1968), pp. 1–48.

Gutman, Harry B. "The Rebirth of the Fine Arts and Franciscan Thought." *Franciscan Studies* 25 (1945):215–34; 26 (1946):3–29.

Lutz, E. "Die Ästhetik Bonaventuras nach den Quellen dargestellt." In Festgabe Baeumker, *Beiträge zur Geschichte der Philosophie des Mittelalters,* supplement, vol. 1 (Münster in Westphalen: Aschendorff, 1913).

Mâle, Émile. *L'Art religieux du xiiie siècle en France.* Paris: A. Colin, 1931.

Marle, Raimond van. *The Development of the Italian Schools of Painting.* 19 vols. The Hague: Nijhoff, 1923–38.

Meiss, Millard. *Giotto and Assisi.* New York: New York University Press, 1960.

Plassmann, Thomas: "The Pointed Arch in Franciscan Theology," *Franciscan Studies* 25 (1945):97–114.

Pouillon, Henri. "La Beauté, propriété transcendentale chez les scholastiques (1120–1270)." *Archives d'histoire littéraire et doctrinale du Moyen Âge* 15 (1946):264–320.

Rickert, M. J. *Painting in Britain: The Middle Ages.* London and Baltimore: Penguin, 1954.

Spargo, E. J. M. *The Category of the Aesthetic in the Philosophy of St. Bonaventure.* St. Bonaventure, New York: Franciscan Institute, 1953.

Ursprung, Otto. *Die katholische Kirchenmusik.* In *Handbuch der Musikwissenschaft* 10 ed. Ernst Bücken. Postdam: Akademische verlags Gesellschaft Athenaion, 1928–34.

Wormald, Francis. "The Crucifix and the Balance." *Journal of the Warburg Institute* 1 (1937):276–80.

Libraries

Bannister, H. M. "A Short Notice of Some Manuscripts of the Cambridge Friars." In *Collectanea Franciscana*, vol. 1, ed. A. G. Little, M. R. James, and H. M. Bannister. BSFS 5: Aberdeen: University of Aberdeen Press, 1915, pp. 124–40.

Guerrini, Paolo. "Due Codici Francescani Bresciani." *Archivum Franciscanum Historicum* 30 (1937):229–34.

James, M. R. "The Austin Friars' Library at York." In *Fasciculus Ioanni Willis Clark Dicatus* (Canterbury: Typis academicus impressus, 1909).

———. "The Library of the Grey Friars of Hereford." In *Collectanea Franciscano*, vol. 1, ed. A. G. Little, M. R. James, and H. M. Bannister. BSFS 5: Aberdeen: University of Aberdeen Press, 1915, pp. 114–23.

Mazzatinti, G. "La biblioteca di S. Francesco in Rimini." In *Scritti vari di filologia in onore a Monaci* (Rome: Forzani, 1901).

Mynors, R. A. B. "The Latin Classics Known to Bolton of Bury, F. S." In *Fritz Saxl, 1890–1948: A Volume of Memorial Essays from His Friends in England*, ed. D. J. Gordon (London and New York: Nelson, 1957), pp. 199–217.

Powicke, F. M. *The Medieval Books of Merton College.* Oxford: Clarendon Press, 1931.

Schmitt, Clement. "Manuscrits de la 'Franciscan Library' de Killiney." *Archivum Franciscanum Historicum* 57 (1964):165–90.

Van Dijk, S. J. P. "Some Manuscripts of the Earliest Franciscan Liturgy." *Franciscan Studies* 14 (1954):225–64; 16 (1956):60–99.

POETRY

Texts

Bettarini, Rosanna. *Jacopone e il Laudario Urbinate.* Florence: Sansoni, 1969.

Bozon, Nicholas. *Les Contes moralisés de Nicole Bozon, Frère Mineur.* Ed. Lucy Toulmin-Smith and Paul Meyer. Société des anciens textes français. Paris: F. Didot, 1889.

Brook, G. L., ed. *The Harley Lyrics.* Manchester: University of Manchester Press, 1964.

Brown, Carleton, ed. *Religious Lyrics of the XIVth Century.* 2nd ed. revised by G. V. Smithers. Oxford: Clarendon Press, 1957.

———, ed. *English Lyrics of the XIIIth Century.* Corr. ed. Oxford: Clarendon Press, 1962.

Campbell, J. J., ed. *The Advent Lyrics of the Exeter Book.* Princeton: Princeton University Press, 1959.

Cawley, A. C., ed. *The Wakefield Pageants in the Towneley Cycle.* Manchester; University of Manchester Press, 1958.

Contini, Gianfranco, ed. *Poeti del Duecento.* 2 vols. Milan, Naples: Riccardo Ricciardi, 1960.

Drèves, G. M., and E. Blume, eds. *Analecta hymnica medii aevi.* 55 vols. Leipzig: Reisland, 1886–1922.

Eberle, Josef, ed. and trans. *Psalterium profanum*. Zurich: Manesse Verlag, 1962.

Greene, Richard L., ed. *The Early English Carols*. Oxford: Clarendon Press, 1935.

Heuser, W., ed. "Die Kildare Gedichte." *Bonner Beiträge zur Anglistik* 14 (1904).

Jacopone da Todi. *Laudi*. Ed. Franca Ageno. Florence: Le Monnier, 1953.

———. *Iacopone da Todi*. Ed. Tressati. Venice, 1613.

Lydgate, John. *The Dance of Death*. Ed. F. Warren. EETS OS 181. London: Oxford University Press, 1931.

McPeek, Gwyn S. *The British Museum Manuscript Egerton 3307*. London and Chapel Hill: University of London Press, 1963.

Meyer, Wendelin. *Franz von Assisi, Sonnengesang*. Leipzig, 1922.

Morris, Richard, ed. "Proverbs of Alfred." In *An Old English Miscellany*, EETS OS 49 (London: Trübner, 1872), pp. 102–38.

Nykl, A. R., trans. *The Dove's Neck Ring*. Paris: P. Geuthner, 1931.

Owl and the Nightingale, The. Facs. reprod. EETS OS 251. London: Oxford University Press, 1963.

Perry, G. G., ed. *Religious Pieces in Prose and Verse*. EETS OS 26. London: Trübner, 1867.

Person, Henry A., ed. *Cambridge Middle English Lyrics*. Seattle: University of Washington Press, 1953.

Raynouard, François J. M., ed. *Choix des poésies originales des troubadours*. Paris: F. Didot, 1816–21.

Robbins, Rossell Hope, ed. *Secular Lyrics of the XIVth and XVth Centuries*. 2nd ed. Oxford: Clarendon Press, 1955.

———, ed. *Historical Poems of the XIVth and XVth Centuries*. Oxford: Clarendon Press, 1959.

Runge, Paul. *Die Lieder und Melodien der Geissler des Jahres 1349 nach der Aufzeichnung Hugo's von Reutlingen*. Leipzig: Breitkopf und Härtel, 1900.

Stevens, John Edgar, ed. *Medieval Carols*. London: Steiner and Bell, 1952.

Stevick, Robert D., ed. *One Hundred Middle English Lyrics*. Indianapolis: Indiana University Press, 1964.

Verona, Giacomo da. *Paradiso e Inferno*. Ed. Luigi Malagoli. Pisa, 1951.

Wright, Thomas, and James O. Halliwell, eds. *Reliquiae antiquae*. 2 vols. London: J. R. Smith, 1845.

Zupitza, Julius. "Die Gedichte des Franziskaners Jakob Ryman." *Archiv für das Studium der neueren Sprachen und Litteraturen* 89 (1892):167–338.

Scholarship

Ancona, Alessandro d'. "Musica e poesia nell antico comune di Perugia." *N. Antologia* 29 (1875):61 ff.

———. *Jacopone da Todi*. Todi: Casa editrice 'Atanor,' 1914.

Anglade, Joseph. *Les Troubadours*. Paris: A. Colin, 1908.

Anglès, Higini. *La Música de las cantigas de Santa Maria del Rey Alphonso el Sabio*. Barcelona, 1943.

Axhausen, Katë. *Die Theorien über der Ursprung der provenzalischen Lyrik*. Dusseldorf: Nolte, 1937.

Bartholomaeis, Vincenzo de. *Le Origini della poesia drammatica in Italia*. Bologna: N. Zanichelli, 1924.

Briffault, Robert. *Les Troubadours et le sentiment romanesque*. Paris: Les éditions du Chêne, 1945.

———. *The Troubadours*. Ed. L. F. Koons. Bloomington: Indiana University Press, 1965.

Brown, Carleton. "Texts and the Man." *Modern Humanities Research Association* 2 (1928):97–111.

Brown, Carleton, and R. H. Robbins. *The Index of Middle English Verse*. New York: Index Society, Columbia University Press, 1943.

Brunacci, G. "Il Codice e l'oratorio dei laudesi." *Polimnia, Bollettino dell' Accademia Etrusca di Cortona* 8 (1931): pt. 1, pp. 873–80.

Cannarozzi, Ciro. "S. Bernardino e la litteratura italiana." *Miscellanea Franciscana* 67 (1967):379–91.

Casieri, Sabino. *Canti e liriche medioevale inglese dal MS. Harley 2253*. Milan: La Goliardica, 1962.

Cellucci, Luigi. "Il Poemeto inglese tratto dalle 'Meditationes.'" *Archivum Romanicum* 22 (1938):67–73.

Chambers, E. K. *English Literature at the Close of the Middle Ages*. Oxford: Clarendon Press, 1945.

Chaytor, H. J. *The Troubadours and England*. Cambridge: Cambridge University Press, 1923.

Chazel, Henry R. *Les Poètes mineurs italiens des xiiie et xive siècles*. Paris: La Renaissance du livre, 1926.

Clair, P. C. *Le Dies Irae, histoire, traduction, commentaire*. Paris, 1881.

Cosmo, Umberto. "Frate Pacifico: Rex Versuum." *Giornate storico della letteratura italiana* 38 (Turin, 1901).

Cristofani, G. *Il Più antico poema della vita di S. Francesco*. Prato, 1882.

Crocetti, C. Guerrieri. *La Lirica predantesca*. Florence: Vallecchi, 1925.

Du Méril, Édélestand P. *Poésies populaires latines du Moyen Âge*. Paris: F. Didot, 1847.

Ecker, Lawrence. *Arabischer, provenzalischer und deutscher Minnesang*. Bonn, 1934.

Fauriel, C. C. *History of Provençal Poetry*. New York, 1860.

Fleming, John V. " 'The Dream of the Rood' and Anglo-Saxon Monasticism." *Traditio* 22 (1966):43–72.

———.*The Roman de la Rose: A Study in Allegory and Iconography*. Princeton: Princeton University Press, 1969.

Fortini, Arnaldo. *La Lauda in Assisi e le origini del teatro italiano*. Assisi: Edizione Assisi, 1961.

Garbaty, Thomas Jay. "Studies in the Franciscan 'The Land of Cokaygne' in the Kildare MS." *Franziskanische Studien* 45 (1963):139–53.

Gastoué, Amédée. *Le Cantique populaire en France.* Lyon: Janin Frères, 1924.

Geary, Beatrice H. N. "A Study of Fifteenth-Century English Lyric Verses . . . with Special Reference to Metrical Form." Thesis, Bodleian Library, 1932.

Getto, Giovanni. *Francesco d'Assisi e il cantico di frate sole.* Turin: Università di Torino, 1956.

Grant, Patrick. "Augustinian Spirituality and the *Holy Sonnets* of John Donne." *English Literary History* 38 (1971):542–61.

Gray, Douglas. *Themes and Images in the Medieval Religious Lyric.* London: Routlege and Kegan Paul, 1972.

Grifoni, O. *Saggio di poesie et canti popolari religiosi di alcuni poesi Umbri,* 2nd ed. Foligno, 1911.

Jeanroy, A. *Savaric de Mauleon: Baron and Troubadour.* Cambridge: Cambridge University Press, 1939.

Laistner, Ludwig. *Golias: Studenten lieder des mittelalters.* Stuttgart, 1897.

Lancetti, L. *Memorie interno ai poeti laureati.* Milan, 1839.

Liuzzi, Fernando. *La Lauda e i primordi della melodia italiana.* Rome: La Libreria dello stato, 1934.

———.*I musicisti italiana in Francia.* Rome: Edizioni d'arte Danesi, 1946.

Manning, Stephen. *Wisdom and Number.* Lincoln, Nebraska: University of Nebraska Press, 1962.

Ong, Walter J. "Wit and Mystery: A Revaluation in Medieval Latin Hymnody." *Speculum* 22 (1947):310–41.

Ozanam, A. F. *Les Poètes francicains en Italic au treizième siècle.* Lyon, 1913.

Pollmann, Leo. *"Trobar Clus": Bibelexegese und hispano-arabische Literatur.* Münster in Westfalen: Aschendorff, 1965.

Raby, F. J. E. *A History of Christian-Latin Poetry from the Beginnings to the Close of the Middle Ages.* 2nd ed. Oxford: Clarendon Press, 1953.

Raisen, Mary Eunice. *Evidences of Romanticism in the Poetry of Medieval England.* Louisville: University of Kentucky Press, 1929.

Robbins, Rossell Hope. "The Earliest Carols and the Franciscans." *MLN* 53 (1938):239–45.

———. "Popular Prayers in Middle English Verse." *Modern Philology* 36 (1939):337–50.

———. "The Authors of the Middle English Religious Lyrics." *JEGP* 39 (1940):230–38.

———. "Friar Herebert and the Carol." *Anglia* 75 (1957): 194–98.

Robbins, Rossell Hope, and John L. Cutler. *Supplement to the Index of Middle English Verse.* Lexington: University of Kentucky Press, 1965.

Robertson, D. W., Jr. "The Doctrine of Charity in Medieval Literary Gardens: A Topical Approach through Symbolism and Allegory." *Speculum* 26 (1951):24–49.

————. *A Preface to Chaucer.* Princeton: Princeton University Press, 1962.

Rozhdestvenskaia, Olga A. (Dobiash). *Les Poésies de Goliards.* Paris: Rieder, 1931.

Scheludko, Dmitri. "Beiträge zur Enstehungsgeschichte der altprovenzalischen Lyrik." *Archivum Romanicum* 11 (1927):273–312; (1928):30–127; *Zeitschrift für französische Sprache und Literatur* 52 (1929):1–38, 201–6.

————. "Orientalisches in der altfranzösischen erzahlenden Dichtung." *Zeitschrift für Französische Sprache und Literatur* 51 (1928):255–93.

Schmitt, Johann. "La Metrica da Fra Jacopone." In *Studii medievali,* vol. 1, no. 4 (Turin, 1905).

Schossig, Alfred. *Der Ursprung der altfranzösischen Lyrik.* Halle: Niemeyer, 1957.

Underhill, E. *Jacopone da Todi, Poet and Mystic . . . 1228–1306.* London: Dent, 1919.

Waddell, Helen J. *The Wandering Scholars.* New York: Doubleday, 1955.

Wardropper, Bruce W. *Historia de la poesia lirica a lo divino en la cristianidad occidental.* Madrid: Revista de Occidente, 1958.

Weber, Sarah A. *Theology and Poetry in the Middle English Lyric: A Study of Sacred History and Aesthetic Form.* Columbus: Ohio State University Press, 1969.

Woolf, Rosemary. "The Theme of Christ the Lover-Knight in Medieval English Literature." *Review of English Studies* NS 13 (1962):1–16.

————. *The English Religious Lyric in the Middle Ages.* Oxford: Clarendon Press, 1968.

HISTORY

Texts

Bourbon, Étienne de. *Anecdotes historiques, légendes, et apologues.* Ed. A. Lecoy de la Marche. Société de l'histoire de France. Paris: Renouard, 1877.

Cambrensis, Geraldus. *Opera.* Ed. J. S. Brewer. 8 vols. Rolls Series 21. London, 1861.

Celano. *S. Francisci Assisiensis vita et miracula additis opusculis liturgicis auctore fr. Thoma de Celano.* Ed. P. Édouard d'Alençon. Rome: Desclée, Lefebvre et soc., 1906.

Eccleston. *De adventu fratrum minorum in Angliam.* Ed. A. G. Little. Manchester: University of Manchester Press, 1951.

Guibert de Nogent. *Guibert de Nogent, histoire de sa vie.* Ed. Georges Bourgin. Paris: A. Picard, 1907.

Gurney-Salter, Emma, trans. *The Coming of the Friars Minor to England and Germany.* London: Dent, 1926.

Jaffé, P., ed. *Regesta Pontificum.* 2 vols. 2nd ed. Paris, 1865.

LeMonnier, Léon, ed. *Nuova istoria.* Assisi, 1895.

Little, A. G. "Chronicles of the Mendicant Friars." *BSFS ES* 3 (1932):85–103.

————. *Franciscan Papers, Lists, and Documents.* Manchester: University of Manchester Press, 1943.

Luard, H. R., ed. *Flores historiarum.* 3 vols. Rolls Series 95. London, 1890.

Moorman, J. R. H. *The Sources for the Life of St. Francis.* Manchester: University of Manchester Press, 1940.

Owst, G. R., ed. "Some Franciscan Memorials at Gray's Inn." *Dublin Review* 176 (1925):276–84.

Paris, Matthew. *Chronica majora.* Ed. H. R. Luard. Trans. J. A. Giles. 3 vols. 2nd ed. London: H. M. Stationery Office, 1872–83; Kraus Reprints, 1964.

Pertz, G. H., T. Mommsen, et al. *Monumenta Germaniae Historica.* Auspiciis Societatis Aperiendis Fontibus Rerum Germanicarum Medii Aevii. Ser., LL., 1826–89; ser., Scriptores, 1826–1934.

Salimbene d'Adam. *Chronica.* Ed. Oswald Holder-Egger. *Monumenta Germaniae Historica,* ser., Script. 32. Hanover, 1905–13.

Sparke, Jos, ed. "Peterburg Chronicle." *Historiae Anglicanae Scriptores Varii.* 2 vols. London, 1723.

Stevenson, J., ed. *Chronicon de Lanercost: 1201–1346.* Edinburgh, 1839.

Thomas of Walsingham. *Historia Anglicana.* Ed. H. T. Riley. Rolls Series 28. London: Longman, Green, Longman, Roberts, and Green, 1863–64.

William of Newburgh. *Chronicles of the Reigns of Stephen, Henry II, and Richard I.* Ed. R. Howlett. Rolls Series 82. London, 1884, vols. 1–2.

Scholarship

Anagnine, Eugenio. *Dolcino e il movimento ereticale all' inizio del Trecento.* Florence: Nuova Italia, 1964.

Bak, Felix M. "If It Weren't for Peter Waldo, There Would Have Been No Franciscans." *Franciscan Studies* 25 (1965):4–16.

Belperron, Pierre. *La Croisade contre les Albigeois et l'union du Languedoc à la France.* Paris: Plon, 1945.

Catholic Encyclopedia, The 16 vols. New York: Robert Appleton, 1907–12.

Clark, James M. *The Dance of Death in the Middle Ages and Renaissance.* Glasgow: Jackson, 1950.

Comba, Emilio. *History of the Waldenses of Italy.* Trans. Teofilo E. Comba. London: Truslove and Shirley, 1889.

Coulton, George Gordon. *From St. Francis to Dante.* London: D. Nutt, 1906.

Cowley, Patrick. *Franciscan Rise and Fall.* London: Dent, 1933.

Davison, Ellen Scott. *Forerunners of St. Francis of Assisi.* Cambridge, Mass.: Harvard University Press, 1927.

Douie, Decima L. *Archbishop Pecham.* Oxford: Clarendon Press, 1952.

Du Méril, Édélestand P. "La Confrèrie des clercs Parisiens du Puy de l'Assumption de Douai." *Memoires de la société Nationale d'Agriculture, Sciences, et Arts.* Ser. 3, bk. 2. Douai, 1914.

Emery, Richard W. "The Friars of the Blessed Mary and the Pied Friars." *Speculum* 24 (1949):228–38.

Foatelli, Renée. *Les Danses religieuses dans le christianisme.* Paris: Éditions Spes, 1938.

Forcella, Vincenzo. *Iscrizioni delle chiese e d'altri edifici di Roma dal secolo xl fino ai giorni nostri.* 14 vols. Rome: Tip. della scienze matematiche e fisiche, 1869–84.

Formoy, Beryl E. R. *The Dominican Order in England before the Reformation.* London: SPCK, 1925.

Fortini, Arnaldo. *Nova Vita di San Francesco.* 5 vols. Assisi: Porziuncula, 1959.

Gebhart, Émile. *Mystics and Heretics in Italy at the End of the Middle Ages.* Trans. Edward M. Hulme. New York: A. A. Knopf, 1923.

Gilbert, F. B. *Agnellus and the English Grey Friars.* London: BSFS, 1937.

Godefroy, P. "Le Tiers-ordre de Saint François." *Études franciscaines* 39 (1927):472–97.

Gougaud, L. "La Danse dans les églises." *Revue d'histoire ecclesiastique* 15 (1914):5–22.

Green, V. G. *The Franciscans in Medieval English Life (1224–1348).* Franciscan Studies 20. Patterson, New Jersey: St. Anthony Guild Press, 1939.

Guiraud, Jean. *Histoire de l'Inquisition au Moyen Âge.* Paris: A. Picard, 1935.

Gurney-Salter, Emma. "Ubertino da Casale." In *Franciscan Essays,* ed. A. G. Little (Aberdeen: University of Aberdeen Press, 1912), 2:108–23.

Hinnebusch, W. A. *The Early English Friars Preachers.* Rome: Sabina, 1951.

Hirsch, Ernst. *Beiträge zur Sprachgeschichte der württembergischen Waldenser.* Stuttgart: W. Kohlhammer, 1962.

Jalla, Jean. *Histoire des Vaudois des Alpes et de leurs colonies.* Paris: Pignerol, 1904.

Jorgenson, Johannes. *St. Francis of Assisi.* New York: Longman's Green, 1912; rpt. 1955.

Karrer, Otto. *St. Francis of Assisi: The Legends and Lauds.* Trans. N. Wydenbruck. New York: Sheed and Ward, 1948.

Knowles, David. *The Religious Orders in England.* 2 vols. Cambridge: Cambridge University Press, 1948–59.

Lambert, M. D. *Franciscan Poverty: The Doctrine of the Absolute Poverty of Christ and the Apostles in the Franciscan Order, 1220–1323.* London: SPCK, 1961.

Landini, Lawrence C. *The Causes of the Clericalization of the Order of the Friars Minor, 1209–1260, in the Light of Early Franciscan Sources.* Chicago, 1968.

Little, A. G. *The Grey Friars in Oxford.* Oxford: Clarendon Press, 1892.

———. "The Sources of the History of St. Francis of Assisi: A Review of Recent Researches." *English Historical Review* 17 (1902):643–77.

———. "The Authorship of the Lanercost Chronicle." *English Historical Review* 31 (1916):269–79; 32 (1917):48–49.

———. *Studies in English Franciscan History.* Manchester: University of Manchester Press, 1917.

———. "The First Hundred Years of the Franciscan School at Oxford." In

St. Francis of Assisi: 1226–1926: Essays in Commemoration, ed. Walter Warren Seton (London: University of London Press, 1926).

———, ed. *Franciscan History and Legend in English Medieval Art*. BSFS 19. Manchester: University of Manchester Press, 1937.

Little, A. G., and E. B. Fitzmaurice. *Materials for the History of the Franciscan Province of Ireland: 1230–1450*. Manchester: University of Manchester Press, 1920.

Maitland, S. R. *Facts and Documents Illustrative of the History, Doctrine, and Rites of the Ancient Albigenses and Waldenses*. London, 1832.

Mallet, Charles Edward. *A History of the University of Oxford*. 2 vols. London: Methuen, 1924–27.

Marthaler, Bernard. "Forerunners of the Franciscans: The Waldenses." *Franciscan Studies* 18 (1958):133–42.

Meerssemon, G. "F. F. Prêcheurs et le Mouvement Devôt en Flandre au xiiie siècle." *Archivum fratrum praedicatorum* 18 (1948):69–130.

Monastier, Antoine. *Histoire de l'Église Vaudoise*. 2 vols. Lausanne: G. Bridel, 1847.

Moorman, J. R. H. *A New Fioretti*. London: SPCK, 1946.

———. *The Grey Friars in Cambridge, 1225–1538*. Cambridge: Cambridge University Press, 1952.

———. *A History of the Franciscan Order*. Oxford: Clarendon Press, 1968.

Muzzey, David S. *The Spiritual Franciscans*. New York: Columbia University Thesis, 1907.

Petry, Ray C. *Francis of Assisi, Apostle of Poverty*. Durham, North Carolina: Duke University Press, 1941.

Robertson, D. W., Jr. *Chaucer's London*. New York: John Wiley & Sons, 1968.

Runciman, Steven. *The Mediaeval Manichee: A Study of the Christian Dualist Heresy*. Cambridge: Cambridge University Press, 1947.

Sabatier, Paul. *Life of St. Francis of Assisi*. Trans. Louise Seymour Houghton. New York: Scribner's, 1894.

Samaran, Charles. "Pierre Bersuire." *Histoire littéraire de la France* 39 (1962):258–450.

Schmidt, C. *Histoire et doctrine de la secte des Cathares ou Albigeois*. Paris: J. Cherbuliez, 1849.

Scudder, Vida Dutton. *The Franciscan Adventure*. London and Toronto: Dent, 1931.

Smalley, Beryl. *English Friars and Antiquity in the Early Fourteenth Century*. New York: Barnes and Noble, 1960.

Strong, A. "St. Francis in Rome." In *St. Francis of Assisi: 1226–1926: Essays in Commemoration*, ed. Walter Warren Seton (London: University of London Press, 1926).

Thompson, E. Margaret. *The Carthusian Order in England*. London: SPCK, 1930.

Thouzellier, Christine. *Catharisme et Valdéisme en Languedoc à la fin du* *xiie et au début du xiiie siècle* . . . . Paris: Presses universitaires de France, 1966.

Thureau-Dangin, Paul M. A. *The Life of St. Bernardino of Siena*. Trans. Baroness G. von Hügel. London: Warner, 1911.

Turberville, Arthur Stanley. *Mediaeval Heresy and the Inquisition*. London and Hamden, Conn.: Archon Books, 1964.

Varga, Lucie. "Peire Cardinal était-il hérétique?" *Revue d'histoire des religions* 117 (1938):205–31.

Vigo, P. *La Danze Macabre in Italia*. Bergamo, 1901.

Whitfield, Derek. "Conflicts of Personality and Principle: The Political and Religious Crisis in the Franciscan Province, 1400–1409." *Franciscan Studies* 17 (1957):321–62.

Williams, G. A. *Medieval London from Commune to Capital*. London: University of London Press, 1963.

Index

The Index is divided into three parts: an Index of Lyrics; an Index of Manuscripts; and an Index of Proper Names, Titles, and Subjects. The Index of Lyrics is itself divided into two parts. Section A lists, by the first line of the complete text, all of the lyrics which are cited in this book, with italicized page numbers indicating *quotation* of all or part of the lyric. Section B lists, by the first line actually quoted in the text rather than by the first line of the lyric, all other quotations of lyrics in the book. The numbers following titles are those assigned to the poems in Brown and Robbins, *Index of Middle English Verse*.

2. Other

II. Index of the Manuscripts

References are to discussions of the manuscripts themselves as well as of poems contained in them. Boldface type distinguishes the MS numbers.

III. Index of Subjects, Proper Names and Titles

Aaron, 235–36
Adam of Saint Victor, 4
Advent Lyrics of the Exeter Book, 15, 17
Agnello[-us] of Pisa, Fra, 47, 65, 122, 169, 170, 211
Alanus de Insulis (Alain de Lille), 3, 15, 92; *Anticlaudianus*, 84; *De planctu naturae*, 84–85
Albert of Pisa, 273
Albertus Magnus, 102–3
Albigensians, 20, 89. *See* Heretic movements
Alexander III, Pope, 36 n. 33
Alexander of Alexandria, 84
Alexander of Bremen, Friar, 70, 71
Alexander of Hales, 83, 170, 247, 249; *IV Glossa* (on Lombard's *Sentences*), 50 (n. 22), 53–56; *Introitus*, 77 n. 45; on the Passion, 53–57; *Quaestio de Sacramentis*, 54; *Quaestiones disputatae antequam esset frater*, 77 n. 45; on the sacraments, 53–57
Alexis, Saint, 20, 35 n. 32
Allegory in Middle English lyrics, 238, 252–59, 263 n. 22
Allen, Thomas, 205–6
Alphonso of Spain, 81 n. 83
Ambrose, Saint, 84
Amiens, Cathedral of, 105
Anglo-Norman poetry, 189, 206, 210–11, 223 n. 79, 228 n. 149, 238, 259, 267 nn. 62, 63; compared with Waldensian poetry, 23; Franciscan, 259; with music, 267 n. 62
Annunciation, in Franciscan poetry, 240 (n. 26); graphic representation (and influence on poetry), 264 n. 26; lyrics, 241, 264 n. 26; lyrics in Wakefield cycle, 178
Anselm, Saint, 84, 168 n. 117; "Cur Deus homo," 53, 247–49, 250
Anthony of Padua, Saint, on *Concordia Scripturarum*, 89–90, 236–37, 262 n. 11; *Dominica II in Quadragesima*, 267 n. 60; *Dominica IV in Quadragesima*, 61 (n. 55); hagiog-

raphy of, 66, 67–68; *In annuntiatione Sanctae Mariae*, 237 (n. 16); *In assumptione S. Mariae Virginis*, 237 (nn. 17, 18); *In nativitate B. Mariae Virginis*, 236 (n. 14); *In purificatione Sanctae Mariae*, 236 (n. 12); on Isaiah, 225; preaching, 17, 89–90, 129, 142; use of poetry, 142; on the Virgin, 60–61, 236–37 and nn.
Anti-clericism, eleventh century, 18–20
Anti-fraternalism, 117 n. 102, 184, 229 n. 158, 273–74
Apocalypse, 43, 84; in art, 107–8, 216 n. 11, 263 n. 23; in Franciscan poetry, 147; and Franciscans, 26, 68–71, 107–8, 117 n. 102, 183, 216 n. 11; and Joachim de Fiore, 69–77; in Middle English Franciscan manuscripts, 205, 238; in Middle English poetry, 294–95, 205, 238–39, 245; poems about, 205, 206–7, 211, 238–39. *See also* Death in poetry
Apuleius, 84
Aquinas, Thomas, Saint, 13; aesthetics, 102–4, 117 n. 91; and Bonaventure, 44–46, 102–4, 117 n. 91
Arezzo, Guittone d', 119 (n. 4)
Aristotelianism, neo-, 91, 92
Aristotle, 84, 190
Arius, 28
Assisan codices (collections of songs), 150, 212; lauds, 141, 143, 145–46 (confraternity poem)
Assisi, confraternities at, 214–15
Athlone Friars, 158, 229
Augsburg *Dance of Death*, 138
Augustine, Saint, 84, 86, 90, 189, 223 n. 84, 258; *Commentary on Psalms*, 84; *Confessions*, 84, 246; *De Civitate Dei*, 84, 258; *De Trinitate*, 84; "Egyptian gold," 29; *Enchiridion*, 84; Franciscan poem about, 167 n. 113; *On Christian Doctrine*, 29, 90 (n. 36); *Retractiones*, 84; *Sermones*, 84; six ages of man, 256; *super*